SLOW BOAT
NEKKID

A 5-YEAR VOYAGE
OF FUN AND ADVENTURE

PHIL PHILLIPS

Additional copies of this book, and two previous books by the author, *Racal and Me* and *Fast Boat Nekkid*, are available from Amazon.com.

This book is dedicated to my son and only child, Grant Edward Phillips, whose young life thus far is already filled with great promise for the future, and to his mother, Mary K. "Kitty" Phillips.

Contents

Maps

INTRODUCTION

Why I Got Nekkid Again

Naked is when you ain't got no clothes on.
Nekkid is when you ain't got no clothes on and
you're up to somethin'.
- Lewis Grizzard

Nekkid suggests an escapade, a lark, spontaneity, passion, a zest for life. Nekkid, in other words, is just plain FUN! At the age of sixty-one, I set about in the spring of 2006 to get nekkid on a 105-foot expedition motor yacht christened *Indigo*. I'm no novice to escaping into the open sea. Two volumes chronicle my adventures: Rascal and Me: A Voyage Around the Eastern US and Parts of Canada Alone in a Small Boat (1999) and Fast Boat Nekkid: An Escapade by Sea from Alaska to Mexico (2005), both available on Amazon.

Along with Grizzard's keen observance, it is this second piece of nautical nonfiction that inspires the title for this narrative. In Fast Boat Nekkid, I describe my affinity for speed, realized magnificently by my six-week jaunt on Rascal, a sleek boat that was all about speed.

In imagining a new adventure, I decided it might be equally thrilling to take it slow. Get nekkid leisurely. I had the time, after all, and the means. Fortune had shone her kind graces upon me in the form of selling my real estate development business to a German fund in early 2006, before the subprime mortgage debacle and real estate market collapse of 2007. With the business sold and my son, Grant, at boarding school, I had time to take a slow trip and venture farther into the watery parts of the world.

So I paid off my debts, shored up my retirement fund, and pur-chased *Indigo*, a 280-ton yacht with twin inboard diesel engines. I outfitted her with the best crew I could find and laid out a route. We would begin the journey by sailing down the coast of Brazil and Argentina, through the legendary Straits of Magellan, around the tip of Cape Horn, and up the coast of Chile before turning westward to the Pacific Isles. In the spirit of the slow nekkid, my world tour would extend into new and wondrous locales. Along the way, I'd inquire about local points of interest and chart our course accordingly. My crew and I would stop wherever we felt called. Whatever the case, we'd travel along in search of the next exhilarating encounter. *Indigo* was fully outfitted and, with a 10,000-gallon fuel capacity, capable of cruising 4,000 nautical miles[1] between fueling stops. Provided we avoided hurricanes, I had every confidence we'd remain afloat.

My wife, Kitty, was accustomed to my occasional extended esca-pades, but was no fan of the open sea. "Follow your dream, and I'll be here," she said. She and Grant would join me multiple times along the way.

Looking back, I suppose Kitty worried for my safety—and for good reason. Though I didn't know it at the time of our departure, we'd be challenged by violent storms, boating accidents, mechanical breakdowns, locust swarms, getting lost in both the desert and the jungle, and, like most great sea adventures, a pirate or two. You can't be afraid of a little danger when you're getting nekkid. That's part of the fun!

---

1. A nautical mile is 2,025 yards, or about 1.15 statute miles.

ONE

Islands of the Caribbean

Barely a week since setting out from Fort Lauderdale, Florida, I had already learned an important lesson about expedition motor yachts: they have lots of complicated moving parts, and sometimes they break.

Something had broken, and now *Indigo* was stuck upon the sandbar of bureaucracy at a marina in Casa de Campo, a resort complex on the southern coast of the Dominican Republic in the Caribbean. Necessary parts had arrived but were being held ransom by the island's ponderous local customs process.

Casa de Campo, Dominican Republic

I whiled away the time playing golf, attending open-air concerts, and touring the nearby town of La Romana. At a piano bar located conveniently not more than fifty yards from *Indigo's* slip, I met Bruno Massidda, a Sardinian tenor and musician and accomplished amateur chef. Bruno visited me and the crew on *Indigo*, where he prepared a delicious pasta dinner for all and regaled us with stories of his years of sailing around the world as an entertainer on cruise ships. After a few too many glasses of an Italian wine, he foolishly invited me to visit him at his home in Porto Seguro on the coast of Brazil, which, in due course, I would do.

INDIGO ITINERARY : FT LAUDERDALE TO FRENCH GUIANA

3,984 nm traveled this portion of trip: 3,984 nm traveled TOTAL
1 nautical mile (nm) = 1.151 miles

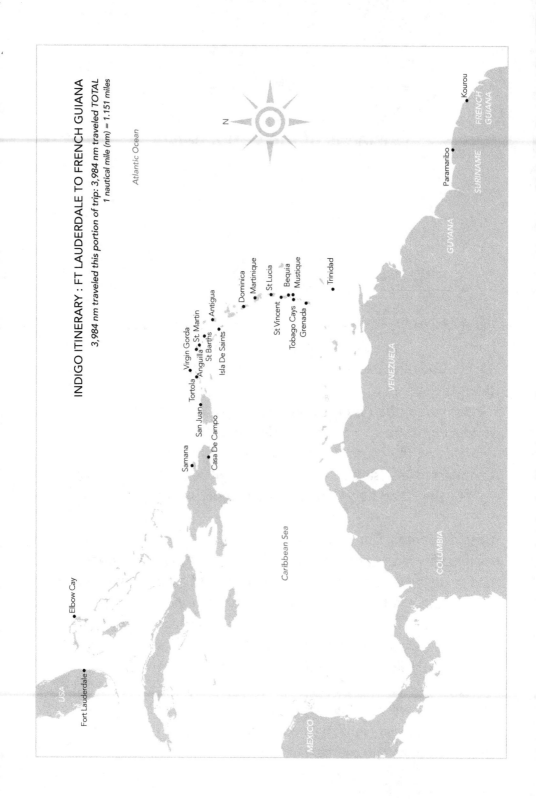

One of the many pleasures of travel is the chance encounter with like-minded travelers from different cultures and the new friendships that spring from these. Over the next few years of our voyage, there would be many others, all memorable and treasured.

One day I retrieved our tender from its place on *Indigo's* aft boat deck and motored about five miles up the beach to the simple village of Bayahibe, where I found, quite by accident, the delightful open-air restaurant/bar owned and operated by Mama Rosa and her husband, Ben Obispo. There, laid up under a shade tree on a soft sand beach and serenaded by Mama Rosa's CD collection of Dominican music, I drank cold Presidente beer, ate Mama's fresh grilled fish prepared local style, watched the fishermen at work, and napped peacefully. Not a bad way to spend a balmy afternoon.

Short excursions like this would become common during our voyage, and *Indigo's* tender was perfect for that. Known in the yachting world as a RIB, or rigid inflatable boat, the tender was fifteen feet long. Like most yacht tenders, it was constructed of heavy duty nylon inflated tubes attached to a fiberglass hull, making it lightweight and thus more easily hoisted by a deck crane and less likely to damage the yacht's hull upon accidental impact. With a 150-horsepower outboard motor, the tender had a top speed of thirty miles per hour and a range of about a hundred nautical miles.

Los Haitises National Park

Still awaiting release of the needed parts, I decided to visit Los Haitises National Park on the island's northeast coast. The coastline of the park is something like you'd expect to find in the South Pacific, with palm-covered limestone islands and glimmering white sand beaches.

Joe, my so-called professional guide for the trip and also the official port captain, turned out never to have been to the park before and so got us lost among the mangroves. I managed to find our way out and also to locate a freshwater river that flowed from a cave. Joe was very impressed.

The outhouse at the park office was a notably quaint affair, mounted at the edge of the beach with its permanently open doors facing into the bay. While sitting on the john, an occupant could offer a friendly wave and big smile to passersby.

Anguilla

June 1 marks the official start of hurricane season in the Caribbean. In insuring yachts like *Indigo*, Lloyd's of London requires that the vessel's owner and crew are to exercise "prudent judgment," as noted in Lloyd's policy. Legal scholars might debate what constitutes prudent judgment, but I presume remaining in the bull's-eye of Hurricane Alley during storm season would be anything but prudent.

Therefore, I knew we'd best get well south of the equator before hurricane season began in earnest. By the time parts were released by customs officials and repairs to *Indigo* were completed, we were already well into May. We had been stranded for more than a month. We had no time to dally.

With clear skies and smooth seas, we hoisted anchor and left the Dominican Republic, cruising through the Sir Francis Drake Channel between Tortola and Virgin Gorda, and wending our way through the Leeward and Windward Islands. We made Anguilla, a sparkling gem in the Caribbean, on May 13, dropping anchor in her bay, as there was no marina.

Were it not for the unfortunate fact that it's located dead center in Hurricane Alley, the island of Anguilla would be an ideal paradise. Without a marina, it isn't especially friendly to yachts, but its beaches lining the western shore are as pure and white and lovely as any beaches could ever be. Not surprisingly, the place is home to two five-star resort hotels.

On the day we arrived, a sailing regatta was underway with colorful spinnakers, adding visual drama to an already tantalizing place. It also added a party that night with the prevalent reggae music prominent on the scene.

Next day, after cavorting about the beaches, I met at lunch a fun group of tourists along with a local couple, he from Germany and she from Egypt. On the spur of the moment, I organized a party on *Indigo* with several local Rasta guys, four local ladies, and the lunch group, all ferried out to *Indigo's* anchorage via tender. The music was cranked up, booze and snacks served, and a fine time was had by all. Next evening, we all met for dinner at a favorite spot among the locals, then headed out to a beach bar and the reggae scene.

Antigua
If there is an island in the Caribbean that can be said to be obviously British, Antigua is it. It is the site of a former Royal Navy base dating from the early 1800s, with wharves, warehouses, barracks, and the like now converted to tourist attractions. Its harbor is lined with bars and restaurants that were mostly empty this time of year. For the tourists, it was out of season, and for the locals it was time to hunker down and await the year's first hurricane.

Dominica
We were happy to hoist anchor next morning and chart our course for Jurassic Park! At least, that's what the island of Dominica feels like. Volcanic and mountainous, as are nearly all the Caribbean islands, Dominica is an ecological wonderland that, viewed from afar, brings to mind the setting for the film *Jurassic Park*, and the closer you get, the more apt the association becomes.

At its northern end, we anchored near the beach in the lee, protected from the prevailing trade winds by the high, jungle-covered mountains. We were met by a local guide in a small skiff propelled by poling, who took me and some members of the crew up a narrow river—or rather, "creek" would be the more appropriate term. Giant iguanas lying about in the trees added to the Jurassic image.

Reaching the end of the navigable stretch and numbed by the incessant drone of guide talk, we stopped at a rude camp that served as the trip's tourist terminal and partook of a local concoction called, with some understatement, "dynamite." The couple who managed the place—really not much more than a wood-roofed pavilion shack—had six kids wandering about, one of whom, the youngest at two years, I called Abe. Without a stitch of clothes on, Abe was preoccupied with peeing on anything in range.

After our jungle river excursion, we arranged for a taxi tour of this ecological dream world. The driver took us up to the top of a mountain into a rain forest where annual rainfall is 350 inches. He led us to a roofless cave with dense vegetation, forty feet above, blocking out the sun. At the cave's entry is a man-made warm-water shower heated by volcanic activity underground.

From the shower, we made our way into the cave, which was flooded to ten feet deep with freezing-cold river water. Swimming deeper into the cave, perhaps fifty yards or so, we encountered at its terminus a substantial waterfall flooding its far end. This, I learned, was used in the filming of one of the Pirates of the Caribbean movies.

Following the cave swim, we hiked up a long, steep pile of boulders to a pool into which an enormous waterfall cascaded from several hundred feet above. The climb was treacherous thanks to the wet, slippery rocks, but nobody fell. As a reward, we bathed in a warm spring heated to about 100 degrees by the underlying thermo-geology.

Dominica has just about every exotic plant and tree that can be imagined. Breadfruit trees, brought to the islands by Captain Bligh on the *Bounty*, are everywhere, as are cashew trees, calabash, cinnamon, and cannonball trees, and a whole lot more. If flora is your thing, Dominica is the place.

For lunch, we stopped at a simple roadside café hanging precariously over a ravine and dined on curried goat—not a dish encountered every day but tasty enough. After lunch, we continued touring the island, finally ending the long, fun-filled day back at *Indigo*.

Saint Vincent

The following morning we set forth from Dominica, and after uneventful stops at Martinique and Saint Lucia, we reached the island of Saint Vincent, where, at its south end, we went ashore and put into action one of the more foolhardy ideas that has ever popped into my frequently off-camber mind. A guidebook of the island said that it is possible to climb an active volcano, called La Soufrière[1], using either of two paths, helpfully described as "harder" and "easier." I failed to note that the word "*easier*" is not a synonym for "easy," and so trouble ensued.

The hike is three and a half miles—challenging, but less than eighteen holes of golf. Could be fun, I thought, something I'd not done before. It also ascends in that length about 3,000 feet—and that was the hard part. Though I have climbed every mountain Florida has to offer, I was unprepared for the upness of this trek. It didn't help that the narrow trail wends through a dense, dripping-wet rain forest.

Our guide, a cheerful fellow who somehow managed to breathe, talk, and climb all at the same time, noted that on this island was one of the few remaining colonies of Caribe Indians, a pre-Columbian tribe noted for their fierceness and cannibalism.

"Are they in this area?" someone asked nervously.

The guide smiled.

At the halfway mark, I cast myself prone across a bamboo bench, gasping for air, my legs turned to jelly. As I prayed for deliverance, the guide announced with sadistic pleasure that now the climb upward would begin.

Begin?

Nearing the top, I could advance no more than five or ten yards without having to stop and heave my lungs in search of tiny doses of oxygen. The last quarter mile or so took us across fields of loose sediment. Now out of the forest, we were in the clouds with wind gusts to forty knots and visibility limited to twenty yards or so.

Finally, at the summit, we peered into a crater with sheer walls rising a thousand feet from its floor. Thanks to the heavy clouds, there was no view of the sea or surrounding countryside. Sitting there trying to resume normal breathing, freezing in the clouds, exhausted, utterly spent, I thought to myself, *Now that was a damn fool thing to do. I'll stick to beaches and cold beer from now on.*

---

1. "Mount Sulfur" in English, and yes, the name is a hint at what lay ahead.

Tobago Cays

June 1 dawned with skies free of clouds and no reports of building storms. Still, it was with a wary eye on the weather that we anchored behind a protecting reef in the Southern Caribbean archipelago of the Tobago Cays. This is, I believe, among Mother Nature's most perfect places. Beautiful islands ringed with white sand beaches lined with coconut palms dot the area, and almost nobody lives there.

On a beautiful, balmy day, I used the tender to explore an islet just a few miles away that was a feature locale in one of the *Pirates of the Caribbean* films. There, I plopped down in the shade of a palm tree for as fine a nap as I've ever had.

That night on a nearby beach, we grilled fish wrapped in tinfoil, returned to *Indigo* when it was done, and had a great meal on the aft deck, caressed all the while by the gentle trade winds. Hard to beat a place like this.

Trinidad

On June 5, we reached Trinidad. As it has never been hit by a hurricane, it marks the southern end of the hurricane belt.

While we were there, Trinidad played Sweden in its first-ever appearance in a World Cup soccer event, and I was privileged to watch the match over a TV in a large sports bar in the capital city of Port of Spain. I was seated immediately adjacent to a fifteen-piece percussion section from the Trinidad & Tobago Marching Band who, at the slightest hint of success by their team, erupted into a cacophony of cheerful rhythmic noise. Trinidad played Sweden to a tie, zero all, and you'd have thought they had won the Cup from the celebrations that day and night. Soccer's a big deal here, and as in many former British colonies, so are rugby and the incomprehensible (to me, at least) cricket.

Originally, we had planned to go to Venezuela to take on diesel fuel, which at sixty-five cents a gallon was a bargain. That, however, was offset by the danger of increasingly active armed pirates marauding in the area. Only a few days before, the longtime owner of a marina near where we wanted to go had been gunned down in a daylight robbery. We decided to bypass the bargain and instead headed for Suriname, formerly Dutch Suriname. Along the way, we would bypass Guyana, due also to its rampant criminal activity.

Motor Yacht *Indigo*

Unless you know more about motor yachts than I did when I started shopping for one, I should point out the difference between expedition yachts and what I call cocktail yachts. The latter are often owned by corporations who use them for entertainment and business promotion. Expedition yachts like *Indigo*, on the other hand, are deep draft boats designed for serious, long-range ocean travel. The very large yachts—say 180 to 300 feet—can do both jobs but often are too large to get into tight places such as some fjords and glacier fields.

The accommodations aboard *Indigo* were spacious and comfortable by nautical standards. From the aft main deck, double doors opened into the salon—essentially a living room, great room, bar, and dining room combined in a single tastefully appointed space. Forward of the salon was the galley, complete with its own smaller but cozier dining area for crew. The main foyer between salon and galley included sets of stairs that allowed easy access to the crew quarters, the bridge and sky lounge/office, as well as to the owner's stateroom. My stateroom featured a king-sized bed, a sofa, a large desk, two bathrooms, and a walk-in closet.

The bridge overlooking the foredeck was outfitted with all the modern gadgetry necessary to keep the captain fully informed and in control. As a bonus, it included a low settee from which guests could watch the proceedings without getting underfoot. The rear of the pilothouse opened into the sky lounge, containing a pop-up television, a desk, and a couch that concealed a pullout bed. In a pinch, this tidy cabin could double as a guest room or entertainment area.

An outside staircase led to the uppermost deck, also known as the sundeck. One of *Indigo's* more noteworthy features was that all of her decks were made of real teakwood, including the sundeck's teak reclining loungers.

The Crew

Of primary importance on a journey like this is the crew, starting with a first-rate captain and a chef who can produce a palatable meal for me, guests, and crew. Both positions were filled prior to leaving Fort Lauderdale with the hiring of Captain Lucas Pelletier and his wife, Jeanette.

Upon joining *Indigo*, Captain Lucas searched for an engineer and eventually hired Sean Reilly. Sean was raised in the tiny Alaskan village of Sand Point and learned his trade working on the crab boats that ply the Bering Sea.

Our twenty-five-year-old first mate, Bobby Hawkins, was a lanky, even-tempered, hardworking guy from Fort Lauderdale and a graduate from Florida State University. On *Indigo*, his duties were to care for the exterior surfaces, tend the anchoring and docking lines, and assist the captain and engineer with repair work. Bobby performed all his tasks with professional competence and a uniformly cheerful attitude.

Our twenty-eight-year-old deckhand, Tomas Maldonado, had spent two years in the Chilean navy before deciding that his future was in the yacht world. He was always smiling, always cheerful and helpful.

Each morning when I arose from my cabin to greet the day, I first encountered the attractive, bright, always smiling face of twenty-seven-year-old Darla McLendon. As *Indigo's* stewardess, Darla brought long experience to the task gained from working in her mother's bed-and-breakfast in Fredericksburg, Virginia, and on other yachts. Her talents at flower arranging, decorative place settings, guest services, and bartending made *Indigo* a five-star yacht in every respect.

All of us got along well together, enjoyed sharing our many and varied experiences, and operated as a cooperative team as we continued south. The equator beckoned.

TWO

Dragonflies and Polliwogs

The long trip from Trinidad to Paramaribo, Suriname, was largely uneventful except for an odd incident that took place one evening at sundown. The sea was calm, the sun was setting, and I was comfortably seated on the upper deck reading a book. The coastal plain of Suriname, some twenty-five nautical miles to the west, was far out of sight.

All was calm until I began to notice that a large number of dragonflies were flitting about. Now, it's not so unusual to see dragonflies on land, at least in my home state of Florida, but here, twenty-five nautical miles out to sea, it was startling.

The number of these critters increased rapidly until they were swarming all over the boat, thousands of them. *Indigo* was caught in the midst of a huge brown, furiously buzzing cloud of apparently irritated insects. Recalling the Hitchcock movie *The Birds*, I went inside, only to watch through the aft salon door as gazillions of these bugs swarmed in a dense fog, clinging to ceiling, deck, and furniture and darkening the air in between.

Next morning, they all lay dead, covering the deck in bug carcasses. I have yet to hear a reasonable explanation for this weird encounter.

Paramaribo, Suriname

On June 13, we made Paramaribo, Suriname's capital city and probably the only place in the country that can be regarded as a proper city. It lies up a large river that we had to enter using a pilot to guide us through the tricky channels. With no marina, we anchored just off the main hotel and took the tender ashore.

Paramaribo is a quaint town, with eighteenth-century Dutch architecture evident in its still-used government buildings. The country is an amalgam of at least five cultures—Indonesian, African, Dutch, Indian, and Amerindian—and the mix is easily seen in the houses of worship. Mosques, Hindu temples, and Baptist and Lutheran churches dot the neighborhoods.

I hired a local guy to drive me on a rainy day along dilapidated, washed-out roads to the site of a seventeenth-century Dutch fort. The grounds were standing in water, as is most of the countryside most of the time. In this part of the world, near the equator, you might think of hordes of mosquitoes, the king of pests. But in all our travels in this area, we never encountered even one, thanks I assume to all those dragonflies.

French Guiana

A *department* of France rather than a sovereign nation, French Guiana has as its capital the town of Cayenne. Since its harbor is too shallow to be accessible by deep-draft boats, we detoured to the town of Kourou. There were no marina facilities, and we dropped anchor in the Kourou River.

One of this place's two notable characteristics is that it's the home of the French space program, a kind of Cape Canaveral in the jungle. The other is that it's the mainland site for day trips to Devil's Island, the notorious French penal colony that served as the involuntary home for many years of Captain Alfred Dreyfus, a man who, in the late 1800s, was wrongly charged and convicted of being a traitor. Devil's Island was featured in the movie *Papillon* starring Dustin Hoffman and Steve McQueen.

I took the tender about twenty-five miles upriver into the interior jungle and there found the banks lined with primitive camps used by the locals as getaways. They had hammocks, cookstoves, raised floors, outhouses, roofs against the rain—but no walls.

Devil's Island

After the river excursion, *Indigo* left Kourou and traveled the few miles out to Devil's Island, now a French national park with a café and quarters for the staff. The first thing I noticed was the abundance of a peculiar animal called an agouti. The size of a small dog, this critter has a head resembling a large rat and the hind legs of a rabbit, a decidedly awkward and unattractive combination. They roam the park grounds at will, nibbling away on the lawn.

Living close alongside these oddballs is a large population of giant iguanas in shades varying from neon green to pewter, some with large warts adorning their already ugly heads. The big guys, like me turned gray by their years, are nearly three feet long and hold a menacing pose while keeping a wary eye alert for predators and prey.

For reasons not immediately apparent to me, the park also contained a pen filled with feathered creatures that seemed most unusual to the island, such as peacocks and quail. It finally dawned on me that these foreign fowl were likely occupying the paddock as a prelude to landing on the park manager's dinner plate.

The whole scene—the old crumbling prison, the agouti, giant iguanas, two overfed raucous parrots, and a barnyard menagerie of other fowl—gives the place the feel of a lunatic asylum whose management has been taken over by the inmates.

Devil's Island is actually part of a group of three volcanic islands clustered close together. The islands are high and steep-walled, natural features that must have discouraged thoughts of escape when this place was a prison. Covered in dense stands of coconut palms, wreathed with stretches of magnificent white sand beaches, and brushed by gentle trade winds, they are also a significant improvement over Alcatraz.

The Equator

It was a moment we had all eagerly anticipated, and it happened at approximately eight-thirty p.m. on June 20, when we crossed the equator. The crew and I were on the bridge, and Mate Bobby Hawkins snapped a photo of the GPS screen at the instant of crossing, thus commemorating on digital memory what we experienced in real life.

In the maritime world, crossing the equator is a significant event, so much so that over many centuries a ritual has built up around it, a rite involving King Neptune and assorted good-humored tomfoolery. Due to somewhat rough seas, we decided to postpone the event until we could lie at anchor out at sea behind the protection of a reef the next morning.

At the appointed time, the crew and I appeared on the aft deck dressed in the costume of our choice. Invariably in these situations, everybody cross-dresses, though just why this should be I can't say. Captain Lucas, as a celebrant of many crossings, was Eric, the brother of King Neptune and the only non-cross-dresser. It was his duty to preside over the welcoming into the fraternity of the first-timers, called pollywogs—something like fraternity pledges—and he did so in style, dressed in toga and white beard.

Pollywogs had been instructed in their formal invitations to appear dressed in a theme beginning with the letter E. A version of GI Jane, Chef Jeanette dressed in camo and toted a machine gun. She called herself Explosive. Darla, the stew, had a beard and frazzled white hair—something on the order of Einstein. Mate Bobby was Eve, she of the Adam association. Our engineer, Sean, covered over in black shoe polish, with black long johns and a black plastic wig twisted into Rasta braids, was Edith, the "Ethnic Exotic Dancer."

Yours truly was stunning, if I may say so myself, in a slinky, clingy, low-cut red dress with matching bra supporting, more or less, enormous boobs. Hooker red lipstick, cheesy diamond earrings, and a full head of Rasta dreads completed the ensemble for E. Z. Duzit of Duzit Escort Services—"Do it on the equator" our memorable advert line.

I couldn't resist asking whether anybody thought the dress made my butt look too big.

Following introductions, we all reported to the sun deck, where Eric conducted the ceremony with appropriate sonorous speech and grave demeanor. Each in turn was first blindfolded and then became the object of various assaults upon his or her dignity, such as being washed down by a hose, sprinkled with flour, and having a raw egg cracked over the head. At the ceremony's conclusion, we were issued official proclamations declaring us members of King Neptune's Kingdom, and thus no longer pollywogs.

All of this strenuous activity worked up appetites that were stanched by breakfast on the aft deck prepared by Chef Jeanette. On a glorious sunny day, seas calm behind the reef, we gave thanks to our good fortunes thus far and eagerly looked forward to great adventures ahead.

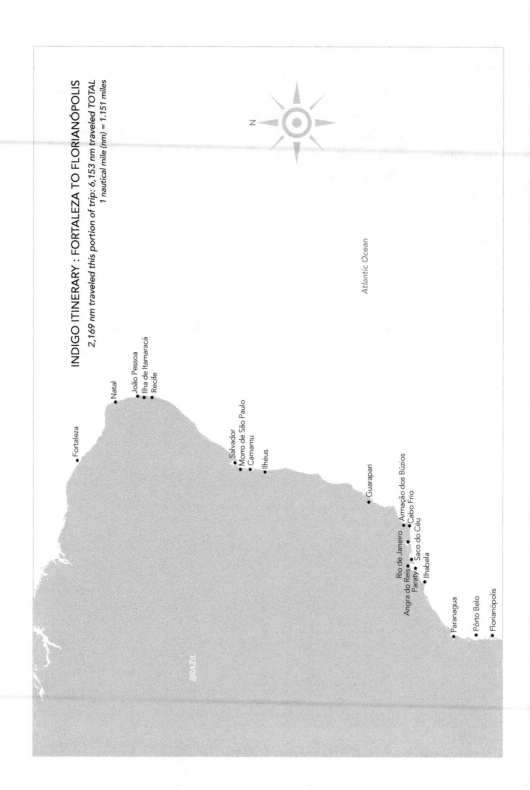

INDIGO ITINERARY : FORTALEZA TO FLORIANÓPOLIS

2,169 nm traveled this portion of trip: 6,153 nm traveled TOTAL
1 nautical mile (nm) = 1.151 miles

N

BRAZIL

Atlantic Ocean

Fortaleza

Natal
João Pessoa
Ilha de Itamaracá
Recife

Salvador
Morro de São Paulo
Camamu
Ilhéus

Guarapari

Rio de Janeiro
Armação dos Búzios
Cabo Frio
Saco do Céu
Angra do Reis
Paraty
Ilhabela

Paranagua
Pôrto Belo
Florianópolis

THREE

Family Fun and New Friends in Brazil

From Devil's Island, we put to sea and traveled a leg of over 1,000 nautical miles. For good reason—piracy and other dangers—we leapfrogged over the northernmost parts of Brazil and past the delta of the storied Amazon River. Especially at its seaward reaches, the Amazon has become a noted haven for pirates. Its enormous length and width is daunting, as well. Vicente Yáñez Pinzón, the first European to sail up the river, traveled a thousand miles before he realized it was not an arm of the ocean. Even 2,000 miles upriver, the Amazon is seven miles wide.

Brazil is larger than the lower forty-eight states, and it shares a border with every other South American country except Chile and Ecuador. Brazil exports immense quantities of coffee, the black liquid that fuels much of the American economy.

Fortaleza, Brazil

On July 29, after five days at sea, we reached the city of Fortaleza, Brazil, the country's fifth largest. From seaward, the place could be Chicago from Lake Michigan, with a solid wall of high-rise condos, hotels, and office buildings extending for many miles across the horizon. We arrived on a Sunday afternoon and anchored off the city's main resort beach.

From our anchorage, we could hear giant speakers blasting Brazilian music to a gathering throng—a lure I was unable to pass up. Mate Bobby dropped me ashore for a walkabout, and it was during this that I learned the cause of the festivities. I had happened upon the annual gay pride parade! And what an event it turned out to be. Thousands of partygoers lined the streets, only a few of whom were obviously gay or lesbian. Kiosks selling everything imaginable were crowded along sidewalks, and soon enough here came the parade: ten semis hauling huge flatbed trailers, each overflowing with music speakers, musicians, politicos, and flamboyant costumes in every shade of the rainbow. My favorite was the guy (or girl?) leading the whole thing dressed as a nun. Nothing surprising there, except that she was pregnant and carried an infant!

Hello, Brazil. I knew I was gonna like this country.

~~~

Kitty, our son, Grant, and Grant's friend Will arrived in Fortaleza to join me in exploring the steaming jungles, mysterious mountains, and bikini-studded beaches. The weather was balmy. South of the equator, technically it was winter—if you count a tropical 82 degrees Fahrenheit as "winter."

It was nearing midday when we ventured out to take stock of the local cuisine at a churrascaria. For those unfamiliar with Brazilian fine dining, in a churrascaria, waiters start the meal by bringing out some sort of drink festooned with limes. Next, a salad bar rich with delicacies is offered, followed by a row of waiters bearing swords that serve as spits carrying every part of the cow, chicken, or pig you've ever heard of and several that I'm sure you have not. If you think I exaggerate, a diagram of a cow with the parts helpfully numbered was present at our table.

The waiters continued arriving with offerings of spit-skewered meats until we were forced to wave them away. *No more! No more!* That, of course, was when the dessert cart arrived.

After the meal, we enjoyed live blues guitar at an outdoor bar while we smoked fine cigars—the boys and me, not Kitty. Then we hailed a taxi to take us back to *Indigo*. Since we spoke no Portuguese and the driver no English nor Spanish, we attempted to communicate with him via the timeless medium of vague gestures and pointing at maps. It must have worked, because in due course we were delivered to *Indigo*.

~~~

The next day, Saturday, dawned clear and fair, apparently business as usual in Brazil. Since it was a perfect day for outdoor excursions, we herded ourselves into a cab, bent on taking full advantage of some attractions beyond the city limits.

About half an hour's drive northwest of Fortaleza is the picturesque fishing village of Cumbuco, known for its palm trees, beach restaurants, fresh fish market, and its extreme sports. Thanks to a peculiar quirk of geography, Cumbuco's coastline features enormous, rolling sand dunes that attract the kind of people who enjoy risking life and limb by hurling themselves through the air on planks. Indeed, we'd come to see—or do, in the case of the younger and more foolhardy members of our party—precisely this.

We conscripted a pair of dune buggies ("boogies" to the locals) and were driven wildly up and down the dunes. In a country largely deprived of winter sports, the Cumbuco dunes serve as a credible alternative. Substitute sand dunes for mountains, boogies for snowmobiles, and sandboards for snowboards, and you'll hardly miss the northern climes.

While Grant and Will continued racing up and down sand dunes, I decided to have an on-the-beach massage. This gave me time to observe the local beachgoers in their native habitat. Brazilian women are famous for their thong-style bathing attire that leaves little to the imagination and much to the appreciative eye. Before rushing to book a Brazilian vacation, however, you should know that the thong is not only the province of beautiful, dark-eyed young women. *Everyone* wears skimpy uniforms at this beach: mothers of five, old men, teenage boys, and gray-haired matrons. For every bathing beauty in a tiny two-piece, there is a middle-aged man with ample back hair and a banana hammock. Despite the prevalence of the Speedo, I can assure you that I saw no Olympic swimmers.

Something else to keep in mind if you're planning a trip to Brazil is the rampant crime. We saw armed hotel guards, electrified security fences, security cameras everywhere, and barred house windows. We'd been instructed by locals to take precautions for our safety: no wearing valuable jewelry or watches while traveling, no traveling alone, and no traveling by night. Tourists are discouraged from walking; better to take a taxi.

At the end of our fun day in the sun, we returned to *Indigo*, showered extensively in an effort to dislodge sand from our more remote crevices, and then indulged our well-earned appetites for meat at a churrascaria once more.

Natal, Brazil

When we departed the Fortaleza marina early the next morning, the sea was smooth—at least as sailors count it—although the waves standing at about five to six feet alarmed Kitty. I assured her that if she spent any time at sea, she'd soon learn to welcome six-foot seas.

The city of Natal was a welcome sight to many eyes. Unfortunately, Natal offered *Indigo* little in the way of good anchorage. In fact, we were discovering that harbors of even moderate quality and depth were in shockingly low supply along almost the entire coast of Brazil. Local captains cautioned us about the lack of places to shelter from the ocean and the even rarer suitable marinas.

At Natal, we made do by dropping anchor off the coast and taking the tender into the city. After a brief tour of the town by taxi, we were delivered to the local "tourism center," a restaurant where the proprietor and his wife spoke halting English. What our hosts lacked in language skills, they more than made up for in the warmth of their hospitality.

For dinner, we went to Camaroes. Though we sat to eat no earlier than ten p.m., families with children trickled in until eleven. The natives certainly maintain a later schedule than is customary in the

US! Nonetheless, the fare was bountiful and the conversation stimulating as we connected across languages and cultures.

João Pessoa, Brazil

Next morning we pushed on to Cabedelo on the Rio Paraiba. Within the river's sheltering embrace, we dropped anchor, kicked back, and took in the resplendent sunset. After a peaceful night's sleep, we boarded the tender and ventured a few miles downriver to the bustling metropolis of João Pessoa. This city has two claims to fame: one is that it is the capital of the Brazilian state of Paraíba, and the second is that it is the easternmost mainland city in the Americas, sited at the tip of the great bulge of South America's east coast.

We returned to the boat in time for a truly incandescent sunset and discovered that we were anchored about a hundred yards from a unique tradition. As the sun bowed its weary head behind the clouds, ten tour buses rolled up to the shore and began disgorging passengers. An impromptu fiesta began as they celebrated the setting sun, complete with chanting and cheering, accompanied by Ravel's *Bolero*. The tune played on a loop over loudspeakers, and hearing it repeated seven or eight or twelve times cured us of any desire to hear it ever again.

Since it was Saturday, Chef Jeanette had devised for us a traditional Brazilian Saturday dinner: feijoada (black beans, rice, and a startling array of salted pork products all stewed together). So far so good. But the meal also featured *farofa*, which resembles, and also tastes like, finely minced breadcrumbs. The locals eat it with everything, but I confess I failed to see the appeal.

Ilha de Itamaracá

We sailed out of the protective waters of the Rio Paraíba and continued our journey south. The weather was perfect, and being in no particular hurry, we traveled slowly, hugging the coast, stopping occasionally to try our hands at fishing (no luck), and generally managing to be exquisitely lazy.

As evening approached, Captain Lucas spotted a particularly desirable specimen of anchorage sandwiched between the mainland and a palm-tree-dotted island. Getting into it, however, required maneuvering about an extensive sandbank on which we soon became stuck fast. Fortuitously, a neighborly boater guided us off the bank and pointed us toward clearer channels. Captain and crew were all apologies, but it appeared that, despite our computers and charts, locals knew this sandbank to shift unpredictably, the better to ensnare unwary travelers. At any rate, by the time the sun began descending in all her finery, we were ensconced in the clear, turquoise waters of our harborage. That night we enjoyed the cool breezes on the aft deck as we dined.

Next morning we learned that the island we had ducked behind was Ilha de Itamaracá, home to Fort of Santa Cruz de Itamaracá, known by tourists as Fort Orange. It was from this island, in 1631, that the Dutch launched an ill-advised invasion of Brazil. In modern times, the island of Itamaracá has become something of a resort, thanks to its languid and tropical beaches. Indeed, *Indigo's* anchorage looked like something straight out of a postcard.

We took the tender to shore and attempted to find a taxi to take us to the town of Olinda, about forty miles away. This took significant time, and the transportation that eventually showed up stretched the definition of "taxi" to its limit: two men in a beat-up van. They did agree, however, to drive us to Olinda, and proceeded to do so at a substantial velocity. At length, our headlong advance was halted so that we could take on not the usual diesel or gasoline but propane gas, a new fuel source to me.

Olinda, when it finally appeared, was standing room only. People and traffic jammed its run-down streets. Though large and perched comfortably on the coast, I presume the town is not a major tourist hub. Nonetheless, we did find a historic area of town liberally festooned with colonial architecture. It seemed unwise to hoof it amid the general bedlam, so we gawked at everything from the relative safety of a propane-powered taxi.

We returned to *Indigo* and spent the rest of the afternoon enjoying the attractions of our little bay, even taking turns to dive off the top of *Indigo* into the warm, clear water below. Then we tied a line behind the tender and did some wakeboarding.

Grant and Will wanted to explore the island, so I took them ashore and agreed to meet them for dinner in a few hours at the Orange Beach Hotel. When I arrived at the appointed time, I discovered that Grant had made the acquaintance of the Dutch woman who owned the place. She, in turn, introduced us to a trio of Dutch archeologists, guests of her establishment.[1] We ate dinner together, and our new archeologist friends told us that they were experts in Dutch fortifications of the seventeenth century, a narrow specialty if I ever heard of one.

As luck would have it, a monthly party for hospitality workers was happening that night, and the hotel's proprietress invited us as her guests.

Next morning, our archeologist friends joined us for breakfast aboard *Indigo*, then took us on a tour of the old fort. Fort Orange, it seems, is only one of the numerous old Dutch forts dotting the coastline in this area. After the Portuguese captured it from the Dutch, they expanded it substantially. At the time of our visit, all that was visible to the untrained eye was the Portuguese part of the fort, but our friends had been busy excavating artifacts from the Dutch original.

For lunch, we found a tiny beachside restaurant, the establishment of a fellow whose acquaintance I'd made at the hospitality worker event. This guy boasted an impressive beer belly and was both the owner and the cook. Imagine a structure with a thatched roof and no walls not fifty feet from the water's edge, surrounded by plastic tables and chairs for guests. Beneath the roof stands a woodburning stove and a small table for food prep, as well as two large metal tubs, one full of small crabs, the other full of large crabs, all clambering on top of each other in a futile effort to escape. For diners not in the

---

1. If you've ever met any Dutchmen, then you know that they are all conversant in English, and probably two or three other languages besides.

mood for extremely fresh crab, nearby sit Styrofoam coolers packed full with ice and fish of all shapes and sizes, including a huge piranha with the sharpest teeth I've ever seen.

We said yes to both fish and beer, and immediately set to work on the latter. The plastic furniture could be moved right down to the water, should you so choose, and we did. Lunch arrived about an hour later—not that we felt the passage of time. At any rate, it was well worth the wait. The fish, grilled whole over the woodburning stove, was mouthwateringly delicious, as were the side dishes. How our host had conjured up sides in his tiny outdoor kitchen remained a mystery. They included fresh tomatoes and onions, rice with green onions and something like scrambled eggs, cold pasta slathered with a tasty sauce, and for dessert, fresh fruit, including the best pineapple I've ever had.

Next morning, we boarded the tender and set out to circumnavigate the island. Seen from the sea, Itamaracá looks every inch an island paradise: tall, elegant palm trees sway over white sandy beaches, and you have the impression that somewhere close they must be shooting a Corona commercial. The stony bulwarks of Fort Orange and the brilliant white walls of the nearby resort hotel peeking through the trees promise precisely the right amount of human habitation, all the homey comforts without too many tourists. The waters that surround the island are breathtaking shades of turquoise and azure separated by sandbars and beaches.

We had encountered no Americans in this area, and very few of the locals on this nameless island spoke English, but we did run into a visiting Swiss family with whom we exchanged pleasantries.

The next morning was quiet, the sky slightly overcast, though not dreary. Captain Lucas put Will and Grant to work cleaning the waterline of the boat, an occupation I wholeheartedly endorsed. Of course, this entailed the boys being in the water most of the morning, so it was no great hardship for them. Grant also spent some time working with Engineer Sean in the engine room. As payment, the crew took the boys to a nearby river in the afternoon for more wakeboarding.

The next two or three days were spent having breakfasts and lunches on the beach, diving off the ship into the emerald waters of the bay, partying, and boating. The boys, I believed, were well on their way to embarking on careers as professional wakeboarders.

Salvador, Brazil

We arrived in Salvador on August 12 and docked at Bahia Marina, the first marina we had encountered since Fortaleza. It was a relief not to have to lower the tender just to get to shore.

Chief among the wonders we saw in Salvador was Sao Francisco Church. While the exterior of the church features a rugged stone cross, the interior is bathed in gold. The walls, pillars, vaults, and ceilings are fashioned of gilded woodwork. Gold foliage decorates the arches, and paintings framed in gold serve as ceiling panels. Cherubim, hands on their hips, peer down from among gold leaf.[2] The entire interior is adorned so ornately and thoroughly with gold that the transept appears to glow in the light.

Morro de São Paolo, Brazil

After saying goodbye to Kitty, Grant, and Will, I begin to explore the areas around Salvador easily reachable by car, heading first to a place that is generally raved about: Praia de Forte, or "Beach Fort" in English. It became quickly apparent that this was another too-cute outdoor shopping mall, a bit like a small and mildly ragged Nantucket, holding no interest for me. Its beach, lined with rocks, is nothing much.

Looking for greener pastures, we made the several-hour trip to the truly delightful seaside resort town of Morro de São Paolo, at the northeast end of Tinharé Island, on the Dendê Coast south of Bahia. We anchored just offshore in a protected bay.

Morro de São Paolo's history is colorful, having been originally settled by pirates and later fought over by the French and the Dutch.

---

2. These swaggering urchins are not quite chaste enough for modern churchgoers, so their wee manhoods have been filed off, doubtless by earnest priests in stiff collars.

The town has no car traffic. Transport is by foot along sand streets— or paths, more accurately—and elevation changes are considerable. Unpretentious restaurants, cozy bars, and the usual shops full of ladies' stuff abound, yet there is an air of authenticity, a slight raffish- ness, that makes the place a joy.

After a long walk along the sunny, windswept beach to a first- class resort, I took a rattletrap bus ride back into town over rough dirt roads, past donkey carts and modest hovels, finally unloading at a sand-floored bar right on the beach. It was out of season, and so the usually oppressive crowds of a popular place like this hadn't arrived yet.

I whiled away two days here under near-perfect skies. It was one of the few places in Brazil to which I'd gladly return.

Camamu, Brazil

We raised anchor and headed south along the Brazilian coast a mere forty miles to Camamu. The village is located up a wide river surrounded by sandbars and breaking surf, making the entry an attention-getting experience. All along its seaward coast are miles of white sand beaches covered over in coconut palms. The shoreline is dotted with substantial homes as well as the simple houses of local fishermen.

It was at one of these that I chose to have lunch. I was the only guest amid a family that included several little kids, a dog, and a loud parrot. The fishermen ply their trade in dugout canoes made from a single tree and exactly resembling the craft used by native Indians a thousand years ago. Several of these, upturned on land, lay in the yard where my lunch was served.

Porto Seguro, Brazil

Seguro means "secure," and the port is certainly secure if you have a shallow-draft boat that allows you to get behind its protecting reef. We didn't, and so we had to anchor behind a reef several miles at sea for protection from the rollers.

After a sloggy ride in the tender, I got into town, where I connected with Bruno Massidda, whom I had met in Casa de Campo. Bruno took me miles up the beach to a restaurant owned by an Italian friend of his. There we had lunch and too many *caiparinhas* while seated on the beach under a sunshade.

In case you're wondering, the *caiparinha* is Brazil's traditional national drink. It's made from *cachaça*, or *pinga* for short, a clear jet fuel distilled from sugar cane, poured over ice into a cocktail glass full of crushed lime slices and a dab of sugar. For variety, you can get the jet fuel mixed with various fruits, including mango, passion fruit, strawberries, pineapple, or my favorite, the fruit of the cashew tree. If ordered with vodka as the active ingredient, it's called a *caipiroska*.

After lunch, Bruno took me to his eighteenth-century town house located adjacent to the fish market. His place was cozy and rustic but delightful, with a small garden out back facing an inland waterway. The home's ceiling beams were hand hewn, still showing the ax marks.

Like Morro de São Paulo, I found Porto Seguro to be something of a miniature St. Augustine, Florida. The shops are open every night, kiosks are set up along the seawall, and the locals and tourists promenade with kids in tow. Later, music and dancing starts in the bars. It's a pleasant town with little crime, and I agreed that Bruno had chosen his new home well.

Isla dos Abrolhos

Leaving Porto Seguro, we headed some thirty nautical miles out into the open Atlantic to a Brazilian national park, a group of four windblown, nearly bare rocky islands called Isla dos Abrolhos, where we anchored in a protected harbor. The islands are uninhabited, and generally uninhabitable, but for a few park personnel who conduct scientific research and operate a lighthouse on the largest of the islands.

For me, the most remarkable aspect of this place was the whales. This whole area was a breeding and feeding ground this time of year for humpback whales preparing to head south to Antarctica. In the morning and evening hours, as we gazed out over the wide sea before us, there were blow spouts everywhere we looked. Hundreds, maybe thousands, of whales were rolling, feeding, breaching, doing the whale thing.

One morning while having breakfast, my eye caught sight of a huge whale breaching nearby, and he repeated this for me three times just in case I missed the first. Several times while underway, we had to slow or veer to avoid hitting one of these sluggish monsters. As we were preparing to leave the harbor, a mama, daddy, and calf came swimming right up to *Indigo* as they lunged through the surf, chasing schools of krill.

Armação dos Búzios

Our next stop, Armação dos Búzios, is on a thorny peninsula. It was a sleepy little getaway for wealthy Brazilians wearied by the hustle and bustle of Rio de Janeiro in the early 1900s. Then Brigitte Bardot vacationed there in 1964, and it became known as Búzios, the trendiest destination for the jet-setting crowd, studded with lovely little inns (*pousadas*), pricey boutiques, sunny beaches, and palatial homes with stunning ocean views.

I decided to stay ashore two nights to give the crew a break. Taking a suite overlooking the bay—and *Indigo*, as it turned out—I relaxed with great food, a hammock on the patio for naps, and reading. The weather was overcast, cool, and rainy. It was, I reminded myself, winter down there.

When the crew and I reconvened aboard *Indigo*, we resumed our southerly course.

Rio de Janeiro, Brazil

From the sea, Rio de Janeiro is one of the world's great sights. Sugarloaf Mountain, the Corcovado with the giant statue of Christ on top, miles of stunning beaches, volcanic rocky islands around its natural harbor, all make Rio a truly world-class city.

Entering at midday, we easily located the marina, situated right in the heart of the city and well protected both from the sea and from the many criminals who ply their trade here. On a ride through town, I was impressed with the many parks, interior lakes, biking paths, and especially the treelined streets. Rio was far more beautiful than any city we had so far visited.

I had invited three longtime friends, Earl Robinson, Pete Cicchine, and Chris Jensen, to join me in Rio and spend two weeks cruising the Brazilian coast with me aboard *Indigo*. From the airport, we traveled by van directly to the boat for a big breakfast, including grits so they would feel at home (and me, too). Their strong Northwest Florida accents were music to my ears.

After breakfast, a tour guide I'd hired took us up Sugarloaf Mountain on a tram to view the city in all its glory. It was a clear day, perfect weather. It was Independence Week, and the beaches were packed with locals. Long lines for the train dissuaded us from taking a trip to the summit of Mount Corcovado to stand at the foot of Cristo Redentor, the enormous statue of Christ watching over the city. We opted to view it from afar.

After a drive through the treelined streets and beautiful parks and neighborhoods of Rio, we enjoyed lunch at Porcão Restaurant, situated on the waterfront of one of Rio's many beaches. Later we enjoyed light snacks at Devassa Bar and Belmonte Bar, both open-air neighborhood places filled with locals and serving great food. After some walking around the area and lots of laughs, we retired to the boat utterly spent.

I could not bring my friends to Rio, of course, without giving them a tour of its world-famous beaches, Ipanema and Copacabana. We set out in the morning, keeping a sharp eye out for the latest in female swimsuit fashions. For lunch, we chose to avoid these crowded places and instead went to Praia Vermelha, or Red Beach, a small place tucked away at the base of Sugarloaf Mountain. There we sat on the sand in rented beach chairs, sipping on cold beer and watching bikinis pass by, and joking among ourselves until it was time to eat at a restaurant right on the beach.

Following long naps on *Indigo* and further tours of the city and extended bull sessions, we dined that night at the famous Marius Degustare on Copacabana Beach and then retired for the night, once again exhausted.

Paraty, Brazil

Early the next morning, we departed Rio's welcoming harbor and forged south along the Costa Verde. Before the morning was well advanced, we called for a halt and took the tender ashore for a walk through the jungle—a prepared nature trail, really—that winds through several tiny fishing villages. At one was Pousada Gata Russa ("Russian Cat Inn"), where we drank fresh fruit juices and whiled away the time sitting on the shore of the cove in perfect contentment.

That evening, just before sunset, we arrived at the village of Paraty, a Portuguese colony settled in 1650 and continually occupied to the present day. This beautiful little town lies at water's edge backed by high hills covered over in thick verdure of an amazing variety. Sandy beaches lined with coconut palms give the place the feel of a remote paradise, which it surely is.

As we eased into the harbor, the sun set behind the town's mountainous backdrop, painting the sky a soft orange pastel. Tied up along the length of the dock were old wooden schooners, replicas of historical ships, painted in vivid colors. The schooners, we learned, were seaworthy and ferry tourists to nearby islands, bays, and beaches.

In town, streets paved with rough granite stones wound among one-story colonial Portuguese buildings. Once devoted to the slave trade, these had been turned into shops, bars, and restaurants. We sampled the offerings of a few bars, and at one enjoyed a combo playing Brazilian music like bossa nova, samba, and MPB.[3]

Before leaving Paraty, we took a tour by van to an old sugar cane farm that also makes *cachaça*. Due to the hot climate and a cornucopia of aggressive microbes, Brazilians distill sugar cane the moment it is harvested. Distilleries like this one are often located onsite. A water

---

3. As they call it—modern popular Brazilian music.

wheel fed by a rushing stream still powers the presses that squeeze the juice from the cane.

Ilhabela, Brazil
Leaving Paraty, we arrived at Ilhabela ("Beautiful Island") at sun-down, in time to locate an anchorage just off the dock of one of the town's several yacht clubs. *Indigo's* hydraulic crane, used for lifting the tender from the deck, had developed a problem, so the captain called ashore and arranged for a local water taxi to pick us up and take us to town.

Right away, we all liked the place. After strolling along its main street into the town square, we enjoyed light appetizers at one restaurant and a main course at another next door. The town is clean, its buildings well painted in pleasing colors, and its shops stocked with upscale merchandise. It has waterfront parks and lots of shade trees. Locals wandered about on this lovely evening.

The next morning, we took a van tour of a small part of the island and stopped along the way at beachfront bars, sampling their wares. At each stop, we were greeted warmly by the owner and offered chairs right on the sandy beach, with umbrellas to ward off the still-rising sun. It was out of season here, so there were few people in sight.

Our last stop for the morning was at a marvelous beachfront resort hotel, a place we all agreed was the best place we had seen yet in Brazil. It has about twenty rooms, all done in fine taste, and the place is well maintained. Leather sofas conveniently located under a shade tree right on the beach were too much to resist. There, seated comfortably, we were served beer brought in silver ice buckets.

We were all so impressed with this place that we changed our plans and decided to have lunch there. Linen-clothed tables were set up for us on the beach in the shade of the trees, where we were seated with our feet in the sand. In due course, we were served an outstanding meal of fresh grilled fish and *picanha*, a cut of beef little known in the US. The design and execution of everything at this hotel is top drawer and artful.

Paranaguá, Brazil

With some regret, we departed from Ilhabela on an overnight voyage to Paranaguá, capital of the state of Paraná. A storm had moved into the area, seas were rough, and the sky rainy with light fog. This important port city is in a bay up a long channel, where it is protected from foul weather.

When we arrived, cargo ships were lined up in a holding pattern offshore waiting for their turn to dock. We detoured up a wide river and anchored off the local yacht club, which sent a water taxi to pick us up for the ten-minute ride to town. Unfortunately, without knowing how many people it would be hauling, the club sent a small aluminum, flat-bottomed skiff. This we filled with six people, some of whom tipped the scales at well over 200 pounds. The ride to shore was touch-and-go as we sat still—very, very still.

At the club, we unloaded, climbed into a taxi, and headed off into town for lunch and a brief walk around the waterfront. Its most remarkable feature is the prevalence of Portuguese colonial buildings, most newly restored, dating from the 1700s. These, together with ancient cobbled streets, give the place the pleasant if shopworn feel of a tourist attraction not yet discovered by tourists.

Returning to *Indigo* in a far larger taxi boat, we decided to make another long voyage, this time to the misnamed Porto Belo ("Beautiful Port"). The weather remained cool, breezy, and overcast, with intermittent rain as we took a taxi ride around the beachfront and promptly decided this place was a little too much like Panama City, Florida. Between stacks of condos, shops sell overpriced knick-knacks. The dreary weather didn't help any of us view it in a more positive light.

Santa Catarina

From Porto Belo, we made our way in still-inclement weather to the famous island of Santa Catarina and its principal city of Florianopolis, called Floripa by the locals. As we had moved south, the economies of the states and towns had grown ever more affluent, the streets cleaner and less potholed. Floripa—and just to the north, Ilhabela—are at the top of this list, with beautiful homes, shops stocked with quality consumer items, and great restaurants. Here there are none of the favelas, or Brazilian ghettos, so common to the north. There is little crime.

The three amigos and I decided to take advantage of a day of brilliant sunshine and clear skies and do a day cruise to a nearby cove. On the way, we spotted a humpback whale lolling about on the surface. Backed by sloping hills with colorful homes and shops along its waterfront, the cove easily resembles a coastal town in Italy.

But there was a sadness in the air, this last day together. I had spent two solid weeks with my best friends of fifty years, and all without a cross word from anybody.

~~~

My time with the three amigos was over, but our stay in Floripa was far from it. *Indigo's* docking for routine maintenance and to repair the recalcitrant crane arm proved to be unexpectedly lengthy and vexing. Partly the long stay was caused by the intensely bureaucratic and snail-paced Brazilian customs department, which took their sweet time processing simple shipments of parts and spares. But far more delay was caused by a local diesel mechanic who, while working in the engine room, left a seawater hose unattached without shutting off the valve. This oversight went undiscovered until seawater had flooded the engine room up to the deck plates.

Now the required repairs were anything but routine. Several electrical systems were extensively damaged, and *Indigo's* pumps had to be entirely rebuilt.

In about two months, the necessary shipments had been rubber-stamped and were ready for pick up in Imbituba. We took the short cruise there, tied up at a massive stone pier, and took on board the shipment of parts and a new outboard motor for the tender as well as a considerable quantity of fuel. At last, we were once again on our way.

Pacific Ocean

BOLIVIA

PARAGUAY

BRAZIL

• Florianópolis

• Imbituba

Viña del Mar •

URUGUAY

Buenos Aires •

• Punta del Este

ARGENTINA

CHILE

• Mar del Plata

Valdivia •

Puerto Montt •

Castro •

• Puerto Quellón

• Puerto Madryn

N

Atlantic Ocean

• Santa Cruz

INDIGO ITINERARY : FLORIANÓPOLIS TO VIÑA DEL MAR

5,332 nm traveled this portion of trip: 11,485 nm traveled TOTAL

1 nautical mile (nm) = 1.151 miles

• Punta Arenas

Ushuaia •

• Puerto Williams, Chile

• Caleta Lientur

• Cape Horn

FOUR

Hobnobbing with Argentina's Rich and Famous

We found nothing remarkable along the southern coast of Brazil on our way to Uruguay, a small, peace-loving, Spanish-speaking country huddled between Brazil and Argentina.

Punta del Este, Uruguay

After an uneventful and relaxing cruise of a few days, we reached Punta del Este, the Palm Beach of South America, on December 10. Rare for the continent, it has a well-protected marina in the heart of town, an easy walk to many shops, bars, and restaurants.

At dockside, I came to meet Enrique Marthi, a warmhearted and charming man who had been a huge help to Captain Lucas in getting us a berth. He was the lead captain of a fleet of seven Italian express yachts of about seventy feet, all nearly identical. At first I took this to be a charter fleet, but later learned that they were the personal yachts of Carlos Pedro Blaquier who, at age seventy, was rumored to be South America's wealthiest man. Why, you may wonder, did he own seven smaller yachts instead of a single large one? He claimed with some reason that if one broke down, he had six others to choose from. While in Punta, he lived on one boat, his wife on another. A third was used for dining and crew quarters, and the others for guests.

I was invited to have lunch with Carlos and his top executives and a few friends on his dining yacht. One long table was set for the dozen or so ladies on board, mostly wives of the executives, and also Cristina, the beautiful and ever-smiling girlfriend of Carlos. Another table was surrounded by the men, with me seated next to Carlos. When I asked why the gender split, Carlos replied with a twinkle in his eyes that "women are good for the bed, but not for the table."

Lunch began with Uruguayan caviar and champagnes, followed by beef and vegetables from Carlos's own estancias (ranches), all wonderfully prepared by Natalia, his personal chef. Fine wines flowed generously. Dessert and coffee followed.

A few days after our lunch, Carlos and his executives came aboard *Indigo* for a tour, and we all enjoyed good company, many laughs, wine, and appetizers prepared by Chef Jeanette.

Through Carlos I met Esteban Caselli, the former Argentine ambassador to the Holy See in Rome and presently the ambassador for the Order of Malta to Peru. Esteban kindly offered the use of his private car and driver—a former federal policeman and now full-time security man—during my upcoming visit to Buenos Aires. He also introduced me to Juan Scalesciani, a wealthy Argentine who made his money in the oil business, sold out to Chevron, and at the time was developing hotels and owned a pharmaceutical company. He was the developer and owner of the fabulous new Palacio Duhau, Park Hyatt, in Buenos Aires, likely the best hotel in all of South America.

In short order, and utterly by chance, I had been introduced to some of the wealthiest and most influential men in Argentina.

I took a car to the surrounding towns of Punta Ballena, La Barra, and the funky, hyper-cool Jose Ignacio. I was impressed with the abundance of modern architecture in homes, hotels, and shops, much of it extraordinary.

I also took the time to visit two of Punta's beaches, Playa Brava, or "Fierce Beach," on the Atlantic side, and Playa Mansa, or "Tame Beach," on the Rio de la Plata side. At the Playa Brava, an impressive sculpture of a giant hand rises from the sand, meant to warn visitors about its dangerous currents and large waves. For me, the light brown sand and murky water of the beaches were uninviting.

Buenos Aires, Argentina

Despite the "Rio" in its name, the Rio de la Plata is by any reasonable assessment an enormous bay rather than a river. This huge divot in the coast of South America is formed by the confluence of the Uruguay River and the Paraná River on the Argentine/Uruguayan border. The silt from the rivers colors the water of this estuary a murky brown. It also has a reputation for unannounced storms. More than 2,000 shipwrecks lie along the bottom of the estuary, dotting the nautical charts so densely that at times they make navigation dangerous.

For these reasons, we were obliged to take on board an official government pilot for the crossing to Buenos Aires. The pilot confidently predicted calm conditions, as did the three separate weather services we consulted.

They were all wrong. Around midnight, a bad storm that had come roaring out of the Argentine Pampas struck the area, and right away, the ports at Punta, Montevideo, and Colonia were closed. Winds climbed to over seventy knots and, blowing over the shallows of the Rio de la Plata, whipped up enormous, sharp-edged waves. Here was an obvious cause of all those shipwrecks.

I was in my cabin attempting (but failing) to sleep as the storm tossed the 280-ton *Indigo* around as though she were a rowboat. One wave knocked us so violently that the glass tabletop in the salon flew off its mount, shattered, and chewed up the woodwork. All the exterior seat cushions flew off into the night. Liquor cabinets flopped open, spilling their contents all over the place.

Finally, Captain Lucas changed course, putting the weather on the bow instead of the beam, and the ride smoothed somewhat for the remainder of the run into Buenos Aires.

As the sun began to color the still-stormy sky, winds continued to blow at thirty-five to forty knots, and the ride remained uncomfortable. Then, across our bow, defining the western horizon, we saw a long, low blanket of dense, dark clouds, the leading edge of an infamous pampero storm front blowing east across the land. In the span of just twenty-four hours, we had been hit by two different storms in something like a pincer.

We were all cheered when Buenos Aires hove into view. I'd never felt more grateful to reach safe harbor!

I was also glad to see Kitty and Grant, who were waiting at the Buenos Aires airport when we arrived. They had come to join me in sampling the sights and sounds of South America's finest city.

Our first stop was lunch at the Alvear Palace Hotel. In the 1930s, or so the story was told to us, a Buenos Aires businessman visited Paris, fell in love with it, and decided to bring a little of it home with him. The hotel was styled along the lines of the Parisian Belle Époque, with sumptuous ornamentation, gilt paneling, and shiny marble floors. The buffet-style lunch wasn't bad, either, and there was plenty of champagne to go around.

After lunch, we met the driver that Esteban Caselli had generously loaned to us for our stay in the city. He was a young fellow named Hugo, and to call him a driver hardly did him justice. He was, in fact, a former federal police officer, and he provided personal security for Esteban. I felt gratified that Kitty and Grant would be in excellent hands during our stay.

Puerto Madera is Buenos Aires's bustling waterfront district. Once a working port, its warehouses have since been transformed into bars, restaurants, and nightclubs, and new construction has sprung up behind them.

This particular evening, however, Grant and Mate Bobby set their sights somewhat lower, visiting the local branch of the Hooters franchise.[1]

The following day, we called upon Esteban Caselli's friend Juan Scalesciani at the Park Hyatt Buenos Aires. Built in the 1890s, the hotel was once called the Palacio Duhau, the private residence of a wealthy Argentine family. Juan's company purchased the old mansion and

---

1. Yes, there's a Hooters in Buenos Aires.

renovated it at a cost of tens of millions. An underground passageway connects the historic part of the hotel to a newer, modern section. The juxtaposition of an ornate Tudor Revival mansion with an elegant structure of modern design is striking.

Fortified with lunch and *lagrima*, we left the hotel and toured the surrounding neighborhood, known as the Recoleta. It has a strong Parisian feel with its broad boulevards, elegant buildings, and numerous parks. There is also a historic cemetery where Eva Peron is buried.

I find that it is always useful to get a native's-eye view of a place, and Hugo was just the right person for this. Next day, I persuaded him to take us on a tour of the city.

Buenos Aires was permanently settled by ambitious Spanish conquistadors in 1580. The city is divided into twenty-eight neighborhoods known as barrios, many of which are quite historic. Hugo took us first to the three barrios of Palermo, Palermo Soho, and Palermo Hollywood, which fancies itself a South American Beverly Hills. Small, "hip" boutiques abound. Then we continued on to San Telmo, one of the city's oldest and most historic barrios. The streets here are narrow and paved with cobblestones. Everywhere street vendors hawk their wares. Hugo informed us that there was a large, open-air antique market on weekends. San Telmo also boasts numerous tango parlors where you can experience Argentina's traditional dance.

Buenos Aires's traffic is, in a word, energetic. While painted lines and street signs adorn the city's thoroughfares, the drivers seem to take little notice of them. Instead, it's every man for himself, a policy that frequently results in hair-raising near misses. Hugo fearlessly braved a 480-foot-wide thoroughfare with eight lanes of hectic traffic running each way. I wasn't at all convinced that we would emerge alive, yet somehow he maneuvered us safely through the maelstrom.

Aside from the automotive mayhem, another notable curiosity of Buenos Aires is the unusual schedule of its residents. Hugo said that a typical routine might be to get home from work and nap until ten o'clock in the evening, followed by dinner at a restaurant at eleven o'clock, and on to a club at two. He said that many people drink and dance until daybreak, then go straight from the club to the office. When Kitty asked how people could possibly be productive after such a night, Hugo answered glibly, "That's why we're still a third world country!"

We soon learned that Argentina, and especially Buenos Aires, has a large population of Italian immigrants. These immigrants have been so influential that the local Spanish dialect has a uniquely Italian flavor.

It was now Christmas Eve, and since we were over 2,000 nautical miles south of the equator, the weather was balmy. I spent the morning exploring the local markets and galleries.

That night, Chef Jeanette and Kitty went to the Buenos Aires Metropolitan Cathedral to attend midnight Mass. The Mass actually happened at ten o'clock so that afterward families could enjoy a traditional Christmas feast and open presents. God only knows what time they must get to bed or if they sleep at all. I do believe that Argentines are an anthropological marvel, a truly nocturnal people!

In the evening, Grant, Mate Bobby, and Captain Lucas went out to get dinner and play pool at that traditional Argentine standby, TGI Friday's.[2]

The next day, Kitty, Grant, and I paid a visit to the Palacio Paz, a stately Louis XIV-style mansion built in the early 1900s. The building materials were imported from France and included marble, exquisite woodwork, extensive gold flake, and ceiling murals. The Palacio Paz is now a private club, the Military Officers' Association. Carlos Pedro sent a retired officer, Alejandro, to show us around.

The Palacio Paz stands in the Recoleta barrio, not far from the Park Hyatt, so after our tour, we had lunch at the hotel. That evening we held a small party aboard Indigo. Guests included the owner of the Park Hyatt, Juan Scalesciani, and his wife, Marta.

~~~

At the top of any list of things to see in Argentina is the world-famous Cataratas del Iguazú, or "Iguazú Falls," located a day's drive to the north on the border between Argentina and Brazil. Again our

2. Yes, there's a TGI Friday's in Buenos Aires.

benefactor Carlos Pedro lent us a hand, chartering a flight that would transport us swiftly to the falls. Hugo picked us up promptly at eight o'clock in the morning and chauffeured us to the airport.

In slightly over two hours, we made our final approach. The pilot did a couple of loops above the falls, giving us a spectacular aerial view. Once on the ground, however, our journey was just commencing. First, we boarded an open tour Jeep to Iguazú National Park and wound our way through miles of lush subtropical forest. We completed the final leg aboard a large inflatable raft that beat its way upriver to the falls. As on any good thrill ride, we were promised that audience members in the front row *would* get wet. We were in the front row.

The Iguazú Falls formed at the point where the Iguazú River tumbles over the edge of the high Paraná Plateau. This perilous shelf and its raging torrents, measuring nearly two miles across, create such mist that we could hardly see the other side. The falls consist of 275 separate cascades divided by islands of lush greenery. Some of these are relatively gentle, and the captain of our raft piloted us through a few of them. The largest is the Garganta del Diablo, or "Throat of the Devil," a raging torrent that plunges 240 feet. That one we avoided.

~~~

Over the next two days, Kitty went shopping, and Grant sampled the nightlife with Hugo's offspring—duly escorted, as promised, by the man himself. I visited the National Museum of Fine Arts, or Museo Nacional de Bellas Artes, whose collection includes sculptures by Rodin and Moore and paintings by Manet, Monet, Gauguin, and Van Gogh.

One evening we had dinner with Esteban Caselli, who had flown in from Punta del Este just to see us. I should mention that while Esteban speaks Spanish and Italian and a few other languages, he does not speak English. To overcome this obstacle, when he arrived at the yacht, he brought along the chief of protocol of the Argentine Foreign Ministry to serve as his translator.

After cocktails aboard *Indigo*, Esteban took us to El Mirasol,

Esteban's favorite restaurant in Buenos Aires. It immediately became our favorite as well. We enjoyed a convivial evening of fine dining, wine, and excellent conversation.

The next evening, Kitty and I dined in one of the restaurants in the posh Faena Hotel and afterward enjoyed a cabaret show, Argentina Imaginings. I confess that I enjoyed the show, especially the ending, when the performers stepped off the stage and into the audience. Before I knew it, I was dancing with a lithe young woman no one would describe as overdressed. I'm afraid I didn't get her name.

There were no concerns about how we would celebrate New Year's Eve while in Buenos Aires. Carlos Pedro invited us to a big shindig at one of his estates, La Torcaza, and sent his driver for us.

La Torcaza is Carlos Pedro's great obsession. He had it designed and built by Italian craftsmen over a period of eighteen years at what must have been a phenomenal expense. From the outside, the mansion is all spare, sharp angles, clad in brick and slate. Elegant statues of lions and wolves guard the immaculate lawn and swimming pool.

The inside of the house is a wonderland of marble from every corner of the globe, polished to perfection. The marble of the floors, walls, even the trim is cut and laid with precision, allowing the veins to run seamlessly one piece to another.

To sustain the immense weight of the marble, the foundation and sides were heavily reinforced. In addition, the marbled ground floor was designed to "float" free from the main structure. Despite this, the overall effect is airy and light.

Carlos Pedro does not actually live at La Torcaza; he only entertains there. In fact, he told me that he'd never spent a single night there. Can't blame him. Homey it is not. Here Carlos Pedro also stores many of the treasures he collected over the years, including china, silver, and ancient Greek and Roman statuary.

During our visit, Carlos Pedro took us down to his immense wine cellar, where he and his son had about 50,000 bottles of wine neatly stacked in climate-controlled racks floor to ceiling. In addition to wine, Carlos Pedro stored in the cellar hundreds of boxes of Cuban Churchill cigars, all made before Castro took over. Carlos Pedro generously gave me a box.

After our tour, we joined the other guests for champagne and caviar, and then we had a light dinner and lots of wine. I suppose when you're sitting on 50,000 bottles, you've got to drink when you can! This put everyone in a jovial mood.

Later, as the evening reached its festive stage, I donned my colorful Bob Marley cap with Rasta locks, wig, and sunglasses, which were such a hit that Carlos Pedro insisted on wearing the getup himself.

We retired back to *Indigo* around three o'clock in the morning.

~~~

Kitty and Grant returned to Florida, and over the next few days, I enjoyed dinner at Oviedo, maybe the finest restaurant in Buenos Aires. I had drinks at Casa Cruz, which could not accommodate me for dinner, even at the bar, because it was so popular. One night, taking leave of my senses, I attended a tango show at the Hotel Faena. Part dance and part play, accompanied by live music, this was even more entertaining than I ever would have guessed.

~~~

Finally, after an eventful stay in Buenos Aires and meeting some great new friends, it was time to continue on with our voyage. On a beautiful day with light breezes, *Indigo* set out from the harbor at Puerto Madero in downtown Buenos Aires and headed toward the Straits of Magellan and Cape Horn.

Mar del Plata, Argentina

We set a course east across the Rio de la Plata and then southeast across the mouth of the Samborombón Bay.

At Mar del Plata, we were greeted by refreshingly blue seas, a nice change from the murk of the Rio de la Plata, and the day was glorious with cloudless blue skies, warm sun, and calm seas—the same conditions that lure thousands of Argentines to the beaches.

I should clarify that a "beach" here is a place on the sea with a large strip shopping mall-like structure housing a bar, restaurant, restrooms, tourist shops, and the like. Out front, along the water's edge, is the real dirty sand beach. Packed together like the proverbial sardines, there is hardly room to move among the hordes. Just landward of that are acres of canvas cabanas, called *carpas*. These are about a hundred square feet each and are rented by the day. In these, the sunbather can change clothes, be served food and drink, nap, and entertain.

One day I took a taxi 120 kilometers north to Pinamar, arriving at seven p.m., just in time for the legal closing hour of the beach bars. Thousands of people who had just spent the day on the beach—the sand even browner than that of Mar del Plata—evacuated all at the same time. It was quite a traffic jam, and with the beach road parallel to the water, there was no way to escape it. Instead, I hiked to a restaurant for a few beers and dinner, and then returned to *Indigo*.

It was now obvious that in Argentina, as well as in most of South America, the summer holiday is much like that in Europe: it all takes place mostly in the same month—August in Europe, January in South America. The result is a crushing load of humanity descending on small places.

Puerto Madryn, Argentina

Having had our fill of tourist season, we raised anchor and endured a storm-tossed cruise to Golfo Nuevo. This gulf is a surprisingly round and sheltered bay carved out of the Península Valdés. In the late 1950s and early 1960s, it was the site of two mysterious submarine sightings by the Argentine navy. On the first occasion, during routine exercises, naval craft received radar pings off an unknown submarine, which they proceeded to chase around the bay for over twenty-four hours before it vanished permanently from their scopes.

Some cynical souls have suggested that the fact that the alarming and mysterious sightings dovetailed with naval requests to the government for new aircraft carriers and other equipment was more than a coincidence, but I will not cast aspersions on the claims of the

Argentine navy. All we can say for sure is that no phantom pings or mysterious periscopes were reported while *Indigo* was in the gulf.

We dropped anchor at Puerto Madryn, an evolving ecotourist center that has grown up so quickly it lacks the disheveled appearance of many South American towns. It's clean and has wide streets, painted and tidy homes, and a few well-appointed shops.

One afternoon I wandered into a local bar and, impromptu, was entertained by a guy with a simple acoustic guitar singing traditional Argentine songs with a few of his buddies. He had a terrific voice and command of the music and was clearly the star of the town. What luck!

During our stay, I convinced an English-speaking driver named Horatio to take me on a day trip to Puerto Piramides. The drive out to the tiny village took us through open pastureland, where I spotted herds of guanaco, cousins of the llama, as well as the occasional rhea, a relative of the ostrich.

Next day, *Indigo* pushed off and headed south. We were now deep into Patagonia, a region comprised of the southern section of the Andes Mountains and the deserts, steppes, and grasslands east of the southern Andes. The climate is temperate rather than tropical, and a visitor is more likely to encounter a cattle wrangler than a cabana boy.

The day was utterly perfect, with low humidity, azure skies, and a calm sea, when we reached a small bay called Caleta Hornos. The water temperature had dropped to the mid-50s, and the wildlife reflected this. We were now seeing penguins, seals, and a variety of birds we had not seen before.

Captain Lucas and I went for a spin in the tender, and I asked him to put me ashore for a hike. The terrain was gently sloping, but the ground was rough, broken shale spotted with thorny bushes and mesquite-like plants. I spotted a herd of guanacos and flushed a Pampas hare from its hiding place. The bones of sheep betray the presence of wolves in the area. The whole place resembles the Asian steppe or southern Utah or Arizona—dry desert, scrawny plant life, all inhospitable to humans.

Returning to *Indigo*, we pressed south once more, toward the fabled Straits of Magellan.

Straits of Magellan and the Beagle Channel
Over the next few days, we made our way south toward Tierra del Fuego in generally calm seas, watching dolphins play in our wake, penguins diving alongside and, for the first time, the mighty albatross soaring gracefully around the boat in search of prey.

At about seven p.m. on Saturday, January 20, we arrived at the eastern entry into the Straits of Magellan. Unfortunately, a heavy fog had set in for the first time since leaving Florida, and we had to watch the offshore oil wells pass by on the radar screen. Still, foggy skies generally mean calm seas, so there were few complaints.

For sailors in the age of sail—that romantic period before the Panama Canal was dug when men were men, explorers were bold, and everyone had scurvy—the Straits of Magellan, a long checkmark of water between Tierra del Fuego and the South American mainland, represented the easiest passage between the Atlantic and the Pacific. Farther south, icebergs and sudden gales threatened the stretch of open sea known as the Drake Passage. The Straits had neither of these. That was not to say that it was all sunshine and daisies for early navigators of the Straits—its channels feature strong tidal currents and, occasionally, dense fog such as what we were experiencing.

After passing by the eastern entry into the Straits, we entered the Straits of Lemaire with the Isla de los Estados off to port. Thanks to good timing by the captain, the Straits were flat calm. We anchored for the night in a protected bay and awaited our daylight voyage up the Beagle Channel to the town of Ushuaia.

Ushuaia, Argentina
The weather broke clean with blue skies alternating with wisps of cloud, a rare condition in these parts, and we wove our way along the international boundary between Argentina and Chile that splits this leg of the Beagle. As we approached the harbor of Ushuaia, widely

regarded as the southernmost town in the world, we were obliged to take on a harbor pilot for the short and obvious channel into the town. This was only the first of many inanities the Argentine—and particularly the Chilean—governments had in store for us.

Ushuaia, a postcard-pretty town of 56,000, is perched in the foothills of snowcapped peaks rising from the waterfront into the forests beyond. Its large commercial dock was filled with cruise ships and container ships alike tied next to one another. At the time of our arrival, the dock was receiving 370 ship calls each year, and the number was growing. The dock was far too commercial for our yacht, though, so we anchored in a small bay off its west side and set off to see the city, getting to shore and back each time by the tender.

I had fully expected Ushuaia to be a ragged frontier town much like the many I had seen in Alaska, but I was mistaken. It's a tidy place filled with great restaurants serving king crab, Argentine beef and lamb, and salmon from Chile and black hake from the Drake Passage. Its many shops cater to the cruise ship trade, but their merchandise is generally of a far higher quality than I had expected.

Ushuaia has two Irish pubs, the Dublin and the Galway, both within an easy walk of the shore. The Dublin is the more popular with the locals, and soon became *Indigo's* shoreside entertainment center of a sort. The town also has a disco[3] called, with a touch of irony in a Catholic country, Saint Christopher's.

---

3. "Nightclub" is the term used here for strip clubs.

FIVE

Glaciers, Williwaws, and Pisco Sours

In late January 2007, Kitty rejoined me in Ushuaia, and one after-noon she and I decided to charter a four-seater Piper aircraft for an aerial tour of the archipelago Tierra del Fuego. Taking off from Ushuaia's airport, we wound our way amid the craggy peaks of Tierra del Fuego, looking down upon remote lakes and a penguin rookery. Far to the south, we saw Puerto Williams, an outpost of the Chilean navy.

When European explorers first came upon this archipelago at the edge of the world 500 years ago, the campfires of the natives seemed to float on the surface of the water in the enshrouding mists, giving rise to its name, "The Land of Fire." Centuries later, the place still retains an air of mystery.

Although the weather services reported that stormy skies and high seas were the order of the day in Drake Passage, you'd never have guessed it by observing the weather in Ushuaia. The morning we raised anchor, it was beautiful and sunny, with a clear view out of the harbor and into the main channel. Even so, of course, we had to pause and wait for a tugboat to deliver a pilot to us who would aid us in navigating these "treacherous" waters. This mandatory service was provided, naturally, at our own expense.

Cape Horn

Once free of the harbor's clutches, we faced a twelve-hour journey to the storied Cape Horn, the southernmost headland of South America. Beyond Cape Horn lie only the storm-tossed waters of Drake Passage, and beyond that is Antarctica. Named after the city of Hoorn in the Netherlands, Cape Horn is located on Chile's Hornos Island at the southern tip of South America, where the Atlantic and Pacific Oceans meet. It was once a major milestone on the route clipper ships took when bringing trade around the world, but the need to follow that route was greatly reduced by the coming of steamships and the opening of the Suez and Panama Canals.

The waters surrounding Cape Horn are notoriously dangerous due to strong winds and currents, icebergs, and large waves, and today sailing around the Horn is considered one of the major challenges in yachting. Some prominent ocean yacht races include sailing around the Horn in their voyages.

We passed Isla Navarino and hung a right so that we could hug its east side. Our plan was to steer almost due south, turn west above the Horn, and go around it from east to west. The approach to the Horn is a bleak and rugged seascape full of barren islands of all sizes—some great, some small, and some little more than rocks jutting from the restless sea. There is little in the way of vegetation beyond a smattering of green clinging to the western side of the islands.

About five o'clock in the evening, we passed Isla Deceit. Cape Horn, a lopsided pyramid of striated rock, stood in the distance, bulging from the sea. We rounded it with cameras blazing, snapping enough pictures to make a runway model blush. On the far side of the Horn stands two man-made structures: a lighthouse and a monument, both fully exposed to the savagery of the wind. We radioed the lighthouse keeper who, pleased to have someone to talk to, regaled us with dreadful tales of foul weather out in the passage. It seemed the storms had still not had their fill of causing misery and woe.

We'd hoped to go ashore, but soon gave up that idea. The weather was clear, but the seas stood tall. There was no safe anchorage, and it would've been a rough ride in the tender. So we passed. Our Chilean pilot reported that although he had made this journey several times, this was the first time he had actually seen the Horn when it wasn't completely enshrouded in fog. Overall, we felt that we had to count it as a win.

When we woke, it was to frigid rain, gusty winds, overcast skies, and sleet, but fortunately, we were well protected in the cove.

Drake Passage

Now it was time to decide whether or not we would attempt crossing Drake Passage to Antarctica. We were within spitting distance of the frozen continent, and it would be a shame to miss the opportunity to clap eyes on it.

The main problem was that crossing Drake Passage would take a couple of days, and the current conditions were nine-to-twelve-foot seas. That may not have been so bad, but the weather service predicted rapidly worsening conditions, including heavy gusts of wind, and behind that lurked an ominous low-pressure front. Just as we were weighing our options, Carlos Pedro called to say he had reports of dire conditions in the Drake Passage and strongly advised us not to attempt a crossing.

Prudence is the better part of valor, or so I once read in a book. Such a policy has never really been my standard operating procedure, but I suppose it's never too late in life to begin learning. Certainly, being caught in a storm on frigid seas full of icebergs and far from any help seemed like a recipe for disaster.

Thus we turned our back on Antarctica and instead laid a course for Puerto Williams, a Chilean navy base and tiny community on an island along the Beagle Channel.

Here we had to deal with Chilean immigration and its rare—even for Latin America—talent for numbskull bureaucracy. No person of ordinary ability could ask on an official form, "Do the rats on your vessel display unusual behavior?"

It's clear to me that the Chilean government functionaries must be the bureaucratic ideal to which all other paper pushers aspire. They wanted to know our plans for the entire time we would be in Chilean waters, every step of the way. This plan, once submitted, would be faxed to Valparaiso, where no doubt it would be rubber-stamped, in triplicate, by whatever department determined that our rats weren't dancing jigs.

Indigo never followed a strict itinerary. However, it was clear that if we didn't knuckle down, we might linger in this bureaucratic hell on the edge of the world for weeks. We jumped obligingly through their hoops, hoping to be released.

After two days we were, but not before they informed us that we would need a Chilean pilot for the supposedly danger-fraught voyage out of Ushuaia's harbor.

Puerto Williams, Chile

Despite all the tourist hype coming out of Ushuaia, Puerto Williams is actually the southernmost town in the world and the true "Fin del Mundo" or end of the world. Apart from that distinction, it is a generally clean but poor fishing village with a substantial Chilean navy base and minor airstrip.

Puerto Williams is also home to the southernmost bar in all the world—actually a partially sunken former navy ship called the *Micalvi*, somehow attached to land by way of a dock. Its bar is a tiny room off the main deck accommodating maybe twenty friendly souls at one time with a ceiling set at just about my height. Cozy it surely is.

We returned to Puerto Williams and dropped anchor to spend the night. In the morning, we fired up the engines and set our course westward.

Glaciers

After several hours voyaging along the Beagle Channel, we entered the glacier region. Here the tops of the gray-green hills glimmered white with slow-moving, hard-packed ice.

For lunch, Chef Jeanette exerted her considerable talents to prepare a special glacier feast—every dish on the table was white. She had planned to serve this meal when we arrived in Antarctica, but since the weather had consigned that scheme to the scrap heap, she rescheduled the menu to celebrate the glaciers.

After lunch, we dropped anchor in Caleta Olla, a sprightly little bud on the northern branch of the Beagle Channel. This well-protected bay is uninhabited but is said to be merely an energetic hike from Ventisquero Holanda, a working glacier.

In addition to dropping our usual sturdy anchor, we tied up to shore with two stern lines specially acquired for this purpose. They were thick and long, and they floated to keep them from fouling *Indigo's* props. Although this was the first time on the voyage we had deployed them, the crew accomplished the task as if they were old hands.

Captain Lucas took Kitty and me ashore in the tender. In our minds' eyes, we envisioned a scenic hike that ended with us standing triumphantly atop the glacier; everything that the light touched would be our kingdom. Alas, we soon discovered that between us and this lofty vision was a particularly soggy marsh and some disagreeably steep hills. Feeling that neither our footwear nor our navigational equipment was equal to the task, we were forced to retreat.

We returned to the boat and reported this, but our tale of woe only emboldened Engineer Sean and Mate Bobby, who decided that, being young and vigorous, they might prosper where we had faltered. So sure were they of success that they took a lighter and a pair of cigars to smoke when they reached the glacier. Not being completely naive, they also took a radio.

When night began to fall and the adventurers hadn't radioed for a pickup, Captain Lucas took the tender out to look for them. He was able to raise them on the radio, but although they glimpsed his flashlight from afar, it was impossible for them to meet up with him.

Captain Lucas retired to *Indigo* to see what word morning would bring; perhaps, I surmised, word of a pair of foolhardy popsicles.

In fact, when the captain arrived onshore the next morning,

Bobby and Sean were waiting for him, bright-eyed and bushy-tailed, and apparently none the worse for wear. We learned that as darkness had fallen, they had become unable to navigate safely or determine their exact location. (Throughout their retelling of the story later, they refused to use the word "lost.") Since they had the lighter, they opted to start a fire and remain where they were. It was chilly, and Bobby was in shorts and sandals with only a fleece jacket to shield him from the elements. ("Cold" was another word they'd stricken from their vocabularies.)

Having retrieved our errant crew members, we shoved off and continued along La Avenida de Los Glaciares, a series of glaciers named for various European countries. Fragments of ice glimmered in the water, and penguins frolicked in our wake. Everywhere we looked, we saw snowcapped peaks hugged by glaciers. The Romanche Glacier, which blankets the top of a series of hills, gives way to a thundering waterfall. With no sign of human habitation, it was easy to imagine that we were the first people ever to have visited this breathtaking place.

Late in the afternoon, we arrived at the enormous Garibaldi Glacier. It was in the process of calving, and the noise was immense. We took the tender right up to where the ice was grinding its way into the channel, and Captain Lucas actually got out and stood on a chunk of ice so that we could snap his picture. Another boat was there, too, the *Karima*, and several of her people were in the water in special dry suits. That water must have been as close to freezing as to make no difference as far as I was concerned; they were welcome to it.

We anchored for the night off a little island while sea lions played on the shore.

The sun slept in the next morning, rising late to shrug off a blanket of fog. *Indigo* now emerged from the Beagle Channel into a maze of islands and peninsulas that form the southwestern fringe of Tierra del Fuego. The water was smooth, and sea birds flew everywhere.

We used our shorelines to anchor in a fjord off Isla Brecknock. Surrounded by nothing but rock and sea and primeval green forest, once more we might have been the first explorers encountering virgin territory. Captain Lucas and I went for a hike up the mountains and discovered a hidden lake in the interior of the island.

That night it was quite windy, and in the morning, the weather added rain to its list of sins. As we left the shelter of Isla Brecknock and hung a left into the channel, we ran smack into some heavy seas, which made for a dreary slog.

In the afternoon, the weather cleared in time for us to enter the Seno Chico, a deep channel carved between rocky prominences topped with two mighty glaciers. The older one was dead ahead, and the younger one was off to our left. Both were ice blue—a color so vivid you'd have to see it to believe it. The glaciers had been calving, and the channel was full of icebergs. We saw another huge waterfall cascading down from beneath the younger glacier. The approach to the older glacier was full of rocks peeking out of the water, and perched on many of these were cormorants, minding their own business. I had the distinct impression they didn't receive many visitors here.

That night we anchored in Canal Magdalena and had a little cocktail party with the crew. The ice in our drinks was real berg ice. It's great stuff, since it hardly melts in your drink. One chunk lasts nearly all night.

The next morning, we headed north up Canal Magdalena toward Punta Arenas, Chile's southernmost city sited on the north shore of the Straits of Magellan.

While sailors favor the Straits because they are more protected than the Drake Passage, navigating them in strong crosswinds is a challenge. That morning a westward wind blew at about thirty-five knots and gusted at higher speeds, making life interesting for us. The crossing took us two hours, but we made it without incident. We arrived at Punta Arenas at four o'clock in the afternoon.

Punta Arenas, Chile

The harbor at Punta Arenas is not well protected, but fortunately, a cruise ship was leaving, and *Indigo* was able to snap up its berth. Captain Lucas, Chef Jeanette, Stewardess Darla, and I went ashore and held a late farewell dinner for Kitty.

"Punta Arenas" is Spanish for the name the original British explorers bestowed on this place, "Sandy Point." More majestic and fanciful names have been dreamed up for the town since then, but the original moniker has stuck.

After Kitty's departure, I spent my time wandering about the vicinity, though aside from its beautiful town square and distinctive, brightly colored metal roofs, there is little about Punta Arenas that's of much interest. Still, I walked the streets, visited the pubs and restaurants, and made a halfhearted attempt at a local disco. The discos there open at one a.m. and close about seven a.m., so their schedule didn't fit with my own all that well.

I was looking forward to the arrival of my old friends Jack Burnell, Steve Halverson, and Peter Rummell for a week cruising the Chilean archipelago. Captain Lucas and crew were hard at work taking on provisions, making repairs, and getting *Indigo* in top condition. They also took some well-deserved time off.

~~~

Captain Lucas and I greeted Jack, Steve, and Peter at the airport, loaded their bags into a rented van stocked with an ice bucket, champagne, and flutes, took them on a brief tour of town, and then delivered them into the arms of the crew.

Chef Jeanette had prepared canapés for our first evening together, matched, as you might guess, with an appropriate wine. Stewardess Darla had the salon and guest cabins immaculately prepared, fresh flowers and all. That evening, we took a brief tour of a few pubs and wandered about the well-kept town square.

For dinner, we selected La Tosca on the second floor of a colonial-era building facing onto the square, then enjoyed a drink in the Shackleton Pub located in the Hotel Jose Nogueira. Converted from a late nineteenth-century mansion built on the town square by a local sheep baron, the hotel was the first place visited by Sir Ernest Shackleton after he was brought to Punta Arenas from South Georgia Island. He had come seeking assistance in getting the remainder of his men off Elephant Island in the Antarctic, a mission at which he famously succeeded.

It was at this pub that I persuaded my compadres to try the Chilean national drink, the pisco sour. The drink has been widely adopted as a South American cultural heritage, so much so that both Chile and Peru claim variations of it as their national drink. The Chilean version is made from pisco, a clear and extremely potent grape distillate, mixed with lime juice and sugar and served cold in a stemmed glass. To me, it tastes much like a margarita, and it has a similarly concussive impact on the brain cells. My pals begged to differ about the flavor of the pisco sour. According to them, it's something on the order of cold, soured pea soup—or maybe sheep dip that has passed its expiration date.

Chilean Archipelago

Following a sound night's sleep for all, *Indigo* got underway on our voyage through the western reaches of the Straits of Magellan and the southern end of the Chilean archipelago. Right away, we experienced the weather that would dog us for nearly the entire trip: dense rain, light misting rain, sleet, snow, cold, high winds, and fog—these intermixing in combinations that varied by the hour. It was the singles bar for bad weather.

As we made our way through the many canals and fjords, we were greeted by a landscape that is stunning by any measure. Snowcapped craggy peaks, heaping blobs of igneous rock, massifs blanketed with dense growth, waterfalls nearly everywhere you looked, wracked and gnarled outcrops of granite, grotesquely formed islands, and glaciers plunging out of the highlands into the sea. Its green cover, where it exists, rises to a tree line hardly more than a few thousand feet high, testament to the harsh winter that was just a few months away.

One day Captain Lucas managed to squeeze *Indigo* into a tight channel where the mountains rose above us all around. Mate Bobby and Deckhand Tomas expertly tied off the stern to trees on opposite shorelines, and we dropped both bow anchors for protection against the ever-present williwaws, sudden gusts of wind that can erupt without warning.

Steve, Peter, and I decided to take the tender and explore the area. Jack was down with some flu-like germ he'd caught on his plane ride and remained behind. After getting pelted with freezing rain, dodging kelp beds and undersea rocks, and churning through tide rips, we decided to go for a hike onshore, although the word "hike" is hardly adequate to describe the event. Landing on a rocky shore— there were no beaches—we tied the tender to a hefty boulder and set out.

The surface underfoot was the most remarkable any of us had ever encountered. It felt like we were walking on giant, soggy broccoli florets. Moss, lichens, and assorted hardy scrub plants had formed a dense carpet of spongy resilience on the perpetually wet ground. As there were no flat places in this entire archipelago, the going was upward, the least favored of the three alternatives. And it was dense with thicket.

When seen through the lens of its weather, the place had an eerie feel, as though it were the living set piece for a Stephen King novel. We were surrounded by evergreen trees stunted and warped by the winds into grotesque shapes, seldom reaching more than twelve feet high. Oddly out of place here were dense tapestries of flowering vines, each flower a pale red bell shape not unlike a honeysuckle. On one of these we spotted a bumblebee of well-nourished proportions. This, along with a very few tiny birds, was the only land-based wildlife we saw the entire trip.

To me, perhaps the most remarkable fact of this area is its complete absence of large animals, quite unlike Alaska with its bear, moose, elk, deer, and much more. Here we saw not a sign of a single large animal. The place was also utterly devoid of humans and their habitations. Even other vessels were rare. We saw one tiny fishing boat, one sailboat and, on the last day, one small cruise ship—all that in a week. If you want to "get away from it all," this is the place to do it.

After stumbling aimlessly through this impenetrable, dripping brier patch, we decided—quite wisely, in my view—to abandon our aging Audubon routine and return to the warm and not incidentally wine-stocked *Indigo*. We had covered in our expedition all of about fifty feet. Lewis and Clark, we were not.

Back on board, we were greeted by the seemingly deathly ill Jack Burnell, he with the pallor of Marcel Marceau and the voice of Joe Cocker. Most of us are familiar with this particular malady. It begins innocently enough with a minor tickle in the throat, an unexpected cough, and the watery eyes. Then it spreads to the hit-by-a-Mack-truck roadkill stage when all hope of a joyful life begins to fade.

We all came down with the Jack Plague, and it hung on through the week, putting a noticeable damper on the festivities. We tried to rally, and we shared potions and nostrums, as apparently we've shared doorknobs and *Indigo* air, but to no avail.

At Puerto Natales, the end of our voyage together, we were all fevered, snorting and coughing—*Indigo's* salon sounding something not unlike a TB ward—and so decided to cancel a planned air charter through three of the finest national parks in South America. It was just too much for everybody, but especially for the guys facing twenty-hour flights home.

So we piled into a van, traveled to the local airport, and I saw them fly off to make their connections. But for germs and weather, it was an enjoyable week with three great friends.

SIX

More Adventures in Chile

During my lengthy stay in Chile, I found the Chileans to be an unfailingly generous people. I was showered with so many gifts during my stay that we created a special storage locker aboard *Indigo* to hold them all. Chileans are also among the world's most genteel and unfailingly polite people. Upon the most superficial of greetings, as to a total stranger on the street or to a sales clerk, they always begin with *"Buenos dias"* or *"Buenas tardes"* or *"Buenas noches"* and end with *"Gracias"* or even *"Muchas gracias."* When two women or a woman and a man meet, even for the first time and even if otherwise strangers, a perfunctory kiss on the cheek is exchanged along with a spoken greeting. When two men already known to each other meet, there is a traditional handshake accompanied by a manly hug, and the same upon departing. They are unabashedly friendly people.

Chile is the most culturally conservative and strongly familial of South American countries. They are nearly priestly when contrasted with the libertine Brazilians. The business class is hardworking, entrepreneurial, and innovative.

Puerto Natales, Chile

Upon one's arrival at Puerto Natales, the question that cries out for an answer is, Why is there a town here? It once was a shipping point for sheep and wool from the surrounding ranches, but now is a town of veggie restaurants and hostels catering to the Birkenstock trekker crowd.

For me, its principal significance was that it was the place where I would get my first haircut in a year. Before *Indigo* left Fort Lauderdale, I had vowed to myself that I would not cut my hair until we rounded Cape Horn. Now that we had done so, I could at last get rid of the tangled and gooped-up thicket of decidedly gray hair before I needed a perm.

In my infantile Spanish, I told the lady in the unisex styling salon what style I preferred to have carved out of the mess, and she did it, more or less along the lines requested. It would do until I could get back home for a tune-up at Cliff's Barber Shop.

Barely two days after the departure of my three friends, a massive high-pressure center moved in over southern Patagonia, pushing out the nasty low that had besieged us for so long and had brought with it rain, sleet, and cold. Glistening, snowcapped peaks stood stark against a brilliant azure Colorado sky.

The beautiful day prompted me to charter the same flight we had canceled only two days before. We circled Torres del Paine's stunning spires now rising from a white blanket, then pushed northward to Perito Moreno and on to Mount Fitz Roy, these last two in Argentina. It was a magical tour as if through the Swiss Alps or the Denali Range on a profoundly breathtaking day.

Chilean Archipelago

In early March 2007, I and the good ship *Indigo* began making our way through the canals of the Chilean archipelago, headed north to Puerto Montt. Along the way, we were once more accompanied by rain, cold, wind, and more rain. We wandered through a geologic maze of granitic upheaval scoured by glaciers, decorated by lava flows, and interwoven by the sea. Each mile was a wonderland of discovery. Snow-laden peaks off in the distance stood guard over igneous blobs, some carpeted in primeval forest, some bare as the day they rose above the sea. Waterfalls abounded, birds skittered and wheeled in the chilled air, and impassable thickets clothed the shoreline.

Adding to this weird and wondrous place was the surprising fact that nary a soul intruded upon our serenity. No habitation of any kind, no trekkers or campers, no RVs,[1] and very few vessels disrupted our sublime experience. Day followed day, rain, cold, and wind always our fellow traveler.

Each evening, Captain Lucas found a quiet anchorage with a water-fall or glacier as our vista. He, Bobby, and Tomas tied off the stern to thick trees onshore. These, with both anchors set off the bow, would protect us from getting blown into the rocks by the sudden bursts of wind exploding off the mountains that surrounded us. Though there were certainly potential perils during this leg of our journey, not once in our travels was our safety threatened, thanks to the good work of the crew.

Up one special fjord, we approached closely to a mammoth gla-cier—at least two and a half miles wide across its face, and watched as enormous bergs calved from the overhangs.

At a northerly point in our passage, the protection of the Chilean canals ended, and we had to pass into the Pacific Ocean for a ways toward our destination of Puerto Montt. Before entering the ocean, Captain Lucas thoughtfully anchored in a quiet cove so we could have a peaceful dinner.

After dinner, just past nightfall, we passed from the calm into the somewhat disturbed Pacific Ocean. I sat for a time on the aft deck tak-ing in the cool night air. Around nine p.m., I went down to my cabin to read for a while before turning in. As in most expedition yachts, the owner's stateroom was located exactly midships—that is, midway between bow and stern—and the top of the bed itself was aligned exactly with the level of the sea outside. This arrangement, sited at the vessel's fulcrum, assures that the bed's occupants will suffer the least possible movement in rough weather.

---

1. There are no roads or even pathways.

Not long after I had turned out the lights, *BLAM!*, a loud concussive noise reverberated throughout the boat, jolting me upright in bed and sending my heart into a spasm of fear. I sprang from the bed, half expecting a flood of water rushing through an imagined gaping hole in the hull, grabbed my robe, and ran out my cabin door, up a short flight of steps to the foyer, and up another to the bridge.

There, in relative calm, stood Captain Lucas and Mate Bobby looking closely at the instrument panel for signs of damage or water intrusion alarms. There were none, either visual or audible. Slowly, after it seemed there had not been the calamity I feared, I regained my composure. After a thorough search of the engine room and bilges, the captain determined there was no hull penetration. From the absence of vibration and unusual noises, he decided the props and prop shafts had not been damaged, either.

Bobby and Tomas then stood on the outer decks and shined lights into the water above the stabilizers, winglike fins that help reduce rolling in beam seas, and there was the damage. The five-inch-thick stainless steel rod that supports and actuates the starboard fin was folded almost ninety degrees up, now nearly flush with the hull, and the fin itself was badly damaged. Something very sturdy had struck it with great force.

From the charts, we knew it could not have been an undersea impediment like rocks. There simply were none anywhere near shallow enough. We were in very deep seas. With searchlights we also failed to locate any floating debris we may have struck. What, then, had caused such damage?

In the early light of dawn, the answer was revealed. Arrayed for miles across the sea in all directions, a vast field of humpback whales were rolling through the choppy seas. We decided it was most likely one of these that struck the stabilizer.

Puerto Montt, Chile

Our next port of call was Puerto Montt, the northern terminus of Chile's inside passage. It is a port town with several decent marinas, one of which we tied up to. It was the first proper marina we had encountered since Buenos Aires, with floating docks, Wi-Fi service, and other amenities we had at one time come to expect. This was also the first time we encountered other yachts in this area, though these were Chilean, most from Santiago.

Since arriving in this northern end of the Chilean canals, we had been impressed with the scenery. Verdant hills rise up from the calm waterways, and well-tended farms, forests, and tidy communities line the horizon. The countryside is much like that of Tuscany or Nova Scotia, or even Austria with a seaside.

While in Puerto Montt, I took one blue-sky day to wander about its public market area. There, stalls of fresh and smoked fish, mostly salmon, clams, scallops, and a variety of other seafoods stand side by side, their owners hawking in a friendly but insistent manner. Other stalls are stuffed with local-made woolens of every description, gewgaws and gimcracks, dust collectors mostly.

One day for lunch, I traveled to Puerto Varas, on Chile's largest lake, and stared across the lake at two volcanoes, both covered with snow and ice, one perfectly conical, much like Mount Fuji in Japan.

Santiago, Chile

While repairs to Indigo's stabilizer fin were underway in the port town of Valdivia, I stayed two weeks in a hotel in Santiago, using the place as a base from which to tour the city and its surrounds.

Santiago is a city of about six million situated against the western slope of the Andes, nearly a two-hour drive from the Pacific coast but backdropped by the stunningly beautiful mountains, a chain of ragged peaks that form the spine of Chile. Santiago surely ranks as one of the tidiest of South American cities, and also is among the tamest. Street crime falls far short of most major cities in Brazil and Argentina. Near my hotel, I was able to wander around many blocks late at night without the slightest hint of threat, though I was cautioned not to do so in other barrios of the city.

I visited the Museum of Pre-Columbian Art, Plaza de Armas,

countless bars and fine restaurants and raucous night spots, and took a private tour of the other major tourist sites.

A side trip to Valle Nevado, one of the many ski resorts within less than a two-hour drive, introduced me to the climatic diversity of Chile. You can water-ski in a lake one day and snow ski in the Andes the next. The city is almost surrounded by vineyards and wineries, and tours of these are a major tourist attraction. Some of the finest wines in the world are produced here, mostly reds, including the memorable Carmenere.

One day while wandering around the centro in Santiago, I came upon a small coffee shop arrestingly named Café Passion. Its large shop window had been fully blacked out, adding to the allure. Once inside, the first sensation was heat. The place was at least 80 degrees. Then there was the dark. For a coffee shop, its ambiance seemed unusually intimate, especially for the midday.

Once my eyes adjusted, it became clear why a coffee shop should be both hot and dark. Behind the counter from which the coffee was being served to seated customers were a bevy of lovelies clad in . . . well, not much. Thong bikinis and airy halter tops seemed to be the uniform of the day. I'd happened upon an institution unique to Chile and confined by law to a few square blocks in the center of the city, called café con piernas, or "coffee with legs." Beats hell out of Starbucks, if you ask me.

Lago Nahuel Huapi, Argentina

After exhausting the opportunities afforded in Santiago, I traveled back to Puerto Montt and from there took a private plane on a scenic flight up and over the dramatic Andes into Argentina, landing alongside the magnificent Lago Nahuel Huapi, the heart of a two-million-acre national park. The largely forgettable town of Bariloche sits alongside the enormous lake (557 square miles), but its saving grace is the five-star Hotel Llau Llau (pronounced in Argentine Spanish as "shau shau"). Sited on a rise adjacent to the lake with dramatic, snow-covered peaks in the distance, it is backed by steep granite walls and pine forests and surrounded by a golf course. Its style is that of a Bavarian resort set in, say, the Arlberg of Austria.

I rented a four-wheel-drive pickup truck to take a long trip through the park on its many unpaved roads, some nothing more than wide hiking trails. Over several days, I wended my way through massive forests of piñon, closely resembling the trees of the Oregon coast, alongside glacial lakes, and around and over Andean peaks, some still draped in piles of snow not yet melted by the coming spring.

The Bavarian-like town of San Martin de Los Andes was an early stopover. With wide, clean streets lined with planted trees and a beautiful city park, San Martin de Los Andes is a major attraction for snow skiers and hikers.

After an overnight stay in a small, friendly hotel, I traveled on through the park forests and over more mountains, returning to the Lago Nahuel Huapi. Along the lake's north shore sits the tiny village of Villa la Angostura. At an inn on the lake's shore, I spent a quiet night dining on an exceptional meal and enjoying the heated pool in its spa.

After spending a week wandering about in Argentina, I drove across the border into Chile, passing through a high mountain pass still lined with twenty-foot-high banks of snow. Border formalities there, as in all Latin countries, were needlessly tedious.

Driving on to the city of Osorno, I turned onto Route 5, the national highway that runs nearly the entire length of Chile. A few hours more, and I at last returned to Valdivia and found that the repairs to *Indigo* had been completed.

Viña del Mar, Chile

The jaunt up to Viña del Mar proved an excellent way for *Indigo* to "shake out" and reconnect with her natural element, for it was a two-day leg, and the weather and waves were mild. Viña, as it is known locally, was no slouch as a destination, either, being more or less a combination of Miami Beach, Florida, and Monterey, California.

We dropped anchor outside the breakwater of the Higuerillas

Yacht Club—*Indigo* being too large to tie up inside. Higuerillas is the largest and finest yacht club in all of Chile. I made landfall at the bar and discovered that we had arrived just in time for one of the yacht club's premier sailing regattas, and many of the club's key members were arriving for the race and accompanying festivities.

I was lucky enough to meet some friendly and interesting people, including Emilio Cousiño, owner of the racing boat *Pisco Sour*, and then the entire crew: Rodrigo, Gato, Pillo, Tato, Juanjo, and Carlos. I also met Jorge Errazuriz, owner of the *Marsetta*, and at dinner one night with the *Pisco Sour* crew, I made the acquaintance of Bernardo Matte Larrain and his wife. I also rubbed shoulders with Sergio Bascunan, a captain in the Armada de Chile, the Chilean navy, and his lovely wife, Paulina.

Oskar Aitken, the longtime president and a founder of the yacht club, invited me to join him for dinner at his condo, which, being mere yards from the club, was easy to do. We had a fine view from his windows of *Indigo* riding at ease outside the harbor at twilight. Oskar told me a bit of his story. It seemed that when he was not busy founding prestigious yacht clubs, he'd acted as legal counsel and financial adviser to no less an imposing personage than General Augusto Pinochet, military coup leader, dictator, reformer, and, eventually, president of Chile.

Oskar also had a role in Chile's economic growth. Chile is a relatively small country but widely considered stable with a productive, growing economy. Oskar helped to push through a slate of free-market reforms under Pinochet, with the advice of a panel of economists from the University of Chicago.

During my stay at Viña del Mar, I attended numerous dinners at the homes of my new acquaintances. In Chile, as in much of South America, the convivial grilling of meat outdoors—what Americans know as a barbecue—is known as an asado. It is so popular as to be a cultural institution. The Chileans favor their asado—usually steaks, chorizo, pork, and sometimes chicken—grilled outdoors, sliced into bite-sized chunks and served with potatoes, salad, and veggies. The meat is far more marbled and fatty than Americans are accustomed to and, as a result, is infinitely more flavorful. Thoroughly lubricated by wines and pisco sours, these events involved much music, dancing, and conversation.

The traditional and hackneyed toast in Chile is the nearly universal "*Salud*," which translates to "Health." A slightly more inventive variation is "*Salud, dinero, y amore,*" or "Health, money, and love." One memorable night I offered up a more raffish toast: "Bigger boats, faster cars, and younger women," which my new friends welcomed with great howls of approval. I was, after all, in a wonderfully macho culture, a world apart from puritanical gringo America. Since my toast was so well received, I made it several more times during my stay in Chile, always to great acclaim. I'd like to think that the toast might have been the legacy, however small, that I left to Chilean culture.

One evening I was coaxed into joining some friends at Club Mediterraneo. A pair of talented musicians played Spanish guitars, accompanied by conga drums playing rumba and flamenco. That was probably where it should've ended, but a woman named Sophia popped out of the audience and persuaded me to attempt the flamenco. I'm certain the sight of an old guy from the Florida panhandle attempting Chile's most traditional dance set Chilean-American relations back by decades. Regardless, I enjoyed myself immensely.

Valparaíso, Chile

Across the bay from Viña del Mar is Valparaíso, and it's easy to see why this city is called the Jewel of the Pacific. Its steeply banked shores are blanketed in a soft yellow glow of city light that sparkles in the night air. Though it retains much of the appearance typical of old port cities, Valparaíso has many buildings of classical architecture. The city rises steeply from the Pacific shores much as San Francisco does, and its historic district is crowded with colonial-era buildings, now brightly painted, lining its steep, twisting roads. The hills are nearly too steep to walk, so at strategic locations are funiculars ("ascensors" in Spanish) for which the city is famous. They are small, wood-framed, brightly painted cabins on rails that move pedestrians up and down the hillsides for a modest price.

Before the opening of the Panama Canal, Valparaíso was one of the most important ports on the west coast of the Americas and a magnet for European immigrants. It was home to Latin America's first stock exchange and its oldest continuously published newspaper. After the opening of the canal, its fortunes waned, but it has staged an impressive renaissance in recent years.

Near *Indigo's* berth was the Argentine navy's tall ship *Libertad*, here for a ceremonial visit celebrating detente between the two countries after nearly coming to blows in the 1980s. One night I attended, along with Deckhand Tomas and Stewardess Darla, a formal reception on the *Libertad* in which senior officers of the Argentine navy hosted those of the Chilean navy along with other local dignitaries. It was a predictably stuffy affair featuring a windy speech from the Argentine ambassador to Chile and a tango danced by the commanding officer of the *Libertad* and his wife.

After the formal reception, I hosted a livelier party on *Indigo* for Sergio Bascunan and other senior Chilean navy officers and their wives. The party, like nearly all I've attended in Chile, got a little wild by conventional standards, but it was great fun as *Indigo* extended her network of friends.

SEVEN

Island Hopping in the South Pacific

After a lengthy stay for some necessary repairs to *Indigo*, we pulled away from the pier in Valparaiso at four p.m. on November 27 and made our way west toward our next destination.

A tiny archipelago, the Juan Fernández Islands lie 413 nautical miles off the Chilean coast. Of its three islands, only the farthest, Robinson Crusoe Island, is inhabited, and this only by some 800 brave souls living in the village of San Juan Bautista.

The islands were discovered in 1574 by their namesake and thereafter for centuries remained bleak dots on the charts, inhabited but briefly now and then by pirates and visited by the occasional navy and sealing ships taking on freshwater. They remained vacant until 1704 when Alexander Selkirk, an irascible Scotsman, demanded to be put ashore on the island and left there. More than four years later, he was "rescued" and delivered to London to great media acclaim that—according to legend, at least—was noted by the writer Daniel Defoe. Defoe, it is said, used the story as the basis for *Robinson Crusoe*, regarded as the first novel of English literature. Recently, in his book *Searching for Robinson Crusoe*, the travel writer Tim Severin concludes after exhaustive research that it was neither Selkirk nor the Juan Fernández Islands that gave impetus to the Defoe novel. This startling conclusion irritates the local tourist industry, nascent as it is.

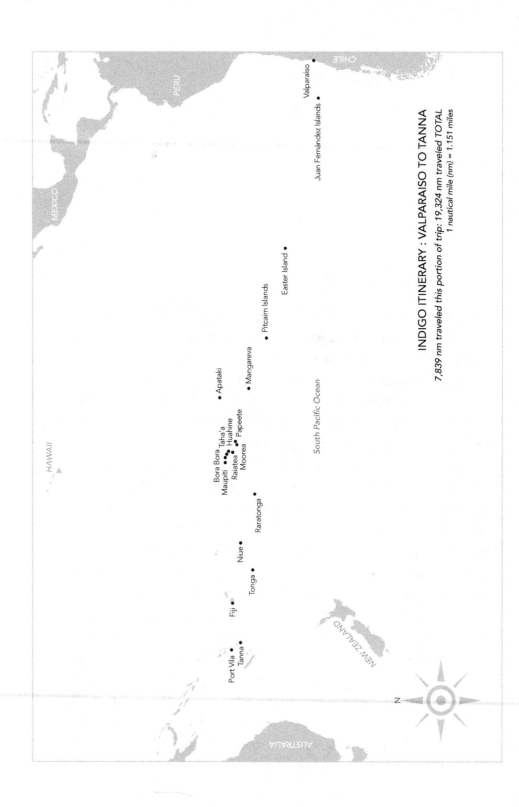

INDIGO ITINERARY : VALPARAISO TO TANNA

7,839 nm traveled this portion of trip: 19,324 nm traveled TOTAL
1 nautical mile (nm) = 1.151 miles

The seas for our voyage to the Juan Fernández Islands, about forty hours from Valparaíso to Robinson Crusoe, were calm by day and almost flat by night. Thanks to the Humboldt Current that flows strongly north along the coast of Chile, the water temperature was 61 degrees. It is this nutrient-rich current that helps make Chile one of the world's largest producers of both wild-caught and farm-raised fish.

Our voyage was generally uneventful except for the several pods of right whales we passed through, some no more than fifty yards from the boat. As we approached the island from a distance, I could barely see it among enveloping clouds. Gradually, though, the island's peaks came into view, dramatically jutting out of the sea to 3,000 feet. The mountainous terrain divides the island into two distinct climatic systems—a verdant jungle and an arid desert. The resulting biodiversity is so unusual that UNESCO declared Robinson Crusoe Island a World Biosphere Reserve. It is said to contain sixty-one times more plant species and thirteen times more bird species than the fecund Galápagos Islands.

Robinson Crusoe Island

As *Indigo* neared the village harbor on Cumberland Bay, the only habitable site on the entire thirty-three-square-mile island, we were struck by the stunning beauty. The mountain peaks in front of us were draped in deep jungle, giving the place the look of a South Pacific island like Bora Bora, yet off to either side were steep cliffs plunging into the sea and covered over with arid desert. Richard Henry Dana, in his seafaring adventure *Two Years Before the Mast*, called the island "the most romantic spot of Earth that my eyes had ever seen."

Upon dropping anchor in the sheltered bay and clearing in with the port captain, I, accompanied by the entire crew, went ashore, where we were promptly greeted by the hospitable Marcelo Rossi, a man to whom we had been introduced by our friends from Santiago. Marcelo was the owner of the inn called Refugio Nautico, to which he took us for a fish barbecue. First came the obligatory pisco sours—the first hint that the party had begun—followed by fresh mero[1] fingers with soy sauce dip and hot empanadas right off the stove. Then we all sat down to the main course consisting of grilled Pacific swordfish accompanied by local veggies.

After lunch, I foolishly hopped aboard Marcelo's ATV and went for a barely controlled spin about the village. Then I, Chef Jeanette, and Stewardess Darla jumped into Marcelo's four-wheel-drive truck for a run up the face of the highest mountain. When we reached a narrow jungle trail, we got out and hiked a mile or so to a glen of enormous piñon trees. The rest of the crew arrived mounted on mules. From the glen, we hiked along prepared trails through a wonderland of flora indigenous only to this island. Elephant ear ferns with leaves the size of serving trays had a texture like sharkskin and stalks rough as corn-cobs. It wouldn't take much imagination to picture yourself on the Jurassic Park island with raptors scampering about.

Returning to Marcelo's inn, we launched phase two of the party. As the sun was setting, a group of four local musicians began playing music indigenous to this island using three guitars, a vocalist, and a set of bongo drums. It wasn't long before your humble servant was dragooned into playing the drums, with rhythmic but discordant results. Soon the island's mayor—or alcalde—appeared with his girlfriend and some other notable locals, and the party shifted into another and higher gear.

Next day, we welcomed the alcalde, Leopoldo Charpentier, a native islander, and the port captain along with Marcelo for a lunch on *Indigo* prepared by Chef Jeanette.

At the meal's end, we said our farewells to this island outpost of Chile and turned our eyes westward. The mystical Easter Island lay some 1,700 nautical miles in the distance.

Easter Island

The trip from Robinson Crusoe to Easter Island took us a full seven days and a wake-up, and we reached our destination on December 7,

1. A species of grouper.

Pearl Harbor Day. Easter is one of the most remote inhabited islands in the world. In keeping with this distinction, we saw along the way not another vessel. No cargo ship, no fishing boat, no military ship. Not even a stray plane soared overhead. We spotted no whales and just a few birds.

Easter Island is surrounded by many hundreds of miles of trackless ocean. Nearly treeless except for a few palms along the coast, most of Easter Island is windswept range grass carpeting a vast uneven rocky topography through which a single paved roadway winds.

What sets it apart, though, are the hundreds of those iconic stone moai scattered about in mostly disorderly profusion, a few standing mute in a line as if troops at attention, a confusion of prehistoric statuary.

The island has a long, interesting history, with mostly Polynesian cultures till the Europeans arrived. It's a province of Chile, called Isla de Pascua in Spanish, Rapa Nui in Polynesian. The population is about 6,500, of whom 60 percent are Polys. Most of the islanders live in the capital town Hanga Roa.

We made landfall at about seven a.m. This was always exciting when we'd been at sea for a week, even when on a fine yacht with a chef and good wine. I could only imagine what early sailors felt when they saw land after months of suffering with gruel and grog.

The sole village lies on the island's lee shore in the southwest corner at one of the few places not atop high cliffs. Its "harbor" is little more than a bight where all vessels have to anchor a half mile from shore. Closer in is an undersea rock shelf on which anchoring is not possible.

After securing *Indigo* in the bay, we were greeted by the usual coterie of local bureaucrats and our shore agent. Through the agent, we'd already secured and paid for 3,500 gallons of diesel fuel, enough to get us to Tahiti.

Once cleared by immigration, I took a small local outboard launch into the village, accompanied by a few members of the crew. This proved to be a thrill ride. As we approached the shore, I saw nothing but enormous crashing waves, great flumes of spray arching into the sky, and a few stout-hearted surfers. But as we drew nearer, I could just make out a gap between the breakers. It was into this breach that my chauffeur delivered us, making a beeline for the rocky shore. Surfing the backs of the combers, it seemed as though he intended to drive us up and onto the rocks—but just at the last instant, a tiny protected boat basin came into view, and after a hard left turn, we floated in its placid waters and I off-loaded at the quay. Fun stuff!

A rental car was waiting ashore, arranged by the crew and our agent. Over the next three hours or so, I took a high-speed and abbreviated tour of Easter Island. The place immediately reminded me of the Dakota Badlands, the Nebraska sand hills, or the Wyoming plains: great sweeping hillocks, deep fissures and chasms, shoulders and hips and undulating pastures, all nearly treeless and grass-covered and all peppered with black volcanic detritus, from baseball to house-sized, left over from explosions of the three volcanoes that formed the island.

It was from this porous rock that the early Polynesian civilization here sculpted the moai, the eerie stone statues for which the island is known. There are a lot of them in all shapes and sizes, most now standing after being reerected for the tourist trade.

After my culture tour and a few photos mugging with the moai, I returned to *Indigo* for a siesta before the night's festivities. I had been pre-introduced by a Santiago friend to a colorful local man, a Chileno with the distinctly un-Chileno name of Andy McDonald. A self-described surfer hippie dude, he was a tall, rawboned guy with a tan and long, scraggly blond hair. He looked as if he'd just stepped off a beach in Southern California.

He approached me with a toothy smile that quickly turned to a sly grin. "Fun night ahead, dude." He and some friends had arranged a full night's tour of the fun spots. It was Saturday night, after all. After ticking off the stops he had in mind and the salient features of each, and getting my enthusiastic okay, he said, "Well then, let's get after it!"

We started at a French restaurant on the waterfront, where we were greeted at the door by the owner, who also served as our waiter. A portly man, he escorted us to one of the numerous empty tables, handed out menus, and took our drink and food orders in a manner that I'll call "dutiful with a hint of snooty." I had the sense he was annoyed that we had interrupted his day by choosing his place to dine.

I ordered a dozen escargot as a starter, which he placed on the table with obvious disdain as though his snails were simply too good to be eaten by the likes of us. When he returned to clear the table, he saw that I had left half of the dish untouched.

"Why do you not eat the food I have prepared for you?" he asked in a haughty tone.

I'm not easy to rile, but in this case my temper spiked more at his manner than at the question, and I retorted, "Why are you such an asshole?"

Briefly taken aback, he recovered his snooty manner and said, to my astonishment, "It is the French way."

From there we hit another restaurant for dessert and coffee, then on to the disco next door. Music was provided by a band playing the modern version of Polynesian music, a kind of cross between bluegrass, country, and Polynesian traditional sounds. It even sounded faintly Bahamian. From there we migrated to Toroko, a local version of an all-night honky-tonk. At somewhere just short of daybreak, I made my way back to the small boat quay with the launch drivers as bodyguards[2] and got back on *Indigo* at about four-thirty a.m.

If you've a mind for it, you can fly to Easter Island in only five hours from Santiago, but the hotel accommodations are pretty basic—and after you've seen the statues, some tablets, and a paltry museum, there ain't all that much to justify the trip. Still, the landscape is lovely.

On the evening of December 10, we cleared immigration and departed from Easter Island bound for Pitcairn Island.

---

2. They had been assigned the task by my thoughtful crew.

Pitcairn Island

For *Indigo*, it was a passage of some 1,100 uneventful nautical miles with gentle seas, wisps of wind, and increasingly tropical skies. The crew and I passed these days in a relaxed stupor of naps, books, movies, fine meals, and wines.[3] These were among the most soporific days I've ever spent, thanks to the warm, moist tropical air and the soft undulations of *Indigo's* motion.

Late in the afternoon of the fifth day at sea, we reached Pitcairn Island. Its sole "harbor," called Bounty Bay, like Easter Island's is nothing more than a bight fully exposed to the seas.

Anchorage in the bay was untenable, so we approached just behind a headland and in the lee. The mayor, Jay Warren, was expecting us after brief VHF conversations announcing our approach. Though the wind was northwesterly, there was a typical Pacific swell rolling in from the south, making our anchorage shy of ideal.

Late in the evening after the winds abated, we relocated to Bounty Bay and anchored not more than 300 yards from the sunken remains of Her Majesty's Armed Vessel (HMAV) *Bounty*. This was the vessel whose mutinous crew and the Tahitians who accompanied them were the founders of the island's current population.

Just to refresh your history, the *Bounty*, captained by the now-famous Captain Bligh, was dispatched from England for the purpose of voyaging to Tahiti. There she was to take on a load of carbohydrate-rich breadfruit and deliver it to Caribbean plantations where it would be fed to slaves dying from malnutrition. When it came time for the *Bounty* to set sail from Tahiti with its load of fruit, twenty-five crew members led by Fletcher Christian mutinied. They captured the *Bounty* and set Bligh and eighteen crew adrift in an open longboat with meager stores and gear.

Sixteen mutineers decided to stay on Tahiti. Nine of the mutineers, including Christian, and six Polynesian men, twelve Polynesian women, and a baby girl sailed away in hopes of avoiding eventual

---

3. No wine for the crew, though. The captain wisely forbade the crew from drinking while underway.

capture by seeking refuge on a remote island. Coming upon Pitcairn Island after an extended search, they discovered that it was wrongly placed on British Admiralty charts 188 nautical miles west of its true location, thus lessening the chance of discovery.

This tiny crew of scoundrels decided that Pitcairn Island would be their home. After off-loading all their possessions, they set fire to the *Bounty*, whose charred hull sank within 150 feet of the present island landing.

The quick-minded reader will have already hit upon the fact that was to be the undoing of this inchoate island community, fifteen men and twelve women. No good could ever come from such a mix, and none did.[4] Trouble ensued with numerous murders, including those of Christian and four other mutineers at the hands of the native island-ers. Literally adding fuel to the fire, one of the mutineers learned to brew potent liquor from local plants. More trouble followed.

Meanwhile, Bligh, in one of history's greatest feats of open-water navigation, managed to get the eighteen expelled crew safely back to civilization. The British navy, never keen on mutiny, sent out a ship, the HMS *Pandora*, in search of the mutineers. Those who had foolishly stayed behind on Tahiti were apprehended and returned to England for trial. On the return voyage, with the bad guys held in a cell called Pandora's Box, the ship struck the Great Barrier Reef and foundered with the loss, among others, of four mutineers. Those remaining were returned to London, put on trial, and most hung or imprisoned.

Pitcairn is a small volcanic island of just 1,120 acres, nearly all of it steeply inclined from the sea. Its surrounding cliffs are dramatic, reaching 500 to 800 feet on average. The interior of the island is lush with wild tropical flowers, trees, and fruits in profusion arrayed among flourishing valleys, soaring peaks, and gentle hillsides.

Pitcairn is the least populous national jurisdiction in the world, with just fifty inhabitants. It may be the most idyllic spot I've ever seen and certainly worth a visit, but for the difficulty of getting there.

---

4. In Christian's defense, three of the Polynesian men were stowaways.

Other than on private yachts or a precisely aimed parachute drop, the only way to get there is aboard the freighters out of New Zealand 3,429 nautical miles to the west that deliver supplies every three or four months, or the occasional cruise ship stopover.

A few years before my visit, a new phone system and Internet connections were installed, and these have been a godsend for communications. The island and most families have their own websites.

The crew and I went ashore in the island's fifteen-foot skiff, which delivered us through the surf to a stout concrete quay. There we were greeted by a goodly number of the island's residents, including the mayor. A stout man of about forty-five, Jay Warren had the natural charm of a practiced politician. He made us all feel welcome and introduced us to everyone in the small crowd.

In general appearance and accent and in most folkways, the islanders are reminiscent of New Zealanders, with whom they have been most closely linked over many years. Island children most commonly go off to schools there, and nearly all of the island's essential consumable supplies derive from there.

Brenda Christian, a direct descendant of Fletcher, and her husband, Mike, kindly took us on a whirlwind tour aboard their ATVs, the principal means of transport. An intricate system of finely graded dirt roads laces through the island's hills and valleys, making access to almost any point possible.

We first visited Adamstown, the island's capital just up the cliff from the quay. There is the town hall, post office, and a museum in front of which there is on display an anchor from the *Bounty*. We then traveled around the island to the edge of various impressive cliffs overlooking a ragged coast and booming surf. Brenda then took us up to the highest point, at 1,100 feet, where the locals have a picnic area arranged on the very spot once occupied by a former US Air Force tracking station. We stopped by the home of Brenda and Mike, the new home of their twenty-two-year-old son, Andrew, and the home of another Christian descendant from whom we bought logoed polo shirts, golf caps, and the inevitable T-shirts. Island homes are generally simple wood-framed clapboard bungalows built from materials shipped from the port in Auckland.

We passed bountiful fields in which grow nearly every fruit found in a grocery store's produce department and then some. Bananas, papayas, pineapples, mangoes, watermelons, passion fruit, breadfruit, coconuts, avocadoes, oranges, grapefruit, lemons, and limes. Vegetables, too, grow there in profusion. Its bee population is said to be unusually placid and one of the few disease-free in the world, with the result that they produce honey of exceptional quality, prized, it is said, by Queen Elizabeth.

After our tour, it was back to the landing, and off we went loaded down with memorabilia. Next stop, just 300 nautical miles west, was Mangareva, the largest island in the Gambier Islands chain.

EIGHT

Fun and Danger in French Polynesia

A colony of France, French Polynesia is one of the most expensive places in the world. Prices of ordinary items are breathtaking, due to duties and taxes imposed by the French. Electricity is so costly that homes and shops are poorly lit and rarely air-conditioned. Most homes have only cold-water showers and the barest necessities of electric appliances.

The Polynesian language, while euphonic, is utterly unrelated to Latin, the root of most Western tongues, and so is learned solely by rote. It is perfectly phonetic, with no silent letters, and has many vowels. The English language gets from Polynesian the word "taboo" (*tabu*), meaning "prohibited" and often seen on no-trespassing signs. It also gets "tattoo" (*tatu*), meaning "to puncture." The place is the original home of body art, as it's now called.

Fishermen in this part of the Pacific employ a technique that to my knowledge is not used anywhere else in the world, though it looks like great fun. In high-speed open boats twenty to twenty-five feet long and variously powered, the captain, usually the sole occupant, stands in a tight cubbyhole far in the bow, just a few feet aft of the bow stem, and steers using a vertical shaft, a nautical version of the joy stick, moved in the direction he wishes to travel. A conventional throttle is at his left hand. When the seas are rough, fish—most particularly the mahi-mahi—rise to the surface in search of food and are thus visible. Spotting a school of them, the fisherman applies power to overtake the fast-fleeing fish and directs his craft alongside using the steering shaft clasped between his knees or in his left hand. He then grabs in his right hand a stout spear tipped with a trident and, with the boat crashing through the rough waves at high speed, hurls the spear at his prey. If it's a strike, he hauls in the catch using a lanyard attached to the spear. Too cool!

Mangareva

From Pitcairn Island, we enjoyed nearly perfect weather and sea conditions, arriving just inside Gambier's fringing reef at sunset on the following day. It was December 17, 2007. In the protection of the reef and the low but sheer volcanic islands, we dropped anchor for a quiet night under a waxing moon and brightly starred sky. Mars hung low on the western sky.

In the light of the next morning, we could see that these surrounding hills were quite different from the high peaks of Pitcairn. These are spotted in copses of evergreens, giving the place at first glance the look of the American Pacific Northwest. Yet along the shoreline are wild groves of spindly coconut trees mixed with pandanus fruit trees and other tropical plants framing gleaming white sand beaches lapped by iridescent blue water. Rising sharply behind the shore are the faded remnants of the ancient volcanoes that created these and most all of the Pacific islands, now covered over in tropical plant life of all kinds.

I accompanied Captain Lucas and Mate Bobby to shore in Mangareva in search of the local police station—or gendarmerie; it's French, after all. After picking our way among the coral heads and pearl farm buoys, we located the cops and checked in. The person in charge was a Polynesian woman who spoke excellent English.

The three of us took an hour to wander about Mangareva in search of logo T-shirts or other curios. We were also looking for electric fans because *Indigo's* air-conditioning compressors had decided, here in the warm tropics, to retire from active service. It was hot and stuffy in our cabins.

The village is but one narrow street along the waterfront lined mostly with modest masonry homes and a few shops, a clinic, the cops, and of course, a monumental church. Everywhere we looked, there were glorious flowers, exotic shrubs, and trees. Rising just behind the street is the rocky and steep former volcano. It is a desultory sort of place.

There are far more French soldiers about than you might expect. Here in the tropics, these putative warriors have been issued one of the more ironic bits of uniform ever to adorn a soldier. It is what can be accurately called short shorts, something like what was once known as hot pants—and in camouflage, no less. The guys looked like the gay cop on *Reno 911*, and I'm being serious here. Had they been designed by Saint Laurent?

After returning to *Indigo*, the crew and I loaded up the tender with a cooler full of iced-down beer and a battery-powered music box and headed off to one of the many beaches within sight. There we spent lazy hours watching the sun set and the tide roll in, beachcombing and snoozing. It was a much-needed break from the strains, such as they are, of yachting across the Pacific.

Papeete, Tahiti

Next day, we hoisted anchor and made for Papeete, Tahiti, traveling through the jewel-like Tuamotu group of islands, coral-rimmed atolls all. It might have been a delightful and largely uneventful cruise were it not for the failed air-conditioning units. Here in the humidity of the subtropics, the balky AC was the source of sweaty discomfort. So our travel from the Gambier Islands to Papeete, Tahiti, grand capital of all French Polynesia, was a trying affair—especially at night when cooling winds abated.

On the first night out, while our engineer, Sean, was on duty, a startling noise interrupted the faint thrum of the main engines. When he and Mate Bobby investigated, they found that a forearm-sized flying fish had leapt over the starboard bulwarks—about ten feet above the waterline—flown through an open sea door, and smashed into the main deck stairway, leaving telltale scales and slime at the point of impact. Dazed, the poor devil lay on the foyer deck for a few moments, then recovered his wits and began to flop about as fish out of water are compelled by nature to do. So vigorously did he flop that he managed to fling himself into the stairway to my cabin, flop-step down the stairs, and deposit himself at my door. It was there that he flopped his last.

Our arrival in Tahiti on the early morning of December 23 marked the end of the 4,400-nautical-mile voyage from Valparaiso, Chile. When we had left there on November 27, the water temperature stood at 61 degrees thanks to the north-flowing Humboldt Current, and we all wore light jackets. Here, the ocean had warmed to 84 degrees, and we perspired in T-shirts.

Tahiti from the sea is a volcanic island with dense jungle growth and peaks reaching to 6,000 feet. On land, it can be driven around in a full day, allowing time to stop at a few of the many local villages that abound along the shoreline. Outside of its towns, the island is breathtakingly beautiful. Aside from the mountains, its principal geologic attraction is an encircling reef. This natural battlement protects a lagoon of always placid water lapping at serene beaches varying in shades from off-white to volcanic black.

Papeete is an unlovely, traffic-clogged, paint-faded port town of 138,000 souls, most Polynesian, French, some Asian, and assorted Europeans and mixed caste. It hosts cruise ships, interisland ferries, and the French navy, among others. Shops along the waterfront all seem to sell pretty much the same stuff: Polynesian clothing, black pearls, tropical flowers, and assorted souvenirs.

Many of the local ladies parade about town with a colorful flower tucked behind an ear. Behind the right ear means available, left ear means taken . . . or is it the other way around? Some women and a few men wear head wreaths of fresh flowers, giving the wearer the air of a fairy queen. It's a style I don't see catching on in the US anytime soon.

While tied to the cruise ship docks in not-so-beautiful downtown Papeete, we watched many vessels come and go. Among these were numerous cruise ships that were doing a brisk business even though this was the off-season. On one memorable day, we looked up from our daily routine to spot the Peruvian navy training ship, actually a smallish freighter, arriving in port with full ceremony. Decked out bow to stern in flapping signal flags, her railings were lined with all the crew in dress uniform singing what I supposed was the navy's or country's anthem.

The 130-foot classic-designed schooner the *Robert C. Seamans* from Woods Hole, Massachusetts, was in Papeete for a few days to pick up a load of young oceanography students. Surely the most picturesque of the visiting ships was the *Star Flyer*, a steel-hulled, four-masted, barquentine sailing ship of 366 feet built in 1991 for the cruise ship trade. At night with all her rigging lit up, she was a magnificent sight on the harbor waterfront, a glimpse into the last days of sailing vessels. The world-famous German-built 295-foot yacht *Ice* pulled into port and docked next to us, followed a few days later by the stunning, hypermodern 220-foot sailing yacht *Maltese Falcon*.

One day Mate Bobby, Deckhand Tomas, and I hopped into a rental car and drove the circumference of Tahiti—ninety miles on a single, mostly two-lane road—in what might have been a local record time of three hours—one of Phil's high-speed culture tours (no museums, no churches). Surfers crowding black sand beaches and dense jungle crowding the highway were memorable sights. But mostly we liked the Tres Cascades, three adjacent waterfalls that crash to earth from jungle-encrusted peaks.

The crew and I explored in considerable detail the nightlife of Papeete. Our favorite beer joint was Tres Brasseurs, which I thought was French for three brassieres—an odd name, to say the least. Captain Lucas, a patient man, explained that the name was not a reference to intimate wear but referred to the three microbreweries the place houses. So much for my French.

We also spent too many hours at the Club Paradise and some

fewer at Club 106, Montmartre, Morrison's, and Ute Ute (meaning "red hot" in Tahitian), all of these just a few blocks from *Indigo's* dock.

By a wide measure, the strangest aspect of Polynesian, and especially Tahitian, culture is its sexual mores. Their practices are thousands of years old, somewhat chastened by the advance of Western culture, yet still widespread. Incest is far more common and indeed more accepted here than anywhere else on Earth. It also is not at all uncommon for a man thirty to forty years old or more to take as his "girlfriend"—for which read "concubine"—a pubescent girl as young as twelve, though more commonly thirteen or fourteen, and this with the permission of and payment of money to the girl's father. The legal age is eighteen.

There are also the mahus. These are young men who, born into a family with an adequate number of boys but lacking in girls, are from an early age shunted off to a female role and, as a result, grow up to be sexually ambiguous or outwardly effeminate.

One night Deckhand Tomas Maldonado and I, among others, were seated innocently at Tres Brasseurs when four charming and very attractive young women joined us. They were clad in the barest necessities of clothing, midriffs fully bared, long lissome legs exposed to the high thigh, eyes and faces made up to a flawless perfection. They flirted and cooed and oohed and aahed until poor Tomas was about to go mad. It was at this point that the bar manager, a friend of *Indigo's* crew, came upon the scene and whispered to Tomas a caution devastating in its implications: "These are not girls, Tomas!" The visions of sugarplums that a moment before had danced gaily in his head now turned to nightmares of Brussels sprouts. Welcome to Tahiti!

One night I left Paradise early and, I thought, alone, leaving Engineer Sean and Deckhand Tomas to occupy the later hours of the night. A few blocks from Paradise, while walking along the main harbor front street, I heard loud shouting behind me and turned around in time to see Sean and Tomas confronting and chasing off a gang of teen punks who had been about to jump me from behind. Comforting to know the crew was looking out for my welfare. They also had the habit of hiring the local club security to keep an eye on us and run off the sloppy drunks.

~~~

Following a Christmas celebration with the crew, I returned to Florida for a much-awaited reunion with the family, attended to some business matters, and caught up with old friends. During this time, the crew addressed a list of maintenance issues while also taking a short cruise (just two hours) to the island of Moorea for a brief respite from their normal routine. I returned to *Indigo* in late January.

Society Islands

Childhood friends Pete Cicchine and Chris Jensen joined me in Tahiti for two weeks aboard *Indigo*.

Upon their arrival, we cast off lines and traveled twelve miles across the Tahiti Channel the lovely island of More, where we anchored in the world famous to Cook's Bay, named for Captain James Cook, who stopped there on one of his voyages of discovery. It is perhaps the most photographed, filmed, and admired bay in the world, and is certainly among its most serenely beautiful. The volcano that formed the island has mostly sunk into the sea, leaving behind the eroded tips of its central vent—now a mountain withered to 2,800 feet.

Pete, Chris and I took the tender out to a tiny picturesque moth (small island in Polynesian) we had spotted on entering the bay. It's alluring white sand beaches and dense cover of coconut palms give it the look of a postcard photo. To our surprise, it was equipped as a public park with showers, barbecue grills, bathrooms, and the like, though on this day we were its only visitors. Onshore, we set up the camp chairs, opened the beer cooler and a large bag of pork rinds, and did yet again what we had done together many times before but so many years ago.

We found a number of long, stout bamboo poles that we decided were there for knocking coconuts out of the tall palms. We tried it but proved inept. Tiring of strenuous activities, we reclined in our chairs, drank beer, and ate pork rinds as we watched the tide ebb and the sun set. At these activities, we were more accomplished.

Just before the sun dropped behind the island's craggy peaks, we took the tender into the large bay adjacent to Cook's, called Baie d'Opunohu. This was the bay used as a backdrop in the filming of the latest version of *Mutiny on the Bounty*, this one starring a young Mel Gibson.

Next day, we went by tender with Captain Lucas to a special spot among the coral heads inside Moorea's fringing reef where large, well-fed stingrays congregated along with blacktip reef sharks. Captain Lucas, who had brought along a bag of fish scraps, hopped overboard in the four-foot-deep water. Promptly besieged by the rays begging for food, he fed and petted them as if they were lap-dogs. Following his lead, Pete, Chris, and I joined him, though with noticeable reluctance.

As the rays dined, word of the banquet apparently went out in the fish world, and sharks began circling, getting closer by the minute to our exposed body parts. When they got within twenty feet and began swimming about in an agitated manner, we promptly climbed back into the tender and went off in search of other adventures.

The island of Huahine is split by an elliptical-shaped lagoon, a geo-graphic arrangement that, aided by a salacious imagination, resem-bles vaguely an important part of the female anatomy. The island's name is the Tahitian slang term for that part. Who says Tahitians don't have a sense of humor?

The island has a population of more than 6,000, engaged mostly in fishing, farming of vanilla and melons, and some tourism. The island's gentle people lead a quiet, traditional way of life far from the drab hubbub of Papeete, and they live on one of the world's most strikingly beautiful islands. From its west shore, the nearby islands of Raiatea and Tahaa, our next destination, are easily visible.

We entered the protected lagoon surrounding Tahaa by way of Passe Iriru ou Maire (try saying that three times quickly), then cruised up to the head of scenic Baie Faaroa. We anchored there in one of the very few bays anywhere in the islands that is the drainage basin for a navigable inland river. Chris and I took two sit-on-top kayaks from *Indigo's* toy storage and paddled up the narrow and quite shallow river. Dense jungle canopied over our path, blocking the sunlight. So exotic was the setting, I would not have been surprised if an ape had swung by on a vine. But after a while, the paddling got tiresome and we headed back to *Indigo*, where we all agreed that kayaks could be improved considerably by the addition of a motor.

Early the next day, we cruised up the east side of the island within its protected lagoon, admiring Raiatea's dramatic peaks 3,300 feet high, passed Uturoa, the largest town in the Leeward Islands and a sometime cruise ship stop, and continued on to the island of Tahaa.

There, our guide, Ivan, drove up a deeply rutted dirt road into dense jungle, where he located a wild hibiscus tree, cut a branch from it with his machete, and from the branch fabricated a wood flute on which he played a tune. He then threw on the ground a wad of the tree's leaves, and we watched as large land crabs, moving at the speed of sloths, came out of their holes to compete with one another in their efforts to drag the leaves into their dens. It was a crab war in slow motion. These same leaves are used as a heat shield over hot coals in a fire pit when cooking fish.

The jungle road climbed to a peak, where there was a small glade from which we could look down into a valley cultivated in pineapples, an important crop for this island. Ivan hacked a coconut from one of the many palm trees and showed us how it should be opened and its contents grated on a steel rasp.

The jungle through which we drove was covered in trees bearing every imaginable wild fruit. There were species of wild bananas, pandanus fruit, breadfruit, aloe, mangoes, papayas, noni, tamarind, tamara, kava, and lots more. Coconut palms are to these islands what weeds are to a garden: abundant and hardy. The stately acacia tree, eaten by giraffes on the plains of Africa's Kalahari, also proliferates. You name it, and it likely grows wild somewhere in Polynesian soil.

Ivan then took us to a copra plantation. Copra are chunks of coconut meat sun-dried over time, then sold to processors who turn the stuff into various oils and emollients.

At tour's end, we rejoined *Indigo* and traveled around Tahaa, still inside the lagoon, to an anchorage just off the Taravana Yacht Club in Apu Bay. Pete, Chris, and I joined the crew for dinner at the club, and next day we took the tender into the town of Uturoa on the north end of Raiatea just a few miles away. Nearly all the shops were closed due to an impending election, but we managed to find a decent restaurant where we ordered the Tahitian dish *poisson cru*, a Polynesian version of ceviche. This is the national dish of Tahiti and consists of diced chunks of raw fish marinated in lime juice and coconut sauce, and mixed with chopped green peppers, tomatoes, and onions.

From the Tahaa shore, it was easy to see the towering peaks of world-famous Bora Bora, to which we would soon be traveling. But not before seeing the seldom-visited remote island of Maupiti.

Entering from the ocean was no easy task. The reef break at the pass was not much wider than *Indigo*, and midway through, it was necessary to make a hard turn to starboard, this while being pushed along from behind by the gentle swell welling up from the sea. But Captain Lucas managed a flawless entry, employing the skill he had acquired over many years at sea.

Once inside, the waters turn from the deep blue of the Pacific to opalescent shades of blues and greens. Maupiti is famous for these waters, so we lowered the tender and went buzzing around the lagoon just marveling at the place. Through the translucent water, it was easy to see spotted leopard rays and eagle rays soaring along and the litter of sea cucumbers and assorted other creatures on the bottom. The fluffy white sand beaches lining this fabulous lagoon are themselves lined with coconut palms whose leaves rustle in the gentle sea breezes. Presiding over all this is the island's ancient volcanic mountain, Teura Faatui, covered over with dense tropical forest.

We had brought a folding table, camp chairs, plenty of cold beer, food, a barbecue grill, portable speakers, and my iPod, and for lunch set up camp on a gorgeous spit of white sand beach under the shade of exotic trees. There we ate grilled fish, drank beer, swam and snoozed, and admired our stunning surroundings—about as fine a way to have lunch as there is.

Maupiti's population is just 1,192, and they've resolutely declined to permit any hotel or resort development, so there are few tourists. As a result, it is the most unspoiled and lovely place imaginable.

Bora Bora

We set off the next morning for the thirty-nautical-mile trip to the tourist haven of Bora Bora.

When the US Navy abandoned Bora Bora at the conclusion of World War II, it left behind an airstrip, now the island's commercial airport, several batteries of shore artillery, a variety of bunkers, Quonset huts, and the like and, in keeping with the Laws of Nature, 116 babies. Its personnel also took home memories of this Eden-like island and its attractive young ladies.

As young men will do, they talked up their memories and deeds, the word spread, and Bora Bora soon became the most famous of all the islands of the South Pacific and remains so today. It is not more beautiful nor its people in any sense more appealing; it just has the cachet. As a result, it also has the finest hotels. St. Regis, Four Seasons, Le Meridian, and others are all there, each with its rooms perched on stilts in over-the-water bungalows and renting at not less than $1,000 per night, food excluded. And that's off-season. They go up to $25,000. Bora Bora also gets all the cruise ships in the area, since no trip to French Polynesia would be complete without a visit here.

Among other pursuits, the people of Bora Bora grow pandanus trees from which leaves are harvested, dried, and formed into thatch for the roofs of all those hotel over-the-water bungalows. When the business, and its related employment, was threatened by the arrival of plastic simulacra with a far lower cost and longer life, the faux stuff was simply outlawed.

In the small island village, I found an aging, Japanese-made six-passenger van parked in the shade of a large palm tree. Its driver, a middle aged, overfed local fellow named Dino, was having a nap. After waking him with a bang on the van's fender, I recruited him to take Chris, Pete, and myself on a tour of the island's circumference, all twenty miles of it. Right off, this proved to be a mistake. Dino was incapable of exceeding twenty miles per hour, left the vehicle in the lower gears too long, and shifted awkwardly—all of which made for a maddening excursion.

The three of us took the tender and zipped off to the St. Regis for a truly memorable lunch in an idyllic setting. Along the way, with your humble servant at the helm, we fetched up on a reef when I misread one of the French channel markings for shoal areas. No harm done— just a few more gouges in the tender hull and a ding in the outboard's foot.

It was a planned convenience that our anchorage was sited just at the dock for the long-famous Bloody Mary's bar and restaurant. It's a large place and friendly enough, but it smacks of mass tourism with busloads of cruise ship passengers arriving regularly. An interior feature of note is its floor of pure white sand, which the owner complained must be replaced every year. Its men's room is, so they claim, rated among the world's top twenty. Whether it deserves this distinction, I can't say, not having visited the rest (that I'm aware of), but it is surely among the most unusual. Hanging in front of the granite trough-type urinal is a chain that when pulled flushes the thing, and hanging from the end of the chain is a finely carved and brightly polished phallus. These can be purchased at shops all over the islands, handmade by locals—an unusual occupation, you'll have to admit.

After Pete and Chris departed for home, I went scuba diving with Captain Lucas and Chef Jeanette in about sixty feet of water just outside the island's outermost reef. Since I hadn't dived in a few years, it took a while to get the hang of it, and when I finally did and began to look around, I saw eight or ten smallish blacktip reef sharks, a few gray sharks, and a wide variety of fish, large and small. All was going swimmingly, so to speak, when there arrived on the scene five very large—about ten feet or so—and menacingly curious lemon sharks, one of whom passed not more than three feet below my fins. We decided then that we'd had enough of shark-watching for the day.

Tuamotu Islands

One cloudless evening as *Indigo* was making her way due east to the Tuamotu Islands, we were treated to one of the many wondrous sights the heavens offer. Just as the day's declining light was shading the sky to a lustrous blue, a glorious full moon was rising directly on the bow. As if this gift were not heavenly enough, the softly glowing Pacific sun was setting directly on our stern. At that ineffably lovely moment, both were poised there at precisely the same height above their respective horizons. Moon fore and sun aft—you could hardly ask for more. Compounding our good fortune, next morning the sun rose on the bow and the moon set on the stern, each perfectly synchronized with the other, a visual duet of astronomic delight.

The Tuamotu Islands are classic atolls that are arranged, as are all the islands in this part of the world, along a northwest to southeast axis. They were formed from ancient volcanoes which have, over many millions of years, simply sunk beneath the sea, leaving only the fringing reefs mounted on undersea plateaus of basalt now supporting flat, palm-covered white sand motus. Where the volcano once stood is now a large lagoon.

To get the flavor of these peculiar islands, we visited Apataki in the northwest end of the chain. In order to enter its lagoon, we passed between two of the numerous enclosing motus through a deep water cut. Prevailing southerly swells and winds caused water in the lagoon to stack up and, under pressure, to blast through the cut, resulting in the saltwater version of white-water rapids, a boiling cauldron of angry sea. The captain steered us carefully down the center of the narrow channel and added power to keep us from being swept sideways and out of control. Because the lagoon is so enormous, we were unable to see from the cut its enclosing motus on the other side, leaving us with an eerie, disorienting sense of passing from the Pacific Ocean through a portal into another and utterly strange body of water.

About three miles into the lagoon, the captain anchored alongside one of the motus in a lovely spot from which we snorkeled among the many coral heads. I took the tender and went exploring and came upon one of the local fishermen with his wife and two sons. They were typical Polynesian, the man and wife short, weather-worn, dressed in faded T-shirts and baggy shorts. The kids, like young people seemingly the world over, wore tattered and soiled faux NBA jerseys over old cotton shorts. Parents and kids were barefoot.

In butchered French, I asked the man where he lived. He pointed across the lagoon in the direction of the atoll's only village, population 430, with a tiny airstrip. He also proudly showed me his second home, a squat box made entirely of corrugated tin sheets, which he used on extended fishing trips. It sported an unlikely satellite dish antenna for the TV he powered with a tiny portable generator. His boat was a tastefully painted open fisherman with new outboard engine. Apparently the fishing business had been profitable.

The Tuamotus are ideally suited for pearl farming, with their large protected lagoons flushed clean by the tides, and pearl farms they have in abundance. Some lagoons are so clogged with the buoys from which hang strings of pearl oysters that it's nearly impossible to navigate through them. But the business has brought prosperity of a sort to islands that otherwise would be destitute.

If you wander into one of the many black pearl shops in Papeete or Bora Bora, you will be struck by how many pearls there are. Great bowls the size of giant clam shells are filled to overflowing with the things. Room partitions made from strings of pearls hang all over the stores. They are plentiful, and more are produced in the pearl farms of French Polynesia every day. Yet despite their abundance, somehow they remain expensive, especially for the high-quality, perfectly round and lustrously colored pearls. My mildly cynical take on it is that there is market rigging going on, something like De Beers once rigged the diamond market.

After a few days anchored in Apataki's sealike lagoon, we returned to Papeete to refuel and take on stores in preparation for the next leg of the voyage, this one to the Cook Islands, a four-day trip west of Tahiti.

NINE

Snakes in the South Pacific

The Cook Islands are an independent country consisting of fifteen islands of varying size loosely affiliated with New Zealand. Rarotonga, the largest and most economically dominant of the group, was our next destination. It was mid-March, 2008.

Rarotonga

This island is best thought of as the top of an enormous ancient volcano standing 17,000 feet above the ocean floor, the first 14,750 feet of which are underwater. The remainder is a group of weathered and eroded peaks, saw-toothed, craggy, and razor-backed, draped in dense tropical jungle. The island's circumference at sea level is just twenty miles, but at a depth of 13,000 feet is thirty-one miles. Like all similar islands in this region of the world, it is surrounded by a shallow lagoon protected by an off-lying reef not more than a half mile to seaward.

In the main town of Avarua is a commercial harbor whose entry is just barely wide enough to permit *Indigo* to enter safely and turn around. At the entry just to starboard is a breakwater made of heavy stones piled above the thundering surf. Perched upon this are the remains of a recent shipwreck, and about a mile to the south is yet another, this one piled up on the reef. Captain Lucas, undeterred by the visual evidence of calamity, guided us to the town wharf with skill.

Ashore, some of the crew and I took a guided tour around the island's circumference that lasted far longer than ideal. ("This is our electric plant. Here is a defunct hotel.") One sweaty day, I walked nine holes of golf on the island's only course, set in the midst of an array of hundred-foot-high, fully guy-wired radio antennae. On five of the holes, you have to hit at an antenna and hope to miss it and its supporting wires to land safely in the fairway.

The crew and I had dinner at several restaurants, one of which included the sights and sounds of wild chickens rooting about and, at sundown, fluttering awkwardly into tree roosts. After dinner, we attended popular festivities at the Banana Court, a bar and disco, where we encountered at the inevitable pool table a friendly group of undersized guys from Fiji and the Philippines here for work.

One of the island's attractions is that its inhabitants speak English, although of the New Zealand variety. After struggling in French Polynesia with my poor French, this place was a dream. It did take some getting used to, though, to see dark-skinned, Maori-like Cook Islanders spouting Kiwi English.

Another pleasing aspect of the place is that it has a pleasing aspect. Yards are tidy, homes and shops painted, gardens neatly tended. The Brits have left their mark. After a few days here, we moved on to the island of Niue ("nu way").

Island of Niue

Niue, at forty miles around and 162 square miles, is said to be the world's smallest sovereign democracy. Although self-governing, *Niue* has a defense pact with New Zealand—though what might be gained from invading the place is not apparent to the casual observer. The Kiwis also provide a heavy subsidy, and perhaps as a consequence, the locals are uniformly heavy. The island's populace is a mix of Polynesian/Maori and expat New Zealanders and Aussies.

From its tourist literature, the crew and I had formed the opinion that this was to be one of our finest stops in all the South Pacific. It has what is reputed to be the clearest seawater on Earth thanks to the absence of muddy rivers, and thus scenic scuba diving. Owing to its substrata of limestone, there are accessible grottoes, caves, and caverns sculpted by pounding surf and the ravages of time. Its diminutive size makes it easily toured in a leisurely day, allowing plenty of time for stops along the way.

What we had failed to take into account, however, was that while the island may sound appealing to us, it apparently is not so to the locals. A population that in 1966 was 5,200, was at the time of our visit something on the order of 1,300, a decline of some 75 percent. Mostly they left for New Zealand, an exodus hurried along by Cyclone Heta in 2004.

It's one thing to read about people abandoning their homeland on such a scale and quite another to see its effects. Driving through the fifteen or so villages of Niue is a trip through dilapidated towns, one after the other, some completely without human habitation. Modest homes layered in black mold, front doors waving in the breeze, yards overtaken by the jungle, windows cracked open to reveal rotting curtains.

In a few villages, one or two families remain out of the many that once lived there. These homes, still modest, at least bear signs of life. Yards freshly mowed, vehicles parked in front, flowers in the garden, freshly painted churches dominating the commons. The whole effect of Niue is something like walking around in a graveyard on a moonlit night, eerie and otherworldly.

I rented a worn-out Jeep wagon and drove with some of the crew on a whirlwind tour around the island's entire circumference. We stopped at a popular swimming hole carved into the shoreside rocks and made our way over treacherous, jagged limestone to ocean-washed grottoes. It was Easter Sunday, and on this deeply religious island no work, or even active recreation, is allowed on the Sabbath. We saw people decked out in their finest, ladies in umbrellalike hats, men in dark suits, but were not able to hear their choirs in the full and harmonious, if dwindling, voices for which the island is noted. For lunch, we stopped at the premier, and only, resort hotel, which I would award a single star. It was an entirely forgettable experience redeemed only by the cliff-top view over the ocean.

Next day, some of the crew and I went for a scuba dive under the supervision of the only dive shop, operated by Ian and Annie, Kiwi ex-pats. Because there is no proper harbor or marina, we drove to a boat ramp where Ian launched from a trailer a fifteen-foot inflatable boat loaded down with all our dive gear. Annie then took us a half mile or so along the reef to a spot where a large pod of spinner dolphins were feeding. Two at a time, we slipped quietly over the side equipped with fins, snorkel, and mask and held on to the boat as Annie powered us to the dolphins. At one point, four of them were riding in the bow wave of our tiny boat, just out of my reach.

The apparently frolicsome pod, with numerous new calves, cavorted for our entertainment until, tiring of us, they went on about the all-important business of feeding themselves. We watched them swimming away through water that was the clearest I've ever seen, visibility reaching to 250 feet.

Following this fun, we went a mile or so away to the ominously named Snake Gully, infamous for its congregation of sea snakes. Along with crocodiles, bears, and sharks, snakes are among my least favorite animals, and the sea snake is surely my least favorite of all. About three feet long with the girth of a garden hose, it has the distinction of being the most venomous animal on the planet. One nip and your bucket is kicked. It took some convincing from Annie to get me into the same ocean with these loathsome critters, and unarmed, too.

The reefs at our dive spot, once among the most florid and lively in the world, are now as bereft of life as the villages of Niue, damaged severely by the 2004 cyclone. There was the odd wrasse, surgeonfish, and spiny lobster, and a few corals had returned here and there, but these were the exceptions. There were, however, many snakes, hidden in rock crevasses in horrible, tangled, writhing masses. Every twenty minutes to an hour or so, they are compelled to rise fifty feet to the surface for a gulp of fresh air, then return to their dens. With many hundreds of the things spread over the comparatively small area of Snake Gully, their ascending and descending made a veritable curtain of poisonous serpents on the move.

Being told by our guide that they are both poor sighted and timid did nothing to reassure me. When she grabbed one and began to stroke it, then invited me to do the same, I declined. They are, it is said, unable to unhinge their jaws as terrestrial vipers do and so cannot nip you except in places like the webbing between your fingers. This, too, offered little comfort as my bare fingers are indeed separated by such webbing.

We left Snake Gully—or Death Valley, as I called it—and moved on to several undersea caves filled with more appealing sea life, like fish.

Then it was on to one of the oddest island groups in the Pacific.

Kingdom of Tonga

Tonga is one of the world's last constitutional monarchies, having declared its independence from the English in 1970. Its population of 120,000 are mostly native Tongans spread over an archipelago of 171 islands, only thirty-six of which are inhabited, divided into three main groups. To the north is the Vava'u, in the center is the Ha'apai, and to the south the Tongatapu group, where the capital of Nuku'alofa (meaning "abode of love") is located—all of which should be called the Unpronounceable Islands. They are a wonderland of utterly unspoiled tropical beauty washed by opalescent sea. While other South Pacific islands have surrendered to the onslaught of modernity and the trampling tourists that come with it, Tonga has steadfastly resisted, though with a depressing effect on its people.

Following a short and calm passage, we arrived in the yacht-popular Tonga town of Neiafu, the main town in the Vava'u group. The islands here are uniformly high but evenly surfaced volcanic promontories, all clad in thick, lush jungle that reaches down the steep slopes to the sea, leaving few places with an accessible beach. The islands themselves are closely spaced, and the sea is deep right to the shore, making it ideal for larger vessels like motor yachts and sailboats. Exploring by tender is fun, since the waters are well protected from the wind and waves of the open sea, and there are few reefs to impale an imprudently steered boat.

The town's waterfront is lined with a few shabby bars and restaurants catering to the owners of the many private sailboats that frequent the area, mostly Kiwis, Aussies, and Americans in thirty-to-forty-foot sloops. In the town itself, just up the hill from the waterfront, there are decrepit, wood-frame buildings, last painted maybe thirty years ago, giving the place the look of a Wild West mining town.

One night when we went ashore to a bar, there were unemployed young men hanging around listening to the hectoring sermon of a street preacher rambling on in Tongan about how the crowd can find salvation. Leaving Tonga would be a start. The crowd was not threatening, and a few even smiled timidly, but it was easy to see that life here lacked much promise.

The Tongans, unique among Pacific islanders, are insular, rejecting outside influence as contrary to the Tongan way. They have chased off foreign investment, declined to trade much with other nations, and made it clear in their policies that they want no truck with non-Tongans. In short, they have always fought a retrograde battle against encroaching civilization with the economic result all too plain to see.

Their diet is best described as opportunistic. They eat horses, dogs, cats, and fruit bats, among much else, and in former times ate each other. Cannibalism was a widespread practice throughout most of the Pacific islands, and the Tongans went about it with considerable gusto. One famous chief bragged that in his lifetime he consumed more than 800 tasty humans, called "long pig." The preferred means of cooking was to bury the hapless delicacy in an earthen oven.

Tongans are among the most religious and priggish people on Earth. Work of any kind is absolutely forbidden on the Sabbath, and strenuous recreation strongly discouraged. Men typically dress in a black skirt hemmed well below the knee with a woven grass mat wrapped and tied around their torso. Shirts are commonly long-sleeved. It is considered an affront to visit a village wearing a hat or sunglasses or to show too much leg or shoulder flesh—for man or woman. Young girls swim wearing two layers of neck-to-ankle clothing, the second intended to cover the inevitable visual effects of wetting the first. Visitors are discouraged from wandering about in shorts, tank tops, and the like lest they give offense.

Outside of the capital and especially in the more forgiving Vava'u group, the rules are far more relaxed. Young teens go about dressed in faux NBA uniforms with baggy shorts, tank tops, and clunky sneakers.

During our brief stay in Neiafu, we were struck by a storm whose winds reached fifty knots even in the well-protected harbor. Our anchor held secure, but trees in the town were toppled and docks blown away. We had known of the approaching storm and had taken timely shelter, thanks to the online satellite-based weather service to which we subscribe. The service kept track of our itinerary in real time, knowing where we were, where we were headed, and at what speed. They sent us—by email, fax, or satellite phone—regular forecasts of wind speed and direction, wave and swell height and direction, barometer readings, and the position and direction of any squall lines, storm cells, and the like, along with advice to change course, remain in port, or seek shelter as appropriate. Since our departure from Florida, they had often directed us away from dangerous conditions. That we were securely anchored in a well-protected harbor when this storm hit was yet another testament to their valuable service.

Fiji

After completing the cumbersome process of clearing out of immigration, customs, and all the other meddlesome bureaucracies, we departed for the two-day travel to the town of Nadi (pronounced, for some reason, "Nandi") on the main island of Fiji.

If you were to count every scrap of soil or rock above high tide, these islands would number in the thousands and you would have one of life's more boring preoccupations. But of these, only 322 are large enough for human habitation, and just 106 actually have people living on them. The remaining 216 islands are prohibitively isolated or lack freshwater and are, it seems, mostly for sale—some at attractive prices, if remote island living is your thing.

About 90 percent of the country's land area is contained within its two largest islands, Vanua Levu and Viti Levu. Of these, the latter is by far the more developed, home to 75 percent of the population and the town of Suva, the nation's capital. The entire country is just a tad smaller than New Jersey, though a good bit warmer and without a Mafia.

Fiji is a polyglot country, but one that is decidedly ill at ease with the *poly* part. It began life eons ago as essentially Polynesian, then migratory and enslaved Melanesians, some Tongans, and even Europeans added to the mixture to make modern-day Fijians. All was just swell until the British, who used to own the place, brought in indentured workers from India to meet a labor shortage. In due course, Fijians were equaled in number by Indians, and this was when the real trouble started. Today, after three coups, military governments, assassinations, disbanded governments, rigged votes—and all of this just since 1987—things are still pretty much a mess.

Suva, we learned from others who have been there as well as from the numerous guidebooks we consulted, is a place where the word "forlorn" leaps easily to mind. Quite like nearly every other town or village we've visited in the South Pacific, the place is said to be hangdog and not a place for the discerning crew of *Indigo*. Instead we opted for the quasi-resort town of Nadi, Fiji's third largest, with its South Florida-like marina and adjoining shops, including some excellent curry restaurants. It even has a Hard Rock Café perched merrily alongside the marina.

After securing *Indigo* to the dock and giving her a thorough washdown, the crew departed for a much-deserved two-day stay ashore at a hotel of their choosing. Being usually cooped up in tiny quarters, working and taking meals at each other's elbows, the crew was delighted to spend some time apart in a commodious hotel room.

One morning I rented a car for a self-guided tour of Nadi. I wanted a glimpse, not more, of a real Fiji town. I passed slowly and observantly along its main street to the far end, and turned around. That was it. It was just another of the all-too-familiar careworn, ill-conceived, scuffed-up places found all over the South Pacific.

At every turn, though, an infectious *"Bula! Bula!"* greeted me. I found this to be one of Fijians' most charming attributes. The Fijian greeting is announced with a vigor not common in the colder, taciturn climes and is always accompanied by an enormous, toothy grin. It surely beat "G'day mate," "Buenos dias," *"Hola,"* *"Bon dia,"* *"Oi,"* and "Hello." Certainly, it was a considerable improvement on "Wazzup."

Vanuatu

Once known as the New Hebrides, Vanuatu is today a collection of spectacular, jungle-cloaked islands strung out across the South Pacific, lightly populated and seldom visited by tourists.

This was the first place we had visited whose people were Melanesians, as distinguished from the Polynesians who dominate every island east of here all the way to Easter Island. The Polys are statuesque, with mocha-colored skin, straight black hair, brown eyes with a vague suggestion of Asian, and a somewhat aloof air. By contrast, if you can picture in your mind a National Geographic photo of an aborigine from Australia's deepest Outback, you will have a pretty good idea of Melanesians. They are short, slight of build, coal black, and have kinky black hair, wide flat noses, and thick lips.

They are also among the most genuinely friendly people I've ever encountered anywhere. If you are driving along a bush road well away from the grimy hubbub of Port Vila, every person in every village along the way will stop what they are doing and give you the biggest, most welcoming grin you could imagine, often accompanied by a fully extended arm wave, frequently with both arms. None of that forearm waggle-wave for them. The kids, with arms fluttering like so many windmills, will yell gleefully something that sounds like

"Yee-haa," which made me wonder if some rednecks had wandered this way recently. These people seem to have not a hint of animosity or a care in the world. In a commercial setting, there is no bargaining or pressure to buy and, as elsewhere in the South Pacific, tipping is thought to be an insult.

The official languages here are three: English, spoken by nearly everybody, some French, and the local pidgin called Bislama. "The beer cooler belongs to me" is rendered in Bislama as "Bia cooler b'long me." "Do you speak English?" is "Yu tok Englis?" This lingo is a corruption of the English they heard from island traders and from the 500,000 American soldiers based here during World War II. Unofficially, though, there are 106 different languages in Vanuatu, of which 81 are still actively spoken, the highest concentration of languages per capita in the world.

Vanuatu today is an independent country, and its politics and government, as common in these parts, is . . . well, colorful. But it has one distinction that can be said of no other country in the world that I know of: at one point it was jointly ruled, get this, by none other than the English and French. Talk about a recipe for trouble. Just to give you the flavor of events then, the Brits insisted that all cars should drive, as in all civilized countries, on the left side of the road. The French, naturally, insisted on the right. So for a while there, people drove on both! The joint agreement was called "a condominium," a word whose etymology I had thought began in South Florida. After a short while, locals here began calling it a "pandemonium," and with good cause.

Port Vila

We elected to visit first the capital town of Port Vila (population 40,000), another scruffy, tumbledown place but one that I grew to like very much partly because of its tastefully planned (if badly disheveled) waterfront. There is a harbor-front park with native specimen trees, pedestrian walk, and shaded benches, but the park is overgrown and weedy, the walk crumbling, and the benches in need of repair. Still, it's a nice place for a stroll, thanks in no small part to the ramshackle cloth market lined with rustic stalls displaying colorful saris, sarongs, and dashikis. Crudely hand-lettered signs offer hair braiding and beading and, oddly, state the time required to complete each of these—a thoughtful though pointless gesture as nobody in the entire country wears a watch.

My favorite place, though, is the dirty, clamorous food market pavilion. Large at about an acre, each day but Sunday the place is stocked to overflowing with every imaginable food found in Vanuatu. There are rolled banana leaves for cooking in earthen stoves and bundles of gurgling land crabs and coconut crabs, taro roots the size of a child, wild fruits of every possible species, enormous tubers caked in mud, the omnipresent kava root, and peanuts freshly pulled from the ground. Among the cooked items are unidentifiable fish fried whole and pots of delicious-smelling stews. Most stalls are managed by a generously proportioned older woman in a colorful but warn and slightly soiled formless dress, who invariably smiles at you even though she knows you have no interest in her inventory. The whole place is alive with the sounds of a bustling commercial market, and I loved it.

Snake!

Experience teaches us a great deal about life and how best to avoid its many tribulations and torments that lie in wait. We learn, for example, that when we hear the expression "Holy shit!" nothing salutary is likely to follow. On a lovely Saturday morning, as I helmed Indigo's tender in toward the town dock at Port Vila, our normally unruffled engineer, Sean, became audibly ruffled, blurting out the ominous exclamation.

Sure enough, no good followed. Besides myself and Sean, Captain Lucas, Chef Jeanette, and Stewardess Darla were aboard. What had attracted Sean's attention—and now justifiably panicked all the boat's passengers—was a slimy and quite deadly black-and-white banded sea snake that had somehow made its way up the anchor line and into the tender's seating area. This is the same species that threatened us on a scuba dive in Niue, the single most venomous creature on the planet. Slithering Death.

Okay, so the thing was only two feet long, but what does size matter? I mean, a 7.62 mm magnum-load bullet is no bigger than your index finger. And what about a syringe of strychnine—to which this serpent is closely, if metaphorically, related?

Now you need to know that *Indigo's* tender was a mere fifteen feet long. Subtract from this the three feet needed to mount the outboard motor and the four feet needed for helm seat and console, and you are left with eight feet that, on this up-to-now stellar day, was cheerfully occupied by five adults and their day-trip gear. Now figure that a two-foot-long deadly snake has a strike radius of, say, a foot and a half, and you come up with a Circle of Death having a diameter of three feet operating in a field of opportunities a mere eight feet long by four feet wide and packed as sardines with potential victims. It's a veritable turkey shoot for the invader. As a killer snake, what more could you ask?

Upon seeing the unimposing but deadly creature slinking over Captain Lucas's backpack clearly in search of someone to kill, great shrieks of impending catastrophe filled the heretofore calm and sultry air of Port Vila, and civil order degenerated. As each person sought to exchange his position for one farthest removed from the fangs of death, and as the creature's slinking continued to compromise the newly selected safe place, a general—and it must be said unseemly—chaos beset the tiny craft.

Your humble correspondent affected the air of one not at all fearful of a horrible and painful death by snakebite. That I was seated at the helm and behind the protecting console may have contributed to this manly pose. But as the slithery devil began to make its way in my direction, there was a notable and, I am ashamed to say, regrettable about-face in my demeanor, though not one accompanied by screaming or anything like that. I just scampered heartily.

Relief came at last when Mate Bobby donned a rubber dry bag over a hand and arm and managed to return the beast to its watery home. Following this, there was a great deal of foot shuffling and aw-shucksing and muttering stuff about how I wasn't really afraid of that little old snake.

TEN

Jungle Diving and Cargo Cults

Human folly has been with us since the dawn of time and comes in two broad categories of misadventure. Perhaps the most prevalent and often humorous of these arises from inadvertence. Within this category, alcohol is a frequent companion. "Hold my drink and watch this." The book *The Darwin Awards* helpfully categorizes only a few of these events for our entertainment. There are many more.

The second, and certainly the more confounding, category is that of purposeful acts undertaken by ordinarily sensible people with forethought and even a touch of planning, though often with a teen-like impetuosity. Included here are such events as, for example, jumping in front of—and attempting to outrun—a thundering herd of enraged bulls.

Pentecost Island
Vanuatu has its contribution to this list, and it takes place once each year on the remote and quite primitive island of Pentecost. I call it jungle diving.

The crew and I, joined by a dozen other passengers all traveling to see the big event, flew one hour north to the island in a twin-engine, propeller-driven plane, one of a small fleet of similar planes operated by Air Vanuatu. The island, as its name suggests, once hosted hectoring missionaries, but the first few to arrive were cooked and eaten. I'm not sure why they let the rest get away.

Upon reaching our destination, the plane landed on a compacted limestone airstrip, and we disembarked at the grandly named Pentecost Island International Air Terminal, an approximately twenty-foot-square hut constructed of a thatched roof, walls of bamboo laced together with strips of wild hibiscus bark, and a bare earth floor. Inside was the Air Vanuatu local office, a scale where all passengers and their baggage are carefully weighed, and bench seating for those awaiting departure.

We were greeted somewhat diffidently by our guide for the day, a chap named Richard, and in due course piled into and atop his extended-cab, raised-chassis, Toyota Hi-Lux four-wheel-drive truck—which, as it turned out, is the bare minimum vehicle with which it's possible to navigate the island's few roads. The four-wheel-drive remained engaged, I noticed, for the entire trip of three miles over roads that were nothing less than a dense quagmire of the slimiest, slipperiest mud it's possible to imagine. The stuff is bad enough in the dry season, but now, just after a monsoon-like downpour the day before, it was nearly impassable in Richard's truck even as he tried, but failed, to stick to the bulldozer tracks helpfully imprinted on its surface. I thought as we churned and slid our way along that the dozer would have been a better choice of vehicle for this ride.

At last we reached our destination: a clearing in the jungle harboring a few ramshackle concrete bunkers with rusted corrugated tin roofs. There we languished in the sweltering sun for an hour or so while the ice in the cooler melted and the beer warmed. We were waiting, our guide said, for the participants in the day's activities to complete a sacred ritual that ancient custom forbade us from observing.

When finally we were summoned forth, we tramped along muddy paths hacked out of the dense jungle until reaching a newly cleared swath of about two acres. The clearing, carefully chosen for the day's events, was on the side of a steep hill and reached to its apex, which as we shall see is a far more important detail than the untrained eye might expect.

Looming awkwardly at the top of the hill was a fifty-foot tower constructed of nothing but machete-chopped trees, limbs, and vines. At heights of thirty, forty, and fifty feet, diving platforms protruded from the tower's face. No nail, screw, rope, hammer, or saw—not a single modern device, part, or piece—was used in building the contraption. A machete was the single concession to modern times.

We learned that at the same time each year, a new tower is built in precisely the same manner under the careful supervision of a master tower builder, who is himself trained in this ancient craft at the knee of a master. Immediately following the one-day event for which the tower is constructed, it is dismantled, and soon the jungle reclaims the cleared land.

By now, you are asking yourself: "Okay, what's this all about?"

Nobody knows for sure just when jungle diving got its start, but it was likely somewhere around a thousand or so years ago, maybe more. We don't know who invented it or why, but that shouldn't preclude us from speculating, and here's my shot at it.

One fateful day in the early dawn of time, a group of teenage boys were sitting around with nothing to do, the sort of gathering certain to produce harebrained ideas. The acknowledged savant of the group, a precocious lad we will call Oswald, complained about the dearth of eligible women in the village.

"The geezers take all the babes, leaving us nothing but sweat hogs," he lamented. "We need to come up with something we can do as teens to prove our manhood and thus get laid a whole lot more than we do now."

Murmurs of agreement rippled among the group.

"What shall we do?" asked Oswald.

Thoughtful ruminations dulled the conversation as primitive brains churned away on the matter. In due course, sheer genius struck the mind of Oswald—an idea so powerful, so persuasive in its elegant simplicity that it survives to this very day on Pentecost Island.

"I've got it! Let's dive headfirst and stark-naked out of the tops of tall towers!"

That single stroke of unhinged brilliance—slightly modified, and I dare say improved upon over the years—captures the essence of jungle diving. Here's how it works today.

To begin the festivities, a group of local young men, all modern descendants of Oswald and his pals, clad in nothing but a breezy penis sheath attached to a waistband, begin stomping about and chanting ancient and indecipherable sacred stuff, a kind of fraternity ritual. Accompanying them is a group of women wearing only grass skirts.

Meanwhile, one of the designated jungle divers climbs the tower to his assigned platform, where an aide secures a vine to both ankles. As the chanting continues, he steps to the end of the platform and raises his arms and head to the heavens, seeking divine guidance for the spectacular folly he is about to commit. As the chanting stops, he barks out what sounds like "what, what, what," probably pidgin for "What the hell was I thinking when I agreed to do this?" He slaps his bare thighs a few times, and then, in the climactic moment, executes a graceful, headfirst swan dive.

As the jungle diver descends toward the ground, the vines uncoil until they reach nearly their maximum extension. Just as the diver is about to strike the ground, the vines cause the platform to shear off with just enough resistance to dampen the fall.

Now the reason for building the tower at the top of a sharply sloping hill is revealed. When our diver strikes the ground, as he is most assuredly about to do, he will strike it a downward, glancing (and thus softened) blow. A keen observer will detect a further improvement on Oswald's original idea. The otherwise hard, compacted soil of Pentecost Island has been fluffed up to offer the diver a more hospitable reception. With all the modern advances upon Oswald's original formula wisely in place, the jungle diver hits the softened, sloping ground at a greatly reduced speed and so lives to enjoy the affections of the village babes wooed by the flamboyant display of courage.

Pentecost Island is the only place in the world where what I have called jungle diving takes place. Nobody knows when it began or what strange compulsion may have come upon otherwise sensible men. My suggestion gained convincing support in the late 1970s when a group of youthful students at Oxford University in England learned of the Pentecost jungle divers and decided to emulate them, undoubtedly to get more girls just as Oswald and his pals intended. From these daredevil students, there developed a further modern refinement to Oswald's genius that came to be called the bungee cord, now commonly known to thrill seekers the world over.

Following the ceremonies and numerous Jungle Dives, all of them leaving the diver unscathed, we sloshed our way to the beach through thick, black, gooey mud, one of us becoming stuck to the knees in the stuff, requiring rescue. There we lolled away some time with warm, badly fizzed beers whose tops and bottoms had become distended from being exposed to the exertions of high altitude during the plane ride. There is nothing quite like warm, fizzy beer drunk from cans that refuse to sit flat on a beach mat.

All kidding aside, I felt honored to have witnessed a ritual that has been a part of the culture of these Melanesian people for eons. Those who organized the event, as well as its participants, were as genuinely warm and gracious as people can possibly be.

On the hour-long flight back to Port Vila, the Kiwi pilot thoughtfully routed us over two active volcanoes. As we approached, I could see great rivers of congealed lava spread tentacle-like down the mountains' faces and into vast lakes of the stuff. The caldera itself was puffing up clouds of sulfurous gasses whose acrid fumes we could smell in the plane. We also saw how large, numerous, and extraordinarily remote are Vanuatu's islands, whose inhabitants live today pretty much as they always have—though they are said not to consume missionaries anymore.

~~~

Every culture throughout the Pacific drinks kava, customarily only men in a casual ceremony whose rites vary among the islands. It is made in the classic version by men masticating sticks and twigs from the kava tree until a slimy, saliva-covered glob develops. Saliva is said to enhance leaching of the essential oils from the wood. The unsightly and decidedly insalubrious glob is then spat onto a perforated banana leaf over which water is poured. The resulting liquid is then drunk from coconut shell halves following whatever ritual happens to be in vogue in the village where it is consumed. Its flavor, something like equal parts kerosene and Vitalis, is unappealing, to say the least.

It is not addictive in the sense of a hard drug, but is in the sense that you will invariably want more of most anything that brings pleasure or relieves pain. It is also made, more hygienically, by grinding and beating collections of kava limbs until a paste evolves that is then mixed with water. Far more conveniently, it is available at your local friendly supermarket in commercial packets of powder that is simply mixed with water. One of these packets claims on its label that the brew is "antibacterial, antifungal, relaxing, a diuretic, an analgesic, antiseptic, anesthetic, soporific, reduces blood pressure, and cures congestion and pain in connection with genitourinary complaints." This is some stuff, an all-powerful magic elixir. All it needs is mixing with gin or vodka, and you'd have the world's most healthful cocktail.

Well, I just had to try it.

Around Port Vila alone, there are said to be over a hundred kava bars, which, at ten times the number of churches, is about the right multiple for a properly organized society. For perspective, however, keep in mind that a kava bar reaches on the scale of commercial enterprise not much above a Tijuana taco stand. All of these bars but one require that you participate in a ceremony, sitting around a huge bowl of the stuff, passing around shell halves and infectious microbes from person to person, clapping once before and three times after each gulp.

I had no interest in subjecting myself to such unhygienic nonsense and so chose the one blessedly ritual-free bar. Some members of the crew and I went by taxi to said bar—really, a shack in a decrepit neighborhood of cinderblock shanties about to be overtaken by the encroaching jungle. The parking lot was bare and potholed, and local guys were sitting around outside in the dark on tree stumps and fallen logs, all in a silent stupor.

Inside, a single bulb hanging from a frayed wire illuminated the bare concrete walls and floor and jungle minimalist interior appointments, dimly lighting an atmosphere that was unhealthful if not actively infectious. I stepped up to the battered card table that served as the bar and accepted a small plastic salad bowl into which the attendant, after collecting payment, ladled a generous portion of kava from a large vat of the stuff.

In the dim light, I looked into the bowl and saw, sloshing around in it, a brown swill that in its hue resembled the waters of the Mississippi River just below New Orleans—though with the exception that there were tiny bits and pieces of unidentifiable, presumably organic, matter floating about in it. Shreds from the kava tree used to make it, I hoped.

With a few gagging gulps, I consumed the entire contents of the bowl, then promptly—and as matters would evolve, foolishly—requested and drank another. I recall a furtive glance from the server that seemed to say, "You don't know what you're getting yourself into, but okay, you paid for it, so here it is."

Standing under the lone light, I said, "Hey, this stuff has no effect on me." That's when things began to go awry. First, my lips tingled and my tongue grew numb and thick. Speech was thus impaired, and coherence suffered soon after. I recall a sort of out-of-body separation of mind from my physical self. I could sense my cognitive skills, such as they were at the time, turning into a gaseous state from whatever state they are customarily found. Now this was odd, but even stranger, my cognitive abilities began to escape through my nostrils and ears and evaporate into the cosmos. Soon I was sure that my IQ had plummeted to somewhere in the range of a school zone speed limit.

Life at that mind speed offers few worrisome troubles, and you don't anticipate events nor concern yourself with frivolous details. I was pleased to be wearing loafers so I wouldn't face the taxing demands of untying shoelaces. Ordinary walking presented no difficulty, but steps up or down required forethought and focused attention.

Alcohol, as life experience has taught us, can lead to aggressive, boisterous, and, in advanced cases, even downright unsociable behavior. Not so with kava. It induces a torpid somnolence that detracts noticeably from conviviality. There is no such thing as a lively kava bar.

Tanna

Located far to the south of Port Vila, Tanna is at once the most remote and primitive of all Vanuatu islands. Its people live today as they have always lived. Those in the bush have one-room huts with a thatched roof and woven grass mat or bamboo walls. Some have floors raised above ground to deter the ever-bothersome rats. Though the men no longer go about dressed only in a penis sheath and the women bare naked, that feature, along with the ubiquitous machete and a single earthen road, is about the only difference between their life as it is today and as it was during the Bronze Age.

The villages, each with no more than ten or so huts, are squalid. There is no electricity and, so far as I could tell, no candles or lanterns. When the sun sets, that's the end of light until dawn. There is no running water other than what flows through nearby streams. Sanitation is a pit for each gender. On the island of Tanna alone, there are twenty-nine different languages—not dialects, mind you, but languages—which, I presume, is one per village. That likely makes inter-village dating problematic.

The local word for the penis sheath is "namba," yet intriguingly there is a tribe on the island called the Big Nambas and another called the Small Nambas. I would have thought the Smalls would have petitioned by now for an official name change or else deserted their tribe for one with a more alluring name.

We had come here to see one of the South Pacific's most remarkable attractions: Mount Yasur—a word for God—said to be the world's most accessible active volcano. I considered this a dubious distinction, as active volcanos are not something that should be high on the itinerary of the prudent traveler. And as you will see, we chose a route that belied the "accessible" claim to a considerable degree.

We piled into a decrepit Toyota four-wheel-drive pickup truck owned by our guide—named Yobill, or something like it—to begin the journey. My choice of the right front seat turned out to be a mistake. Its adjusting mechanism was stuck in the most forward position, so my knees were jammed against the dash. The window was stuck half-open, thereby blocking much of the fresh air needed on the sultry night and precluding me from hanging a casual arm on the sill.

What recently had been a decent dirt road, one vehicle wide, was now a considerable mess. Torrential rains a few days before had washed deep gullies, sharp-edged craters, and corrugated chasms into its surface, limiting our speed to about ten miles per hour. These surface conditions jostled and bounced us with a vengeance for the entire distance and turned what should have been a forty-five-minute pleasant excursion into an hour and a half of sustained misery.

We arrived near the volcano just at dark, forded a small stream, and traveled across a mile or so of gray volcanic sand fields. In the middle of these, there loomed into view in the headlights a man standing by the road dressed nondescriptly and toting a machete. Yobill announced that this man was the volcano gatekeeper appointed by the chief of the tribe that owned the surrounding land and demanded payment of $25 per head. Unfortunately, we had no funds with us, but we persuaded him that we would leave money for the chief in town next day.

As we were chatting with the gatekeeper, the low-hanging night clouds and the smoke and fumes swirling up from the volcano's crater were eerily lit by periodic flashes of brilliant red as the sound of thunder rolled at us down the mountain slopes, sights and sounds at once ominous and thrilling.

When at last we reached the end of the wretched road, the last quarter mile over terrain I thought only a tank could manage, we were in a wide field of volcanic waste. There, Yobill parked the truck, and we hiked 200 yards up a trail littered with detritus strewn there by recent eruptions.

On reaching the pinnacle, we peered cautiously over the crater lip into what can only be described as Hell on Earth, the wrath of Satan, the place Baptist preachers harangue their flocks about. Indeed, it looked like the place my dear mother once told me I'd go if I didn't change my ways. *Well, Mom,* I thought, *I didn't change, and sure enough here I am.*

All around the steep, conical slopes of the crater lay chunks of fiery, glowing embers which, moments before, had erupted into the cool night air. At the pit of the crater cone was a roiling, amorphous mass of molten rock that had oozed its way up from the Earth's mantle far below, a thermo-luminescent quagmire. There erupted from this every few minutes a volcanic burp of smoke and steam and poisonous fumes so powerful that we felt its shock wave standing there on the rim. Following the explosion, an enormous geyser of globular molten rock would spew wildly into the air high above us, getting and holding our attention.

Our guide cautioned us not to wander far. Should the wind direction shift unexpectedly, as it often does, the light blobs of superheated viscous fire that lit up the sky could be blown in our direction with deeply painful and maybe deadly results. Nobody wandered. A week earlier, an unfortunate Japanese tourist had been struck and sustained serious injuries. It will not surprise you to learn that medical facilities on Tanna Island are not all that a visitor might hope for.

~~~

Once we had absorbed the arresting scenery offered by this glimpse into the bowels of Earth's furnace, we took our leave lest the winds change. Mount Yasur had overawed us, and we were deeply grateful for an experience never to be forgotten. Even the one-and-a-half-hour night ride back to *Indigo* could not dampen our spirits.

In a world with no shortage of offbeat religious sects, tiny Tanna Island is home to what must surely be one of the most bizarre: a cargo cult. These are systems of belief—almost hallucinatory it would seem—all in Melanesia, in which it is thought that the object of their worship will one day come to them bearing a plentiful cargo of useful goods like home appliances, never mind that there is no electricity with which to operate them. You can laugh, as I'm sure you are prompted to, but I'm not making this up. The world's last remaining cargo cult is right here on Tanna Island not far from Mount Yasur. Their messiah is a white guy whom they call John Frum, a name I'm guessing that is a corruption of something like, "Hi, my name is John from California."

The story, as I gathered it, is that a small, slight white man with green eyes landed here at a place called Green Point in 1938, probably an island trader. At that time, the island was beset with charmless, sanctimonious missionaries who strictly forbade those in their thrall to practice any of the fun stuff they had been practicing for a thousand years. Talk about party poopers. No longer could they drink kava, dance, worship any of their pantheons or, most distressingly, swap women for sexual purposes.

Well, our man Frum shows up and says, "Lose the Bibles and go back to your ancient practices, and as a reward I'll return with an immense cargo of material goods that will make your life a whole lot better." Within just three years, half the island had forsaken Christianity.

Another John Frum, this one a mountebank, appeared in 1943 proclaiming himself King of America and Tanna, clearly a man with a gift for self-promotion, and had an airfield cleared from the jungle to accommodate his cargo planes that he said would soon arrive with all the promised goods. So far no such planes have arrived, but who knows?

Again, in 1945 a navy Seabee from Florida arrived claiming to be a John Frum emissary and had himself a fine old time with the island at his feet. Today the believers dance, sing, drink kava, and I suppose swap women, and pray for the reappearance of John Frum. He is thought to be an American, and so the worship practices include iconography like American flags and such. This annoys the Vanuatu government, which has tried but failed to eradicate the peculiar cult. Getting rid of the missionaries would be far easier . . . and more humanitarian.

New Caledonia
Imagine stepping from the most backward-looking, primitive African village onto the welcoming, fragrant byways of, say, Palm Beach's Worth Avenue, and you will pretty much have in your mind the startling transition from Vanuatu to New Caledonia.

This place has a powerful and, I have to admit, welcomed Wow! factor. Its road system is thankfully well-paved, striped, marked for traffic, and pothole-free. It would be the envy of any US state, marred only by the inexplicable French affinity for speed bumps and roundabouts. There are classy restaurants, first-class marinas, manicured parks, lovely beaches, a verdant countryside, tres chic shops, and sparkling vistas.

We had arrived at the Pacific outpost of the French Riviera, and what a delightful place it was.

People who know me would say that sometimes I'm a touch reproachful of the French. But I would here like to pay them their due, to balance the books so to say. The French have given to human civilization some of the highest attainments in the fields of literature, art, philosophy, mathematics, and architecture. Descartes, Diderot, Pascal, Bayle, Fermat, Renoir, Voltaire, Flaubert, and many more have enriched the tapestry of intellectual and artistic life, and we should be eternally grateful for these contributions.

But there is one achievement that stands far above even these, a contribution to modern humanity so lofty that it puts all others in a pale light. I'm sure that as a person of sophisticated and refined taste, you will have no trouble agreeing with me that at the very pinnacle stands the topless beach.

To grasp the enormity of this contribution, picture in your mind the finest painting imaginable—maybe it's a particular Renoir or Degas.

Its surface is flat, it doesn't talk to or smile at you, indeed it is entirely inanimate and tacked to the wall in a dull, deadly quiet museum. Now for contrast imagine a comely and shapely young woman relaxed supine upon a colorful beach towel, her generously proportioned bare breasts, themselves fine works of art of inexpressible delight, swathed in the sunlight of the Pacific subtropics. Now I ask you, which of these will draw the largest, most attentive crowds? At which will aficionados exclaim their approval most enthusiastically?

I believe you begin to see the persuasive power of my argument. And best of all, New Caledonia is blessed with many of these wondrous beaches, each just waiting for a sunny weekend when enthusiasts can applaud high achievement. It really is a wonderful island, and its capital city of Noumea just the right antidote for the Kingdom of Tonga.

ELEVEN

The Slow Nekkid Down Under

I am pleased to report that *Indigo* and her crew managed to achieve one of the highest distinctions possible in the arena of international game fishing. It is an achievement toward which we labored almost daily, employing our collective skills to this glorious end, an attainment so superior that it is unlikely to be excelled at any time in this or the next century.

Let me explain.

By the time *Indigo* reached Brisbane, Australia, she had traveled just over 20,000 nautical miles, or about 23,000 statute miles. During a significant portion of this voyage, her crew deployed one—and sometimes two—deep-sea fishing lines to which were attached the most modern, technologically advanced, and alluring lures that one could buy. In the fish world, these were tight skirts and plunging necklines. These lines were dragged behind *Indigo* in the conventional manner of this sport, sometimes with the lures far behind, sometimes closer in, and the vessel's speed was altered in search of the ideal that would attract our quarry. Lures that dive, lures that skip and skim, lures that wiggle and wink and shake their hips were all employed in an honest and concerted effort to attract a strike.

And yet, thanks to our superior and award-winning skills, not

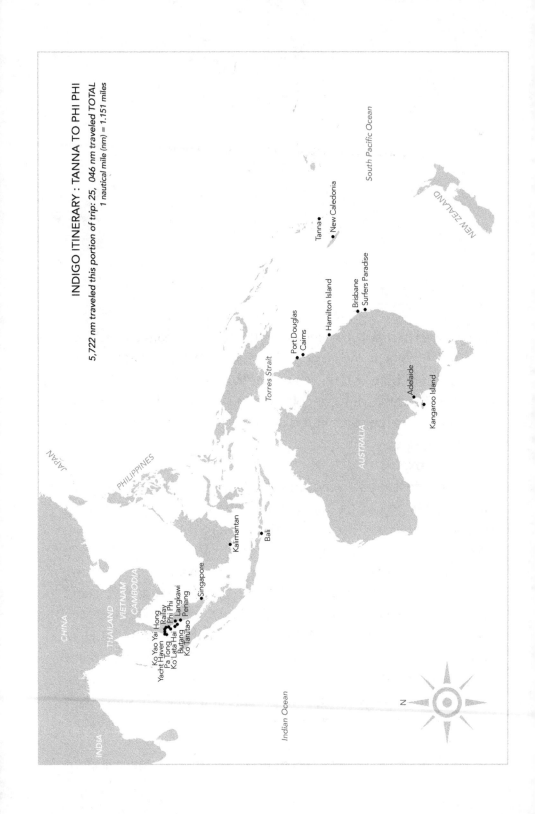

INDIGO ITINERARY : TANNA TO PHI PHI

5,722 nm traveled this portion of trip: 25, 046 nm traveled TOTAL
1 nautical mile (nm) = 1.151 miles

a single fish was boated, nary a one, zip, nada. There was a solitary strike, but to our good fortune, the line quickly parted and our string of success was preserved.

This manner of fishing I have termed eco-angling, the objective being to preserve the endangered creatures of the sea while attempting seriously to catch them. When I reflect on how many of the ocean's finest game fish were spared the pain and indignity of being snatched from their watery homes, an air of self-righteousness comes over me. Twenty thousand nautical miles without a catch is truly a high achievement. I think of it as *Indigo's* contribution to a better planet. We await an award from Greenpeace.

Brisbane, Australia

We sailed into Brisbane on May 2, 2008. It is a great city, and it also had the facilities we needed for some serious refit work on *Indigo*.

A little background.

Ever since its initial construction, *Indigo* has carried the yachting world's highest and most stringent classification: Lloyd's 100 A1. One of the many excruciatingly detailed requirements for maintaining this seal of approval is that the vessel must undergo a major Lloyd's-monitored refit and survey each ten years, a period that expired just as we pulled into the Marine Industry Park, downstream on its eponymous river from Brisbane.

Prior to our arrival, our engineer, Sean, had visited the various refit yards, talked with the major tradesmen and material vendors and, with the captain's added research and concurrence, recommended this yard for the extensive work we would need. A work program was prepared with detailed cost and time estimates, a bid process was initiated, and tradesmen and vendors chosen. We also employed Scotty, a highly competent Aussie engineer who knew all the vendors that would be involved, as an assistant project manager.

Indigo was lifted out of the water on a 300-ton travel lift and moved into her new home, a 200-foot-long fully enclosed metal shed in which scaffolding was erected and work was begun. Over the five and a half months from early May to mid-October, the refit was duly and competently completed, on time and on budget.

Though the work list was quite extensive, the main items were these:

» Overhaul both main engines.

» Replace both generators with new, more advanced units.

» Replace the tender, which had become tatty from extensive use.

» Repaint the entire vessel, top and bottom, in a handsome dark blue on the hull and soft white on the superstructure.

» Overhaul the heating, air-conditioning, and water-making systems.

» Design and install a new sun canopy and cocktail seating area on the boat deck.

» Repair and replace, as needed, sections of the teak deck.

» Add upgraded bridge electronics.

» Turn and balance the props and shafts, and align these with the main engines.

» Strip all teak cap rails and tabletops down to bare wood and varnish with fourteen coats of UV stable, high-quality yacht varnish.

» Rebuild both stabilizer wings.

» Make cosmetic improvements to the interior spaces, including carpet and drapes. Replace all upholstered ceiling panels and refinish interior wood decks.

For the first several weeks of the refit, I stayed in central Brisbane in a room on the twentieth floor of the tired but well-located Stamford Plaza Hotel. Situated on the Brisbane River Walk alongside the Botanic Gardens and just a block from the many cafés, restaurants, and bars of Eagle Street Pier, it was an ideal location from which to wander about the city.

With a population of just under two million, Brisbane—or Brissie, as the Aussies call it—is the smallest of the major cities, the only one in the state of Queensland, and, as the northernmost, the one with the most appealing year-round climate. Two of Queensland's largest and finest universities are in Brisbane, giving the place a youthful energy, especially in the nightclub district called Fortitude Valley. On most weeknights and every weekend night, the place has the look and feel of Bourbon Street during Mardi Gras. Block after block of nightclubs, bars, outdoor cafés, strip joints, and public parks are thronged with wildly exuberant college kids doing what they do, often until five a.m. Oddly, or so it seemed to me, each place has a stringent dress code. Flip-flops, sandals, and tank tops are not permitted, among much else. Few of the celebrants wear denim or T-shirts.

During my many months of roving about the country, I found Australians to be generally polite, well-mannered, possessed of an easy humor, cordial, and, with some exceptions, neatly dressed.

The country, roughly the size of the lower forty-eight states, has a population about equal to that of Florida plus Atlanta. It also is the fourth most urbanized country in the world. Combine these stats, and you get a country that outside of its cities is nearly empty, filled only with either vast desert or vast sheep and cattle ranches ("stations" in Aussiespeak) the size of small states. With all that vacant space available, the country is the world's leading exporter of beef and has a major mining industry that digs up huge quantities of coal, copper, and assorted other minerals.

In Brisbane, I could never shake the image of Australians as a mass collection of people cloned from the characters in *Dobie Gillis, Leave It to Beaver,* and *Ozzie and Harriet* with a healthy dash of *Mayberry RFD.*

Like Americans of fifty years ago and those from the upper Midwest today, they have a refreshing natural geniality and guileless innocence that I found appealing.

Gold Coast, Australia

After exhausting the possibilities of Brisbane and in search of new adventure, I booked a room at the sumptuous—if excessively ornate—Hotel Palazzo Versace situated at the north end of a roughly twenty-mile-long stretch of chockablock beach towns known as the Gold Coast, population a little over 600,000.

To reach the hotel from Brisbane, I drove about thirty miles toward the coast on a multilane expressway, following the helpful road signs. I had formed a picture of the Gold Coast in my mind that consisted of low shanties with peeling paint, sandy streets, greasy spoons, burger joints, and seedy pubs. In this mental image, surfer dudes and beach bunnies lazed about. After all, the main town of the many that stretch along this coast carries the jaunty name Surfers Paradise.

I couldn't have been more wrong! Cresting over the last rise in the highway, I was greeted by a skyline of high-rise development reaching along the coast to the distant horizon. Near the center—in Surfers Paradise, my rustic beach village—was at seventy stories what was reputed to be the world's second highest residential building, surrounded by similar if less-grand condominiums and hotels. At nearby Broadbeach, there is an Aston Martin dealership and Bulgari, Hermes, and Louis Vuitton shops, sleek outdoor cafés, several casinos, and a beachside pedestrian walk.

Its pristine beach, stretching along Australia's east coast for many miles, is great for sunning, surfing, and idle walks. The seawater, at about 70 degrees, is a touch chilly for my taste, but that doesn't seem to bother the locals.

Main Beach is by a measure the best neighborhood on the Gold Coast, and its Tedder Avenue is nicely landscaped and lined with generally good-to-excellent restaurants, all with outdoor seating, and a few bars and pubs. Best of all, it is just a ten-minute walk from the hotel.

Broadbeach, where the casinos are found, has a few good restaurants of which the best is Lauxes[1], owned by Pete and JoJo Third, with whom I became friends. He is originally from a small town in New Zealand, and she grew up on the Gold Coast. They had spent the previous fifteen years owning and running restaurants in Nagoya, Japan, of all places.

One day while lunching on Tedder Avenue in Main Beach, I met a group of guys ("blokes") and girls ("sheilas" though you have to be careful with this one as it can be taken as pejorative) who kindly invited me to join them next day for a swim at the beach. That seemed like a pleasant way to waste a few hours until, while at breakfast on the appointed morning, I read a front-page story in the local tabloid about a great white shark that, just the day before, had been hauled up out of the surf on the very beach where we were to swim. The article remarked that this one was somewhat larger than the one dragged ashore a few days before.

Well, that was all I needed to cancel my swimming plans for the day, thank you—or any other day, for that matter. This country's coastal waters are teeming with sharks. Its inland bays and lagoons, too, though sharks are just one species of the many lethal predators that lurk along Australia's shores.

Surfers Paradise has its own predators: the two-legged variety. It also has boisterous nightlife, souvenir shops, crowded outdoor cafés, and more than a few strip joints. It is, in short, a fun place—though as with much in life, a place that requires some self-restraint.

Growing weary of the ersatz glitz of the Gold Coast, I drove two hours north to the quaint and charming village of Noosa, which is something like Naples, Florida, was maybe thirty years ago. With its beach, adjoining national park, and blocks of stylish shops and restaurants, it is the quiet refuge of choice for the cultured swells of Sydney, Melbourne, and Brisbane.

On another day, I drove an hour west into the foothills of the Great Dividing Range, a spine of mountains separating the low coastal

---

1. In case you didn't notice, it's "sexual" spelled backward.

plains from the vast bushland, or "woop woop" as the Aussies call it. The several villages that dot the area are reminiscent of the quaint towns of western North Carolina, with rustic shops selling things like antiques, toffee, and hooked rugs. There at Mount Tamborine, set deep within a rain forest, was a restaurant where I had lunch in the cool shade of massive eucalypts. There are more than 700 species of these trees in Australia, and they are by far the most common tree. As the pine is to the Deep South, so the eucalypt is to Australia.

Sydney, Australia

In early July, Kitty and Grant joined me for a month-long tour of the eastern half of Australia by car and plane. We flew into Sydney first and spent a week or so there seeing all the must-see sights. Our hotel, the Shangri-La, recently redone in the manner of, say, a Hilton, had by far the finest vistas of any hotel in the city. From its upper floors, and especially from its club floor lounge, we could see the sunrise over the Pacific, the harbor entrance called the Heads, all of the eastern harbor, the iconic Opera House and Harbour Bridge, and most of the western harbor.

In my humble judgment, Sydney is one of the world's finest cities and one of its most beautiful. What makes the place so special is its enormous and dazzling harbor, really more a huge fjord, with arms, bays, and inlets jutting from it in all directions. The shoreline rises steeply with the result that almost all housing has a magnificent view of the harbor and its active ferry and private boat traffic. The city's central business district is easily and pleasantly walked, with parks large and small in profusion. As you might expect, the harbor front is tastefully developed. Crime is not a matter of much concern.

We visited the city's renowned zoo, where a private guide explained the habits of some of the bewildering array of strange creatures that inhabit the country. The cuddly koalas, for example, sleep twenty hours a day and eat only the leaves of certain species of eucalypt. They sleep by wedging themselves into a fork in the limbs of the tree whose leaves they have been chomping. More often than you might think, they become dislodged and plummet to the ground, usually far below, thus becoming their own worst predator. This should not be surprising coming from an animal known to have an intellect not all that much higher than a clam. To their credit, however, koalas are also one of the few animals of this country that are not injurious or lethal to humans.

On a day when the wind blew over forty knots, we unwisely chartered a small sailboat and huddled together in chilly discomfort while the skipper coasted along some of the city's elegant neighborhoods. On other days, we toured the various seaside neighborhoods, including Bondi Beach, toured the famous Sydney Opera House, and walked across the Harbour Bridge.

The city center has several nineteenth-century, multilevel shopping centers, all tastefully designed and spotlessly maintained, loaded with stores selling every product you might want. We wandered around Darling Harbour and through the sea life and wildlife exhibits there.

It is in these exhibits that you begin to appreciate what a dangerous place Australia can be. Of the ten deadliest snakes in the world, seven are in Australia. It has two species of deadly jellyfish (jellyfish, mind you!); lethal spiders; a tiny blue octopus that is instant death; heaps of hungry sharks (including the great white); shrubs, thorns, and trees that can put a serious hurt on you; and of course those hyperaggressive saltwater crocodiles, who have an offshore range of ten miles.

Recently, a local man who had been checking his crab pots in a North Queensland river failed to return to his camp where wife and son awaited him. A search turned up his camera, sandals, and a huge slide mark in the sand made by the twenty-foot croc that dragged him into the river. This is a common event. Often it's campers in their tents or imprudent fishermen in small canoes who fall victim to the wily man-eaters. Beaches in northeast Australia have signs warning of both the jellyfish and the crocs. It is odd and disconcerting to see miles of pristine beach washed by warm, inviting sea in which nobody is swimming.

Before departing from Sydney, we drove an hour or so west into the Blue Mountains, which are not true mountains at all but actually more like low, rambling foothills. They get their name from the pale haze that lingers in the valleys caused, it is said, by oil in the leaves of the eucalypt trees. There we stayed a few nights at the venerable Lilianfels Blue Mountains Resort and Spa from which we could gaze out over some of these wondrous, pastel-tinted valleys.

At a nearby tourist attraction, we rode a cable car down to a valley floor and wandered around a maze of boardwalks set in a dense rain forest of enormous towering eucalypts. What pure delight. So outsized were all the trees and plants that it seemed as if we were in a scene from *Honey, I Shrunk the Kids*. The air was dank and cool, the winter sky obscured by the tree canopy high above. Here and there were abandoned coal mines, their entrances boarded up and nearly undetectable among the giant fern leaves and dense shrubs. Helpful signs told us what species of flora held our attention at that moment, and a map kept us from getting lost among the boardwalks. What began as a most dubious exercise turned into an afternoon of joyous discovery—one of those quirky things that happen to travelers now and then.

Melbourne, Australia

From Sydney, we flew to Melbourne, its arch competitor for national honors as best place to live. Following a six-hour flight delay, we arrived on a cold, rainy day, common in the winter months. In fact, this weather is common any time of year, as the city is on the shore of the Great Southern Ocean. The next land mass south of here is Antarctica, and it is not all that far away.

Melbourne has a more diverse population than Sydney, with many inhabitants of Greek heritage, and the slightly dilapidated, two-story wood-frame aspect of, say, Providence, Rhode Island. There are modern high-rise glamour buildings, to be sure, and an enormous casino, but they seem out of place, carbuncles on the landscape. It has none of the visual appeal of Sydney.

Weaving through the central business district are bafflements of pedestrian alleyways lined with tiny eateries, specialized food vendors, and offbeat shops no larger than a generous walk-in closet. Aromas of exotic foods waft through these confining spaces hurly-burly with lunch crowds and bewildered tourists.

Our tour guide took us to see the most important landmarks, parks, and public spaces obligatory for the first-time tourist.

The Great Ocean Road
Our planned stay in Melbourne at an end, we took a rental car and drove four days on the Great Ocean Road—a misnomer, as only a small part of its length is actually along the water, the rest a long, straight ribbon through vast cattle ranches and farms. On one of these, we spotted our first—and as it would turn out our only—wild emu. This giant, flightless, and extraordinarily fleet-footed bird is, as with much else in Australia, dangerous to humans. Continuing along the way, we stopped overnight in various tiny seaside villages, none especially memorable.

Following directions from our Melbourne tour guide, we pulled off the highway and drove down a local residential street to an unassuming golf club whose fairways and parking areas were crowded with a large family of kangaroos. Loitering about innocently, and with the blank look of a stunned mullet (a wonderful piece of Aussie slang), these strange creatures barely noticed our arrival.

Next day, we observed a herd of "roos" hopping across a field like large brown fuzz balls on pogo sticks, a sight so hilarious we broke out in spontaneous laughter. These animals are so numerous as to be pests and are a considerable road hazard, often hopping unexpectedly in front of speeding vehicles.

Kangaroo steaks are available in many restaurants, but the meat has the consistency and flavor of an old doormat. These animals do have one useful role to play in Australia, however. In some select tourist shops, a person of discerning taste can buy a beer opener with a handle made from a kangaroo scrotum. It's a fun tool for the home bar, sure to generate spirited commentary.

Again following the directions of our tour guide, we managed to catch glimpses of koalas in the wild—though spotting comatose gray blobs high up in the limbs of a tree does not rank high in the wilderness experience. Wallabies, the smaller cousin of the kangaroo and just as pestilential, are plentiful. We never saw a wombat. These lumbering marsupials resemble a small bear with stubby legs, though one with the stout and unyielding anatomy of a tree stump. Of all Australian animals vying to become the Road Kill Most Harmful to Vehicles, the wombat is the hands-down winner.

On the subject of peculiar animals, the national shield of Australia prominently features both the kangaroo and the emu. The reason for this, our guide patiently explained to me, is that these are the only two animals in Australia incapable of walking backward. Though it was of anatomically moderate interest, I didn't see why this peculiar handicap should qualify the beasts for iconographic immortality until he added, a bit peevishly, noting my bewildered expression, "Don't you see? They can only move forward, just like the country."

Kangaroo Island

Our only purpose in visiting the city of Adelaide was to catch a plane from there to Kangaroo Island. The flight took us over a narrow strait separating it from the mainland. We were met at the modest airport by a car and driver sent from our destination: the new, super-chic eco-resort, Southern Ocean Lodge. An hour's drive away, the place was about as remote as it is possible to get on the island.

When at last we arrived, the long trek seemed worthwhile. With its one-floor, modern, monochromatic design, and its location atop a seaside cliff, the resort blends neatly into the island's low brush and rocky terrain. The rather high, all-inclusive rates include small, guided group tours to the island's most prominent natural features.

I decided that instead of watching sea lions mating on the rocks below the resort, something that I had seen often enough in Alaska (it ain't all that interesting), I would instead take generous advantage of the resort's "free" bar and the massage parlor, also known as a "sumptuous spa." Besides, it was really cold, wet, and blustery outside, and given a choice between watching sea lions in those insalubrious conditions and a warm bar and massage . . . well, it was not really a difficult decision.

Uluru-Kata Tjuta National Park, Australia

Back in Adelaide, Kitty departed for home in Florida. She had prior commitments there and wished to give Grant and me some time together. After a three-and-a-half-hour flight from Adelaide to the Red Centre of Australia, Grant and I landed nearly dead center in the continent at Yulara, a village whose sole purpose is to serve visitors to the Uluru-Kata Tjuta National Park. This part of the country, an unimaginably vast empty desert, gets its name, the Red Centre, thanks to heavy concentrations of iron oxide in its soils and rocks. There is so much of the stuff here that scales of rust encrust many of the rocks.

Uluru, also known as Ayers Rock, and Kata Tjuta are the aboriginal names for the two enormous, smooth-surfaced and strikingly red rock formations that comprise the principal attractions of the park, both of these sacred and still revered in the aboriginal pantheon. There we spent four days and three nights (quite long enough, thank you) at the splendid safari camp-style Longitude 131 resort, our home base for tours of the iconic rocks, surely the most photographed natural wonders in the country.

Our guide was—I am not making this up—half-Irish and half-aboriginal. He had long, curly, reddish hair pulled back in an unruly ponytail. He wore a pale green, long-sleeved shirt and baggy, knee-length matching shorts. On his feet were lace-up, over the ankle, well-worn boots. The overall effect was of a hardy Irish outdoorsman. His accent was backwoods Aussie, though his manner was genial and helpful.

With him leading the way, we toured Uluru, walking partly around its base at sunrise, a spectacular time of day in this endless desert, but damn cold and breezy in July.

As we drove from one sacred rock pile (forgive the diminution) to the other, your ever-alert and keen-eyed writer spotted a herd of feral camels grazing among the desert roughage. Imported into Australia in the nineteenth century as a means of crossing the woop woop, today something like a million of the creatures wander around in the Red Centre.

Port Douglas, Australia

Grant and I, having had enough of large piles of red rocks, flew three hours to the northeast coastal town of Cairns, where a driver met us and whisked us along a scenic coastal highway forty-five minutes north to the touristy but pleasant town of Port Douglas.

With it as our home base, we rented a car and drove an hour or so north into the magnificent Daintree Rainforest, the world's oldest continuously existing rain forest. Here at its visitor center, we spent a delightful and informative several hours walking through a patch of the dense foliage on boardwalks thoughtfully installed for us tourists. Every thirty feet or so along the walk were helpful signs that explained this and that about the mind-numbing array of plant and animal life right before our eyes. You can also rent, for a modest fee, an electronic device that tells you in impressive detail much more than most of us would care to know.

Heading north from the visitor center, we drove along the coast on a paved road just barely wider than one car, wending our way enveloped in dense canopy. At intervals along the road were those yellow, diamond-shaped caution signs that warn you of potential road hazards. We had seen lots of these with the silhouette of a kangaroo (and in Patagonia, one with an enraged bull and another with a guanaco), but this was our first encounter with what appeared at first to be a caution concerning a very large chicken. This was puzzling until, resorting to our guidebook, we learned it was not a chicken but a cassowary, the large, flightless, and quite aggressive bird peculiar to Australia. The cassowary, in keeping with the least admirable trait of the Australian animal kingdom, will attack—and on occasion kill—humans.

Near the end of the pavement, we came upon Cape Tribulation, so named by Captain James Cook whose ship, *Endeavor*, came to grief on a patch of the Great Barrier Reef just offshore. He and his crew put ashore and lived here for many months until they could make repairs and be on their way again.

Next day, we boarded a ninety-foot catamaran with about forty other people for a snorkel trip on the Great Barrier Reef. Just getting out to the first dive site took about an hour. The Great Barrier Reef is not a single reef, as the name suggests, but a patchwork maze of separate reefs, some miles apart, stretching for a thousand miles along the northeast coast. Of the three different sites we visited, I dived only on the first, as the water at less than 70 degrees was too cold for me, even with a short-sleeved wet suit on, while the ever-intrepid Grant dived on all three—without a wet suit. In the clear, shallow water of the reefs, coral colors were vibrant and reef fish plentiful. Many of the species were new to me. At that time of year, the water was too cold for the deadly species of jellyfish, and we were, according to the guides, too far offshore for the crocs to reach us. I hoped they were right. Sharks, they said, are plentiful in the deep passes between reefs but don't hang around the shallow water in which we were diving.

~~~

Grant had returned home to Florida by the time the refit work on *Indigo* was complete. Upon boarding the now-revitalized yacht, the crew and I departed from Marine Industry Park and traveled down the Brisbane River, out into the ocean and south a bit to enter the inlet at Southport, then on to the Marina Mirage adjacent to the Versace Hotel.

We arrived just in time for the annual funfest called Indy Week. Twenty-four Indy race teams had been loaded into three 747s and flown to Brisbane, off-loaded, and trucked to the Gold Coast. A winding road course was laid out among local streets, grandstands were erected, and the infrastructure needed for three days of practice and racing was built.

Race weekend itself is about the most Sybaritic, wild, drunken orgy you could imagine. Every hooker in Australia shows up, and the balconies of the many high-rise condominiums that line the race-course are a full-on (a favorite Aussie intensifier) live porn show. This year, according to the local newspaper, the cops decided that it was okay, though not encouraged, for women to flash their breasts or even go topless, but they would not tolerate oral sex on public bal-conies. Spectators, they said, should exhibit proper decorum. Yeah right, mate!

As usual, I managed to meet a lot of new friends on the Gold Coast. It was during Indy week that we had on board *Indigo* five parties in six days, of which four ended no earlier than three a.m. and one went on until the sun came up. That stands as *Indigo's*, as well as my own, record for sustained celebration.

On the Saturday night of race weekend, I sat at a dinner table with a group of twelve in a restaurant packed with tables of raucous peo-ple having a fine old time. The adjoining bar and the crowds waiting for seats were standing room only.

Into this melee walked three twenty-something young guys clearly sloshed. First they yelled as loud as they could to gain the crowd's attention, then, at just the right theatrical moment, they stripped all their clothes off, tucked their manhood between their legs, and paraded around hooting and hollering, all to the joyful delight of the crowd—until the security men came over, returned the boys' clothes, and gently escorted them outside.

Capricorn Coast, Australia

On November 1, following the end of Indy week, we departed the Gold Coast through the Southport inlet on our way to Great Keppel Island at the southern end of the Whitsunday chain.

As we made our seaward approach to Keppel, we could see, strewn across the ocean surface for many miles in all directions, a brown, fetid sludge. This, we learned, was the result of a periodic coral spawn.

Next day, we made our way to Hamilton Island, supply depot for the Whitsundays, and docked in its marina in the midst of a small village of bars, restaurants, and tourist shops. Just over a small rise is a garish monument to early 1980s architecture, a fifteen-floor concrete hotel dominating the otherwise one- and two-story residential development set in among the eucalypts. None of it is especially tasteful or even memorable, and much of it brings to mind military housing.

This chain of islands was formed eons ago when the sea flooded a mountain range, leaving just the tops protruding above the surface. Today, evergreen forests and volcanic rock cover their foreshores, broken here and there by beaches. The islands are reminiscent of those in the Inside Passage of British Columbia, and not at all tropical as I had expected.

Next day, we coasted along the well-known Whitehaven Beach, a strand of sparkling white sand several miles long and unspoiled by any sign of human habitation. Captain Lucas anchored *Indigo* offshore of a small hideaway beach just around a headland from Whitehaven and set in a national park.

We took ashore all of our usual beach gear and set up in the shade of some palms with the beach all to ourselves. While seated in the palm shade guzzling ice-cold beer and noshing on pork rinds, listening to some snappy beach tunes on the portable iPod speakers, I heard heavy-footed rustling coming from the underbrush just next to our camp. Now if we had been almost anywhere else in the world, this noise would not have prompted even a moment of thought. This being Australia, though, I instinctively went on high alert, and that turned out to be a good thing. Just behind us, not ten feet away, was a matched pair of four-foot, wicked-looking lizards, black with yellow spots, forked tongues stabbing the air in search of, we guessed, stray pork rinds.

These hideous escapees from Jurassic Park, called goannas, while not lethal to humans, nevertheless can be seriously hurtful. If you try to run from them, they will chase you down, scamper up your back, over the top of your head, and down your front, all with long, sharp claws. The recommended tactic is first not to run from and thus provoke the devils. But should they attack, you're supposed to lie down, and they are supposed to simply run over you. We decided instead to hide the pork rinds in the beer cooler so they couldn't smell our treasure, and sure enough they returned to the bush, leaving us free of claw scars.

Next day we continued on our way toward Cairns, cruising over blessedly flat waters protected from ocean swells by the Great Barrier Reef. Along the way, we were joined by ten of the largest bottle-nosed dolphins I've ever seen, each at least fifteen feet long and wide through the girth. For half an hour or more, they frolicked in *Indigo's* bow wave, leaping, twisting in midair, darting here and there. At times, six would cluster together just in front of the bulbous bow, and a few of these would twist around playfully, looking directly up at us with what seemed like bemused expressions. It was quite an impressive and unforgettable display.

I noticed that when the dolphins were in the bow wave, they stopped propelling themselves and appeared to glide along as if going downhill. A vessel pushing its hull through water also pushes in front of it a pressure wave that carries with it whatever happens to be within its influence. It was in *Indigo's* pressure wave that the dolphins hitched a ride.

Cairns, Australia

Cairns is a mostly tourist-driven small town, though the largest along Queensland's northeast coast. Its marina, one of the finest we had encountered since leaving the US, is within a short walk of the town center, and dockside facilities include many open-air restaurants and bars. As if to underscore the dangers of its seashore, the Cairns town center features an enormous swimming pool surrounded by a white sand faux beach. It's the only place you can go for a refreshing dip without fear of being consumed by a croc or stung to death by a jellyfish.

Several times during our stay in Cairns, I drove a half hour north to visit the delightful seaside resort village of Palm Cove. Its low rise and tasteful design, shaded beach walks, elegant inns, and restaurants contrast sharply with the high-rise sprawl of the Gold Coast. Here, too, though the entire area has miles of near-perfect beaches washed by the warm waters of the subequatorial Pacific, I saw not a single person swimming in the sea.

~~~

It would not be fitting to leave Australia without remarking on its delightful contribution to the English lexicon: Aussie slang. So plentiful are the laconic, offbeat, truncated words that there is a hefty dictionary devoted to the subject. All the daily newspapers, including *The Australian*, perhaps the best of the broadsheets, use slang freely, even in headlines.

Some articles I encountered used slang so abstruse as to be unintelligible. One referred to the local law enforcement problem of "p-platers hooning." To understand what this means, you have to know that adolescent drivers with a restricted license are required to display a license plate beginning with the letter p, and "hooning" is street racing, or hot rodding.

Here for your enjoyment, if not inclusion in your everyday vocabulary, are a few more of my favorites:

>> "Stunned mullet" means roughly the same as "deer in the headlights."

>> "Good on ya" (maybe the most useful and fun expression) means "good for you."

>> "Stoush" or "blue" is an argument.

>> To "shout" means to pay a bill, as in "I'll shout for the beer."

» A "tinnie" is a metal skiff.

» A "stubbie" is a bottle of beer.

» A "drop kick" is a seedy male.

» "Brekky" is breakfast.

» "Gos" is "gossip."

» "Sus" is "suspicious."

» "Arvo" is "afternoon." (I once got a text message from an Aussie friend saying he'd see me in the arvo. When I asked the hotel concierge, "Where the hell is the arvo?" great howls of laughter followed.)

There is an entire category of slang terms in which half or more of a proper word is simply lopped off, often followed by the letter "o." "Ambo" is an ambulance driver, "journo" is a journalist, "servo" is a service station, "dero" is a derelict, and "unco" is uncoordinated. These are only a few examples.

TWELVE

Indonesia—Rain Forests, Orangutans, and Elvis

We left Cairns in late November 2008 and cruised north along the coast over the bathtub-flat Pacific still protected by the Great Barrier Reef, passing Cape Melville and Lizard Island among many other landmarks. Low coastal mountains sprouting clumps of arid vegetation, tide-washed islets, coral reefs awash—all these and more glided past us each day. We watched the sun set over a land hardly touched by humans, and each night watched the Southern Cross light the sky.

Soon we rounded Cape York at the extreme northeast corner of Australia, passed through the Torres Strait, a choke point for shipping traffic in this part of the world, and headed due west over the Arafura Sea. After a few days, we detoured slightly to the northwest into Indonesian waters and the Banda Sea, a course change that got us out of head winds and a steep chop.

Near the far eastern end of the Indonesian islands, we came upon a volcanic cone protruding from the sea and, as we drew near, could see that it was very active. From its maw, great flumes of dense, dark cloud burped from the cone, and eruptions of white steam ballooned into the sky.

Indonesia is now, and over the Earth's geologic history has ever been, seismically active. Sited on the Pacific Rim of Fire, it has numerous active, dormant, and extinct volcanoes. One notable eruption in 1816 not far from Bali exploded with the force of 60,000 Hiroshima-sized A-bombs and killed 100,000 people. And then there was the world's largest bang when Krakatau exploded in 1883, sending up columns of ash nearly fifty miles high and spreading it as far as Singapore, 500 miles away.

At the time of my visit, Indonesia was the fourth most populous nation in the world. It's also one of the most congested nations, with a density of people four times that of the UK, concentrated mostly on the island of Java. With its bewildering array of languages, cultures, races, tribes, political parties, and religions, it must be said that the country is a big mess and seems always to have been so. Corruption and cronyism are endemic, and the threat of military domination hangs over its political institutions.

The population, spread over 17,000 islands, is 88 percent Muslim, with the rest divided among various sects of Hinduism, Buddhism, Christianity, even animism. Its people are comprised mostly of light-brown Malays and darker-skinned, fuzzy-haired Melanesians. Just 3 percent of Indonesians are Chinese, and they are, as everywhere in Southeast Asia, by far the wealthiest and best educated and are, perhaps accordingly, resented.

Island of Bali, Indonesia

To enter Indonesia legally, we were obliged to visit the main port at Bali before setting foot on Indonesian soil. Bali is a small island of just 2,100 square miles and can be driven around in a long day. It is by far the most tourist-friendly island in all of Indonesia, and its population of 4.2 million, unlike the rest of the country, is 95 percent Hindu. For Westerners, this means they are tolerant of alcohol consumption and other un-Islamic hedonist habits.

The locals are quite small in stature, light brown in skin color, and invariably affable and polite. They can't be called good stewards of their island, though. When most of us think of Bali, our minds fill with images of a tropical paradise, lovely white sand beaches, and palm fronds fluttering in gentle breezes. Alas, the reality is quite something else. The beaches, of which there are many, are colorfully dotted with every manner of plastic flotsam, from Pepsi bottles to discarded grocery bags and beer six-pack holders. Spars, rotted fishnets, and assorted other detritus complete the picture. While we were there, the first fifty feet or so of the surf was a dingy, tobacco-brown murk lapping at the shore, into which I saw not a person venture, not even the locals. This, we were told, was a temporary condition brought on by unusual tides. Beach sand was mostly dull pewter.

The island's roads are okay, and many even have landscaped medians. But their entire length is lined with squalor and dilapidation broken only here and there by bizarrely out-of-place modern buildings. Traffic is a chaotic blur of motorbikes three and four abreast on a single lane wending in and out of dense, creeping thickets of autos and trucks. Lane striping is treated as merely decorative, or at most suggestive, and sidewalks are either nonexistent or unusable.

One evening as the crew and I dined at a local restaurant in Jimbaran, seated on the beach with a calm sea lapping at our feet, we watched in wonder one of the fabulous nuclear sunsets for which Bali is famous. Its brilliant kaleidoscope of colors is the delightful result of minute dust particles blown from the Australian desert mixing with warm, moist sea air.

As we finished dinner, three strolling Balinese musicians led by an Elvis impersonator (really!) came to our table and performed. Elvis was not more than five feet tall, weighed at most a hundred pounds including guitar, and had a gyrating hip swivel and glorious sweeping ducktail. He and his band put on a show that delighted us all, doing faithful renditions of "Hound Dog," "Jailhouse Rock," and "Blue Suede Shoes."

Anchored just beyond the breaking surf were colorful fishing boats with the upswept prows and jaunty pavilions one might expect on an ancient Egyptian ceremonial barge. Onshore near these was a crude encampment of huts, where the fishermen often slept between outings, tended to nets, and partied into the night.

I rented a car and ventured an hour and a half north to the artsy historic town of Ubud. Along the way, we passed through many miles of rice paddies and through charming, tidy villages whose general aspect was far superior to anything we saw in the touristy areas.

In Ubud, I stayed several nights in a slightly worn Four Seasons perched on a cliff overhanging a deep ravine of dense jungle. On the first night, I visited a local jazz club where Balinese musicians sang blues, and another where small brown guys dressed in combat camouflage and draped in bling sang James Brown hits. The second night out, Captain Lucas and Chef Jeanette kindly hosted me at Ubud's finest restaurant for a meal of local delicacies.

What I find most remarkable about Bali's countryside is that each of the many tiny villages along the way is devoted to a different cottage industry. At Ubud, they manufactured—and that is just the right word—art objects in a bewildering array of choices, everything from Holiday Inn schlock to brilliant Picasso copies to Henry Moore knock-off sculptures. Roadside stands making and selling the stuff are lined up along both sides of the road for more than a few miles, each with its own specialty.

Other villages devote themselves to ornate wood carvings. I stopped at one of these and visited a gallery displaying an immense collection of works of astounding artistry. One piece stood about four feet tall and maybe three feet on a side at its base. It was a carving of a Balinese peasant man seated in a full squat, a traditional cloth tied around his head, wearing farmers' short pants and no shirt. His poignant face showed the wear of his hard life. Held up in his left hand was a wicker basket containing a finely detailed fighting rooster. None of this might be thought particularly notable until you learn that the entire piece was carved by hand from a single block of wood, including the rooster within the basket, and all without any plan other than what was in the artist's mind. Every other piece in the large gallery was equally elaborate.

Other villages along the two-lane highway specialize in ceramic roof tiles, silverwork, landscape decorations, large pots for flowers and plants, outdoor furnishings, religious icons, and much else. Each artisan is descended from a line of artists who were themselves taught the intricacies of their craft by their forebears.

Island of Borneo, Indonesia

In dense rain forests on Borneo and on nearby Sumatra are found all of the world's wild orangutans (Malay and Indonesian for "forest man") and on Borneo alone, all of the world's wild proboscis monkeys. Hoping to see these in their natural habitat, we cruised several days to the south shore of Borneo, the world's third-largest island, traveled a short distance up the shallow, muddy Kumai River, and anchored alongside a deserted beach out of the main channel used by aging wooden freight boats carrying supplies to primitive villages farther upriver.

It was on the Kumai that we saw for the first time the ubiquitous local boats, called long-tails, that we would soon see all along our journey into Southeast Asia. These vary in length from twenty to ninety feet, though most are at the shorter end of this range, have shallow keels, are built of local wood, have a narrow beam, and are double-ended—meaning pointed at both bow and stern.

But their most curious feature is their propulsion. Each is powered by a gas or diesel engine, from lawn mower to car sized, mounted at the stern on a small platform that both tilts and swivels. The aft end of the motor is connected to a long propeller shaft that extends up to twenty feet behind the stern with a two-blade prop attached. At the forward end of the motor is a shaft gripped by the helmsman, tilted up or down to raise or lower the prop and swiveled side to side for steerage. When underway, the helmsman maneuvers the gripped shaft in such a way as to keep the prop about halfway above the water surface, resulting in an aerated plume of prop wash behind the craft, thus the name "long tail." The arrangement results in a small, fast boat that's inexpensive to own and operate, reliable, easy to repair, has an extremely shallow draft and a prop that can't be easily damaged on the ever-present reefs. They are used by fishermen, freight haulers, and tour operators.

From our anchorage, I took *Indigo's* tender fifteen miles up the narrow, winding Sekonyer River lined with pandanus trees and dense malarial jungle. My destination was Camp Rimba. This rude collection of huts and interconnecting boardwalks raised four feet above the wet jungle floor, once a zoological research station, is now a primitive eco resort. Its staff all come from a nearby village that is accessible, as is the camp, only by river.

My room was one of the few with air conditioning, powered like the rest of the camp by a single generator turned on at five p.m. each day and off at ten a.m. I wore long pants, long-sleeved shirt, hat, and liberal doses of high-DEET insect repellant to discourage the malaria-carrying mosquitoes and other nasty bugs.

On a stroll along the boardwalks, I came upon a family of proboscis monkeys and raucous gangs of pesky macaques, the hooligans of the primate world. With a thunderous harrumph, an enormous male orangutan, apparently in a quarrelsome mood, announced his presence and captured my attention. Hanging from vines with arms and legs fully extended, his aggressive posture and loud grunts were intended to warn me away—a ploy that worked well. Following my guide's advice, I averted my eyes, lowered my head in a gesture of submissiveness, and backed away while the big guy glowered at me, sure that I had romantic designs on one of his numerous babes.

Next day, I traveled in the tender another ten miles into dense rain forest up an increasingly narrow river, at places no more than twenty feet wide. Along the way, I passed a few colorful putt-putt tour boats, closely resembling Humphrey Bogart's *African Queen*, taking a few brave tourists deep into the Tanjung Puting National Park, home to some 5,000 orangutans. Other than these and a few locals in dugout canoes, the river was empty of human life.

My destination that day was Camp Leakey, named in honor of the famed paleoanthropologist Louis Leakey. Dr. Leakey, in his time, was mentor to Jane Goodall, who studied chimpanzees, and to Dian Fossey, who studied gorillas. He also was mentor to Dr. Birute Galdikas, who undertook an extensive study of orangutans and established Camp Leakey, naming it in her patron's honor.

When I finally arrived at a dock near the camp, I was greeted by a wet and tired team from the BBC there to film a series on gibbons. They had been at it for six months, which seemed to me like quite a long time to be filming gibbons, and lived in a smallish local boat tied to the dock.

At the head of the dock is a sign warning visitors not to swim in the river. A few years back, a research assistant, hot and sweaty from a day's work, dived off the dock into the river seeking relief and was promptly devoured by a crocodile. Pythons are another menace, killing more than a few village children every year. But these pale in comparison to the toll of diseases—like dengue fever, malaria, typhoid, typhus, all the hepatitis varieties including E and Japanese B, rabies from monkeys, schistosomiasis, TB, amebic dysentery, and giardiasis—to name but a few. Indeed, there is hardly a tropical disease not found in the rain forests of Borneo, an idyllic setting for viruses, bacteria, fungi, and parasites, and the assorted animals and insects that transport them.

Owing partly to the prevalence of these diseases and partly to a diet deficient in complex proteins, the villagers who work in the camp are the smallest people I have ever encountered. Two women who worked in the dining hall, both age twenty-five, looked as though they were twelve. Neither was taller than four feet, and both were extremely slight of build. Male camp workers were only slightly larger.

Walking from the dock over the flooded jungle floor on a raised boardwalk, I soon came to the camp where Dr. Galdikas lived and worked for many years. In a light rain, I walked deeper into the forest and soon came upon a mother orangutan with a baby slung upside down under her body. She and her adolescent child were perched on the low limbs of a nearby tree. Soon they descended from the tree and began ambling along a forest trail, paying little heed to my presence even when I stood next to them. For a time, I walked along with them side by side on the narrow trail, until they wandered off into a dense thicket in search of forage. It was thrilling to encounter these placid great apes roaming wild in a Borneo jungle and worth the long travel to get there. As for the aggressive, territorial, and apparently jealous males, my brief encounter with one was quite enough to keep me away from any orangutan singles bars.

THIRTEEN

Singapore Days and Langkawi Nights

We left the Kumai River anchorage on December 18. Entering the Java Sea on our way to Singapore, we promptly encountered bad weather. Winds blowing at twenty-five to thirty knots across the shallow sea, mostly just sixty to ninety feet deep, caused the waves to steepen to fifteen feet or so and become knife-edged and widely spaced. Even worse, they came at us directly on the bow. The result was three days of violent heaving and pounding.

Everybody on board got seasick—even me, for the first time. My skin turned clammy and pale, and a tight knot formed in my gut. I lay on my back on the salon sofa, closed my eyes, and tried to will the feeling away—which of course didn't work. It was a miserable ride, the worst in more than 25,000 nautical miles.

Singapore

The city-state of Singapore owes both its existence and its spectacular achievements to the Straits Chinese who founded it and dominate its daily life.

As we approached the massive harbor, we could see what appeared to be tall buildings extending across the entire horizon. Then, as we drew nearer, what had seemed to be buildings turned out to be the ramparts of a vast fleet of empty cargo ships lying at anchor in the roadstead, idled by the global recession. I've never seen so many ships gathered together in one place in my life, an impressive and sobering sight.

Singapore is the world's busiest port. In keeping with its status, entering it by vessel is much like flying into Heathrow. Captain Lucas was required to check in to port control, which monitored us on radar and directed us into traffic separation zones, instructed us to allow faster vessels to overtake on one side or the other, set speeds, and permitted other vessels to cross our path. Even though so many ships sat unused with only skeleton crews, the radio crackled with activity.

Captain Lucas guided us skillfully through the maze of ships into our berth at the Keppel Bay Marina, set in the midst of an enormous modern condo development. During our stay, we paid many visits to the numerous restaurants and bars at the end of the floating docks.

It's easy to see why Singapore has been called Disney World with a death penalty. The city has the florid landscaping of Disney World, and its buildings are well-maintained. If you like a city to have an over-lay of smog, graffiti-decorated public spaces, and urban squalor, you won't like Singapore. If you find slums rustic or quaintly charming, if windblown trash adds for you an air of festivity, if you enjoy the thrill of risking a mugging, then you'll find Singapore unsatisfactory.

The city does have capital punishment for certain crimes, but no, you won't be hung for dropping a cigarette butt on the sidewalk. There are, however, enforced laws against chewing gum, spitting, littering, urinating in public, smoking in public places, jaywalking, and failing to flush the toilet. In the recent past—and on occasion now—you could be caned for any of these offenses. Fines are up to $500 for public smoking and $1,000 for littering. Public displays of affection and a scruffy appearance, once misdemeanors, now still draw frowns of disapproval. Hanging is reserved for serious offenses such as mur-der, kidnapping, and drug trafficking.

Singapore is Southeast Asia's shopping center with enormous high-rise malls dominating the midtown skyline. Our favorite of these was its least imposing. Orchard Towers, located in the very heart of the prime addresses, is a careworn, four-story affair with small floor plates and a central atrium served by escalators. Its shops are mostly Indian and Chinese tailors, cheap-jacks, and a few restaurants.

By a wide measure, though, Orchard Towers' prime attraction is its plethora of energetic nightclubs and bars. And of these, the most incongruous for me was a country and western bar that specialized in honky-tonk music. I could never go in the place without breaking out in a big grin. There's just something comical about short, brown-skinned Asian bar girls parading about the place, their faces barely visible under enormous western hats, singing along to Patsy Cline or Hank Williams.

The Chinese New Year celebration was in full swing while we were in Singapore. This two-week-long party featured colorful dragon parades, lots of fireworks, concerts appealing to every possible taste, various exhibits of Straits Chinese culture, and hawker stalls selling every manner of street food.

I visited a Chinese Buddhist temple and was awed by its elaborate ornamentation—a snippy modernist might call it ostentatious—and the sophisticated elegance of its interior spaces: red-lacquered walls with hundreds of gold recesses, each holding a miniature Buddha; a ceiling of three stories to accommodate a twenty-foot-high, gold-leaf-encrusted stylized replica of the great Buddha himself, and two lesser figures at his side; congregants genuflecting deeply while waving aromatic joss sticks in the hope the Great One will grant them good fortune, long life, and happiness. It all made the most ornate Christian churches of Europe seem primitive and clunky by contrast.

A service was going on in which offerings of fruit and other food and drink were being made to ancestors awaiting their return trip to Earth. Saffron-cloaked monks chanted mantras to bless the offerings and their intended recipients. Both tourists and worshippers walked about the building with a reverential air, but the place was thronged, and this in midweek.

There was a fund-raising effort underway. One of the ways to entice money from the pockets of the ever-frugal Chinese was through the sale of miniature Buddhist gods associated with the year and month of a person's birth. By using a handy guide, I determined that I was born in the year of the rooster, which meant that my god was, I must confess, the most fearsome-looking of them all. His skin rendered in ceramic was a middling blue, which I was told was an artist's way of depicting black, and fangs protruded from the corners of his snarling mouth.

In addition to shopping, the other obsession of Singaporeans is food. Some of the world's finest restaurants are here, for sure, but it's the street vendors, or hawkers, that serve up some of the best and least costly food. Some of it didn't sound particularly edible—like pig's organ soup and bird's nest soup and fried dung beetle—but for the most part it was delicious and fun.

One of the world's oldest food courts is found in downtown Singapore. Housed in a huge open-air pavilion constructed of wrought-iron filigree, Lau Pa Sat buzzed with local and tourist diners and occasional entertainment. One night the place was invaded by a troupe, some of whom were the motive power for a thirty-foot red paper iconic Chinese lion that slinked serpentlike among the cheering crowds, chasing away evil spirits and bringing good fortune to all. Another guy, dressed in a fantastic costume and mounted on high stilts, strutted about tossing candy to the adoring crowd.

I was in the shop of a tailor to pick up some slacks I had ordered when another troupe invaded, also outfitted as a red paper Chinese lion. To the accompaniment of clanging cymbals and discordant drumbeats, it slunk around the shop, bringing good fortune. What amazed me was that this was an Indian Hindu shop. There is an easy tolerance here for religious differences.

I visited Singapore's world-renowned zoo to take in its Night Safari. This was a forty-five-minute tram ride along a dimly lit trail around which various wild animals lazed about in relaxed indolence—well-fed, I hoped. They were contained within their respective compounds by hidden electrified fences extending a few feet above ground. What I found especially remarkable was that the natural prey of many species were just across the tram path, each clearly visible to the other.

The zoo, as well as the civic center/concert hall, were ingeniously designed to serve both their essential functions and also, this being Singapore, as shopping malls. I attended a classical piano recital by a twenty-four-year-old Chinese woman who had been voted one of the world's most talented pianists under thirty. The huge and acoustically refined performance hall anchors one end of a large, multistory shopping mall filled with bars, restaurants, public spaces, and shops. Also within are venues for live theater, art films, pop concerts, opera, and symphonic and chamber music. Though there was a dearth of tourists when I was there, the place was alive with crowds attending one or another of their chosen art forms, wandering about the riverfront or dining outdoors. It is one of the finest and most financially sensible combinations of fine and performing arts with commercial interests I've ever seen. Smart guys, these Singaporeans.

While I don't usually get excited by flowers, I did visit the Botanic Gardens' world-famous National Orchid Garden where, in hothouses intended to emulate the wet, tropical climate in which these plants are most at home, and in tastefully manicured outdoor beds, this lovely and amazingly variant and wildly colorful species is celebrated.

Another of Singapore's many allures is its vibrant—if a bit stolid—nightlife. Along the quays lining the Singapore River is a nearly endless supply of glittering entertainments featuring bars, restaurants, and nightclubs for every taste. These are filled every night of the week with gleeful throngs of locals and a few tourists celebrating late into the night.

There is a tendency, either through Buddhist-inspired self-regulation or laws imposing prudish standards, to a mildly irritating "golly gee whiz" wholesomeness. A single example will suffice.

At the historical riverside Clark Quay is a cabaret-style nightclub featuring performers that you might expect to find headlining the entertainment at a Southern Baptist convention. The show I encountered featured four attractive and quite innocent-looking women prancing about on stage dressed in mid-calf flouncy dresses, breasts fully enshrouded, reminding me more of Annette Funicello in her Mouseketeers days then, say, Madonna. Together with the male lead singer (think of young Perry Como), they performed schmaltzy show tunes. This sort of '50s-era innocence is quite common in Singapore. I didn't stay long; that honky-tonk bar beckoned.

Strait of Malacca

Fully rested after several weeks in Singapore, *Indigo* and her owner and crew departed on February 11, 2009, and set off up the Strait of Malacca.

The Strait is one of the principal choke points for international vessel traffic, especially for ships traveling between Asia and Europe and North America. As a result, our radar screen was active. There were ships all over the place. But, as we had seen back in the harbor, most were anchored along the shore, idled by the recession. For miles and miles, the Malaysian side was a mass parking lot of empty ships.

Going back several centuries, the Strait has been a hotbed of piracy. These days the bad guys have become ever more brazen, attacking huge cargo and even tanker ships in broad daylight, climbing up anchor chains to kidnap members of the crew and hold them for ransom. It has not yet reached the level of the Gulf of Aden, but it's still a dangerously active place.

Spotting trouble early is essential to repelling an attack, so during our transit, we posted double watches and equipped the outside watch with alarm devices. We were never threatened, though as we arrived at our destination, headlines carried the news that the day after we passed through the Strait, a band of brigands had boarded a tug in midday, captured its captain, and was now holding him for ransom. Just blind luck had kept us out of the newspapers that day. Or was it the contribution I dropped in the box at that Chinese Buddhist temple back in Singapore? Maybe, just maybe, my ugly, snarly, squatty little god for the year of the rooster was watching over us.

Island of Penang, Malaysia

Our first destination after Singapore was the island of Penang. Giving offense to self-respecting oysters everywhere, it bills itself as the Pearl of the Orient.

The guidebooks say that the island of Penang is one of the most visited and best-known corners of Malaysia, and the only one of the country's thirteen states to have a Chinese majority. Having once been a British colonial outpost, the capital city of Georgetown now has a collection of buildings from that era that would be impressive were they not sprinkled about in a maze of tumbledown shops, seedy hostels, and flyblown street food vendors. Just a few blocks away, a long strip of incongruous high-rise beachfront condos defiles both the sky above and the squalid landscape below.

The place is not without its attractions, though. It was fun to be pedaled about the narrow streets and alleys of its historic area in a trishaw (bicycle-powered rickshaw) watching the vibrant nightlife scroll by at a stately pace. The once-eminent Eastern and Oriental Hotel, a sprawling affair built in 1884 and tastefully restored a few years before my visit, is a delight. During its heyday, it was often the haunt of Rudyard Kipling, Noel Coward, and Somerset Maugham, among other notables of the time, the names suggesting that it may have been a forerunner of today's gay-friendly resorts.

But what I gained most from Penang was an appreciation for the Chinese—or at least those of Penang's past known as the Straits Chinese. Dotting the central area of the town are elaborate clan houses built by prominent Chinese families almost solely for the purpose of extolling their economic and reproductive success and paying homage to ancestors. The Khoo family's clan house is the grandest of these, a wildly flamboyant, colorful jumble of dragons, lanterns, gargoyles, bronze filigree, ornate columns, ceramic figurines, red-lacquered surfaces, and copious amounts of gold leaf. By America's Puritan minimalist standards, the architecture and interior spaces are vulgar, but astounding nevertheless. On either side of its main shrine room are smaller rooms whose walls are adorned with brass plaques bearing the names of family members and listing their academic achievements. *Khoo Yung Foo, Master of Science, Botany, Michigan State University, 1983; Khoo Mao Doo, PhD, Mathematics, University of California, Berkeley, 1979.* These extensive, patriarchal families value higher education and economic success and are not shy about trumpeting their attainments.

One night I took the crew out to what the guidebooks described as a lively outdoor bar with good music. In sultry night air, we sat in the place on rickety plastic chairs, chickens pecking at our feet, surrounded by a scruffy crowd of locals and backpackers all listening to a Malaysian band murder what, in more skillful hands, would have been tolerable music. The girls reported that the female restroom there won the prize for Most Noxious (you don't want to know the details). I thought to myself that if the female restroom was so awful, the men's room must have been a disease-ridden cesspit, it being a universal Law of Nature that the female is invariably more fastidious than the male in matters concerning sanitation. Street food vendors were busy nearby selling stuff that smelled enticing but looked unhealthful.

On another night, I took everybody to what was reputed to be a premier restaurant located in a restored mansion. The place looked okay as we arrived, but inside it had the vapid air of an inner city school cafeteria. Service was prompt, and the spicy Malay curry dishes tasted as you would expect. The place was owned and operated by a Muslim family, however, so it served no alcohol. Mate Bobby was dispatched with instructions not to return without cold beer. Ever reliable, he came back in fifteen minutes with two plastic bags filled with iced-down beer.

Island of Langkawi, Malaysia

Our last stop in Malaysia was the lovely, duty-free island of Langkawi, where we docked at the Royal Langkawi Yacht Club alongside some impressive yachts and local boats. At the head of the docks was a fine restaurant, and nearby were all the services you could want. This clearly was a different place from Penang, and a welcome change.

To give the crew a break and time to attend to various boat issues, I chose to stay a few nights at a new, architecturally stunning, and mostly vacant Four Seasons. The staff, almost all Muslim, don't eat pork, nor will they work anyplace where it is eaten or served. Breakfast at the hotel, accordingly, features such unappealing items as chicken sausage and turkey bacon. Thankfully, though, they are cheerfully indifferent to serving vital spirits. You can get sloshed—they'll happily serve up all you can handle and then some—but they won't themselves ever touch the stuff.

The island's excellent roads wind through a bucolic countryside of jungle-covered hills, cultivated rice paddies, and roaming water buffalo. Modest homes and shops along the roads are orderly, their yards swept clean of the random trash common among third world habitations.

Langkawi is predominantly Muslim, and it shows. Walking along the commercial streets, the first thing you notice is that everybody is dressed in traditional Muslim garb, and their garments are spotless. In the shops, they greet you with a friendly but somewhat distant manner, not unlike that of a man greeting his urologist. You have the distinct sense that your non-Muslim presence is merely tolerated for the economic benefits you bring, nothing more.

I must say, though, that by any measure their culture suffers far less from the social pathologies that bedevil most third world nations. Their low rates of disease—especially HIV—alcoholism, divorce, and the like are commendable and due in large measure to the strict conduct required by their religion.

What I did not much care for is the corollary of this salutary life, and that is the obvious regimentation that comes from a state-imposed religion, the tenets of which reach far deeper into its believers' daily lives than most non-Muslims could abide. Outside of the resorts, almost everyone adheres fairly closely to Islamic dogma, with the effect that vivacity is absent and differentness is not welcomed, let alone celebrated. But they seem quite pleased with their ways, and it's surely not my place to say how others ought to live.

We moved *Indigo* from the yacht club a few miles away to Cenang, one of the more popular beaches, lined with low-rise hotels and apartments.

While roaming the beach one day, I came upon a startling sight. Four youngish, giggling girls fully enshrouded head to toe in brightly hued burqas, faces barely visible, were wading into the ocean carrying snorkel gear. I found a shady spot, sat on the sand, and watched in wonder as, fully clothed, they went about snorkeling over an inshore reef. In stark contrast, in the all-Muslim Maldive Islands, it's common for Muslim women vacationing there from rigidly Islamic countries to sunbathe in bikinis. They and their husbands happily indulge in the evil spirits, too, but they won't touch pork.

After exhausting ourselves with nightlife, we moved *Indigo* to the remote east side of the island and dropped anchor in a spot aptly named Hole in the Wall. With the tender, we found the narrow slot in the steep cliffs from which the place derives its name, and entered through it into a maze of mangroves and lagoons encased in a natural box of steep-sided cliffs and jungle. Along one shore is a strip of floating restaurants, some abandoned, all looking forlorn. One of the lagoons passes through a low cave about 150 feet long.

At another place along the island cliffs, low tide revealed a cave that, from its deepest recesses, I could detect the faint glow of light. I worked the tender carefully through, avoiding low-hanging stalactites, and came out the other end into a hidden lake with water of the most lustrous emerald green. So high were the enclosing cliffs that it seemed as if I was at the bottom of a huge well. The incoming tide would, within a few hours, flood the cave and block my exit, so I didn't linger there as long as I would have liked.

I confounded the crew a bit one night by taking the tender out for some stargazing. It was such a pleasure to be out on the open water alone, to turn off the outboard motor and all the lights and just drift on the outgoing tide. The heavens didn't disappoint. Over the course of an hour or so, I watched a resplendent display of shooting stars streaking across the sky over the Andaman Sea. With miles of mangroves nearby, I began to wonder if they were home to saltwater crocs and if they could leap out of the water and snatch me from the tender. Without reflecting much longer on the matter, I concluded the otherwise pleasant excursion and returned to *Indigo*. Later I learned that there are indeed crocs among those mangroves, but there seems to be a difference of opinion on their talent for leaping.

After taking on a full load of duty-free fuel and provisions in Langkawi, we set out for Thailand.

FOURTEEN

Thrills of Thailand

Without a doubt, Thailand is among the best places *Indigo* visited on her long voyage. It attains this distinction mostly through its people, who are among the most gentle, serene, and kindly I have come across. When you encounter a Thai, even in the most perfunctory circumstance, you're greeted by hands clasped together prayerlike, fingertips nearly touching the chin, head slightly nodded, a gesture called the *wai* (pronounced "why"). The greater the difference in age or social status, the deeper is the nod from the younger or less-prominent person. With this gesture of gentility comes the all-purpose "hello" (in phonetic Thai, sounding like "sweaty crop" spoken by males and "sweaty ka" by females) expressed in a soft lilt. The smile of welcome that accompanies this gesture is almost always genuine—or at least you will think it is. If they know your name, you are called, whether male or female, by the honorific "Kuhn" followed by your first name. Thus I would be Kuhn Phil and my wife Kuhn Kitty.

It is a serious social infraction to raise your voice, which will be taken as a sign of both your incivility and your low regard for the listener. They are anxious to avoid giving offense, and so when asked a question that calls for a direct answer—perhaps an answer they worry might offend you—they resort to indirection. This can be maddening to a Westerner until you come to appreciate the self-effacing culture and adapt yourself to it.

In struggling to understand these remarkable people, I came to the conclusion that their easy serenity is due in part to their essential nature, quite different from the nearby Burmese, Laotians, and Cambodians, but mostly to their religion. To paraphrase G. K. Chesterton: Thailand is a nation with the soul of a Buddhist temple.

Thais are 95 percent Thai Buddhist, an adaptive strain of Buddhism that mixes their ancient history and animist practices with traditional Buddhist teachings of the Theravada sect. Though called a religion, Buddhism is essentially a transcendental philosophy. There is no compulsion to attend temple, contribute money, or live in a particular way. You are free to do as you like, live as you wish. Monks are teachers to help you along the path toward nirvana but not to hector you or preach to you.

Thais are remarkably modest and fastidious in their dress and public behavior. Despite the hot, humid tropical climate, they are always neatly turned out, wear spotless garments, and practice good hygiene no matter their station in life. Thais outside of the more cosmopolitan Bangkok and popular beach resorts usually swim fully clothed, rarely wear shorts, and never wear tank tops. Couples don't hold hands in public or otherwise display affection toward each other. There are many other social and language conventions, taboos, and matters of religious etiquette, not easily apprehended by an outsider, that make the Thai culture rich and varied. They also offer the visitor a minefield of opportunities for social blunders.

The social elites of Thailand, as with other countries of Southeast Asia, are part Chinese and as such have generally lighter skin. This fact and its corollary—the darker your skin, the more you will be thought of as a common laborer—leads to noticeable efforts to block the sun. Ever since Bali, I had been seeing people riding along on motorbikes, working in the hot sun, even strolling along a street, covered in clothes more suitable to fall in New England. Long-sleeved shirts buttoned to the neck, broad-brimmed sun hats, and even shrouds draped over the head and tied under the chin are common, and it's not to prevent skin cancer. Chemist shops are filled with emollients and pills intended to lighten the skin. Thais will even remark to each other about their skin color. One Thai lady who uncharacteristically liked to sunbathe said she was frequently asked, "Why are you so black?" We whites lie in the sun all day trying to acquire the color of fried chicken while they want to look like raw chicken.

Butang Islands, Thailand

It was early March 2009 when we sailed into the Butang Group in the fifty-one-island Ko Tarutao Marine National Park. It remains one of our favorite stops, with lovely beaches and glimmering clear waters barely discovered by tourists.

On one of my favorite islands, Ko Lipe, a gently arcing beach set deep in a cove is lined with a few midrange, single-story resort hotels, some bungalows, and inviting sand-floor bars. I landed the tender there and wandered along the water's edge, exchanging casual greetings with the long-tail drivers and chatting with a few of the pasty white tourists from places like Australia, New Zealand, Germany, and, as always in Thailand, Scandinavia.

The seawater in the Butangs was the clearest any of us had ever seen. One afternoon I went snorkeling on some reefs near our anchorage, a time of day when the surface was undisturbed by breeze. So perfectly transparent was the water that I had the sensation of flying through clear, clean air rather than swimming in a sea. The reefs, as everywhere else we would go in Thailand, held a menagerie of colorful sea life. Every conceivable species of reef fish, large and small, darted about or meandered among the coral, many in dense schools.

The Butang islands mark the southerly beginning of a long chain of the most geologically remarkable and visually arresting islands anywhere in the world. The limestone karst islands of the Andaman Sea were shaped by the millennia into squat hatboxes, columnar shards, high mesas, and grotesque statuary cleaved by deep fissures and caves and undercut by erosion. If islands were precious gems, the Andaman Sea off Thailand's west coast would be Tiffany's.

High up on these islands' sheer faces is a species of tiny bird that builds its nests with the usual sticks and twigs but, oddly and with regrettable effect, cemented with their own saliva. The nests of these birds are the essential ingredient in bird's nest soup so treasured by the Chinese, and it's the saliva that is said to make it so delectable. I'll have to take their word for it.

Throughout these islands, we came upon rude shacks housing the men who gather the nests for profit. Peering into caves and tunnels, it's common to see intricate networks of bamboo poles used to shinny up rock faces, enter the otherwise inaccessible interior nooks and crevices, and gather up the valuable nests.

At the northernmost end of the islands, four freshwater rivers draining Thailand's western highlands converge and empty into the Andaman Sea. The resulting brackish water interacts chemically with the limestone karst, turning the sea from its customary deep, clear blue to opaque emerald, adding still more visual drama to this already dramatic place.

At the delta of the four rivers sits a tiny fishing village built entirely on stilts and anchored floats. I took the tender there for lunch one day at one of its numerous waterside open-air restaurants. Upon my arrival, the owner offered a photo op with local sea eagles perched on my shoulders, this for the price of $2.85, which seemed like a bargain to me.

On the menu was a variety of fish, all described as "live," which gave me pause as I've always preferred to dine on fish that are inarguably dead. Nonetheless, I ordered one just to see what it was all about and became further alarmed when the waitress showed up with a bamboo serving tray on which were four fish, sure enough alive and flopping about in the manner of, well, fish out of water. These, I learned, had been plucked from an underwater holding pen in which, just moments before, they had been swimming happily about.

Eventually it became clear that no, these were not to be served up raw and squirming. They were offered so that I might choose the most delectable and prescribe the manner of its preparation. This I did in something like pidgin sign language with the result that I enjoyed one of the finest—not even to mention freshest—seafood dishes of my life.

Islands of Ko Phi Phi Don and Ko Phi Phi Leh, Thailand

From the Butangs, we traveled a short distance to Ko Phi Phi Don and Ko Phi Phi Leh, known in phonetic translation as Big Pee Pee and Little Pee Pee, names apparently not chosen by the local chamber of commerce. Big lies on a small beach lodged tightly between two karst hills. It is home to a dense thicket of motels, bungalows, bars, restaurants, and miniature shops arrayed along a bewildering maze of brick walkways, all newly built since the deadly 2004 tsunami. Fun bars and plenty of restaurants for every taste and budget line its two waterfronts, each facing onto a cove. We anchored in the north cove, took the tender into the village, and had a grand old time eating, drinking, and funning.

Big's apparent role is to provide commercial support for visitors there for scuba diving and sightseeing on Little, just a mile away. A fleet of long-tail boats, dive boats, and speedboats ferry tourists between Big and Little all day long, and it's well worth the trip. Development is forbidden on Little, with the happy result that its numerous secluded lagoons, shaded beaches, and scuba sites remain pristine. It is where the movie *The Beach* was filmed—or at least scenes from it—a fact extolled in every brochure on the area.

Entered through narrow openings in the karst cliffs, the lagoons of Little are almost fully enclosed by 300-foot walls rising straight up from pools of shimmering green water. Hidden beaches, copses of local forest, jumbles of rocks, and opulent reefs make this a dazzling place. While we were there, the world's economy was in the tank and the tourist trade suffering, yet still the place was crowded.

Island of Phuket, Thailand

After the Pee Pees, we cruised a short distance to the epicenter of Thailand's west coast fun spots, the large island of Phuket. Its west coast is a thirty-mile-long stretch of superb beaches strung along the coast in bights. During our stay, we anchored off most of these, tendered to shore, enjoyed exotic dinners, visited some of the many bars and other attractions, and had a great time.

Through our agent, Asia Pacific Yacht Services, I employed a Thai man named Kuhn Nong to drive me to the many—and often hard to find—choice spots. He was a soft-spoken, mannered gentleman who was always neatly dressed and respectful of others. His English, though shy of fluent, was adequate to the task of escorting me around and keeping me mostly out of trouble. He helped me choose wisely from among a bewildering array of diversions, some more innocent than others.

What I especially like about Phuket is its diversity. Each beach is set within a town having its own unique personality, ranging from funk to posh. Most are furnished Euro-style with rows up to six deep of colorful umbrellas shading lounge chairs, and all are lined with thatched-roof huts offering inexpensive Thai massages and with simple restaurants featuring Thai dishes, beer, and wine.

Some of Thailand's finest restaurants are found on Phuket, often in the five-star resort hotels. One night Kuhn Nong took me and a few crew members to a fabulous public restaurant overhanging a high cliff from which we watched a flamboyant sunset over the Andaman Sea. Though the climate tends toward muggy, this place, like most, was not air-conditioned because of the high cost of electricity. Evening breezes bring relief, and eventually you just don't notice the absence of air conditioning.

Of all the towns and beaches along Phuket's west shore, my favorite is Surin Beach. It is here that three of the top hotels in Thailand are found: the Amanpuri, the Banyan Tree, and the Chedi, all within easy walking distance from each other. Along its beach under the shade of tall palms and banyans is a stretch of every kind of restaurant and bar anybody could wish for, from tres chic to rustic, some owned by Germans, others by Irish, most by local Thais. There is even a reggae bar.

There is one other beach on Phuket that cannot go unremarked. Patong has a long crescent beach and a handsomely landscaped promenade, but these are not the features for which it is famous. Each night at six p.m. the town's main thoroughfare, called Bangla Street, and most of its side streets, are closed to traffic. From that point on until the wee hours, the place is about as wild and debauched as any you could imagine, though in a playful way. It's something like Bourbon Street in the New Orleans French Quarter during Mardi Gras without the parades, multiplied by about four. It's also lots of fun.

I went to the Bangla district several nights, always with Kuhn Nong as my trusty guide. He and his family owned a small but popular bar there called U2, so he knew the traps awaiting the unwary. Each time I went, I couldn't suppress a huge, euphoric grin, as though I was six years old and it was Christmas morning. The streets were packed with tourists and locals alike shambling along, some like me gawking in amazement, others drinking or singing or cheering. Still others clustered around pole dancers or street performers or lined up at the pushcarts of street food vendors.

Groups of confused guys wagered among themselves on which of the dancers were true females and which were lady boys. Magicians and street musicians played the crowds, and enterprising fellows with endangered species perched on their head offered up their creatures for photo ops. Tarted-up hookers strutted, garish lights flashed, raucous music blared, and hordes of unruly celebrants shouted above the brassy din and drank themselves silly as aromas of Thai curry and garlic prawns hung in the warm, tropical air. It was a raffish wonderland of raw, unrestrained energy, a place where inhibitions are bound and gagged and locked safely away . . . and a place that quickly had me mesmerized. I loved it.

Bar girls in the Bangla district outnumbered patrons at the time we were there. We called them "long time girls," as in "Hey, meesta, you buy me cell phone, I love you long time." At one typical bar, I bought drinks for the crew and generously tipped the several girls serving us, in return for which I was invited to join a group of them dancing suggestively around a brass pole—an invitation that I accepted, thus adding another to a long list of my improvident choices. After watching my performance, marked as it was by a wild flailing of limbs and done at a rhythm not exactly in accord with the music, the crew agreed with the girls that although I got high marks for vigor and an inexplicable self-assurance, my future lay in other directions.

One of the most curious attractions of the Bangla district is the transvestites who come there to show off their beauty. At a curbside arcade is a raised, open-air dance floor about twenty feet square on which the "girls" take turns gyrating feverishly, often three or four performing at the same time. The locals say that the only difference between the transvestites and real girls is that the trans are more attractive.

One evening I went to the area's finest transvestite cabaret show held in a large, well-appointed theater with plush seats and wide aisles. For an hour and a half, I was entertained by acts in which there was not a single female. You would never know it, though. My favorite acts—and the crowd's, too—were a Tina Turner impersonator and a mime of a Japanese geisha. As my seat was on the front row, center aisle, I and a few other members of the audience were the recipients of cheek kisses from several of the "girls" who mingled among the audience. After the show, the cast lined up outside for photo ops.

With Kuhn Nong's assistance, I was able to discern the only outwardly visible means by which you can tell a transvestite in full costume from a true female. It's the feet. Men's feet are, of course, larger and less sleek than those of a woman. There's no surgical treatment available to hide this difference. Otherwise, you just can't tell.

No visit to Patong—or to Thailand, for that matter—is complete without a visit to a show in which unusually talented females withdraw from their vaginas an astounding array of items, including Ping-Pong balls, live fish, a live bird, and much else. It's not clear yet if this talent will be welcomed into the Olympics anytime soon, but you never know. It is a considerable improvement over synchronized swimming, though.

Railay Beach, Thailand

On the mainland coast east of Phuket is the fabulous Railay Beach, described by our guidebook in accurate but overwrought prose as "the most stunning beach in all of Thailand. It's home to emerald silk water punctured by surreal limestone formations, honey-hued beaches, and psychedelic sunsets." It is surely that. Its premier resort has a bar at beachside, with many of its tables set in an adjoining cave, and others placed in the welcome shade of palm trees. I had dinner at its restaurant on a night that featured a fabulous show of ethnic dances performed to traditional music—not usually my favorite entertainment, but in this case spellbinding.

Each day, specially equipped long-tail boats nose onto the beach selling Thai lunches prepared on small grills, a sort of floating version of a food truck. If it's luxurious sunbathing on nearly perfect beaches you're looking for, this is the place.

Just seaward of Railay Beach is a collection of karst islands in a national park frequented by day-trippers from the small nearby town of Ao Nang. One of these features a prominent rock formation that, with a little imagination, resembles the neck and head of a chicken and is thus known as Chicken Island.

On its main beach are a few thatch and bamboo huts where an extended family of park rangers live and supplement their meager incomes by selling cold beer and hot lunches to the tourists. We engaged the family to prepare for us a home-cooked sunset dinner with fresh fish, Thai chicken, local veggies, grilled squid, and fruit salad. The fish and squid had been pulled from the sea that very afternoon. With the entire island to ourselves, we helped the ranger family set up wooden tables on the beach as the tide receded, and on these they served up at water's edge one of our most memorable meals ever.

After dinner, I shared a wee bit of my treasured Jameson eighteen-year-old Irish whiskey with the family's patriarch, who had declined wine and beer. He was a dignified, broad-shouldered man in his sixties. He wore the traditional men's black sarong and a white, short-sleeved cotton shirt—roughly equivalent to a Westerner's smart casual. Neither of us spoke the other's language, but we managed to talk in rudimentary fashion. I complimented him on the fine life he and his family had made for themselves. He thanked me and grinned in agreement. A fine life indeed.

Just as the sun set, we were treated to the sight of thousands of fruit bats leaving their cave high up in the hills above us, circling overhead, then flying across the nuclear orange sky on their way to the mainland to feed on the fruits and insects there.

We also visited the tourist-crowded James Bond Island, so named because one of the Bond movies, *The Man with a Golden Gun*, was filmed there many years ago. Following that, we anchored at a resort called Six Senses, and from there took a local taxi—really just a pickup truck with a canopy and bench seats in back—miles into the jungle across the island to a thatched-roof, raised-floor open-air restaurant.

Live fish in a plastic bucket were brought to our table fresh from an underwater holding pen so we could choose the exact fish we fancied and specify its manner of preparation. The overused term "fresh seafood" will never have quite the same meaning. Forewarned that it was Muslim owned, we brought our own wine, to which they had no objection. In true Thai fashion, they even refused our offer to pay a corkage fee.

Chiang Mai, Thailand

Wishing to explore a bit more of this country, I booked a flight on Thai Airways from Phuket to the northern city of Chiang Mai. My guidebook describes it as a "lively mountain city filled with ancient temples, modern chic, and loads of culture classes," that last part not especially inspiring. It has more than 300 Buddhist temples, far more than any US city of comparable size has churches. Very little in life is more certain than that any place with one temple for every seven people is not a place in which the baser spirits are apt to run loose. An inquisitive mind is then set buzzing when it discovers that alongside this dismaying surplus of temples sits Chiang Mai University—packed with 20,000 students who, if they are anything like their US counterparts, are resolutely devoted to the loose running of baser spirits.

Just outside the city is a Four Seasons resort hotel, where I stayed two nights. Set along the perimeter of a working rice farm thirty minutes from town, the hotel is a tastefully designed, rambling affair with superb rooms, each with a balcony looking over densely landscaped grounds, flowing creeks, and of course, rice paddies. If I were to return to Chiang Mai, as I would very much like to do, I would instead stay in town, closer to the sights and sounds and loose-running baser spirits of the city. Not to take anything away from the Four Seasons, but lying about gazing upon lethargic water buffalo plowing rice paddies is a bit bucolic for my taste.

A stroll through Chiang Mai's vibrant night bazaar was a memorable experience. Each evening, a part of the central city is closed to traffic, and along these streets are erected hundreds of stalls offering an astounding array of stuff. It's a popular place for the Thai hill tribes to peddle their handicrafts, for artists to sell their works, and for street entertainers to perform in front of an enthusiastic audience. There are stalls offering the traditional Thai foot massage, and lines of pushcarts from which street food vendors dish up aromatic local favorites. It's about as bustling a thoroughfare of commerce as there is anywhere.

FIFTEEN

From the Golden Triangle to Bangkok

Still in the mood for exploration, I rented an SUV and headed some 200 miles or so down the road to Chiang Rai. Primary roads in Thailand are uniformly excellent and well signed both in Thai and English. Outside of chaotic Bangkok, drivers are mindful of the speed limits—a bit *too* mindful, if you ask me. Here and there are police checkpoints searching for contraband, drugs, expired licenses, and illegal immigrants from Myanmar and Laos.

Scenery along the drive was more arid than I had expected, the habitations less scuffed. Agriculture is devoted to pineapples, melons, and various truck vegetables, these offered up at roadside stands. But for signs in Thai over commercial shops and the like, I could have easily been driving through, say, central Mississippi, though Thai roads are better.

At Chiang Rai, I turned onto a secondary but still nicely paved road to Chiang Saen, a sleepy town on the Thai side of the Mekong River. Just across the river by ferry is Laos, though if you are Thai, you will have to stress your brain to come up with a reason to go there. It would be like living in San Diego and wishing for a trip to Tijuana.

The Golden Triangle

I followed a narrow country road along the bank of the Mekong to a village that, for commercial exploitation, has adopted for itself the name the Golden Triangle. The term actually encompasses a large area of Myanmar (formerly Burma), Laos, and Thailand that, in recent history, had a nefarious reputation for being one of the world's largest producers of opium poppies and the drugs made from them. These are still a major crop in Myanmar and Laos, and are still cultivated in remote areas of northern Thailand. But the Thai queen and her government have taken enormous and quite successful steps to wean Thai, mostly hill tribe, subsistence farmers off the stuff by introducing alternative crops, job training, and rehabilitation clinics. The Thai police have largely chased off or killed the warlords who controlled the trade for so many years. Tourism has now replaced opium as the local industry in the tiny village of the Golden Triangle.

As I was dining at a restaurant on Railay Beach a week or so before visiting northern Thailand, a personable fellow came by hawking colorful hats of a sort that might come out late at night at a party that had got into its spirited stage. Lampshades have been overdone in this arena. With the aid of an interpreter, he said that he was from one of the hill tribes of the Golden Triangle area and, with the candor of a man who had already done penance for his offenses, confessed that he had formerly raised and sold opium poppies and also had become addicted to the drugs they produced. He said that the queen had helped him kick the drug habit and helped him and his family learn new trades, which included, in his mother's case, the hand sewing of these unique hats done in a zippy style peculiar to the hill tribe of which he and his family were members.

I bought two hats, which were, for a short time, among my most prized treasures from Thailand. I say "a short time" because what the man neglected to mention was that one of his newly acquired skills was the art of flimflam, a skill at which he had clearly risen well above the level of journeyman. While visiting the Golden Triangle, I learned that these hats were not hand sewn by his mother as he had sworn and were not in the style of any known hill tribe. Instead, I was disillusioned to discover that they were mass produced in a Chinese factory and sold all over Thailand to unwitting tourists like me. Still, they were particularly handsome hats.

I wandered around the waterfront of the Golden Triangle, took photos of a giant statue of Buddha perched on the bank, and browsed through the souvenir shops.

Soon growing bored with this, I drove a few more miles along the bank to a tiny road marked only in Thai, turned there, and soon found myself on a rutted dirt trail that suggested I might be lost. Just as I was looking for a place to turn around, I spotted a small, dusty wood sign mounted on a simple pole pointing the way to my destination: the Four Seasons Tent Resort.

Turning at the sign, now on a seriously potholed pig trail, I continued along a hundred yards or so to the bank of a muddy, fast-flowing river, the Nam Ruak, where by prior arrangement the welcoming staff of the hotel stood in the bushes waiting to greet me. Nowhere in the world is there an entry into a five-star resort hotel quite as unobtrusive.

My meager luggage was loaded onto a finely built long-tail boat whose driver, apparently a fan of stock car racing, took me at a bracing speed downriver to the resort's landing dock. From there I hiked up stone steps to the reception area, where a cool and welcome drink, ice-cold face towel, and genial greetings awaited.

My room was a tent of a sort. Its walls and roof were of a sturdy canvaslike material to be sure, and the flooring, bathroom, and furnishings tastefully suitable to the rustic safari motif. But by any measure, it was a sumptuous accommodation and a welcome improvement over the tents I once occupied while serving in the US Army. This would be my home and base camp for two nights of what would prove to be a remarkable but too-brief adventure.

While at the resort, I became proficient at riding an elephant. The resort has a small school staffed by expert mahouts, the term for elephant wranglers, and some twenty animals of varying age and size who are sacrificed to the beginning student. My elephant, a large and thankfully docile creature named Yuki (Japanese for "happy"), much to my amazement followed the commands I shouted—in Thai, no less. These were helpfully printed on a card worn around my neck in case the words didn't leap to mind. She turned left and right, backed up, and stopped, all as I instructed. She also adjusted her stance to three different positions, each of which allowed me to climb onto the back of her neck by a different route.

With the elephant, as with all animals of the lower orders, it's essential to ingratiate yourself right off, to establish that you mean it no harm but have thought of it always, along with the dog, as among man's most endearing friends. This is best done by feeding it at close range, which in the case of the pachyderm is a task not to be taken lightly.

As I approached her for the first time, making sure to keep my feet out from under hers, Yuki sniffed me thoroughly, seeming to sense my benign intentions and the quality of my aftershave. I patted her head and trunk and whispered flattering words in her oversized ears, being careful not to say anything about her weight, a subject on which the female elephant is known to be sensitive.

In feeding elephants, you are coached by the resort staff to stand a comfortable distance from its gaping maw, to offer stalks of sugarcane for it to wrest from your grasp with its trunk, and whatever else, not to tease it by feigning a game of keep-away. When it comes to food, the elephant has little humor. From the manner in which Yuki gnawed at the sugarcane, there was the suggestion of Bugs Bunny munching the carrots of Elmer Fudd.

Upon graduating with high honors from the mahout course, an achievement of such distinction that I was presented with a parchment certificate attesting to it, I was ready for the big time. After I mounted up in proper form, legs straddling her neck, knees clasped together with feet behind her ears, we set off on a two-hour trek through the jungle, our pace best described as stately. Intelligent as beasts go, the elephants of Asia don't wish to use up their limited supply of energy by darting about unwisely.

In due course, we came to the same muddy river I had traveled down the day before on my way to the resort. Kicking her gently behind the right ear, the indication for a left turn, I directed Yuki over the river's bank and into the cool waters of its flowing stream. This evidently agreed with her—so much so that she just couldn't bring herself to stop despite my increasingly desperate commands that she do so. She kept going until her entire body, and nearly mine, was completely submerged. Her head tossed about a bit more exuberantly than I would have preferred, and her trunk, now like a submarine's periscope, rose out of the current as if it were a gray serpent gasping for air. She got her mouth out of the water and did a few of those elephant trumpets often heard in Tarzan movies, but these of a cheerful sort.

Soon tiring of her brief swim, she acceded to my wishes and headed for the high ground but not before filling her mouth and trunk with water and expelling it an impressive distance into the air. Yuki was having a ball, and so was I.

After cavorting with elephants, I retired to the bar in time to watch the sun set over Thailand's tightly controlled, closed border with Myanmar and, just across the Mekong, it's more laxly monitored border with Laos. In the distance, I could see long-tail boats plying the Mekong and farmers behind ox-drawn plows and, in the foreground, the resort's livestock grazing in the meadow. Off in the distance, dark, rain-laden clouds were forming and beginning their march across the landscape. No scenery anywhere could be at once so pastoral and so exotic.

Next day, I met up with one of the resort's tour guides, an amiable, gracious gentleman named Kuhn Tee, a nickname indicating the youngest son from a family of Chinese heritage. About thirty-five years old, he spoke fluent English, Thai of course, some Laotian, and Burmese. As with Kuhn Nong back in Phuket and so many other cultured Thai Buddhists I had met, Kuhn Tee displayed the serene, untroubled air commonly found in men who have recently won the lottery and paid off their creditors.

Together we set out on an event-filled tour of the local area that, though brief, was one of the most memorable of my travels.

Our first foray was a speedy ride downstream in the resort's long-tail boat, passing by frowzy Laotian villages, kids frolicking in the turbid river waters, fishermen in dugouts, and freshly plowed fertile fields. In short order, we came upon the wide, muddy waters of the Mekong River, which is to Southeast Asia what the Mississippi is to the eastern US. Turning north on the Mekong, Kuhn Tee directed the boat driver to a point midstream where the borders of Laos, Myanmar, and Thailand meet. Other long-tails passed by, some filled with tourists, others with farmers transporting crops and almost certainly contraband to market, all apparently oblivious to the convergence here of these national boundaries.

Back on land, we visited the huge and quite modern—and I must say impressive—Hall of Opium built by the Thai government. It is the world's leading exhibit and research facility for the study of opiate use. Anything a person could want to know about poppies, opium, heroin, drug addiction, and drug history and its use can be found here in balanced and tasteful displays. If your aspirations run in the direction of profitable but unlawful careers, there is a quite-detailed exhibit explaining how valuable drugs are produced from these seemingly innocent flowers, enough information to get you started in the business.

Following our river trip, we climbed into a Land Rover and drove to the village of Chiang Saen, where we transferred to a more suitable "tuk-tuk," a three-wheeled, motor-powered conveyance with two passenger seats. Aboard this, Kuhn Tee and I went to the town's farmers' market to gaze upon strange and noisome creatures, many of which are more usually encountered floating in formaldehyde in a biology lab. There was a tub filled to overflow with squirming dung beetles and another with recently deceased grub worms. In other tubs were writhing masses of shiny, slippery serpents, which I identified as deadly snakes but he called edible (though most assuredly not by me) freshwater eels. Bloody gobs of offal—lamb brains, pig stomach, and sausage factory floor sweepings—added color if not allure. Salad seemed like a good idea for lunch.

Our next stop was one of the many ancient Buddhist temples that dot the area. It seemed a bit shabby to me, as if fund-raising had not gone well of late, but who was I to complain? After all, the head monk for the area was there, a buddy of Kuhn Tee, who asked if I would like for the monk to administer a blessing of good luck, health, and prosperity. Sensing an opportunity, I asked if I could maybe instead be forgiven for past infractions, which I assured him were of the most inconsequential sort. In that way I could start out with a clean slate and take my chances with luck, health, and prosperity. Kuhn Tee replied that no, Buddhist monks, unlike Catholic priests, don't erase past misdeeds.

Not wishing to seem ungrateful, I knelt before the monk, who sprinkled special water on me while chanting his blessings—a bit long-windedly, I thought, but maybe he figured I could use the extra help. A short, slight-framed man with the obligatory shaved head, saffron robe, and smiling, gentle manner of the Buddhist monk, he went about his ministrations with apparent devotion even though knowing I was a Westerner with no intention of converting to his religion.

When the chants finally stopped, I held out my right wrist, around which he tied a little piece of white string with a knot in the middle as a talisman.

Outside the temple walls were a few stalls from which ladies of several hill tribes were selling their handicrafts. From my close examination, aided by Kuhn Tee's knowledgeable eye, it soon became apparent that the items offered here were of exceptionally high quality and finely made. The tribeswoman, commenting on a particularly handsome quilt I was admiring, said that it had been stitched by hand and took the better part of a year to complete, a claim with which Kuhn Tee agreed. Its stitchwork was done in the manner of needlepoint but with finer threads in a wide variety of vibrant colors describing elaborate geometrical patterns peculiar to the Yao tribe.

After a round of perfunctory negotiations, I bought the thing for *Indigo's* salon, where I knew it would add a cheerful splash of color to an otherwise monochromatic room.

On my final day of adventure in the delightful and learned company of Kuhn Tee, we visited the nearby town of Mae Sai. There we stopped in at a jade factory where the semiprecious stone, mined mostly from the northern reaches of Myanmar, was cut, shaped, and polished into every manner of human decoration. For me, jade is forever associated with bric-a-brac and the dust collectors found in the homes of doddering grandmothers. Sold mostly by Oriental souvenir shops, the stuff long ago lost any appeal it might once have had. Still, I have to admire the artistry that goes into some of the more intricately carved pieces.

Myanmar

My next stop with Kuhn Tee turned out to be an entire country once called Burma.

Just over a short, narrow bridge from Mae Sai through a customs and immigration post is Tachileik, one of the few towns of Myanmar open to the outside world then. Since my visit, the country has opened up quite a bit more.

With the huge advantage of Kuhn Tee's Burmese language skills at my side, we parked the resort's car and walked across the bridge, passed through the border formalities, engaged a dilapidated tuk-tuk, and headed out into Myanmar.

It's called the Land of a Thousand Pagodas with good reason, so of course we went first to an enormous golden Buddhist pagoda situated on a hill overlooking the town and the river valley. There we bought from commercially reticent vendors incense, a nosegay, and a tiny bird enclosed in a simple bamboo cage. Then we walked around the pagoda's base until we found a small shrine devoted to all those born on Tuesday—one of whom was me. Buddhists believe that those born on particular days possess certain favorable characteristics, which we carry throughout our lives.

Poised at my Tuesday shrine and with Kuhn Tee as my guide, I performed the required unction involving pouring precise amounts of water on Buddha's hands and a lesser amount on my designated animal god, who resembled an irritated hound dog rendered in colorful ceramic in the Chinese gargoyle style. I then placed the flowers in a nearby stand and lit my incense sticks and waved them about in a solemn manner, hoping nobody was watching. Finally, I opened the door to the birdcage, setting it free, a supposed gesture of my goodwill, or karma, directed at one of the smallest and most helpless of Mother Nature's creatures. Before leaving the pagoda grounds, we stopped at an enormous gong, which I rang the required nine times using a hefty log.

My future thus secured, or so I judged, and all set right with Buddha, we departed.

Our next stop was a Burmese Buddhist temple, where to our good fortune, an event was going on in which young boys were being initiated into their required temporary service as monks. It was all very casual, with moms and dads and sisters and extended families hovering about and fussing over the robed lads, more like the first day of Little League than a solemn religious occasion. The temple, as the town itself, was a touch derelict compared to most of those in Thailand.

Our last stop in Myanmar was at a demonstration village depicting the daily life and culture of the Asian hill tribes. There are ten (though possibly up to twenty—the matter a point of some debate among the experts) of these tribes living in mostly remote villages spread throughout much of Southeast Asia. Seminomadic subsistence farmers with no national identities, each tribe has its own language, customs, style of dress, and spiritual beliefs.

Northern Thailand is home to six of these tribes, who live much as they have for the past 200 years—or at least they do if you don't count their newly acquired skill at fleecing unsuspecting tourists by selling them colorful hats.

The village we toured featured only women and young girls living in typical huts and dressed according to the style of their tribe. Men dress pretty much as Thai farmers, but women wear vividly colored and intricately patterned clothing, usually accompanied by headwear, some of which you wouldn't be surprised to find perched on the head of a royal attendant to the Court of St. James. Women of one tribe, the Karen, also called the long-neck people, affix brass rings around their necks beginning at a young age, adding rings as they mature. Those of other tribes have equally exotic fashions from which the wearer's tribe is easily discerned if you have skill in the subject.

After a brief stroll through the little village, we were escorted to a small outdoor pavilion. There, young girls and older women dressed in their respective tribal costumes danced to the innocent rhythms of their tribe—which, to be candid about it, reminded me of the Disney tune "It's a Small World." Hip-hop, it was not. Their dances were just simple steps and twirled arms that even I might have been able to pull off. Still, it was fun to watch.

Following the show, we got a few photos with the dance troupe and made a modest contribution to the village welfare. Well, I imagined it was modest until I learned later that the average annual per-capita income in Myanmar is $470.

With our Myanmar tour at an end, I went back across the Thai border with Kuhn Tee, collecting on the way one of the world's rarest passport stamps, and there said a heartfelt goodbye to my guide, whose knowledge, language skills, and genial manner had contributed enormously to one of the best experiences in all of my travels.

As he went on his way, I climbed into the comfortable and blessedly cool Land Rover and was driven to the airport in plenty of time for my flight to Bangkok.

Bangkok, Thailand

Bangkok is not my favorite city in Southeast Asia, nor is it likely to be anybody's. Crowded, noisy, and traffic-choked, there hangs over it a visible mixture of smoke, particulates, and hydrocarbon fumes that passes for air. Its streets are a befuddlement, made more so by the local practice of changing their names every few blocks or so.

On the plus side, the place is largely free of petty crime, save for a few enduring scams to which only particularly dimwitted tourists are likely to fall victim. And there is that matter of Thai food. It's almost impossible to get a bad meal there.

I stayed two nights at the iconic Mandarin Oriental Hotel, as fine an establishment as there is in all of Southeast Asia, though directly across the river is the equally fine but more contemporary Peninsula.

I didn't do too much in the city, as I was not up for the wild club scene, which only gets going at midnight. And after two spirited nights on Phuket's Bangla district, the city's four riotous party districts held little appeal.

However, there was one excursion that made my stay there memorable, largely due to my fortunate encounter with another guide, the highborn, matronly, and charming Kuhn Diamond. With her guidance, I spent several hours wandering about the inner sanctums of the Grand Palace, ceremonial home to the king and queen. With the stern air and officious manner of a US Marine Corps general, Kuhn Diamond chased away pesky hawkers with a glare and instructed traffic cops that it was high time they stopped the flow of cars to allow us across the street. You dare not get at odds with this formidable woman.

The 236 wall-enclosed acres of the palace grounds are stuffed with more than a hundred buildings, the most important of which are those that accommodate the fabled Emerald Buddha, a royal throne, and the royal residence. Their architecture is an odd mixture of styles, but the terms *ostentatious* or *garish* come to mind. The visitor is requested to dress conservatively, which means arms and legs fully clothed, to refrain from taking photos inside some buildings, and always to be respectful. The whole place is said to be for Thais something akin to what Washington, DC, is for Americans. Judging from its colossal waste of the Thai treasury, I'd say the analogy is just about right.

Following my brief, and largely uneventful, stay in Bangkok, I returned to *Indigo*. On April 15, we hoisted anchor and set off on the next leg of our voyage.

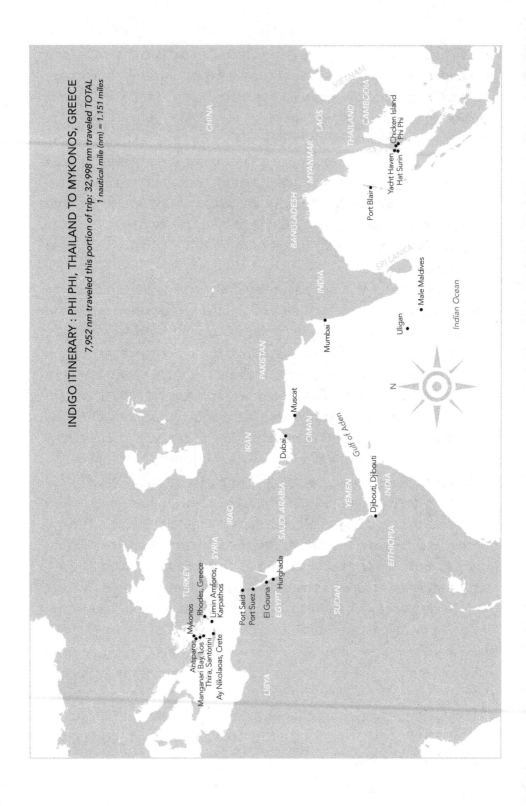

INDIGO ITINERARY : PHI PHI, THAILAND TO MYKONOS, GREECE

7,952 nm traveled this portion of trip: 32,998 nm traveled TOTAL

1 nautical mile (nm) = 1.151 miles

SIXTEEN

Cow Pies and the Streets of Bombay

Our route to Bombay, India, took us past two island groups, the India-owned Andaman Islands and the Republic of Maldives.

In the English language, a single word can tell us much about a place. When we read that the Sahara is a desert, for example, our mind conjures a reasonably accurate image of it. Likewise, if we say Palm Beach is manicured, we can quickly grasp the meaning.

For the town of Port Blair, capital of the Andaman Islands, the single descriptive word is "shithole." No other term adequately conveys its essence. There is nothing quite like a town that allows cows to roam freely about the commercial areas, yet doesn't bother to clean up after them. It makes walking the poorly lit streets at night hazardous lest you step on a freshly deposited output, and it gives the place an unforgettable stench.

Many of the islands are off-limits to tourists, the better to protect the indigenous Jarawa people. We were warned that, should we be so unwise as to land the tender on some of these without proper introductions and ceremony, we would be attacked by the Jarawa who live there, bows and arrows their weapons of choice.

Unwilling to risk life and limb, we decided to remain aboard *Indigo* while waiting for a cyclone in the area to clear out. Once the skies and the sea were calm, we enjoyed an uneventful eight-day crossing of the Bay of Bengal to the colorful city of Malé, capital of the Maldive Islands. Among the most geologically unusual of countries, the Maldives are a constellation of some 1,190 islands and islets—more if you count those visible only at low tide—spread within twenty-six enormous coral atolls.

Malé, with a population of 130,000 almost entirely indigenous people, all Muslim, is shoehorned into an island just over a mile long and a half mile wide, making it one of the most densely populated places on Earth. But for protecting seawalls, much like those around New Orleans, the first floors of most of its tall, narrow, colorful buildings would be awash.

I took a seaplane from Malé to a remote, one-acre island a half hour's flight west, and there spent a few nights at what was billed as a five-star but was more accurately a three- or perhaps on its best day a four-star establishment, called W Resort and Spa. I had one of those over-the-water bungalows that are all the rage there and in Polynesia, and a deck out back of it from which I could gaze at the sea life below—though an hour of this sort of thing is about all a sane man can endure. After that you begin wondering just why it was that you came here and what it is exactly that you're supposed to do.

So I whiled away my time at W Resort, working feverishly at every diversion the place offered in the hope of fending off the earlier stages of lunacy. The plane taking me back to *Indigo* arrived just in time.

Bombay, India

There is first the matter of the city's name: Mumbai or Bombay. In 1995, a far-right, xenophobic political party, apparently in an irritable mood, changed the city's name from the classic Bombay, a pusillanimous gesture at ridding it of the last vestiges of the British Raj. Nevertheless, English-speaking Indians still call it Bombay, and so will I.

We knew the city was near long before we actually saw it. It was the sea that gave the first hint of arrival. Slowly the water beneath *Indigo* began to change from the radiant blue of the Arabian Sea through various hues to an unhealthy looking dusty green. As we drew nearer, expecting to see a skyline, instead we saw only a toxic vapor lying in a thick blanket across our path. At a distance when we should have seen signs of a city, it still seemed as if we were gazing through pale brown gauze.

A tour with an educated, English-speaking guide was enough to confirm for me that the people of India, despite years of overwrought hokum in the commercial journals to the contrary, are desperately impoverished. It was a sobering encounter with destitution on a scale I had only read about. Everywhere we went, beggars seeing the small, aging Mercedes stopped at a light invariably tapped on its windows offering up contorted limbs, skeletal toddlers, or just an anguished face in hopes that we might give them alms. Only the practiced, steely heart of a native can endure these pathetic scenes without feeling deep and sincere sorrow for their plight. I tried to brush them from my sympathies as the driver and guide did, but in this I was wholly unsuccessful. Yes, some of it is well-practiced scam for sure, and in this fact the locals take heart. They tell you how cunning the beggars are and how they really aren't as poor as they pretend to be. But after a day of driving around, I remained unconvinced.

The hotel where I stayed a few nights was the unquestioned finest and located in one of the city's poshest neighborhoods, an area in which can be found most of the best restaurants, bars, and clubs. In the very same block on which this grand hotel sits, I was repeatedly accosted by emaciated beggar women toting equally emaciated infants. In the late night as I returned from a foray, I found these poor wretches asleep on the bare sidewalk, infants nearly nude and without the enveloping arms of their mothers, passersby like me stepping over them with hardly a glance. And this was by no means unusual.

My best day in Bombay was spent walking five hours in the sultry heat from my hotel along busy, feculent streets and busier and even more feculent sidewalks to the stock exchange, a noted retail store, and several shops along the way. It was a far more enlightening experience than the car and guide because I managed to get up close to the people and their way of life. I smelled and touched and heard the sounds of city life in ways you can't from a car.

I ate lunch in Peshawari Restaurant, named for the region of Pakistan that is said to be the spawning ground and hideout of the most fanatic of the Islamic jihadists. It also served up one of the tastiest meals I've ever eaten anywhere. In response to an innocent question from my waiter, an Indian, I made a mildly derogatory but accurate remark about radical Islam, which earned at my departure the hateful glare of the restaurant's owner. I didn't say, "Fuck you!" but it would have been a fine time to do so, and I wish that I had. Still, it was great food at a reasonable price.

In the crowded streets outside the stock exchange stood a lone disheveled security guard, hired by the exchange to deter thieves, I suppose. He wore a soiled, rumpled uniform shirt bearing sewn-on badges identifying his employer. His untucked shirttail was draped over badly worn, also soiled, baggy trousers that gathered at his sandaled feet. For protection of the commercially important building, he carried a dilapidated, rusting twenty-gauge, single-shot shotgun whose vintage was, I judged, about the middle 1900s. If armed robbery is your line of work, the Bombay stock exchange would make an appealingly soft object for your talents.

Sidewalks in Bombay seem not to be intended for pedestrian traffic. They are marked by fractured pavement, crushed curbs, and holes deep enough to break a leg. They are also the bedroom, living room, and parlor for the people who live on them. You have to be careful where you step. I saw on these sidewalks a man getting a haircut and shave, shoes being repaired, sandals being made, laundry being done, piles of cheap jeans being sold, midday naps being taken, and, most popularly, aromatic foods being cooked and served to long lines of eager customers.

With all this going on, walking along a sidewalk in central Bombay is next to impossible, so people naturally migrate to the streets, with a predictable effect on vehicle traffic.

What I learned during my brief stay was that much of the social calamity that is Bombay has little to do with its people. After all, they came here from the hinterlands in search of a better life and are, to a most surprising extent, industrious and law-abiding. The whole place bustles with the energy of people eager—even desperate—to make an honest buck but struggling against the nearly insurmountable barriers of religious and caste discrimination, government's strangulating hand with its attendant corruption, and intense poverty.

I came away from Bombay glad that I had visited the place. I would go again, making sure to walk the streets for hours. I would also spend a month or so touring the rest of the country. But in the end, if India were a stock, I would not buy it. Its government has a stranglehold on life owing to its socialist heritage and is not likely to let go. The absurd caste system, about which nobody wants to talk except to act as if it doesn't really exist, only makes everything worse. I'd buy China or Singapore instead.

SEVENTEEN

Palace Hotels and Uppity Sheiks,
or My Time in the United Arab Emirates

For a vessel to travel from Bombay to Dubai, it must pass through that sector of the Western Indian Ocean called the Arabian Sea, then along the coasts of Pakistan and Iran, through the Gulf of Oman and the Strait of Hormuz, and into the Persian Gulf. For *Indigo*, it would be a voyage of six days, longer than it might have been thanks to high winds and heavy seas.

All was well aboard *Indigo* as she departed from Bombay. Grime from the city's fetid air had been washed away, and she glistened in the morning sun. The crew went about their duties with a noticeably jaunty step, and there was an air of eager anticipation at the prospect both of leaving Bombay and arriving in Dubai.

As we entered the Gulf of Oman, a prelude to transiting the Strait of Hormuz, a British Royal Navy destroyer passed us going in the opposite direction. Captain Lucas got on the radio and inquired about pirate activity in the area. He was assured by the officer on watch that while there had been a considerable number of pirate attacks in the nearby Gulf of Aden, a fact we and the rest of the world knew only too well, there had been none in the Gulf of Oman, the Strait of Hormuz, or the Persian Gulf.

The officer said, however, that from sundown and on into the night, we would see many small outboard-powered boats running back and forth across the Straits. These were smugglers operating with the tacit approval of the Omani government, delivering contraband into Iran in defiance of the West's embargo.

He also gave us the phone number in Dubai of the Coalition Task Force patrolling the Gulf of Aden to combat piracy there. He said that we should call them to arrange a sailing date and routing through a so-called secure corridor in the pirate-infested waters. The Coalition was composed of twenty ships from various blue-water navies of the world patrolling the Gulf, though unfortunately not under a unified command.

The officer went on to say that should we come under pirate attack, we should call the Coalition office or any nearby Coalition warship, and they would scramble the nearest "assets"—meaning armed helicopters—to chase off the pirates. I would have preferred that instead of "chase off" he had said "sink," but we would be glad to take whatever help we could get.

We passed through the Strait of Hormuz without result and, as the British officer had said we would, saw lots of small boats traveling at high speed between Oman and Iran delivering smuggled goods—for a handsome profit, no doubt.

Next day, as we were cruising along in the Persian Gulf making for Dubai, a US Navy amphibious assault ship, the *USS Boxer*, came blowing by us doing about thirty knots to our nine. The *Boxer* was designated the flagship of Combined Task Force 151 patrolling the Gulf of Aden against pirate attacks. As it zipped past, I instructed Captain Lucas to raise the large American flag we keep at the ready for gala ceremonial events. No sooner had he got it up the mast than the *Boxer* gave us three impressive blasts on its horn, and its crew began waving cheerfully. When a vessel transits the Persian Gulf, surrounded as it is with troublesome countries, it's reassuring to know that powerful friends are nearby.

Dubai, United Arab Emirates

In 1965, the emirate of Dubai was a sleepy sandbox of a place. That year, RAF pilot Lt. Terry Michaels flew a mission there requiring him to land at its airport, a single sand strip hardened by oil sprayed over its surface. Following protocol, he made a low pass over the strip to be sure no camels or goats had wandered onto it, then landed.

What he encountered was empty, blistering desert and a small town along an estuary called Dubai Creek, from which pearling, fishing, and trading had long been conducted. There were no buildings over two floors, and few paved roads. Most inhabitants, including the sheik, preferred spending their time in tents far out in the desert, herding camels and goats just as their forebears had done.

Nothing Terry Michaels saw when he climbed out of his plane could have foretold the Dubai of today. The year after he landed, oil was discovered, and everything changed.

My impression of the place, based on spending several weeks wandering about in the desert; in hotels, malls, and nightclubs; and talking with expats and locals, is that Dubai is not so much a city as it is perhaps the world's most grandiose real estate development project.

At the time of my visit, Dubai had what was claimed to be the world's tallest building, the Burj Dubai (now named the Burj Khalifa). Adjacent to that is what until recently was the world's largest shopping mall, the Dubai Mall. It has since been exceeded by the Mall of the Emirates, which boasts 1,000 shops, parking for 10,000 vehicles, and Ski Dubai, the world's largest indoor snow park, containing 6,000 tons of manufactured snow and five runs, of which the longest is a quarter of a mile.

Not far from the mall is the Burj Al Arab, a hotel a thousand-plus feet high with a sail-like structure, perched upon its own man-made island. The Palms, a collection of islands dredged and filled and arranged into the shape of a palm tree, is one of the largest man-made developments in the world.

Work was well along on 300 man-made islands, each in the shape of a country and arranged in the shape of a world map. Since then, development of this project has stalled. At that time, a person could buy his or her own "country" in the World at prices that ranged from $10 million to $45 million. The project will require 426 million cubic yards of sand and a seventeen-mile-long breakwater. At more than twice the size of Disney World, Dubailand, when completed in 2020, will be the world's largest entertainment attraction. There is also the world's largest retail store under one roof. And on, and on it goes.

Dubai, as these projects attest, is a land of superlatives. Everywhere you look, there are new buildings. Condominiums, hotels, offices, and retail stores have sprung up from the desert, many arrestingly modern in both their exterior and interior design and impressive in their scale. Set against the cloudless, radiant sky of the Arabian Peninsula, they mark Dubai as the business, shopping, and entertainment center of the Middle East, the sprawling, random, visually incoherent Los Angeles of Arabia.

Set as it is upon a wide, flat desert and strung out along the Persian Gulf, you would have thought that site planning a new city for Dubai would not have been all that taxing. Apart from Dubai Creek, there are no tortuous waterways flowing through it or mountains around which it must wind. A simple grid pattern would have done nicely.

But Dubai is as orderly in its arrangement as a plate of spaghetti. Roads twist and turn and meander, local streets and expressways collide and crisscross, and all are laden with hopeless snarls of dense traffic. Anyone foolish enough to suppose that brilliant engineering and planning could forestall the traffic jams common to large cities everywhere would be disheartened when driving around Dubai. The place is a transportation mess.

Adding to its list of "world's biggest" claims, at the time of my visit, Dubai had every appearance of the world's biggest real estate disaster. What most struck the eye was the vast number of partially completed buildings and abandoned foundations that stretched out across the desert and lined the handsome new roadways. One-third of the world's supply of tower cranes were in Dubai, and virtually all of them stood idle, hundreds of them perched atop derelict structures

194

reaching out to the horizon like tombstones in a vast cemetery. Malls were nearly empty, shops were boarded up, restaurants were shuttered, hotels were vacant, laborers and office workers alike had departed for home.

Growth has resumed since then, and Dubai is slowly but surely making a comeback.

The sheik of Dubai, when before the economic crash he gazed at himself in the mirror, must have imagined that his was a particularly handsome visage, one so becoming that it should be shared with others. And so the major roadways of the emirate are dotted with quite large, illuminated images of that face, the better to remind passersby of his eminence. It is a vision, however, from which the average viewer is likely to recoil. Aquiline nose, tight-lipped smirk, jawline accented by a thin strip of black beard in the style fashionable among sheiks, eyes like oysters that have been dead for some time. The hyena whose meal has just been snatched away has a friendlier demeanor.

Antisocial behavior seems to be contagious in Dubai. When staying a few nights at the magnificent Raffles Hotel, it was my habit to visit the lobby bar at the hour when civilized men take the first of their evening's refreshment. There, gathered in groups of four and sporting the unimaginative dress of the Arab sheik, were coveys of Arab sheiks, all Saudis. At their tables were piled heaps of dates and chocolates which, from their girth, I concluded comprised much of their diet. None drank alcohol. Just why four grown men would gather in a bar at happy hour and sip fruit juice, I can't say. To the Western mind, it would be much the same as attending a wild party in the company of your mother. Surely the practice contravenes some fundamental Law of Nature.

Each night as I walked past them, and despite their contemptuous glares, I turned on the easy Southern charm for which I am known around the world and offered an affable "Good evening, gentlemen," giving them the benefit of considerable doubt on this last matter. Not one of the supercilious twits had the courtesy even to acknowledge me. They just continued to glare, then turned away in barely concealed disgust—a Saudi sheik disdaining an infidel. When I approached one with a harmless question, as a Western tourist customarily would do, he waved me away imperiously as though I were a guttersnipe. It was for such people that the expression "arrogant asshole" was coined.

It is a helpful—and so far as I could tell largely accurate—rule of thumb that the civility of an Arab is inversely proportionate to the wealth of the country from which he hails. By this measure, Omanis are sunny and genial while Saudis are disdainful and arrogant.

I managed to wander about a few of the shopping malls in Dubai and, as I said, spent a few nights at the Raffles. I spent a few more at the hippest new lodging, the Address Hotel, located across a man-made lake from the towering Burj Khalifa. At appointed hours each evening, a show of dazzling flickers and beams of multihued lights and dancing geysers of water, choreographed to booming strains of some musical refrain or another, burst from the lake to assault the senses of innocent bystanders. One of these unfortunate displays—said to be the world's largest, of course—erupted quite without warning as I was seated in idle comfort at the poolside bar of the Address Hotel, taking in the night air and admiring the latest feminine swimwear. For a fleeting moment, I thought I had mistakenly wandered into an E-Ride in the kiddy section of Disney World, until a particularly fetching bit of swimwear walked by and brought me to my senses.

Wafi Mall, attached to Raffles, is said to be Dubai's, if not the world's, most luxurious mall. Bearing up this assessment, *Indigo's* stewardess, Darla, wandered into a clothing store there, one of whose offerings was a pair of denim jeans priced at $2,000. The salesperson said she could be assured that this pair of jeans was one of a kind. Senseless extravagance of this sort was, until the financial calamity, common in Dubai.

On one particularly hot and thus ill-chosen day, I ventured into remote desert, where I raced up and down the dunes on an ATV, recalling the beach buggies of my youth on the dunes of Pensacola Beach. I then boarded a Toyota four-wheel-drive SUV for an hour of what is known as "dune bashing," which means more racing about over dunes, but in air-conditioned comfort. This was followed by a visit to a tourist-friendly rendition of a desert Bedouin encampment.

Though offered the chance to ride a camel, and ever prone to making improvident choices, I nevertheless declined the chance to make another. Instead, I elected to sit on a rug in the sand and watch a belly dancer perform. In the stodgy Emirates, this is about as close as it's possible to get to a strip show, and though not exactly robust entertainment, it was a considerable improvement over camel riding.

Dubai is now, and likely will remain, the place in which I paid the highest price I have ever paid for a simple lunch. Wishing to take in the mildly garish interior spaces of the iconic Burj Al Arab Hotel and wanting also to see the Palm Islands developments from above, I booked a table at its restaurant on the top floor. For a modest plate of lamb something-or-other, cheese and crackers, and two glasses of ordinary white wine, the tab was $300. As for the interior spaces, their essence is captured nicely in a single statistic: among much else, they incorporate 86,111 square feet of 22-karat gold leaf. No more need be said.

Abu Dhabi, United Arab Emirates

A hundred miles from Dubai down a magnificent four-lane, divided, lushly landscaped, illuminated, and ornately fenced highway is Abu Dhabi, capital of the United Arab Emirates. If Dubai is to the United Arab Emirates as Los Angeles is to the US, then Abu Dhabi is New York—or more precisely Manhattan, the region's cultural and intellectual center. There are plenty of tall buildings, hotels, and a few malls, but the arrangement of these is more deftly done than in Dubai, more artful, and its general aspect is more pleasing to the Western eye.

In choosing a land over which you and your (male) descendants will be the ruling sheik, it is essential to select an area under which there is a great pool of oil and over which there are few people with whom you are obliged to share it. The antecedents of the current sheik of Abu Dhabi were extraordinarily lucky at getting it right on both counts. Of all the oil underlying the United Arab Emirates, which together have the world's sixth largest reserves, 93 percent is in Abu

Dhabi. An ocean of black gold underlies its vast desert, making it the Fort Knox of the United Arab Emirates. Abu Dhabi accounts for about two-thirds of the roughly $400 billion UAE economy. Of course, the distribution of the wealth is anything but equal. Genetic proximity to the ruling sheik matters most.

In America, the fenced enclave of luxury that we know as a gated community is now commonplace. In Abu Dhabi, there are single homesites the size of one of these entire communities, and these, too, are commonplace. Driving along a leafy boulevard, I passed one measuring a half mile along the roadway and the same in depth—about 160 acres. It was surrounded, as are all residences in this part of the world, by enclosing masonry walls, a tradition left over from the days when nomadic Bedu erected rustic wind fences around their encampments. These walls, though, are anything but rustic, measuring about twenty feet high and elaborately ornamented. At the main entry, as with the gated communities of America, are small platoons of armed sentries standing behind locked gates.

The property I'm referring to is owned by one of the many brothers—fifteen or so—of the current sheik of Abu Dhabi, all themselves sheiks. Inside are four identical homes of about the size—and from what I could see, of about the same architectural style and elegance—of a middling 1970s US airport terminal, maybe 50,000 square feet, each the home of one of the sheik's four wives. In managing more than one wife, the one essential rule is that each must have bestowed upon her a scrupulously equal degree of splendor. Show one even the tiniest of favoritism, and even Allah cannot save you from the hell to follow. More modern—and it must be said wiser—men make do with one wife, if that.

Other signs of the sheik's great wealth abound. The Sheikh Zayed Grand Mosque, completed in 2006, rises from a nearly vacant desert, blotting out the horizon. Three monumental domes of white sandstone are the eye-catching centerpiece of this house of worship, said to accommodate within its interior and courtyard spaces up to 40,000 supplicants.

Ostentation is the unifying theme. The mosque houses the world's largest (see what I mean?) single piece of carpet—handwoven, of course—and the world's largest (and again) crystal chandelier—by Swarovski, with whose work the sheiks of United Arab Emirates seem particularly enamored.

This is one of the few Middle Eastern mosques that permits non-Muslims to tour during restricted hours, so I took advantage of this opportunity. Visitors are required to dress conservatively: a long-sleeved shirt and long trousers for men, and complete covering from head to ankles for women. Traditional black robes, called abayas, are loaned at the door. Shoes are removed before entering.

The mosque's interior, as you might guess, is both monumental and sumptuous. The experience of standing on the world's largest carpet beneath the world's largest chandelier under the largest of the three domes was something like I imagine it must have felt to stand in the gargantuan hangar that housed the Space Shuttle just prior to launch.

It is an impressive structure on a colossal scale, and an engineering marvel. But it's devoid of the warm glow of spiritual embrace that you would expect from a place of worship.

Then there is the Emirates Palace Hotel. Of all the hotels I've ever stayed in, this is by far the most opulent. Built and owned by the Abu Dhabi government (read "the sheik thereof") as a residence for visiting dignitaries, it has the feel more of a palace than of a hotel. During my stay, it was about 10 percent occupied, yet not a single service had been cut back. There were far more staff than guests. It is apparently not an investment from which profit is expected.

The hotel's 302 rooms and 92 suites sit on 250 of the choicest and most elegantly manicured acres in the entire Middle East. Each of the rulers of the Gulf countries has his own private suite on the top floor, and enters the grounds through a monumental archway only slightly less grand than the Arc de Triomphe in Paris. The hotel features its own superyacht marina, along with every other amenity that can be imagined.

Pure, soft white sand was hauled in from Algeria to build a perfect beach, from which footprints are swept daily. Its two house cars are new Rolls-Royces. In one of its shops, you can buy handmade hunting rifles at $500,000 and up and custom knives starting at $50,000. The walk from my room in the east wing to the spa in the west was six-tenths of a mile across wide expanses of glittering marble interrupted here and there with enormous columns topped with capitals trimmed in gold leaf. Where lightbulbs would be expected, Swarovski chandeliers hang. With it all, the place comes close to—but never crosses—the line between tasteful splendor and philistine flash.

Sudden wealth, alas, does not bring with it the refinement of taste the West has been honing now for many centuries. Homes throughout the United Arab Emirates, no matter how grand their scale, are for the most part merely unattractive, and more than a few are obnoxious blights. Without exception, they are built of cement block covered in stucco, have a flat roof, and are enclosed by the ever-present wall. Though mostly painted an inoffensive white or beige, a few reflect their owners' unfortunate venture into the world of color. In all my wandering around the United Arab Emirates, I never once saw a home I would wish to call my own, especially not one owned by a prominent sheik.

In the summer months, the United Arab Emirates is humid along the coast, arid inland, and searing in both. I was there in July, when daily temperatures routinely hit 120 degrees, rising often to 130 and more, dropping at night to the high 90s and low 100s. It's a pizza oven without the aromas. Water temps in the Persian Gulf hover at around 95 degrees, too warm for a pleasant swim.

It is the months of October to April that bring tourists to the shores of Dubai and Abu Dhabi. Temperatures then decline from blistering to balmy, and the humidity becomes bearable. In the desert, nights grow cool enough to require a sweater.

Still, despite the better weather during those months, I would not choose to return to Dubai nor to Abu Dhabi. They are for the tourist seeking warm, sunny beaches too much like Miami or Fort Lauderdale.

To me, they are big, glitzy, traffic-choked places without an offsetting appeal. Brazil and Thailand remain my favorites, in part because both offer a simple, nearly rustic, way of life; warm, gracious people; and exceptional local food and entertainment. Neither has condescending sheiks nor the annoying strictures of Islam.

EIGHTEEN

New Friends in Oman

With Dubai in our rearview mirror, we traveled the Persian Gulf along the north side of the Musandam Peninsula, transited through the Strait of Hormuz, and made our way to the ancient city of Muscat, Oman. What was meant to be a brief stop for supplies and fuel would turn into a month-long visit and one of the most memorable of the entire voyage.

A Son's Treachery

In 1970, Oman was a weak, poor, backward country ruled ineptly by a feudal tyrant, Sultan Al Sayyid Said bin Taimur. Within an area equal to that of New Mexico, there were just eight miles of paved roads, one hospital, and one school. Its literacy rate was 5 percent. Tribes in the interior were in open rebellion fueled by ancient rivalries and by avarice arising from the expectation that oil would soon be discovered. In the southern region of Dhofar along the border with Yemen, a Communist-inspired insurgency had gained a foothold and was advancing.

In that year, the sultan's only son, Qaboos bin Said, arising from the torpor of his virtual house arrest in the palace at Salalah, overthrew his father in a coup with the aid of the sultan's own personal guard and a detachment of British troops, and banished him into exile. The deposed sultan was only the latest victim in a long, bloody tradition of betrayal and treachery among the Arab tribes, commonly orchestrated by close family members. "Father knows best" is a sentiment that evidently doesn't enjoy popular acceptance in the Arab world.[1]

The Sultanate

The new sultan, who was educated at England's Royal Military Academy, Sandhurst, among other institutions of higher learning, promptly began what must surely be one of the world's most dramatic transformations of a country. Today Oman is an absolute monarchy, a police state over which the sultan has tightfisted control. He has appointed himself head of the ministries of state, defense, and finance, and is deeply involved in the affairs of these and in much else. In other words, nothing of consequence happens in Oman without the sultan's approval.

But to the good fortune of its people, Sultan Qaboos bin Said has turned out to be a wise—though by no means a selfless—ruler, a despot of mostly benevolent instincts, who, using a growing stream of oil and tax revenues, has turned the country into a modern state. Its several thousands of miles of highways and roads, its bridges, ports, electric transmission, and generating and water-producing facilities are as modern and well-maintained as any in the US, many better. There are modern schools and universities teaching eager young Omanis the finer points of engineering, technology, medicine, and commerce.

The sultan is said by the locals to arrogate to himself something like 10 percent of the country's revenue for his own entertainment, but this estimate comes from people who are handsomely paid for their loyalty. Other—and I believe more accurate—estimates suggest an amount closer to 50 percent goes into his piggy bank. With half, or even a meager 10 percent, of about $20 billion a year, you can have a lot of fun.

1. I use the term "Arab" in its narrowest sense as one who is a native of the Arabian Peninsula and speaks Arabic.

In addition to ten enormous palaces scattered about the country, each approached along miles of lavishly manicured, tastefully illuminated and flagpole-lined boulevards, he has an unknown number of villas here and there in other parts of the world. The *Al Said*, his largest yacht in a fleet of about thirty vessels, measures 324 feet. He keeps it docked in the ancient town of Muttrah, a few miles down the road from the marina where *Indigo* was berthed, fully staffed should he wish to travel on short notice.

Sharing runways and flight control apparatus with the proletariat's international airport, there is an entire separate airport, complete with verdant landscaping and handsome design, called, of course, the Royal Airport. Its hangars are filled with his numerous private planes, also fully staffed and ready to go. The Royal Air Force is always available to escort him, should he feel the need.

As one who enjoys classical music, he assembled the Oman Symphony Orchestra from scratch, staffed only with Omani musicians who, until they were recruited, had never played a note. When he travels, they accompany him to provide private and ceremonial entertainment. Evidently the sultan's tastes have not risen to sufficient heights of refinement for him to appreciate the dulcet tones of American country music, but it's still early in the country's march toward a more advanced civilization.

While I was there, the Royal Opera House was under construction in the diplomatic area of Muscat. I was sure that upon its completion it would be among the world's most magnificent, and a superb venue in which the sultan could enjoy another of the fine arts in which he is keenly interested. Being sensible people, though, Omanis, upon hearing their first operatic performance, will likely want the building converted to other, more pleasurable pursuits. Rock concerts, monster truck events, demolition derbies, professional wrestling matches, and Grand Ole Opry shows are just a few of the many possibilities. As I said, though, Oman has a way to go up the civilization ladder before they may find higher levels of entertainment appealing.

Not a single commercial or government building is built in Oman without the sultan's personal approval, though from what I've seen of many of these, he ought not to make too big a point of this. The story is told of one five-star hotel that was built with his approval but painted a color he disliked. He ordered it repainted a more appealing (to him) hue, and it was. He dislikes the sound of beeping car horns so common elsewhere in the Middle East, so all over Muscat are signs forbidding horn tooting. Ports, highways, neighborhoods, airports, libraries, mosques, schools, universities, and much more have been thoughtfully named by the sultan for himself, confirming to his countrymen what a really swell guy he is.

If in your next life you are offered your choice from a list of vocations, I heartily recommend that of Sultan of Oman. Easy job; good pay; lots of palaces and other perks; your own army, navy, and air force; great boats and planes; and about all the power you could want. Everybody laughs at your jokes, and you own the internal revenue service into whose collections you can dip whenever you like.

But as the sultan's father experienced—and the experiences of most other Arab sheiks, emirs, kings, and assorted potentates attest—watch your back, particularly at family gatherings.

The People of Oman
Unlike Dubai and Abu Dhabi, Oman has striven to preserve its unique culture, at least to the extent that's possible in the face of galloping modernity. It has few glittering towers and no claims to have the world's largest this or that. Omani people, unlike many other Arabs, are a warm, genial, easily smiling lot with a reluctant tolerance for Western ways. As a rule, they don't drink alcohol, but they don't really mind if you do so long as you confine it to your hotel or a few licensed restaurants and bars, and you don't make a fool of yourself. Drunk driving will land you in jail for at least two days for a first offense, provided it's minor, longer if there are aggravating circumstances. In Muscat, there are a few nightclubs of a tame sort, nothing like the wide-open Dubai scene. Local friends told me that when traveling with your wife in the more puritanical interior, you had best have

your marriage license along if you plan on staying in the same hotel room.

As with most Arabs, Omanis tend toward prudishness in the matter of dress, asking that men and women cover themselves decently in public. I found it odd that in a hot—and along the coast, humid—climate, men don't wear shorts or even short-sleeved shirts. Instead, they wear the long white traditional Arab robe, called a dishdasha, topped off with a peculiar, richly embroidered brimless pillbox hat borrowed from Africa during the time when Zanzibar was an Oman colony or, on occasion, a turban with one or another color and pattern. Indeed, these constitute the official uniform for all government service, except the police and military. For footwear, open-toed sandals are all but universal. At ceremonial events, Omani men wear a decorative belt into which they insert the iconic curve-bladed dagger called a khanjar.

Omani men tend to be more stylish than other Arabs. While they are most frequently seen wearing white robes, they also wear robes in muted shades of yellow, red, gray, and brown, all solids, often trimmed with piping of contrasting color. And there is no end to the color and pattern of those pillbox hats. Young men seem to prefer robes in bold but generally colorless plaids.

Women in public nearly always cover themselves from the crown of their head to the bottom of their ankles in black—and thus needlessly uncomfortable—abayas. Many single women choose to cover their entire face with a black scarf, leaving only an eye slit showing, while married women may reveal their face. The black abaya is required dress inside a mosque, but otherwise its color, style, and even whether to wear it at all is a matter of choice.

Twenty or so years ago, and in the more conservative inland areas still today, all Omani women wore brightly colored and intricately patterned abayas. But then, perhaps following the lead of Manhattan styles, the women of Muscat and other coastal regions all turned to black. It was a change in fashion made entirely by choice, not by the dictate of Islam or by the command of their husbands.

While wandering through the shopping malls and souks of Oman and the United Arab Emirates, I always wondered how there could be so many shops selling ladies' clothing, shoes, and makeup when there were no women to be seen wearing the stuff. Only later did Omani friends reveal the (hidden) truth, especially when they complained of their wives' expensive tastes. When Omani women meet at special social occasions involving family and friends, the abaya is not to be found. Instead they are outfitted in stylish, bejeweled dresses along with expensive shoes and matching bags that would be the envy of any American woman. These are also often worn underneath the abaya and thus seen only by the woman and her husband.

The preference for a black abaya when combined with Islamic/Arab prudery makes for an interesting scene around the resort swimming pool. There you can see expats or tourists in bikinis swimming along-side Omanis fully draped in black abayas used in lieu of swimsuits.

Muscat, Oman

The ancient port city of Muscat is the capital of Oman as well as its largest city. The city itself isn't all that interesting, but a mile from the marina where *Indigo* was docked is a particularly notable hotel, one with a deserved place in the book *1,000 Places to See Before You Die*. The Al Bustan Palace Hotel, as it is known, had been recently reopened after being closed two years for major renovations.

In the hotel's piano bar, I came to know Mr. Rao, the bar's long-time manager. As an irrepressible raconteur and master networker, he introduced me to two gentlemen of upper Omani society: Zahran Al Rugeishi and Fahmi Al-Harthi, from whom I learned much about Oman and its people.

Zahran had angular facial features, prominent Arab nose, and swarthy complexion. He always wore the traditional dishdasha robe in summer white with gold trim and sandals. He was an articulate, highly intelligent man with a serious but friendly demeanor. Like half of all working Omanis, he was employed by one of the federal minis-tries, though just which he would never say. He has traveled widely and along the way mastered several languages including Spanish, Italian, and English.

One day after we had become casually acquainted, he paid me the considerable honor of inviting me to his home for a traditional Omani breakfast, to be followed by a guided tour of his modest village, called Izki, the historically important town of Nizwa, and some other nearby attractions.

Rare is the man who requires wine with his breakfast, so for this reason alone, when dining with the abstemious Muslims, the morning meal is strongly to be preferred. We sat on the floor in the men's sitting room of Zahran's and his wife Aziza's handsome home with a traditional Arab morning meal spread before us. There was a soupy yellow lentil dish; stacks of freshly baked Arabian bread of a sort that when folded properly serves both as a pusher and as a spoon; piles of various dates and fruits; another style of bread, this one more doughy and eaten with honey poured over it; and a dish of a classic sweet, fudge-like dessert called halvah made from dates, brown sugar, cardamom, and other ingredients.

All of this is eaten using only the fingers, thus presenting a challenge to the Western diner whose mother spent years demanding that he keep his hands either in his lap or grasped around a utensil. No Arab meal is possible without coffee, the ever-present elixir of welcome. They drink it from demitasse cups and mix it with cardamom, which gives it a sweet but pleasant, somewhat exotic flavor, although it's not nearly as strong as I had thought it might be.

I met Zahran's father, a distinguished man with a neat gray beard. He was dressed in a white robe, carried the traditional camel stick, and wore around his waist an artfully made silver belt into which was inserted a very old and intricately decorated Khanjar, the silver Omani curve-bladed dagger, a necessary possession for any adult male. Zahran's three handsome sons, ages ranging from five to eight, added a note of liveliness to our breakfast.

Electricity, which only recently reached the village, is expensive and so is used sparingly. Though the new house has a few air-conditioning units of the wall-banger variety, as do most of the finer homes, they are used only at night in the bedrooms to facilitate sleep. Prior to this, it was common for families to sleep in the open on the roof in the summer.

During our breakfast, the air conditioners were not running, windows remained closed, and no fans were in use, with the predictable and uncomfortable result that the temperature was in the neighborhood of 85 degrees and the air still. For Omanis, this is quite normal; for me it was nearly stifling.

~~~

Another gentleman I was introduced to in Muscat was Fahmi Al-Harthi, editor-in-chief of several slick tourist magazines and of the English-language daily newspaper the *Oman Observer*. He is also the chief of all propaganda for Oman and a confidant of the sultan. On the night we met, he was at the Al Bustan Palace Hotel, having just collected a high honor for his professional achievements, a memorial of which he carried proudly. His appearance and manner are that of a kindly university professor, something he should know about, having spent what sounded like a fun-filled seven years as a student obtaining a degree in political science from a Cairo university. We hit it off right away and quickly became good friends in that fortuitous way that happens when you travel.

He was reluctant to talk about his own convictions, but it's clear that Fahmi is a pious man, though not one to proselytize. He adheres to Oman's prevailing faith, the Ibadi sect of Sunni Islam found only in Oman and parts of North Africa. Its most distinguishing feature, for the Westerner, is its tolerance of other beliefs. There are in Muscat places of worship to accommodate Protestant, Roman Catholic, Hindu, and even Shiite Muslim and other religions—though not, as you might guess, Judaism.

Omanis, in contrast to many other Arabs, are also more tolerant—or maybe I should instead say less intolerant—of what they perceive to be our Western corruptions such as drinking to excess, engaging gleefully in licentiousness, and wearing clothing that fails fully to envelop the body. "Sanctimonious" is not a word that would occur to you in describing most Omanis, though it accurately describes many other Arabs.

At several dinners on *Indigo*, Fahmi and I explored our differences, his hopes and fears for Oman, his sense of its future, his family and tribe, and much more. I found him to be a thoughtful man whose opinions are carefully formed and artfully expressed.

Of all that I learned from Fahmi, I would have to say the most important was his notion that the seemingly stark differences that separate much of the Arab world today from the West, and that separate its own constituent sects from each other, are merely transitional. It is clear to him that in the span of just one or perhaps two generations, most of these differences will either disappear altogether or become greatly attenuated.

I met Fahmi at his home one morning and we set out on a daylong trip through the region of his youth, with him serving as my personal guide. We stopped first at the tiny village outside of Rustaq, where he spent much of his childhood. There we met his aunt and a few cousins of the Al-Harthi tribe. The aunt, a grizzled lady of about eighty years, was seated on the floor in the entry hall of her modest home, sorting through a bundle of freshly picked dates. Outside and inside temperatures were hardly different, the former about 110, the latter 95. Wisely, she sat in front of a fan turned to its highest speed.

Just behind her home were the remains of her and her husband's former residence, built in the ancient manner using sun-dried mud to cement and encase stones. Its rooms were tiny, no larger than a modern walk-in closet, the ceilings high to dissipate the heat. Fahmi said the home was more than 400 years old and had been in his family all that time.

Close by was a grove of date palms watered in the traditional manner by an open sluiceway fed from a well. The design and building of these sluiceways is done exclusively by a single tribe using exactly the same techniques that have been employed for a thousand years. Though revered by Omanis as an important link with their ancient culture, the design is badly flawed as the water, a scarce and costly resource in the desert climate, is exposed to considerable evaporation. Modern pipes would be far preferable.

In all of my visits to small villages, what struck me most was the absence of people walking about. It was just too hot in the summer. The small groupings of modest homes, with the inevitable mosque and a few commercial establishments only a few steps up the ladder from the lemonade stand, were not so much sleepy as comatose. On Fridays, however, men—and only men—could be seen in traditional dress walking along the streets to the mosque, a veritable riot of activity by contrast.

Fahmi and I also visited a natural spring boiling up inexplicably from the base of a dry desert mountain on which there was not a sprig of green growing anywhere. It is a centuries-old oasis that once supported the surrounding villages and has now been made into a public park surrounded by groves of date palms. On the day of our visit, it was crowded with families, their shrieking kids frolicking in the cool stream.

Oases of this sort are found throughout the Arabian Peninsula, and at each is a village often dating back to the birth of Christ. Oases were the functional equivalent of today's gas stations, and knowledge of their locations was crucial to survival, especially for the nomadic Bedu. Some of these oases can be found in the midst of many square miles of arid, sand-blown deserts, while others are in and around the valleys and deep gorges of the mountains. Why water should come bubbling up at these odd places from far below the most inhospitable of terrains, I cannot begin to say.

Nizwa, Oman

I reconnected with Zahran Al Rugeishi and we drove into the newly restored historic town of Nizwa, once the center of open rebellion by the area's tribes against the present sultan's father. Zahran's uncle served as governor of the province during those times, and his family was accordingly deeply involved in the effort to overthrow the sultanate and install an Islamic form of government. The rebellion was put down with the assistance of the always-shrewd British, whose RAF dropped a few smallish bombs on some nearby villages just to focus the minds of their recalcitrant citizens.

Now, he says, all is forgiven. The sultan is doing a good job of bringing a better life to the Omani people (for which read "sharing the oil loot") and for this, he and his tribe, the Al Rugeishis, are grateful. Never mind that the sultan has lots of guns and the people none.

Any doubts that Oman was once rived by tribal anarchy are put to rest by the briefest of travels around the country. There is no town, village, or dusty corner that doesn't have its fort and accompanying watchtowers from which tribes keep an eye out for the raiders from other tribes intent on stealing their camels or goats or settling a festering blood feud.

Indeed, these forts and redoubts, now tastefully restored, are something of a tourist attraction. I never came upon such forts in all my driving around Oman that I wasn't taken with the thought that I had stumbled upon the film set of an Errol Flynn movie. Surrounded as they invariably are by acres of densely clustered date palms and sited upon strategic high ground, they evoke exotic images like those from the 1939 film *Beau Geste*.

Their architecture with its emblematic crenellations remains the dominant theme of Omani residential and commercial design. When the low wall surrounding the flat roof of your new home features a series of battlements from which rifles can be fired at attackers, and all the homes in all of the other neighborhoods are similarly equipped, it says much about your forebears.

After touring the important fort at Nizwa, we traveled to the top of nearby Al Jabal Al Akhdar, using all the gears in my rented four-wheel-drive SUV, eventually reaching an elevation of nearly 8,000 feet. There, in cooling breezes, we could look out over the sun-drenched, desiccated valleys and scattered villages far below.

NINETEEN

The Back Roads of Oman and Abu Dhabi

A modern map depicting each of the seven United Arab Emirates, as well as Oman, is an inexplicable jumble of enclaves, exclaves, and twisted boundaries. Bits and pieces of these two countries are separated from the rest, lying about helter-skelter for no apparent reason. Not even the most grotesque of America's gerrymandered congressional districts is as confusing. You can drive north up the coast of the Gulf of Oman from Muscat to a point near the tip of the Arabian Peninsula, where you pass into a detached bit of the emirate of Sharjah. Just thirty or so miles farther along, you come to another unhitched piece, this one from the emirate of Fujairah. Continuing along, you reach another severed chunk of Sharjah adjacent to a postage stamp exclave of Oman, then some more of Sharjah, Fujairah, and another tiny piece of Sharjah.

Finally, you reach the spectacular mountains of the Musandam Peninsula, mostly but not entirely under the sovereignty of Oman. If you were to set off across this peninsula, you would encounter stand-alone pieces of the emirates of Ajman, Ras Al Khaimah, and Umm Al Qaiwain. What, you may ask, as I did, is the source of this bafflement?

It is the result of a devil's brew that includes a long and bloody history of tribal feuds and shifting allegiances, avarice from the prospect of oil revenues, and the skillful skullduggery of the British

Foreign Office and Western oil companies. In just one among many examples, a long and bitter war between Dubai and Abu Dhabi over oil-rich domains was not concluded until the 1960s. None of the boundaries in the region were firmly established until the early 1970s, and then only with the aid of the British.

No understanding of this part of the world would be complete without reading the incomparable story of Wilfred Thesiger's travels through much of the Arabian Peninsula from 1945 to 1950. In his book *Arabian Sands*, he recounts his journeys by camel and on foot while living among the Bedu.[1] Using them as his guides, he crossed the Empty Quarter, the world's largest sand desert, twice, and roamed through Yemen, Oman, large parts of Saudi Arabia, and what are today the Emirates—all before oil was discovered and the SUV replaced the camel. He witnessed firsthand the startling savagery of desert justice, the rampant thievery, the hatreds, jealousies, and age-old blood feuds of the desert and coastal tribes.

Trouble at the Border
Wishing to see more of a country I had come to like very much, I took an hour-and-a-half flight from Muscat to the southern resort town of Salalah, where I rented a four-wheel-drive SUV and set out to explore the nearby Dhofar Mountains and desert.

After a two-hour drive north, I came to the remote, dusty town of Thumrait, where I stopped for lunch. It was around 110 degrees outside, so I tried to find a restaurant with air conditioning. At first I had no luck. None of them offered anything more than a few fans, yet they were crowded with laborers, mostly Indians and Pakistanis, chomping away—on hot food, no less. Finally, I located the only air-conditioned restaurant in town, though it merely had a single inadequate wall-banger aided feebly by an overhead fan. In such a setting, my hopes for a memorable meal were not high, so I was happily surprised when the proprietor set before me one of the most mouth-pleasing lunches of my Oman visit.

1. More commonly today called Bedouin.

I noted that I was the only diner using utensils. All the others followed the traditional custom of using their fingers to hoist or shovel food into their mouth. To the Westerner, this is likely to bring up memories of fraternity house food fights, though here the diners carefully washed after the meal and returned to gainful employment.

After lunch, I walked next door to a ramshackle bank branch where I converted dollars to Omani rials, then drove westward into the desert over a new paved highway on which mine was almost the only vehicle.

My destination, 120 miles away, was Al Mazyunah, the border outpost for crossing into Yemen. I knew the country was said to be dangerous, most especially for Americans, but my Omani friends had told me that it is one of their favorite places on Earth, a place of quiet beauty and endless charm, and so convinced me to attempt a visit.

Oman's topography is the result, over many millions of years, of ocean flooding, violent upheavals, fractures, erosion, and deposition. As a result, it is today a scenic wonderland, often of unspeakable beauty, though one that is almost entirely lacking in natural vegetation. It's as if you took the mountains and deserts of Arizona and Nevada and stripped from them every bit of topsoil and everything green. What's left is a scabrous, flinty landscape in hues of gray, blue-gray, ochre, pale red, and peach.

It was through this country that I drove, past high mountains, over low hills, down into gorges and gaps scoured by ancient rivers. I passed through a wide and perfectly flat desert plain on which thousands of camels roamed, seeking the rare bit of edible scruff for nutrition. This was, and remains today, a part of the ancient route used by the Bedu tribes as they made their way in summer from the vast inland deserts to the shores near Salalah. Along the way, I spotted black goat-hair tents pitched by modern Bedu in the open desert, flaps closed. At nearly 120 degrees, it was searing outside my vehicle, so just how they could endure such heat inside a dark tent, I can't even venture a guess. In other places, more modern-minded families, apparently descended from the upper reaches of the Bedu intelligence scale, were camped in lighter canvas tents pitched under shade trees with SUVs parked outside.

At the Yemen border, I was aided by a guard who had lived for a time in Miami and spoke passable English. He checked me out of Oman and drove me in his official truck the few miles to the Yemen checkpoint, where he insisted on serving as my interpreter.

Contrasted with the Omanis, the Yemeni border guards were slovenly and ill-tempered. They all had their cheeks stuffed with khat, a mild narcotic made from the bark of a local tree, and sat around in their sweltering offices, most of them squatting on their haunches.

After much animated conversation, the Omani guard said the Yemenis refused to allow me to enter the country because I had no visa, and the man who issued these (read "collects the bribe") would not return until eight p.m. Besides, they said, there was a war going on between separatist elements from South Yemen and the Yemeni government, and another between several warlords. They also said that al-Qaida was actively searching for Western tourists on whom they wished to inflict punishment for being infidels—like me, for instance. Accordingly, they said, it was very dangerous to drive where I wished to go. He said that if I was lucky, the bad guys would stop me, force me out of the vehicle, and steal it, leaving me stranded in the desert. If I was unlucky, they would simply shoot me. When I asked if the Yemeni border guard could at least stamp my passport, he refused and sent me rudely back to Oman.

Disconsolate from missing out on a part of Yemen that had been highly recommended to me and that I had read about in Thesiger's book, I headed back toward Salalah, once again driving across the splendid desert and mountains of Dhofar. Upon reaching the coast, I drove to Wadi Dirbat, an oasis fed by a lethargic stream now turned into a local park. Families were picnicking on its banks, kids splashing in its stagnant pools.

Oman's landscape is characterized by its mountains, gravel plains and deserts, coastal plains, and wadis. This last feature is a well-defined dried riverbed marked by the rock-strewn bed itself, the beds of tributaries that once flowed into it, and a meandering course. There are thousands of them spread all across the country, and their names and locations are well known to Omanis.

On the sporadic and rare occasions when rain falls, these wadis quickly fill and become raging torrents whose containment is a major engineering problem in Oman. Many villages I visited are protected from these cascades by thick concrete revetments or banks of stone riprap. Despite these and other efforts, every year hapless tourists— particularly those with poorly chosen campsites—die from flash floods.

Salalah is noted all across the Arabian Peninsula as the place to be during the summer monsoons. Around late July to early August, climatic conditions and a peculiar geography combine to cause dark, wispy clouds along the coast which, when they encounter the nearby mountain range, result in rain. Nowhere else in the world that I'm aware of is rain an occasion for visiting the beach for the purpose of standing in it and celebrating its arrival, but that is just what happens in Salalah.

As soon as word gets out that the season has begun, brief though it is, the hotels promptly fill with Arabs who have had quite enough of radiant blue sky, relentless searing heat, and abundant sunshine. Marked as it is by strong and persistent winds blowing onshore and by thundering surf, the rainy season is not conducive to swimming or even wading. Most Arabs can't swim anyway, so people just go there almost literally to stand in the rain.

Standing in a downpour, whatever may be its appeal to the locals, did not for me hold much promise. It's the sort of thing that, back in Florida, is just not done much, even on a golf course. So I hopped in my SUV and drove down the coast to the forlorn village of Mirbat, once a thriving center of the frankincense trade, and there stumbled upon a restaurant that I was sure, judging from the number of cars out front, must be one of its better places to dine.

As the menu was in Arabic, and nobody in the place spoke English, I concluded that tourists didn't get down this way often. That suited me just fine. I held up the menu, closed my eyes, and pointed to a dish, which when it arrived turned out to be one of the finer meals I had in Oman. I still don't know what it was, nor do I even know from what animal its contents were derived before landing on my plate, soaking in a stew of unidentifiable (by me) herbs and spices, but it sure was good.

Frankincense trees are found throughout this part of Oman, and their sap is still harvested for processing into perfume. But the aroma is far too powerful and sickly for the Western taste. Thesiger reported in his book that Arabs in the desert, after defecating, clean themselves with sand (now that's hardy!), then use the smoke from burning frankincense to improve their aroma. It's desert Air Wick. For the person who goes many weeks between ablutions, and more importantly for those who find themselves in the company of such a person, I'm sure it has its appeal. But beyond that, I can't recommend the stuff.

Musandam Peninsula, Oman

After returning to Muscat and getting some rest, I traveled by car northwest along the Gulf of Oman coast, passing through various emirates before arriving at the dramatic scenery of the Musandam Peninsula. At the extreme end of this geographic apostrophe is the Strait of Hormuz, across which, just forty miles away, is Iran.

A few miles north of the Musandam town of Dibba, the paved road gives way to a graded gravel surface that winds its way up a wadi into the mountains. A short distance up this road, I came upon a modest sign indicating that I had arrived at my destination, the Six Senses Resort at Zighy Bay, where I would stay two nights.

Only recently completed at the time of my arrival, it is the latest rendition of the current vogue in resort hotels, known generally as eco-resorts—or as I prefer to call them, primitive camps. In exchange for the payment of large sums of money, these places offer you the opportunity to live for a short time pretty much as some specific tribe of indigenous people did about a hundred years ago. At Zighy Bay, this tribe is the mountain Bedu.

My car was parked in a dusty, ramshackle shed of the type in which you would expect to find lawn maintenance equipment—were there any lawns. I and my bag were loaded into an SUV, and I was driven up the steep face of a mountain on narrow, unpaved switchbacks, over the crest, from which there was a magnificent view of the tiny beach below and the Gulf beyond, and then down more switchbacks to the resort nestled in a corner of its eponymous bay.

Anybody who happened to stumble upon this resort would assume that it was a Bedu encampment that had been abandoned long ago, possibly as the result of a bloody tribal battle from which it never recovered, so artfully does its design and the choice of its building materials mimic the primitive motif.

My room, directly on the beach, housed not a single piece of furnishing that did not closely resemble something that had been purchased secondhand from a defunct summer camp for boys. Its plumbing hardware was painted a flat black and felt as though sand had been generously mixed in with the paint. Visual screens, ceilings, and shaded areas were all built of desiccated and unpainted sticks and twigs gathered nearby, just as the Bedu once built these. There was no landscaping save the planted date palms, no hardened pathways for walking around the place, and little in the way of outdoor lighting. Exterior walls were made from chunks of stone which, until they were cemented into place, had been lying about the site. None of the buildings had been painted.

From Zighy Bay, I drove north up the wadi over a poorly graded surface barely wide enough for two cars to pass, enclosed by sheer, parched cliffs. Here and there were the authentic ancient hovels of Bedu goatherds constructed in much the same manner and of the same materials as my resort room, which made me regret that I had not stayed in these and thus saved a lot of money. They were not air-conditioned, however, and water would have had to be fetched from a well.

An hour's drive later, after passing through deep canyons barely wider than the car and over high mountain peaks from which there were stunning panoramas, I came upon an Omani military checkpoint with lowered crossing arm. Here I was told that going farther up the Musandam was not permitted by the military, and taking the alternate route also was not allowed because my Emirates visa didn't reflect the proper stamp.

Despite my pleading, I had to retrace my drive, pass out of Oman into the Emirates, and travel on new highways to my destination: the Bab Al Shams Desert Resort in Dubai.

On the way there, south of Dubai, I passed by a square mile or so of desert which had been divided into many enclosed pens in which camels were bred, raised, and trained solely for the purpose of racing them against one another. The sport in Arabia is no less popular than is horse racing in America, with the additional similarity that millions are paid for the best animals. I also drove past the enormous stables where the sheik of Dubai breeds and trains his racehorses.

The resort is an older established place, something of an institution among the people who know these things, and is a decided improvement over Zighy Bay. Among its amenities is a well-known outdoor theme restaurant where you can sit on the desert floor, eat local foods, watch belly dancers, ride camels, and buy cheesy souvenirs. Though grateful for the opportunity, I passed it up and instead spent my time in the air-conditioned interior.

Al Ayn, Abu Dhabi

The next day, I drove two hours (one more than necessary because I got lost) to the surprisingly agreeable—and in the midst of the desert discordantly verdant—city of Al Ayn in Abu Dhabi. It is the ancestral home of Sheikh Zayed bin Sultan Al Nahyan, former ruler of Abu Dhabi and founder of the United Arab Emirates, who lived there in the family palace until moving in 1965 to more commodious accommodations. Oil money was flowing in, after all.

Calling the old place a palace is an exaggeration. It comprises an area of no more than two acres surrounded by a ten-foot stone wall through which there is but a single entry with a massive gate. His and his family's modest former living quarters are on the second floor, to which the sole access is by way of a narrow staircase, the better to deter potential assassins. This sensible feature is a reflection, and daily reminder, of the violent, untimely end to which sheiks seem particularly susceptible. Of the fourteen previous rulers of Abu Dhabi, only two died peacefully of natural causes while still in power. Eight were murdered and four driven out, all in consequence of rebellions instigated within the family.

Just to remind me of this past, one of the sheik's sixteen sons, brother of the current ruler, was in the news for having severely beaten, whipped, and jabbed repeatedly with an electric cattle prod an unfortunate man whom he accused of misdealing. To be thorough, he also ran over the man with his SUV.

The Al Ain Museum, once I found it amid all the new roads being built, was a worthwhile stop. It traced the cultural history of the Abu Dhabi and Emirati people and some of their dress, beliefs, and practices—though it glossed over their habit of engaging in pointless tribal wars, their talent for treachery, their rampant camel thievery, and their pervasive religious bigotry. Only oil has saved them from a secure place in world history's backwater. I much prefer the people of Oman to these.

TWENTY

Pirates on the High Seas

Throughout this writing, I have attempted to affect a carefree, jocular tone that I hoped would convey to you the tone of life aboard *Indigo* as we disported ourselves among the world's fun spots. In this chapter, you will find the tone lacking the accustomed frivolity as I prepared for what amounted to a potential firefight with thugs bent on armed robbery during our passage through the Gulf of Aden.

The Threat of Pirates and a Nervous Crew

In thinking about the risk of a pirate attack, I had done some homework and learned that in the first quarter of 2009, there were forty-one attacks on vessels transiting the Gulf of Aden. Of these, only five were successful. What I did not know, because I could find no source of reliable data, was how many vessels transited the Gulf during that period.

While I was wandering through the desert, a British naval officer from the Coalition Task Force visited *Indigo* at the marina in Muscat and met with Captain Lucas for nearly two hours to assess the risks. During that meeting, he supplied the missing number, informing the captain that each day on average, 200 vessels pass through the Gulf.

For me, this was a startling bit of information. From sensational press reports, I had formed the speculative notion that the risk of an attack was somewhere north of 25 percent. Now, with the missing essential piece of the calculation in hand, it became clear that the risk was not 25 percent but in the vicinity of .02 percent. Put another way, during the first quarter of 2009, 18,000 vessels passed through the Gulf, and of these, 17,959 did so without seeing a pirate.

Thus when I returned to *Indigo* at the Muscat marina, I was surprised to find that Captain Lucas, Chef Jeanette, and Stewardess Darla had stirred themselves into a frenzy over the fear of wicked pirates. All three resigned effective upon reaching the next port. Even after I carefully explained the now-evidently minuscule risks, they adamantly declined to change their minds. Though I committed to hiring two armed security men experienced in guarding vessels in the Gulf, they still refused. Engineer Sean would have none of it, and Mate Bobby and Deckhand Tomas, after some persuasion, elected to remain aboard.

I was fortunate to find well-qualified replacements, and we welcomed on board our new captain, Steve Hubbard, and our new stewardess, his wife, Gillian. Both have a great deal of experience in all aspects of yachting and are affable professionals. Most importantly, neither of them was spooked at the prospect of traveling through pirate-infested waters. We also welcomed on board our new chef, Camille, a cute young French Canadian who was living in Fort Lauderdale when we called upon her.

Bridge Over Troubled Waters

Captain Steve found, and we hired, two security guys to join us for our upcoming voyage. Both were from South Africa, and both were experienced in escorting vessels through these waters. John Mason, age forty-three at the time, was a former infantry officer in the British army and senior official with a security firm that, until recently, had a considerable presence in Iraq, where he served for a number of years. Lloyd Bernard, age twenty-eight, was a former British

Royal Marine with more vessel security experience than his age suggested.

Together, John and Lloyd conducted a thorough security audit of *Indigo*, examining our CCTV system, radio communications equipment, exterior steel and aluminum structure and its vulnerability to small arms fire, fire suppression systems, and the like. They developed a written security plan for the voyage, acquainted the crew with its features, and drilled them in its finer details.

When *Indigo* had departed from Fort Lauderdale in March 2006, we had on board two AR-15 semiautomatic assault rifles, the civilian version of the standard fully automatic military M-16 in which I was trained during my army service; a twelve-gauge, pump-action shotgun; a Glock 9 mm semiautomatic pistol; and a supply of ammo for all. These I had purchased solely to get us through the Gulf of Aden, and had carried them on board in a hidden cache from the time we left Florida. Now I was glad I had done so. Without these weapons, I'm not sure I would have taken the chance of confronting armed pirates.

John and Lloyd field-stripped and reassembled the weapons and found that they were in perfect working order, which I knew from having done the same thing myself sometime back. They loaded the primary and extra magazines with ammo and stowed these, together with the ceramic-plated body armor jackets I had purchased, in the sky lounge office on the bridge deck, where they also had sleeping pads.

They drilled the crew, teaching them where they should muster when an alarm sounded and where they should go from there—into one of the forward crew cabins—and what they should take with them—the few items they would most desperately desire while sweating away several months in a Somali prison hut. They instructed the crew to lock the cabin door behind them and not to let anybody inside. This cabin was to serve as a last-ditch citadel in the event pirates boarded us and took over.

John and Lloyd also collected all our passports and wallets and hid them away. Of particular concern were mine, Engineer Sean's, and

Mate Bobby's, since the pirates had reportedly declared a vendetta against Americans after three Somali brigands were nicely dispatched by American snipers, an event dramatized in the film Captain Phillips. It was suggested to us that, should it come down to it, we should adopt an accent that would mask our nationality when speaking to pirates.

None of this set well with me. It had within it the suggestion that we would allow pirates to board and take over my vessel. I felt strongly that I needed to establish with the crew, and with the security team, my firm rejection of this apparently defeatist attitude and instead insist on an aggressive approach.

I told them that I would not consent to hiding out in a citadel while my vessel and crew, to say nothing of my beloved self, were under attack by thugs. I insisted that I would be on the bridge when there was any action and that under no circumstances were they to allow any pirates to invade my yacht. I told them that if they had qualms about shooting pirates during an assault, I did not and would gladly shoot them myself if need be. There would be no compromise, no negotiation, and no capitulation. I knew that up against pirates in small fiberglass skiffs, even armed with AK-47s and RPGs, we had distinct advantages. All we needed was a firm resolve and to spot the attackers early.

In conducting my own security inspection, I noted that the two stairwells leading from the aft main deck down to the swim platform were open, leaving a clear line of sight—and of course line of fire—down the port and starboard catwalks where we as defenders might be standing. To remedy this, I had Engineer Sean cover these openings with sheets of one-third-inch steel plate secured in place.

From the Coalition Task Force, I had gathered one bit of important information: the pirates are all Muslim. When they captured a Saudi oil tanker, they got into a lot of trouble for attacking fellow Muslims, and ultimately returned the ship and crew to their owners. With this in mind, I had the crew purchase a full-sized official flag of Oman, which we would fly during our passage through the gulf. We also had purchased Arab headscarves for John and Lloyd. I already had an Omani white robe and pillbox hat, in which I cut a fine figure, if you don't mind my saying so. With these, we would at least suggest to pirates viewing us through binoculars that we were Omani Muslims and that, with lots of other targets around, they should accordingly pass us by in deference to their fellow religionists.

Spotting possible attackers at a distance was a key to our security plan, so Captain Steve set up a watch schedule that called for one man at the helm and two on deck, each assigned a particular sector for which he had responsibility. We knew from the Coalition Task Force that most attacks occur at dusk and at dawn and come from both Somalia and from Yemen, which were to the south and to the north, respectively, of our anticipated course. These times of day and these sectors, then, would receive our concerted attention. I sometimes personally joined the watch on deck during the early evening and night hours just to add another set of eyes and ears.

We had on board a superb set of night-vision binoculars that employed both light-gathering and infrared technology. These, along with a pair of conventional binoculars, were on deck at all times. Each man on watch had a VHF radio tuned to the channel we used for intra-crew communications.

We obtained from the Coalition Task Force the phone numbers for both the conventional cell phone and single sideband phone that we were to call in the event of attack. These numbers were printed on labels in bold letters and attached to the phones and to the instrument panel on the bridge. We also had a portable satellite phone with its battery fully charged should other means of communications get knocked out or fail. These were all backup measures, though, for the marine VHF radio, our primary means of communication. There were two of these on board, both fix-mounted and connected to high antennae on the mast, and numerous smaller handheld but effective portable units.

Officers of the Coalition Task Force told us that as soon as we spotted what appeared to be pirates, we should call them, giving our vessel name, position, course, speed, the direction from which the attack was coming, and the number of attacking skiffs. They said they hoped to be able to have an "asset," by which they meant armed helicopter, on the scene within thirty minutes or less from the time they received the call. This would require us to hold off an attempted boarding for at least thirty minutes.

I concluded that while it was mildly comforting to have the Coalition warships patrolling the area, it would be foolish to rely on them. Ultimately, we had to look out for ourselves.

The waters of the Gulf of Aden are at various times of the day full of Yemeni and Somali fishermen running around in boats identical to those employed by the pirates, so it's important to be able to tell one from the other. Fishing boats, the Coalition told us, have no more than two men on board while pirate boats have four to six and usually a long boarding ladder easily visible. Otherwise, it's hard to tell them apart. Just to complicate matters, we learned that all fishermen carry the ever-popular AK-47 for their own protection.

Our plan was that, once we identified a suspicious-looking small boat as being on an approaching course, whether or not we could confirm that it was full of pirates, we would sound an alarm that would alert all crew not assigned to specific duties to muster in the citadel room. We would also sound another very loud alarm with its annunciator mounted outside on the mast to alert the approaching craft that we had spotted them. At this point, John and Lloyd would grab their weapons, don their body armor, go out on deck to pre-selected positions, chamber rounds of ammunition, and be prepared for whatever might ensue.

They chose to be on the bridge deck for their firing positions. That would give them a higher elevation, though I thought it was unwise because the entire superstructure of Indigo is constructed of aluminum, through which small arms fire passes easily. I would have elected, and fully intended myself, to stand behind the one-third-inch steel plate of the main deck bulwarks, a solid railing, forty-two inches high around the deck's outer perimeter. I had always assumed that it was resistant to any small arms fire, but John said that he thought a 7.62 mm NATO round fired from an AK-47 would penetrate it. These are high-velocity rounds able to pierce light armor, but not our ceramic-plated body armor—or so I was assured. But we didn't know whether the pirates were using these or other lower-powered rounds. Whatever the resistance of steel plate, it was considerably greater than that of thin-sheet aluminum.

Once we had identified an approaching boat as a threat, we would assume that pirates with predatory intentions occupied it. At this point, John and Lloyd would cut loose first with flares from our Very pistol, aimed in the manner of a warning shot. If that failed to divert the attackers, they would fire a fusillade from the AR-15s aimed into the air to alert the pirates to what we hoped would be for them the unwelcome news that we were armed.

Our prediction was that upon gaining this knowledge, the pirates, known to be pickers of low-hanging fruit and not known to be suicidal, would abort their attack and go off in search of softer targets. During this time, the bridge watch would call on VHF channel 16 to alert the Coalition of the perceived attack and also call the phone numbers we had been given.

In the unlikely event that the pirates chose to open fire, John and Lloyd would do likewise, taking careful aim and firing in single shots as required by the weapons' limitations. The skiffs at which they would be firing have no protection whatever for their occupants— the expression "sitting ducks" seems appropriate—while John and Lloyd, when on the bridge deck, would be able at least to hunker down mostly out of sight. On the main deck, they would be all but invisible and somewhat protected by the steel bulwarks.

We were highly vulnerable, however, because the superstructure, which houses the all-important bridge, is aluminum rather than the steel plate of ships. If that were hit by a few wild rounds, they would pass through, perhaps damaging communications, vessel control, or other systems, even injuring a crew member on duty. Somewhat more worrisome was the RPG, or rocket propelled grenade, which when it strikes a target explodes with terrific force, doing far more damage than a small arms round.

We knew from John and Lloyd that the Somali and Yemeni pirates had grown somewhat more sophisticated of late, had begun employing coast watchers to detect the movement of potential target ships, and had planted spies to alert them to opportunities. With this knowledge in hand, we took the precaution of casually announcing to the marina staff, most especially including the dock boys, that we were headed for Dubai, in the direction opposite to our intended course.

Gulf of Aden

With all our preparations completed, we departed the Muscat marina on August 10, 2009, and headed for whatever lay ahead. I was confident that we had done all that could be reasonably done to ensure a safe voyage and that no matter what we might encounter, we would come through it just fine. I have to confess that I also felt eager to get on with it, as though embarking on an exciting new adventure— which, come to think of it, was just what I was doing.

The Coalition Task Force has established within the Gulf of Aden something called an Internationally Recommended Transit Corridor, or IRTC, often miscalled a "secure corridor." In truth, nothing about it is secure. The zone has, for the pirates, the beneficial effect of concentrating potential targets within a narrow belt, thus saving them the bother of wandering about aimlessly in search of one. It also concentrates the meager resources of the Coalition.

The IRTC consists of eastbound and westbound lanes, each five miles wide and 490 miles long. Between these is a separation zone, much like a median strip on an interstate highway, that is two miles wide. A distance varying between thirty and sixty miles separates the outer limits of the IRTC from the coasts of Somalia and Yemen, meaning that a pirate skiff setting out from the coast could reach the zone in as little as an hour. Because *Indigo* traveled at around nine knots while large ships traveled at more than fifteen, we were assigned to make the passage within the separation zone, well clear of faster vessels.

Hoping to gain some incidental protection from a thusly aroused Omani military, we elected to travel west along the Oman coast to Salalah, near the border with Yemen, before venturing out into the Gulf and taking up our initial position in the IRTC. I believed that we should have little if any confidence in the supposed protections of the Oman military, as their force was so small and the area of their territorial waters so great. As a result, we transited the coast on full alert.

Once we arrived at the eastern end of the IRTC, we notified the Coalition Task Force of our position and speed and updated that information every three hours thereafter. The captain decided to illuminate *Indigo* at night with only the barest navigation lights, a decision to which I objected but in the end with which I reluctantly concurred. My thought was that we were in no danger at all of colliding with other vessels, since we could see them easily on our radar and they could see us on theirs. By using these lights, I felt that we were simply broadcasting our presence to the pirates.

Our passage through the Gulf occurred during the season known as the summer monsoon, whose principal characteristic is a dry wind blowing night and day from the southwest at up to thirty knots. Seas kicked up by this wind make it difficult if not altogether impossible for pirates in small craft to operate, a fact in which we placed great hope. We thought we could not have picked a better time of year in which to make our passage.

In arriving at this mild delusion, however, we had failed to take into account the ever-present workings of Murphy's Law, which chose our first night in the IRTC to make its appearance. On that night, the wind speed dropped sharply, the seas abated and, as if to mock our false hopes, a full moon rose into a clear sky. So luminous was the night sky that our high-tech night-vision equipment was useless. Conditions could not have been more genial for the pursuit of armed robbery at sea.

Apparently poised for the occasion, the pirates fired up their outboard motors and set out from their ports in search of treasure. During the four days and three nights that we were in the IRTC, considered the area with the highest risk of attack, we overheard on the VHF attacks on three commercial ships. Two of these attacks came from Somalia, and one from Yemen. In each case, two or three pirate skiffs with four to five armed men in each approached a ship and opened fire, aiming at the bridge.

In one attack, the bridge windows were shattered and a radar beacon damaged by automatic weapons fire, and a rudder was damaged from what must have been an RPG round. We overheard all of this when the master under attack called the Coalition to request assistance. His heavily accented voice, tense with emotion, gave the Coalition warship nearest him the information they needed to launch a helicopter to come to his aid.

Meanwhile, the pirates, knowing they had only a short time within which they must board or be chased away, attempted to board. The shipmaster reported that he was commencing evasive maneuvers, but his turns were initially so severe that they had the effect of slowing him considerably, which would make boarding easier. Seeing this, a nearby shipmaster told the man that he must make his turns more deftly so as not to slow his forward speed, an adjustment he quickly made. He also constantly reported the position of the pirate skiffs, which the master under attack could not see from his vantage point on the bridge. As the pirates tried to board, the ship's crew hit them with a powerful stream of water from the ship's firefighting system, which was enough deterrent to hold them at bay until the Coalition helicopter arrived to chase them away.

The other two attacks were similar to this one, and neither was successful. In both cases, a Coalition helicopter arrived quickly and chased off the attackers. Two of the attacks took place on the same night, our first night in the IRTC, and within just a short time of each other. It seemed as if we had mistakenly wandered into the wrong end of a shooting gallery.

Listening over the VHF to the sounds of these attacks at night in *Indigo's* darkened bridge was, I have to admit, thrilling. The tense voice of a fearful shipmaster calling the Coalition for help, the Coalition radio operator's calm and distinct diction as if he were placing an order for takeout food, the helpful suggestions from nearby shipmasters, the helicopter pilot talking over the sound of whirring rotors asking for details about location and direction and giving the worried master an estimate of his arrival time. These sounds reverberated around *Indigo's* bridge and in the minds of her crew and myself.

All of us were intense, as alert as it's possible to be, ready in the event we should be the next target. The crackling of the VHF and taut voices of well-trained men going dutifully about their business, punctuated by intervals of ominous silence, these replaced the easy jocular banter that is the usual sound of *Indigo's* bridge. At times, I worked myself into a quiet but murderous rage at the utter cowardice of these scum who lurk about in the dark firing on unarmed people. The whole experience got my blood up in a way that no events in a usually humdrum, secure, comfortable life can match. All that said, I also have to admit that I loved every exhilarating second of it.

In the deepest recesses of my mind, there is regret that we were not attacked. It was Churchill who said there is no thrill quite like being shot at without result. I have been shot at, and I am pleased to say, without result. On one memorable occasion, a severely irritated—and need I mention intoxicated—Cajun fired two blasts from his shotgun which, though aimed in my general direction, instead tore gaping holes in the atmosphere. Then there were all those live-fire exercises during my military training that had the desired effect of encouraging the soldier to keep his head down.

I wanted not so much to get shot at as to shoot back at contemptible thugs, to frighten them as they had frightened so many others, and if it should come down to it, to put a few rounds into their skiffs or zinging over their heads or, if needed, into their miserable bodies to see how much they liked it.

Indigo made it through without a scratch, for what I believe are three reasons. The first is just pure dumb luck. In both lanes of the

IRTC, there was a constant stream of very large ships, brightly lit up at night and easily visible in the day. We saw with our eyes and with the radar hundreds of them, yet there were just three attacks. The odds, in other words, worked in our favor.

Another reason pirates did not attack us was that traveling in the separation zone between the two major shipping lanes meant that, coming from either Somalia or Yemen, they would have to travel at least five miles beyond the outer limits of those lanes and in doing so pass across a target-rich stream of ships just to reach us. Even though we were illuminated at night, they could not have seen us from a distance, since our masthead light was low to the sea, standing only about thirty-five feet in the air. They would have had to stumble upon us by accident.

One final reason I believe we avoided trouble was that from a distance in fading light, and particularly at night, we resembled a warship on patrol. Our faint minimal illumination was similar to that employed by the warships, and our slow speed matched that of a patrolling navy vessel. Our size, much smaller than a commercial ship, more closely resembled that of a navy corvette or coastal patrol vessel. A pirate coming upon us at night would not know quite what to think of us. We would be for him a highly unaccustomed sight, possibly fraught with risk, so he would be most likely to move on to targets he could understand and with which he has had experience.

After clearing the western end of the secure corridor in the Gulf of Aden, we set a course for Djibouti—the name of a country and also the name of its capital city.

TWENTY-ONE

Lost in Djibouti

Once a French colony, Djibouti is today an independent nation of the most meager sort whose minor port supplies its landlocked neighbors and the Coalition's warships.

Just a bit larger than New Jersey, it is a dreary, festering sore of a country, one of the hottest, most arid, most inhospitable places on Earth. With an unemployment rate of 60 percent in urban areas and 83 percent in rural areas, virtually no industry or arable land, few natural resources, a life expectancy of forty-three years, a neighborhood that includes Somalia, Ethiopia, and Eritrea, and an economy deeply in debt, all in arrears, the place has little to recommend it. The population of half a million is comprised of two African tribes, the Somali and Afar, who only recently concluded a civil war.

As I had never seen a country of such unrelenting dereliction and grim poverty, I directed us there. I just had to see what the place was all about.

Djibouti

It will not come as a surprise to learn that in Djibouti there is no yacht marina. As a consequence, we were assigned a berth in the dilapidated commercial port alongside small, rusting freighters that, with the aid of swarms of stevedores, were loading and unloading their cargos. The first thing I noticed was that everybody, in addition to being black, was extraordinarily slight of build. They resembled a Kenyan marathon runner recently recovered from a bout of intestinal flu. Two of them, prone and stacked on top of each other, wouldn't have made a decent speed bump. I don't think there was a single man in sight whose weight could possibly have exceeded 110 pounds or whose height exceeded five and a half feet—and these were the men with jobs.

Though slightly built, the people of Djibouti are uniquely blessed with a handsomely sculptured physiognomy. There is a delicate quality, an elegant fineness of detail that makes them attractive, the result of genetic heritage found only in Djibouti and Somalia. They are blessed with little else.

On our first night, I took the crew, plus our protectors, John and Lloyd, to dinner at a restaurant on the shabby town square. Called La Chaumiere, it had the air of a place that had been regularly overlooked by the local health inspectors, and it came complete with a snotty French waiter who also, as it happened, was the owner.

Quite a while back, an undernourished and overworked draft animal of some description, possibly an ox, had expired after a long and arduous career. It was a sinewy piece of this unfortunate beast that appeared on a plate in front of me, forever putting to rest the dubious notion that French cuisine is superior. With no ax at hand, I had no adequate means of cutting off bite-sized pieces. Even if I had been able to do so, my jaws would not have been up to the task of masticating them. So I ate the fries and drank the barely drinkable wine.

The Road to Somalia

Next day, there appeared at *Indigo's* door by prior arrangement a modern SUV, behind the wheel of which was a smallish local driver whose name I never quite got. His was a physique that a pugilist would have been pleased to see on his opponent. He wore trousers so baggy on his diminutive frame that only when he squatted could they have made contact with his legs. We were told by the agent who had arranged for the car that the driver "speaks English," by which he evidently meant that the man had been taught to announce the word "English." Only in this limited and unhelpful sense could he have been said to speak the language.

John and Lloyd, both wiser in the ways of Africa than I, were to be my companions for the day's travels, the goal of which was to drive across the Djibouti outback to the Somali border and, if possible, pass into that country and return from it unharmed. That it was known to be both war torn and ironically the home of the very same pirates who had plagued us only added to the allure. I should point out, though, that Somalia is a sizeable country, that the regions in which the pirates are active and those in which the war zones are located are not where we proposed to travel, and that accordingly our destination was not as foolhardy as it may first appear.

We made our planned destination known to the driver, who by various grunts and gestures indicated that he understood and knew the way there, which was, we figured, about thirty miles away. Shortly after setting out, we turned off a paved road onto a rough track, passing by a collection of primitive market stalls. These ramshackle huts, all unpainted and with dirt floors, were arranged in helter-skelter fashion and housed more supine souls resting in their shade than goods.

From the moment we set off, there was in our driver the suggestion that he had only recently climbed off a camel and got behind the wheel of a motor-powered vehicle. After he had stalled the car many times in a flawed attempt to coordinate clutch and accelerator, and had convincingly demonstrated his fear of exceeding ten miles per hour, I relieved the man of his duties and consigned him to the cargo compartment. As he was a frail, gangly man, he fit into it nicely. Lloyd drove from then on.

Continuing down the washboard road, we passed through heaps of trash, mechanical wreckage, and assorted rubble, veered around a newly deceased camel that appeared to have been struck by a vehicle, and a somewhat less recently deceased, and so more redolent, goat that seemed to have met with a similarly violent end. For the Muslims who make up 95 percent of the country, an animal may not be consumed unless it has been killed in an approved manner that, judging from these unmolested carcasses, doesn't include getting run down by a car.

After a distance of some five miles or so, there were no more trash heaps. In their place was a vast monotony of desiccated scrub, dotted here and there with low, scabby hills. At various places along the roadside, there appeared quite inexplicably a man squatted on his haunches under a scraggly tree ill-suited to providing the shade he sought. When we waved, he waved back, though only after a pause long enough to suggest that he had given the matter more thought than it demanded.

At another point along the way, a goat-sized, four-legged creature with impressive horns bounded across the road in front of us. According to Lloyd, our designated African wild beast expert, this was a Thomson's gazelle, a species peculiar to Africa and first revealed to the world by one Joseph Thomson. How this particular animal had thus far escaped the hungry clutches of the natives I couldn't say, but it seemed to be quick afoot, a useful talent for animals in these parts.

We saw lots of wandering camels and goats that appeared to be feral but probably belonged to someone. Here and there were isolated stone huts, none larger than a two-man camping tent that in their design appeared no different from what you'd expect in a Bronze Age hovel. Near these was usually a man, a woman, and a kid or two going about some domestic task.

Quite far along the road, we came to a miniature village of about ten of these huts arranged in no order at all. Women in colorful robes and kids with runny noses paused to stare at us. When we stopped, the kids ran up to us with hands out, shrieking and laughing and rapping on the car windows for attention, thus adding a cheery tone to a decidedly bleak place.

We had wondered where these isolated, desperately poor people got their water. There was no sign of it anywhere. But here in this village we saw a small standpipe from which flowed a steady stream of freshwater in which a woman was washing clothes and kids were playing. Nearby was a large white plastic tank, apparently set in place and kept filled as, I was sure, a secondary source in the event the well should run dry. The well's pump—and the small field of solar panels that powered it—were gestures of technology startling to behold in the Djiboutian desert.

After traveling some two hours through the blistering heat with no sign of the Somali border, we began to harbor the uneasy sense that our driver had no idea where the country might be. There was a disconsolate feeling of the kind you might get if you found yourself driving around in Oklahoma unable to locate Texas. Surely we had missed a turn somewhere.

But as always seems to happen in such cases, we just pressed on, unwilling to give up the ground we had gained even if it had been gained in the wrong direction. Of course, we had no map and no GPS, and our driver stuffed in the back had shown himself to be a man from whom it would be pointless to ask corrective directions. Stopping to ask directions of strangers, never an attractive option for the deter-mined explorer, was out of the question as none of us spoke a word of French or Arabic, Djibouti's official languages, to say nothing of the tribal tongues of Somali or Afar.

Under these less-than-appealing conditions, it seemed to me that pressing on was the right choice. After all, Somalia had to be out there somewhere.

In due course, we came upon a large village containing sixty or seventy of those ancient stone huts, some newer cement structures, and a school of a strikingly out-of-place modernist design sporting a bright blue metal roof. In the single-lane, unpaved, and still very rug-ged road that passed in front of the school were two of the most unnecessary speed bumps I have ever encountered—one of which we managed not to see in time, with predictable results.

While passing through the village, we saw ladies wearing colorful and richly patterned clothing carrying babies whose swaddling was much the same, offering a striking contrast with the uniformly black abayas and white robes of the United Arab Emirates and Oman.

Near the road, a few people had gathered around two camels with brightly colored saddles fashioned from carpet. As we watched, a statuesque woman of about twenty stepped out of a door with an infant in her arms. Her robe was of a deep red cloth that hung to the ground, and her matching scarf was tied in such a way as to leave only her face exposed. She had high cheekbones, a delicate jaw, lips of which a professional model would be proud, and a long and shapely neck. The smooth, ebony skin of her face surrounded clear, conspicuously white eyes which, to my astonishment, she focused on me with an intense, lacerating glare of hatred. It gave her the appearance of one who regularly communes with the netherworld—a place to which it was clear she wished to consign me.

John and Lloyd explained that, to African tribal people, a person attempting to photograph them is a person attempting to deprive them of part of their soul. Unaware of this opportunity for cultural blunder, I had been attempting to take her photo. Clearly, she disapproved. I don't know that she hexed me, but I can say that since that moment I have been experiencing various annoying tics and rashes.

The road on which we had traveled to this village, such as it was, ended there, washed out by a rare downpour years ago and still unrepaired. We had come literally to the end of the line in the Djiboutian desert and still had not found Somalia. It is the rare occasion when a small group of experienced travelers, including one highly trained in such matters by the British army, another by the Royal Marines, not to mention still another—your humble correspondent—by the US Army, is unable to find an entire country.

But this was one of those uncommon events, so we turned around and drove the many bumpy miles back to *Indigo* and the well-earned refreshments that awaited us.

In the later stages of refreshing ourselves that night, and after a great deal of vigorous if not deeply thoughtful discussion, we arrived at the only possible conclusion as to how we had misplaced an entire large country. A voodoo curse had been placed upon us by the witch woman from the village.

Still later, I discovered that the one-lane dirt track we had followed is designated National Highway 5, that the village at which we turned around is called Holhol, and that the blue-roofed schoolhouse is the College of Holhol. I also learned that, had we continued down Highway 5 as our collective instincts directed us, we would have arrived not at Somalia but at Ethiopia. Oops!

With the briefest glance at a map, we would have seen that Highway 2, the coast highway out of Djibouti City, would have delivered us in just fifteen miles to the elusive (for us) Somali border after a scenic drive along the shores of the Gulf of Aden. But knowing where it will end before setting out deprives a journey of spontaneity and the secret thrill that comes from happening upon the unknown. The route we unwittingly chose, though it would never have gotten us to our desired destination, was the route to adventure.

I returned to *Indigo* very happy that I had stopped in Djibouti, and given the right opportunity, I would gladly return there again. Next time, though, I would employ a driver who was more familiar with modern contrivances such as motor vehicles. I would also refrain from snapping photos of the local babes and take with me an antidote for curses.

Next stop: Egypt.

TWENTY-TWO

Ancient Ruins and Old Bones

Leaving Djibouti, we transited along its coast in calm seas and passed into the Red Sea through the Bab el-Mandeb Strait, translated variously as the "Gateway of Anguish" or "Gateway of Tears." With Djibouti and Eritrea on one shore and Yemen on the other, the doorway into a large body of water lined with countries that are on nearly every list of the world's least desirable places to live richly deserves the names however translated.

About 60,000 years ago, the strait was quite shallow and narrow, and was accordingly the route thought to have been chosen by the first anatomically modern humans in their earliest migrations out of Africa. Today the small island of Perim divides the strait into an eastern channel two miles wide and a hundred feet deep, and a western channel sixteen miles wide and 900 feet deep. As we passed by the island using the wider channel, dozens of small outboard-powered runabouts darted back and forth across our path, suggesting the possibility of pirates on the hunt. Though this area had had few attacks, John and Lloyd donned their bulletproof vests and took up positions as I strolled around on the boat deck in full Arab regalia just in case.

Off to our starboard was Yemen, currently the site of considerable and seemingly endless tribal conflict, and the home of an active al-Qaida insurgency. Lloyds listed the country among those while in whose waters our insurance coverage was suspended.

Farther along was Saudi Arabia, whose port city of Jeddah I wished to visit—until I learned that private vessels were not welcome there. Strictly abstemious, in keeping with their Wahabi Muslim practices, Saudis do not permit alcohol anywhere in the country, not even in hotels or resorts, and *Indigo* was nothing if not a floating warehouse of sporting refreshments.

To our port side was first Eritrea, then Sudan, both popular for a variety of human misery, including genocide, starvation, and disease.

Hurghada, Egypt

After plunging headlong through steep combers for six tiring days, we arrived at the Egyptian port of Hurghada, and there endured the rarely pleasant immigration and customs procedures and paid the necessary bribes without which in Egypt nothing happens. The waterfront of the town's well-appointed marina bristles with new retail and residential development of the most colorful and eye-pleasing design, but is alas far from fully occupied.

Just behind this facade of hipness is quite another scene. Everywhere you look in the town, and stretching for miles along the Red Sea shore, there stands the stark evidence that the financial calamity of 2007 to 2009 hit here, too. From appearances, it seemed to have hit even harder than elsewhere, Dubai perhaps excepted. The skeletal remains of half-finished apartment blocks, windblown beachfront foundations, and sites newly razed but vacant cluttered the landscape. Adding to the picture of devastation, there were no tourists. Streets were nearly vacant of pedestrians, shops were without shoppers, and restaurant staffs were idle.

Egyptians, according to my Omani friends who have lived there for extended periods, are famously humorous and cheeky. Attesting to these qualities, Mate Bobby was escorting Chef Camille, a winsome young woman, along the harbor esplanade when a shop attendant standing outside asked him, "How many camels did you pay for such a fine woman?"

Then there are all those ruins of the ancient Egyptian civilization.

Mark Twain, no fan of the grandiose compositions and religious themes of Renaissance art, nevertheless took an extended tour of Rome and its many art treasures from that era. At its conclusion, he said, "I never felt so fervently thankful, so soothed, so tranquil, so filled with blessed peace as I did yesterday when I learned that Michelangelo was dead."

As Mark Twain felt about Michelangelo, so I felt about the ancient Egyptians—and, as our voyage through the Mediterranean would soon reveal, the ancient Grecians, Romans, Minoans, Assyrians, Phoenicians, Ottomans, Persians, Etruscans, and many more bygone litterers. I was greatly pleased that all are now dead and can no longer clutter the countryside with their moldy detritus—or piles of rocks, as they are more accurately described.

This part of the world is a colossal junkyard, a vast cemetery of failed civilizations whose vestiges provide employment for the archaeologists who uncover them and anguish for the students who study them. They also are a magnet for tourists, though just what enjoyment is gained from traveling thousands of miles to stand in hot, sweaty lines for the privilege of gazing upon jumbles of stone, I have never understood. It does not seem to me to be a diversion suitable to the well-balanced mind.

Egypt is furnished, to the extent it is furnished at all, with attractions of the most severe simplicity. Without those attractions, such as they are, there would be no cause whatever for the discriminating traveler to visit the place, easily the least appealing and most venal of all the countries I have toured. On any list of the world's most inhospitable, impoverished, corrupt, desolate, scorching, or repressive countries, Egypt will be at or near the top of all these. It is Djibouti with a river.

On the Road in Egypt

We were docked only about a hundred miles from the city of Luxor, home to an array of ancient ruins, so I supposed that, notwithstanding my aversion to them, I should go there, see a few and, following the customary practice among tourists, absorb then quickly forget pointless facts about them.

Of much greater interest, I thought, would be seeing remote villages, the Egyptian desert, and the Nile and its valley. To get there, the tourist has two choices. He can rent a car and drive himself, or he can hire a car and driver from a government-affiliated firm. The first is outrageously expensive and, somewhat alarmingly, requires the tourist to wait until enough vehicles assemble into a convoy that heavily armed military vehicles then escort. Travel by military convoy, seldom an enterprise undertaken without some misgivings, is necessary for protection from the country's cheerless and censorious religious fanatics, whose hobby, judging from past events, seems to be gunning down unarmed tourists of the non-Muslim variety, like me.

But a convoy is such an awkward way to get about that I chose the second option. My driver for the few days of the planned excursion was Mr. Sayeed, a tall, distinguished, smartly dressed fellow in his middle years, whose grasp of English was adequate. He had one attribute, however, for which I was especially grateful. He was a man who paid commendable attention to the small-but-important details of personal hygiene. Passengers riding across deserts in air-conditioned automobiles prefer drivers whose attitude toward these matters is more than merely slapdash.

Setting out from the harbor, we zipped along the coast highway with the Red Sea shoreline to our left and low desert hills to the right. Along the shore were miles of still more defunct real estate projects in various stages of incompletion, a few completed but vacant hotels and condominiums, and lots of vacant sand. The desert on our right consisted largely of vacant sand, some of it piled high, some arranged in sinuous undulations, some of it immense, flat, and extending to the horizon, none with a hint of vegetation.

Luxor, Egypt
Twenty or so miles south along the Red Sea, we came to a large roundabout and a line of traffic waiting to get through a military checkpoint.

When it came our turn, surly soldiers holding mirrors on the end of staffs probed our car's undercarriage while others peered into the engine compartment and trunk in search of contraband weapons. They checked my passport and the driver's identification papers.

At both ends of the checkpoint, soldiers with automatic weapons glared down on us from concrete pillboxes mounted atop ten-foot-high columns. As the traffic snaked its way around protective barriers, a platoon of heavily armed soldiers loitered nearby. What I could not know at the time was that this was but the first of what would be at least a dozen of these checkpoints through which we would pass on the way to our destination. The military armed camp motif of Luxor's gateway failed to elicit in me that hopeful anticipation customarily experienced in the jaunty holiday outing. It suggested more the entering of a maximum-security prison.

Emerging from the parched, sandy desert, we passed quite abruptly into the Nile Valley, a region having the blackest, most fertile soils on Earth. The result is that for the entire length of the river, the valley is a cornucopia, with every imaginable crop growing in profusion. In the squalid, congested villages, rude houses constructed of sun-dried mud bricks stand side-by-side with those built of concrete frames and masonry bricks, all flat-roofed and of the simplest design, window openings merely dark voids without glass or screen. Dusty, trash-strewn paths wind among the shelters, providing laneways for farm animals and their masters alike.

Stunted, imperturbable donkeys provide much of the motive power and transport. I observed one of these hapless—and not at all handsome—creatures pulling a two-wheeled cart loaded down with three cheerful little guys, each about eight years old, and a great heap of sugar cane. The kids were having a fine old time of it, though from the animal's dour demeanor and dispirited gait, I got the impression that he was none too pleased with his lot in life.

No sooner had I snapped a few photos of the rustic lads then all three in unison thrust out their hands, palms up, as if on command from some deeply embedded Egyptian gene for cupidity. Practicing for a career in government, I supposed. This was not the first, nor would it be the last, upturned palm I would see.

In a memorable moment, we passed a full-grown man clad in a traditional Arabic robe riding one of these undernourished donkeys, a common sight. Though the man was of just average height, so slight was the donkey's stature that the passenger's sandaled feet were nearly dragging the ground. As there was no bridle or reins, he held in his right hand a stick with which to encourage the beast to move along and, when needed, to change direction. To that point, the scene has not changed in 2,000 years. It was his left hand, though, that captured my attention and, in a symbolic way, captured the essence of Egypt. In it, he held a modern cell phone on which, while ambling along on his donkey, he was intently text messaging.

At about 600 yards wide, the Nile was narrower and a good bit swifter and bluer than I had imagined. Signs cautioned me not to jump in, but failed to mention that a prominent reason for this was the likely presence of crocodiles. The Nile version of these beasts are the second largest on Earth, after the dreaded saltwater crocs of Australia, not uncommonly growing to an impressive twenty feet and 2,000 pounds. Swimming in the Nile is not a popular pastime.

Next day, Mr. Sayeed drove me to a tattered parking lot set amid a plowed field from which crops of some kind had been recently harvested. There, just a few steps away, stood great heaps of stone about thirty feet high arranged, in this case, as three enormous statues of ancient Egyptian potentates sitting stiffly upright in straight-backed chairs, folded hands in their laps. Mr. Sayeed wished to park so that I could get out of the car, walk up to their base, and see the statues up close. I dissented, however, saying that I saw no reason to extract myself from the comfort of an air-conditioned car to join a line of people staring vacantly at a sight I could see perfectly well from where I sat. I mean, how close to them must a person get to gape at three large statues, and for how long is it necessary that he do so? A drive-by sighting was quite enough for me.

"Onward," I said.

We next pulled into the crowded parking lot in front of the monumental Temple of Hatshepsut artfully carved into the face of a mountain to honor a pharaoh queen of that name. Widely considered one of the "incomparable monuments of ancient Egypt," it is certainly an impressive relic. Gazing upon it, ideas for my own interment began to take on imperial tones.

It was here that, in 1997, six jihadists massacred sixty-three innocent tourists, all of course in the glorious name of Allah. Because of this atrocity, security at the temple was so tight and the lines so long that I didn't bother getting out of the car. Once again, I could see the place in pleasurable comfort, cool refreshments close to hand.

Continuing our speedy tour of Luxor, we stopped next at the Valley of the Kings—really just an overly large, pretentious cemetery cut into the desert, a gated community for the dead. I stood in line with busloads of sweaty sightseers—Scandinavians, Brits, Germans, as always Japanese with clicking cameras, no Americans—baking in the midday sun.

When it came my turn to pay the entry fee, I asked the ticket seller to name three of the many crypts that were, in his opinion, the most appealing. He immediately stopped selling tickets, leaving the long line of customers to stand idle in the blazing heat, and escorted me six steps to a shady spot. There he wrote three names on the back of my ticket and promptly extended the Egyptian salute, palm up.

All three of the crypts the man suggested were more or less the same and had the effect of reconfirming my aversion to ancient ruins of any sort. Each featured a long, low-ceilinged, featureless corridor that slanted down into the desert floor, ending at a cubicle that once held the sarcophagus of some notable or another. That was it. There was about the crypts the suggestion of a storage depot for ammunition or possibly nuclear waste, but not much else.

We drove past the Temple of Karnak and several other stone shambles, which I waved at as we sped past. Coming to a stop at a museum, I entered and found it to be a place where the macabre-minded tourist can view the desiccated remains of corpses dug from the cemetery I had just left. From recumbent midget mummies, some bearing the expression of a belligerent fish, it appeared the life of a pharaoh had had its disadvantages. It also appeared that ancient Egyptian dentistry had room to improve.

Having had quite enough of gruesome corpses, I hurried back to the hotel bar and there, my customary aplomb restored with the aid of a cool glass of beer, swore that I and ancient ruins would hereafter be forever strangers.

Suez Canal

The casual student of history, when he reads about the colossal engineering achievement of Ferdinand de Lesseps and the building of the Suez Canal, is likely to form in his mind a vision of monumental proportions, a scene that inspires awe at what man has accomplished. He will imagine something on the grand scale of the Eiffel Tower, the Burj Khalifa, a modern offshore oil platform, or a nuclear-powered US aircraft carrier.

Upon seeing the canal, however, quite another and decidedly less memorable, even dispiriting, vision will come to him. It is a ditch. To be sure, it is a long, wide, deep ditch, bristling with military installations. It is 120 miles long, 79 feet deep, and 224 yards wide. Its banks are of white sand piled there from its original and successive excavations, and the scenery beyond, extending to the horizon, is wide, flat farmland of the Nile Delta. Driving down an interstate highway in Kansas would provide greater visual stimulation than passing through the Suez Canal.

To enter the Canal, Captain Steve contacted Canal Control on the VHF radio, who took note of our displacement, draft, and anticipated speed and assigned us a position in a northbound convoy. A detachment of personnel from Control soon came aboard and required the captain to prove that we could maintain the speed we had reported and that *Indigo* was a reliable vessel unlikely to break down during the passage. With this done, we sat at anchor for many hours until late at night, when Control called and instructed us to fall into line behind a large container ship and maintain the assigned position and speed.

Traffic in the canal is one-way, reversing every twenty-four hours. Along its length are two lakes, the Great Bitter Lake and the Ballah Bypass, into which vessels in transit are shunted when the direction of flow reverses.

At four in the morning, we pulled into the Great Bitter Lake as instructed and there spent hours riding at anchor surrounded by featureless flat delta. When the direction of flow again reversed, we reentered the canal and resumed our slow cruise to the Mediterranean Sea.

Port Said, Egypt

At the north end of the canal lies the city of Port Said ("sah-eed"), where we tied up at the local version of a yacht club. As the canal divides the city just about in half, a system of ferries is required to accommodate routine vehicle traffic. Our dockage at the club was right alongside the ferry terminal, giving us a close-up view day and night of city traffic, both vehicles and ferries.

I took several walks through the nearby neighborhoods at both day and night, and toured the city by car. From these experiences, I can report that there is nothing wrong with the place that high explosives would not cure. Sited on the shore of the Mediterranean just above sea level, the city affirms that the melting of polar ice caps will have some beneficial effects on the human condition. Port Said would make a fine reef.

Some of the crew hired a van to drive three hours into Cairo, spend a day there, and return. Knowing of that city's reputation from my Omani friends, I declined to go along and, it must be said, wisely so. Their reports confirmed all that I had ever heard or read on the subject, none of it complimentary. A city that employs herds of pigs to roam through its streets consuming garbage is a city that a man of the civilized world should avoid. That it is also home to great heaps of ancient rocks and the consequent throngs of sightseers attracted to them further adds to my low opinion of the place.

Leaving the Suez Canal and Egyptian waters and entering the Mediterranean Sea brought to all on board the relief felt by the man who extricates himself from the cesspit into which he has accidentally fallen. Cool breezes wafted over the deck, rays of a kindly sun shone down upon *Indigo*, warming her and her passengers and, if we'd had any on board, daffodils would have danced in the wind. Little else in life brings such ineffable pleasure or is so therapeutic to the human spirit as a departure from Egypt.

TWENTY-THREE

Greek Islands of the Aegean Sea

Wishing to make amends for blighting the earth with Egypt, Mother Nature graced it with the Greek islands of the Aegean Sea. On this leg of our voyage, we would see many of these islands, each with a distinctive personality, some with more appeal than others. They were uniformly parched, thinly treed, and their soils and shorelines rocky. Though praised around the world, especially in Europe, their beaches were more soil, pebbles, and rocks than glistening white sand.

Despite all this, I liked most of these islands and look forward to visiting them again someday.

Rhodes

Capital of the Dodecanese archipelago, Rhodes was the first of the Greek islands we encountered traveling north from the Suez Canal. There we docked in the heart of Old Town, an ancient, fortified town surrounded by high stone walls, now a UNESCO World Heritage site. Unlike Egypt, where crumbling remains are the passive object of gawkers, here the remains have been restored to their former grandeur and profitably employed as a tasteful outdoor shopping mall and entertainment center with medieval castle theme. Of all the ancient walled towns I would see in the Mediterranean—and there would be many—Rhodes was among the best and one to which I would gladly return, though only in the off-season.

On the day of our arrival, Old Town's delightful, if bewildering, maze of pedestrian walks, lined with shops, cafés, and bars, was filled with wandering tourists recently decanted for the day from the several cruise ships in port or from the convoys of mammoth tour buses that helped to clog the streets. Situated conveniently among these winding laneways are important museums housing permanent displays describing the island's long and bloody history, all clearly marked and thus easily avoided.

Though Old Town is appealing, its unimaginatively named neighbor New Town is not. Hip in the 1970s, New Town today is decidedly down-market. Like nearly all the Greek islands, Rhodes is a favored destination of backpackers, youth hostel habitués, and assorted budget-minded travelers on package tours. For Brits, a two-week cheap and cheerful studio package in New Town, including airfare, cost as little as $520 at the time. Scandinavians, Italians, and the notorious Brit lager louts, among others, swarm to New Town in the summer months to pack themselves onto thin strands of stony beach, drink themselves into oblivion, and in general wreak havoc upon the local population. Their preference for low-cost meals, I learned, has a depressing effect on the offerings of local tavernas.

As an example, for lunch one day I selected what appeared to be a mid-level New Town establishment pleasantly situated on a plaza by the harbor. This was, as it turned out, a poor choice. Swayed by its charming setting, I had forgotten the universal truth, distilled from many years of experience, that the man who dines at a Greek restaurant called Zorbas is destined for gastronomic disappointment.

Having had enough of Rhodes's New Town, I rented a car and went off seeking solace in the hinterlands. For this trip I took along no map or GPS and did not ask for directions. I instead relied entirely on my keen innate sense of direction—though with some trepidation, as it was this same keen sense that had failed me so ingloriously in the Djibouti desert.

Nothing of particular note happened during my brief sojourn, with one minor exception. At a tiny village high in the burnt hills, I came upon a tavern with an outdoor terrace shaded by pines and overlooking the luminous Aegean Sea far below. It was crowded with large, noisy families out for their Sunday lunch and looked inviting, so I joined in the fun, taking one of the few available seats.

Only then did I realize I had crashed a private party, a blunder that a minimally observant person would have foreseen. When I tried to avoid embarrassment by sneaking away, the celebrants would have none of it. They laughed heartily, welcomed me to the festivities and, as neither of us spoke the other's language, engaged me in a cryptic conversation of the see-Spot-run variety, accompanied by wild gesturing that would have made a mime shudder.

Next day, continuing my excursion around the island, I happened upon the comely village of Lindos, its narrow walkways and whitewashed homes clinging to a steep hillside above the sea. There you can walk—or emulate an Egyptian villager and ride a donkey—down a steep staircase to the rocky shore and back up to the village square. The up part of the trip makes the donkey a plausible alternative.

I lunched that day at Mavrikos, located on the village square perched on the edge of a high cliff, all of its tables shaded by a leafy arbor. Still run by the same family that founded it in 1933, it rates among the top five restaurants outside of Athens, an assessment with which I fully concur. My lunch that day was one of the finest meals I had eaten ashore in a very long time and, with soft breezes wafting in from the sun-dappled sea, one of the most agreeable places I have been.

Crete

At Crete, the largest of the Greek islands, we docked in the town harbor of Agios Nikolaos, rendered in English as Saint Nicholas—or in other words, Santa Claus Town. Once known as the Saint-Tropez of Crete, it is today worn at the edges but in a pleasing way. Like all of Greece, it has ancient ruins, but here they are not so prominent as to define the place. The crew and I all liked the town very much and were pleased to spend a few days there.

Just down the road from the harbor is what may be the only legitimate five-star hotel in the Greek islands, the Elounda Mare, where I spent a few lazy days to give the crew some needed rest. One of the hotel's numerous attractions is a bar cut out of—and partly recessed into—the rocky shore, a sort of seaside cocktail cave. At sunset, the view from its terrace across the Gulf of Mirabello to the high, arid Sitia Mountains is one of the most pleasant and serene anywhere. With lights from tiny villages twinkling high on the mountain face, the last rays of sun painting a golden sheen across the placid Gulf, cool water lapping happily at my feet, refreshment at hand, it was not possible to be more content.

Wishing to see more of Crete, I rented a car and drove on an expressway to yet another medieval walled town, this one called Iraklion. It is the site of an ancient Minoan civilization which littered the island with, among much else, the celebrated ruins of Knossos. These I happily bypassed in keeping with a pledge never again to inflict on myself ancient ruins that have not been converted to a frolicsome use or that fail to offer a happy hour.

I visited a museum of note that displays relics of the Minoan civilization and managed to weave my way through its crowd of visitors in less than five minutes. What it displays are unidentifiable shards of pottery, some spearheads and arrowheads, and assorted chunks of marble that have become detached from crude, disfigured sculptures. Most of the stuff I saw looked as if it had been recovered from a Minoan landfill but should have been left there.

It did not take long to get the gist of the town, filled to near overflowing with yet more cruise ship and tour bus throngs, so I moved on to the town of Hania (or Chania) near the western end of the island.

A guidebook describes this as "simply one of the most beautiful of all Greek cities," and I have to agree. Hania is an elegant town of eucalyptus-lined avenues, miles of waterfront promenades, and shady, cobbled alleyways of medieval vintage. Its warren of narrow, paved walkways, twisting staircases, and hidden courtyards yielded surprises at nearly every turn. These were a bit narrower than others I had walked—so narrow that on some of them I had to step aside to let oncoming pedestrians get by. Where there was adequate room, cafés and wine bars set up tables and chairs outside, which on balmy nights was the preferred seating. The result was a pleasant air of festivity that lightened my steps and put the town firmly on the list of places to which I one day wish to return.

Santorini

Santorini is one of the world's most visually stunning islands and is certainly the most extraordinary island in the Aegean Sea. Its principal village, Fira, a dazzling, whitewashed jewel, clings precariously to the edge of a 1,100-foot cliff.

At the base of this cliff, we tied *Indigo* between a mooring buoy and a quay, since anchoring here is impossible due to depths deeper than our anchor chain is long. Sensible travelers wishing to conserve their energy will choose to reach the village from the quay by a cable car while the younger generations and other foolishly over-energetic visitors will hike up the absurdly steep and long staircase. Those wishing to mimic an impoverished Egyptian villager may choose to ascend astride a bedraggled donkey.

The island is all that remains of a volcano that exploded long ago, leaving behind the enormous depths of the bay where its caldera once was, and the precipitous cliffs. Set against the azure sky and sea, the enchanting village laced with winding pedestrian paths is at a distance about as lovely as a Greek village can be. Up close, it is just another tourist-choked outdoor shopping center, this one hanging dramatically at the edge of a lofty promontory.

Employing my well-developed instinct for homing in on fine bars, I walked into Franco's as if by genetic command. Any questions as to its suitability were promptly put to rest by its helpful claim to be the World's Best Bar, an assertion I found no cause to dispute. Unlike most bars in the upper echelons, which favor the more sophisticated compositions of honky-tonk, Franco's is the only bar I have ever encountered that plays only classical music. Mozart string quartets, I have to admit, blend nicely with the tranquil views of distant islands and unruffled sea.

Differently from most other Greek islands I had visited, Santorini has some great restaurants. It also attracts serious artists and musicians. One night I attended a chamber music concert featuring performers drawn from the National Symphony in Athens and sat through most of it.

Patmos

With a harbor too small to accommodate large cruise ships and with no airport, Patmos is far quieter during the season than the larger islands, and, for that reason alone, I liked it very much. On our first day, I went for lunch to a beachside café where I sat under the shade of leafy trees, indulged in a glass of local wine, and gazed vacantly over the Aegean.

Soon enough, I began talking with a German lawyer from Aachen seated at a nearby table with his lady friend. As the wine flowed, the three of us then began talking with Katrina and Labros, a young couple from Athens also seated close by, and eventually all five of us sat together for lunch. That night, they all joined me for cocktails and dinner aboard *Indigo*. Katrina and Labros invited me to visit them when my voyage brought me to Athens.

One of the numerous and quite popular beaches on Patmos is famed for being densely covered by dark, egg-sized stones worn smooth by the elements, a feature that makes it surely among the oddest beaches on Earth. So coveted are the stones that signs warn bathers not to make off with any. To tread over them requires heavy-soled shoes and a wary step lest you break a leg, and to lie upon them in the manner of a sunbather, it seemed to me, surely would require an anesthetic. Though highly regarded by some, it did not seem like much of a beach to me. I will take the sugary soft white sands of Northwest Florida any day.

Patmos is most famous as the site of a celebrated grotto where Saint John is said to have authored the Book of Revelation in 95 AD. It also is the site of the imposing Monastery of St. John, which to my good fortune was closed on the day my new friends attempted to drag me there. Walking about in monasteries is not for me the stuff of a stimulating day.

At other islands, we anchored overnight rather than go ashore. These included Karpathos, Ios, and Andiparos. These provided opportunities for barbecues with the crew, swims in remote lagoons, and general indolence.

We would see more Greek islands when we reached the Ionian Sea, but for now we entered the waters of Turkey and headed for the city of Bodrum.

TWENTY-FOUR

Turkish Delights

My travels in Turkey would turn out to be a benevolent pool of water on the parched earth of my innocence. I liked the country and would happily return there. This is an opinion contrary to the one I held before arriving—one I had derived from a fuzzy, incomplete, and in some areas downright wrong grasp of the place and its people.

Bodrum, Turkey

We arrived in the vacation port town of Bodrum in mid-September. This was to become one of my favorite places. Its harbor, anchored at one end by a fortress built in the early 1400s, is enormous and, at the time of my visit, packed with at least 400 boats of every description, but mostly with the classic wood-hulled Turkish sailing vessel called a gulet. Tourists from all over the world charter these, with or without crew, and in them travel in high style and comfort among the islands and coastal villages of the Turkish Riviera. There are also a surprisingly large number of privately owned vessels, mostly sailboats, whose owners live elsewhere most of the year but come to the Riviera in their free time.

The town's most appealing feature is a corniche that makes a graceful, tree-shaded sweep around the harbor's edge. Lined up

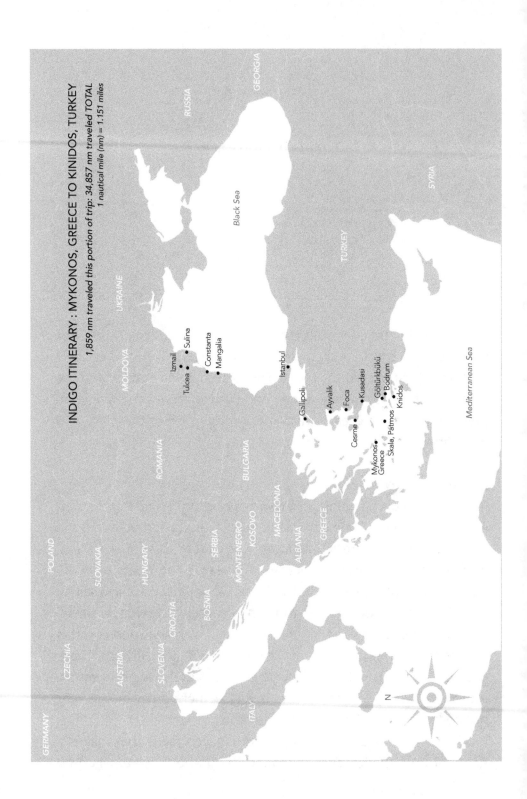

INDIGO ITINERARY : MYKONOS, GREECE TO KINIDOS, TURKEY

1,859 nm traveled this portion of trip: 34,857 nm traveled TOTAL
1 nautical mile (nm) = 1.151 miles

along its landward side are bars, cafés, a few nightclubs, stylish shops, and restaurants serving almost any kind of cuisine you could want, which together make up the epicenter of Bodrum's lively scene, night and day. Along its harbor side is a superb leafy park and pedestrian walk that, from early morning until the later hours, is filled with people enjoying the balmy weather and harbor sights.

For the energetic fun seeker, there is an entire seafront strip of bars which the city, with a taste for simplicity, named Bar Street. Customers of these places are mostly tourists; indeed, many of them are open only during the summer season. Near Bar Street is a strip of waterfront restaurants, all featuring alfresco dining, and a warren of pedestrian walks lined with shops selling merchandise of nearly every description, including knock-offs of luxury-branded goods.

Upon arriving in Bodrum, some of the crew and I visited an outdoor bar/restaurant called the Marina Yacht Club conveniently located just a hundred yards from our dock. That night it featured a live show under the stars by one of Turkey's most celebrated pop groups performing such traditional Turkish favorites as "I Left My Heart in San Francisco." It amazed me that the audience members, mostly in their twenties and thirties, who I would have thought wanted more contemporary, vigorous music like techno or hip-hop, were thrilled with the group. They applauded at length in a most mannerly fashion, as if at a cricket match.

I was also surprised to note that everyone in the audience, and those on stage as well, was dressed in modest, tasteful clothing. Neither the ghetto thug nor the slut puppy style has come to Turkey. I found this to be true everywhere I went in the country, even in the clubs and bars of Istanbul. Public rowdiness and impassioned displays of affection, too, are always well within the bounds of an appealing propriety. To be sure, these observations do not apply to the alien throngs who invade the town in summer, most particularly the notorious Brits.

Islam, I believe, is the reason for this unexpected but welcome deportment. A relaxed conformity to conservative community standards I found also prevalent in Malaysia, Dubai, Abu Dhabi, and Oman. It was common in Singapore, but there the result of a strict regulatory regime. On the Redneck Riviera of my native Northwest Florida, restrained behavior of this sort suggests a hangover from the night before, but the fun there is more stimulating.

Both commercial and residential buildings in Bodrum are required by law to have two square floor plates of equal and modest size stacked one atop the other, to be built of concrete covered in stucco and painted white, to have a flat roof with low parapet, and to employ simple punched openings for windows and doors. No curves, such as radiuses at corners or arched openings at windows and doors, are permitted, nor are decorative rustications or appliqués of any sort.

The result of this flawed effort at cutesy conformity is that the town from a distance looks like giant sugar cubes that have been indiscriminately scattered across the landscape. At street level, though, there is enough variation in shop fronts to offset some of the monotony. Many Greek islands and other towns along the Turkish Riviera impose similar restrictions with similar results.

Needing to get through an exploration of the Black Sea before the onset of its wicked winter, we hurried along the coast, stopping at the most important of the towns. These included Türkbükü, Kuşadasi, Foça, and Ayvalik. All were fine seaside resorts and made for pleasurable layovers. Çeşme, in particular, is an appealing town much favored by the wealthy of Istanbul.

Close to Kuşadasi are the ruins of Ephesus, once the second largest city in the Roman Empire after Rome itself, and noted for its role in biblical events. There is a claim the Virgin Mary lived there for a time. If the government had had the good sense to turn the place into an entertainment and shopping center in the fashion of Old Town on Rhodes or Hania on Crete, I would gladly have gone there, but as they hadn't, I didn't.

Alaçati, Turkey

I rented a car and drove one day to Alaçati, a quaint village of one-story design constructed of hand-hewn stone, with cobblestoned pedestrian paths meandering through it. There, I stayed a night in what had once been a Christian mission, whose chapel now serves as the breakfast room. Not having spent much time in missions, I found the experience disconcerting but pleasant.

A large cross is mounted on the wall over the main entry door, and another on the wall of the chapel. There is even an outdoor bar, a thoughtful touch not often found in missions. The crosses and the bar are, for this Muslim country, an emphatic announcement of its ecumenical tolerance of Western religions and its acceptance of sporting refreshment, both gestures of modern Turkey's convivial spirit.

By good fortune, I arrived there on an important religious holiday for Turkish Muslims, a weeklong celebration of the family marked by eating meals together and visiting the old folks—a version of Thanksgiving. Along the pedestrian paths of Alaçati, the restaurants and bars were filled with families seemingly having a great time, all dressed smartly, kids scrubbed clean and well behaved. It seemed as if I had stumbled onto an annual Parent Teacher Association appreciation dinner.

Cappadocia, Turkey

A UNESCO World Heritage site, Cappadocia is a region within the high desert plateau of central Turkey that is home to both ancient subterranean towns and the most geologically bizarre landscape on Earth. Millions of years ago, there was beneath the region a vast aquifer through which rivers of freshwater flowed, carving a honeycomb of caves, grottoes, shafts, chimneys, and tunnels. A seismic uplifting of the entire area caused the water to drain out and the honeycomb to dry. Much later, ancient peoples, beginning several thousand years BC, began excavating the honeycomb below ground, adapting it for use as a safe haven from their enemies. Because the honeycomb is not stone, but densely compacted volcanic ash called tuff, excavation was comparatively easy. When cave-like rooms are cut into it, tuff does not collapse as soil does but retains its structural integrity without need of bracing and ceiling timbers.

In this formicarium-like, below-ground realm, there once lived many thousands of people, including early Christians from about the first and second centuries AD, there to escape marauding armies intending to plunder, convert, or enslave them. Once burrowed into these hideouts, they were hard to find and, if found, impossible to get at. With plenty of food stored for just such invasions, water readily available, the capacity to make wine and bread, and chapels and altars with which to practice their religion, they could hold out indefinitely.

So far, archaeologists studying the area have discovered forty of these underground towns, many extending more than eight levels totaling 240 feet below the Earth's surface and accommodating up to 20,000 people. There are almost certainly more of them yet to be found.

Above ground, there is still more to see in Cappadocia that is equally astounding. Thanks in part to the peculiar qualities of tuff, the area features some of the most extravagant contortions of landscape imaginable. There are fields of perfectly shaped cones standing up to 130 feet high, atop each of which is precariously balanced a single great block of stone. These fairy chimneys, as they are known, look as if they belong in a Disney theme park.

Wide expanses of the area's stony surface resemble frozen waves and fields of giant, phallus-like columns. Everywhere you look are openings in cliffs, cones, and mesas marking the entrance into homes dug by the villagers of long ago. A modern, five-star hotel mimics the caveman motif by offering rooms dug deep into cliffs, if you don't mind staying a few nights in a cave. We spent just one night in Cappadocia, but I would gladly go back and would spend at least three days to see it all properly.

The Dardanelles

Following those all-too-wholesome few days in Alaçati and surrounds, I returned to Bodrum, boarded *Indigo*, and set out for Romania, Ukraine, and Bulgaria by way of Istanbul, the Bosporus Strait, and the Black Sea. On the way to Istanbul, we passed through the famous Dardanelles, a long, narrow passage as little as three-quarters of a mile across, into the Sea of Marmara, two bodies of water which, along with the Bosporus, link the Mediterranean and the Black Sea.

The Dardanelles is one of the most strategic bodies of water on Earth and has a correspondingly bloody history. Near its western, or Asiatic, shore lie the ruins of ancient Troy, which, in keeping with my sensible distaste for ruins, I declined to visit. Archaeologists, in any event, have uncovered seven different civilizations there, one on top of the other, and cannot say which of these featured in the Trojan Wars.

On its eastern, or European, shore is a museum I visited dedicated to the sorrowful events of the Battle of Gallipoli, whose triumphant hero was a then-obscure lieutenant colonel named Mustafa Kemal, later known to the world as Ataturk. Perhaps the most remarkable and accomplished leader of the modern era, he almost single-handedly forged the modern Republic of Turkey, today a secular, thoroughly liberal, Western state. It is tragic irony that the man who freed Turkey from the puritanical grip of the Islamic clergy, including their ardent abstemiousness, should die of cirrhosis.

Istanbul, Turkey

In my opinion, Istanbul is one of the world's great cities. Built upon hills that rise up from the iconic Bosporus, it also is breathtakingly beautiful, especially seen at night from a vessel or from atop one of the hills. So insistently Western in manner and appearance are the citizens of Istanbul that a visitor would be forgiven for thinking he was in Manhattan. Only the seldom-seen headscarf and the presence of mosques and the calls to prayer suggest Islam.

One of the best things about my visit to Istanbul was that Kitty, whom I had not seen for too long, joined me there. During our extended stay, I drove by a few of the required tourist stops, like the Hagia Sophia, Topkapi Palace, Blue Mosque, and others and waved. Fleets of tour buses in the parking lots and long lines at the ticket kiosks forewarned me of what I could expect should I be so foolish as to visit these places. Kitty, far more tolerant of crowded places than I, went to all of these in the company of a tour guide.

The one concession I made to ancient history was to join Kitty in a joyful visit to the Grand Bazaar and Spice Market. Until a new Dubai mall came along, the bazaar was the world's largest indoor shopping mall. Completed in 1496, it is still the oldest and, by a wide measure, the most fun. The place is a befuddling maze of fifty-eight pedestrian boulevards, streets, cul-de-sacs, paths, and hidden courtyards with over 3,000 emporia, including too many carpet vendors. Even with a map at hand, I never could figure where I was in the maze, so I just pressed on until eventually seeing the proverbial light at the end of the tunnel signaling an exit.

More than 300,000 visitors a year wander up and down its laneways under high, vaulted ceilings, gawking cheerfully at the merchandise while being hectored by shopkeepers eager to lure them into their stores. "Hey, mister, you buy this nearly authentic designer watch for your beautiful wife." A few of these guys were happy that I had come along. I bought a faux sultan's robe of blue velvet adorned with ornate gold-colored embroidery, shields, curlicues, and appliqués. It was said to have been handmade in an Uzbek village, though my guess is machine-made in China. It was a costume sure to be worn by the Sultan of *Indigo* late in the evening at appropriately celebratory parties. I also bought an authentic, and somewhat timeworn, handcrafted ornamental headpiece of the kind Genghis Khan once wore, along with a few other additions to my hat collection.

On another day, we visited the city's famous fifty-yard-wide pedestrian shopping street called Taksim. What impresses the first-time visitor right off is the dense river of people flooding this boulevard of commerce. To escape it, you are obliged to flatten yourself against a building on either side—and even then, you are likely to be jostled by eddying currents of humanity.

At one end of the street lies an old, slightly seedy neighborhood perhaps six or seven blocks square, which, we were astounded to note, is devoted entirely to the retailing and repairing of musical instruments. Some shops deal solely in percussion, others in brass, and still others in woodwinds. As you might guess, many specialize in guitars of every description. Piano and organ vendors, too, are numerous.

A weekly visit to a Turkish bath is, for the Turk, an essential part of life, which he will forego only under the most extreme circumstances. Every hotel offers these, but the locals more commonly use public facilities. Wanting to see what this cultural experience was about, I decided to have one of these baths. Just to be certain of a superior experience, I chose the spa in the venerable Hotel Çırağan Palace.

As directed by an attendant, I entered a large steam room whose floor, ceiling, and walls were covered in marble, a fountain in its center gurgling away. There I was greeted by the young woman who was to administer the bath. She wore a modest white uniform, and from her physique, I gathered that she had been recently employed as a village blacksmith. Nude, though with a towel discreetly wrapped around me, I lay upon a marble bed complete with marble headrest—though to be truthful, rest is not what a head does when lying upon marble.

She began dousing me generously with warm water followed by dense fluffs of warm, soapy bubbles, after which she set upon me in a particularly vigorous fashion with a slab of, I believe, concrete block. Had she spoken English, I would have requested that once she could see organs through what was left of my outer crust, she should feel free to desist, but as she did not, I did not, and she kept at it.

After an hour of this, there was not much skin left on yours truly, or so it seemed to me, although I felt better about my condition when I failed to detect pools of blood on the floor. Finally, the blacksmith poured cooler water over me and announced that that was it. This mild form of personal abuse is what women call exfoliation, though

I suggest that the version of it I had just endured is best called defoliation. Dermatologists, using sandpaper, call it dermabrasion and charge a small fortune for it. You could get the same effect at considerably reduced expense and less pain by jumping naked off a speeding motorcycle onto a concrete highway.

Before my arrival in Turkey, if anyone had asked me what country I thought designed and produced the world's finest toilet, I would have said the US, or maybe Germany, Japan, or Holland. In these countries are found, I thought, the ultimate attainment in man's quest for perfection in this underappreciated device. Yet, I would have been sorely wrong. The award for the pinnacle of achievement goes to Turkey. In all of my travels, never have I come across a bathroom appliance that comes so near to attaining perfection as the toilet of Turkey. So nearly flawless is it that all toilets in Turkey employ the same ingenious design, the result no doubt of a government mandate ordering that all its citizens should know, and in a most personal manner experience, the joy of their country's unique achievement.

Upon first encountering one of these wondrous inventions, I observed that it had one obvious feature not found on the everyday toilet: a small, stainless steel spout, about the size of a little finger, protruding horizontally from the rear vertical surface of the bowl rim. Without giving this discovery any further consideration as a more cautious man would be inclined to do, my attention turned quickly to something truly peculiar. Protruding from the bathroom wall near the toilet was a knob of the kind used on a water faucet for opening and closing the tap. What, I wondered, was a knob of this kind doing stuck to the bathroom wall?

A person who is both curious and impulsive comes to learn that life will now and again throw little surprises his way. When I reached down and gave the knob a vigorous twist just to see what would happen, an impressive geyser of water shot upward from that steel spout, reaching nearly to the ceiling, a gusher that, before I could shut it off, thoroughly drenched the bathroom and me. It was in this accidental and slightly embarrassing fashion that I came to appreciate what, in retrospect, should have been obvious. The Turkish toilet is a masterful blending of the toilet and the bidet into a single, all-purpose unit. The rest of the world's toilets are far behind, so to speak.

Although it is nearly perfect, there is a helpful accessory for the Turkish toilet I found appealing and heartily recommend. In bathrooms of the better establishments, the water coming out of the spout is pre-warmed, providing a less bracing experience. There is nothing quite like a blast of chilly water up the fundament to awaken the groggiest of morning risers.

Meals consumed daily by the ordinary Turk are the essence of the acclaimed Mediterranean diet, sure to please a cardiologist and to impoverish a cardiac surgeon. I have no wish to be overly critical of this cherished cuisine, but I have just a slight quibble with it. Each morning when I took my breakfast, I found myself facing a plate covered over with deftly sliced green cucumbers and red tomatoes, leaves of lawn-green lettuce, clods of red radishes, slabs of sickly white cheese, oily black and green olives, and walnuts—where scrambled eggs, bacon, biscuits, and grits should be. An exuberantly colorful salad for breakfast, however healthy it may be, seems to me a poor way to start a day.

There is one more suggestion I would like to offer the Turkish people that would go a long way toward improving the impression the country makes on its visitors. In countries like America, residents are accustomed to churches that insist on the ringing of bells. Thoughtfully, this pealing comes just once each week, lasts only a few minutes, and occurs at an hour when most of us are awake. Anyone for whom the ding-donging of bells is offensive can easily avoid it by the simple expedient of locating his residence at a sufficient remove from any offending church. Whatever may be your opinion of churches that ring bells, there are only a few of them that do it, and they have gone about the business in a manner about as congenial to the civil order as it is possible for bell ringing to be.

In Turkey and every other Muslim country, however, a clergyman, chosen I believe for his especially disagreeable voice and powerful lungs, calls the faithful to prayer five times a day, nearly every day—in Arabic, mind you—and does so through overly amplified loudspeakers erected all over town on which the volume has been turned to the level generally associated with torture.

You just cannot get away from it, and therein lies the problem. It is bad enough that this goes on five times a day nearly every day, but appalling that the first of these comes just at dawn most mornings. This, to my way of thinking, is not the hour at which the sensible man wishes to be awakened. It is a practice inconsistent with the scheme of universal happiness and needlessly offends the visitor to an otherwise fine country.

So I suggest that the morning call to prayer should be done using text messaging or possibly email. With this one simple reform, the Turkish people would endear themselves to visitors, most especially to those spirited partygoers who, at the early morning call to prayers, have only recently climbed into bed.

TWENTY-FIVE

Romania, Bulgaria, and Turkish Nymphs

In late October, we departed from Istanbul and passed through the Bosporus and into the Black Sea, leaving enough time to visit Romania, Ukraine, and Bulgaria and travel some ways up the Danube before winter set in.

Separating the Asian and European continents and cleaving Istanbul, the Bosporus is just nineteen miles long and, at its narrowest point, 766 yards across. To transit the strait, vessels over 1,000 gross tons must travel single file through its marked channel, the direction of traffic flow reversing every six hours. Because *Indigo's* size is considerably less than the minimum, we were permitted to travel against the flow of vessels but outside the marked channel, which gave us the flexibility to set our own speed and wander closer to shore when we wished.

The voyage north through the Bosporus was a joyful experience that none of us will forget. Kitty and I sat on the uppermost deck, astounded at the scenery that passed before us. We passed under its two colossal bridges, dodged the many ferries that ply between the banks, and took in the sights of its striking shore lined with stately old mansions, grand hotels, historic buildings, and restaurants offering outdoor dining. All the while, we basked under a radiant, early fall sky that failed to hint at what lay ahead.

No sooner had we exited the Bosporus than the skies turned the color and texture of steel wool, the winds became brisk, and the seas rose in an effort to deter us from our destination.

Constanta, Romania

After an arduous, four-day voyage, we at last arrived at the Romanian port city of Constanta, and there docked at the largest and most modern commercial port on the Black Sea. What struck us all upon entering its breakwater was that, apart from a few scraggly Romanian naval vessels, we were the sole occupant. Its few miles of seawalls had no vessels secured to them, and its fifty or so giant container cranes were idle and obviously had been so for some time. Built in the hope of creating jobs, the port instead consumed an enormous amount of the country's little capital. After it was built, the country's leaders learned that there are few products produced in Eastern Europe the rest of the world wishes to buy, and that a global recession devastates trade and shipping.

The consequence of this unfortunate combination of economic blunder and bad luck is that Constanta, never a garden spot, remains a hapless, dreary city. Dilapidated and unkempt Soviet-era apartment blocks line the streets and, judging from the looks on the faces of pedestrians I observed, hopelessness has taken a firm hold. It is among the dreariest places I have visited.

By contrast, just down the highway is the smaller, bustling town of Mangalia, home to an enormous shipbuilding yard owned by the Korean giant, Daewoo. While nobody would ever call Mangalia an attractive town, it has jobs building ships.

Not only is the Danube River up which we cruised not blue, as Johann Strauss II apparently imagined it to be, it is a disgusting, dull green. The second longest river in Europe, the Danube flows through ten countries and four capitals, facts that, together with the water's insalubrious appearance, discourage swimming in it.

We traveled through the marked channel of the Danube's Black

Sea delta upstream as far as we could go before it grew too shallow, and there stopped for two days at the ramshackle town of Tulcea. From there, outdoorsmen and tourists venture into the vast delta, a UNESCO World Heritage site, to watch birds, catch fish, sleep in tents, and while away the last days of summer. What a person would do in Tulcea during the bitter cold winter, I cannot say. Get out, if he could, I suppose.

Sulina, Romania

Our next stop was a curious little town called Sulina on a branch of the Danube. The only way to get there is by boat from Tulcea, which makes it an appealing place for those seeking respite from the summer throngs. Its waterfront is a handsome new esplanade, nicely landscaped, with comfortable park benches on which the almost certainly unemployed pedestrian can sit and watch the river traffic. On the other side of the water, just a hundred yards away, is a line of unattractive single-family cottages that look as if they may once have been getaways for Soviet apparatchiks or maybe hideouts for criminals on the lam.

Our next stop was the Ukrainian town of Izmail. At its riverfront sits an incongruously modern and notably unattractive terminal building constructed to accommodate all the tour ship passengers the government was sure would wish to behold their town. As far as I know, no passenger has appeared and none is likely to do so. The terminal at Izmail sits, as the port at Constanta sits, without benefit of customers.

As Kitty and I walked off the boat, a friendly woman greeted us. She was the coach of the girls' high school basketball team, had the day off, and offered to take us on a brief tour in her car, a relic of uncertain vintage.

She took us to see some lovingly maintained and strikingly colorful Russian Orthodox chapels, small, handsome buildings with ornate interiors sporting the characteristic onion-shaped domes. For contrast, we then visited in the center of town a ragtag collection of stalls that function as a seasonal market for just about anything you might need to live in Izmail. It is the local version of a flea market.

Overall, I regret to say that the town does not amount to much.

Bulgaria

Kitty and I rented a car and explored the Black Sea coast of Bulgaria, which held a few surprises, most of which were of the pleasing sort, one not.

Our first stop was the slightly shabby but pleasant city of Varna, the nation's third largest. Its pedestrian boulevards and streets lined with outdoor cafés, an enormous seafront park, and a sandy beach give it the tranquil air of a coastal resort, while its youthful population of 30,000 university students gives it vibrant energy. Leftover from the Soviet era are grand statues celebrating the brave men and women of the proletariat.

From Varna, we drove south along the coast through numerous resort towns in varying states of disrepair. These beaches, and the hotels and apartments nearby, are mobbed in the summer with holidaymakers from all over Europe eager to take advantage of the low prices Bulgaria offers. With alluring names like Golden Sands and Sunny Beach, the towns seem in their visual aspect to be clones of beach towns on the Florida coast of the 1960s.

We stayed overnight at decent hotels in Nesebar and Sozopol, which both feature beautifully restored and commercially active old towns on peninsulas jutting into the sea. What we both found appealing is that these towns are fully functioning villages where people live, work, and play and are not merely museum pieces to be gaped at.

As I said earlier, our experiences in Bulgaria were of the pleasant sort, with one exception. That exception occurred one night in the village of Nesebar. After Kitty had gone to bed early, as is her custom, I took our rental car up the road to an inviting outdoor café for my usual evening cigar and nightcap, and then took in the night air with a stroll. Returning to the car, I drove around the town to get a sense of it, and on my way back to the hotel, the car in front of me abruptly pulled up in the middle of an intersection, revealing on its side the unmistakable markings of the constabulary.

Busted!

When the mind is confronted by Bulgarian police checking for excessive alcohol consumption, it calculates the stratagems available to it, assesses the probability of the success of each, and selects the two or three most likely to keep it and its owner out of the slammer.

"Me no speak Bulgarian," seemed at the time to be a foolproof ploy, one that would most certainly elicit in my captors a warm empathy for a good but misguided man and citizen of a prominent country beloved by all Bulgarians.

Then one of the cops gave me a look which, had he been Marshal Earp of Tombstone, he might have bestowed upon a horse thief. Scratch ploy number one.

The officers used forceful gestures and an irritated manner to indicate that I was to blow into the breathalyzer rather than, as I was in the midst of doing, play it as if it were a banjo.

Ploy number two, bribery, I scratched right away. Using surprisingly sound judgment under the circumstances, I determined that the penalty for this infraction, if reported, would almost certainly exceed by a measure of many months, perhaps years, the penalty I might face for driving under the influence.

Ploy number three, beg for mercy, was the solitary arrow remaining in my quiver, and I deployed it in such a way that, had I been on stage, the house would have been brought down with cheers. But it, too, failed.

The single Jack Daniels Manhattan, plus half a bottle of wine with Kitty at dinner more than an hour before, resulted in a score of .08. Recalling the sensible limit of .10 that prevailed back in Florida years ago, I nodded to the cops in the style of the gracious victor, the man whose innocence has been proved beyond doubt, and turned to walk away. Only then did I learn—through a translation rendered by a helpful bystander—that in Bulgaria the legal limit is not the prudent .10 of my youth but .08, and that the tie most definitely does not go to the miscreant.

Oddly, I was allowed to drive the two blocks to my hotel and to keep the car keys.

Next day, I reported as directed to the sergeant of the local police force, a man with the close-cropped hair, square jaw, and tight-fitting black leather jacket without which the Bulgarian police chief is incomplete. With a halting translation provided by a fellow lawbreaker, the chief said that the usual punishment for the initial infraction is three days in the hoosegow.

"This is very serious," he intoned, to which I nodded in the style familiar to the parents of teenage boys suggesting deep remorse and a solemn promise never to do such a foolhardy stunt again.

After much falderal, paper shuffling, standing in line, and the like—all part of the punishment, I suppose—the police sergeant levied a fine of $300, which I happily paid.

~~~

We returned to *Indigo* and voyaged south from the Black Sea just in time to escape a winter that already had announced its presence. Our transit of the Bosporus this time was on a cool, clear night under a luminous full moon, one of the most thrilling scenes imaginable. Lining the shore and covering the hillsides that rise steeply from the narrow gorge are thousands of tiny glittering lights of private homes and the flamboyant ornamental lights of commercial and government buildings and important historical structures. Moving silently through the narrow corridor are navigation and cabin lights from ships, ferries, and pleasure craft. To this is added the wildly theatrical lights that illuminate the strait's two enormous bridges. At night under a fulgent moon, the Bosporus is about as dazzling a spectacle as it is possible to imagine.

~~~

After seeing Kitty off, I accompanied *Indigo* from Istanbul to its winter headquarters at a yard in Bodrum, organized a few things there, and returned homefor my own winter hiatus.

The Turkish Riviera

I rejoined *Indigo* in early April 2010, long before hordes of tourists would descend on the area in July. Spring along the Turkish Riviera, where Bodrum is located, is a delightful time of year. Indeed, few places on Earth are more agreeable. The air is crisp and free of humidity, the sky radiant and clear, the towns peaceful and somnolent.

Before setting off on our planned voyage, I rented a car and drove a half hour from Bodrum to visit the villages of Yalikavak and Gümüşlük, noted for their exceptional seafood. I dined on the most delectable whole fish pulled that morning from the sea, grilled to perfection over a wood fire, and served with side dishes chosen from a wide assortment of hot and cold items, called *mezzes*, all expertly prepared. It is nearly impossible to have a bad meal anywhere along the Turkish Riviera, just one of its many attractions.

While in Bodrum, the crew had the benefit of the expert assistance of Ilker Varder, whom I came to know. He owns a yard just out of town, where he builds and repairs sailing yachts and charters his and others. These are mostly the classic wood-hulled Turkish vessels, generally 60 to 120 feet, found by the hundreds in marinas all along the Riviera.

Ilker comes from a notable family in Turkey. He graduated from the best schools in Istanbul, then embarked on a career in business. He and his father, a pious man, are estranged over the son's apparent lack of sufficient devotion to Islam. It is a tension especially common in Westernized Turkey, and entirely the result of the declining role of Islam in modern daily life. While the young do not renounce their religion as such, they see it as merely another facet of their lives, one to be kept in balance with education, career, and family. Thus, for example, rather than attend prayers five times each day six days a week, plus the midday compulsory Friday prayers—thus leaving little time for anything else—Ilker and many of his generation attend only the Friday prayers or none at all.

Turkish Nymphs

After wandering about the countryside a bit more, we cast off the lines and began our spring and summer tour of the Med by coasting along the Riviera in a generally eastward direction. We visited numerous towns and villages, tiny islands, and remote bays. These included Knidos, Bozburun, Marmaris, Dalyan, Göcek, Fethiye, Gemiler Island, Kaş, and Kekova.

All of these are delightful places nestled into the foreshore beneath steep, arid hills amid ruins of Greek, Roman, and Ottoman or Byzantine origin. There is scarcely a protected harbor or lofty promontory that is not pockmarked with these ruins, so thoroughly did the ancients clutter the landscape. Amphitheaters are all over the place, something like drive-in movie theaters of their day. Though more than a thousand years old, they appear as if they have been only recently left to the ages.

In the towns are narrow, winding pedestrian lanes lined with retail shops, ending here and there in shady squares of outdoor coffee bars and restaurants. Along their waterfronts are crisply landscaped promenades where the locals take in the night air, beginning around six. Several generations of families join with friends in relaxed groups and stroll along, talking enthusiastically about one thing or another, giving the towns an agreeable, wholesome character.

Göcek was a favorite stop. Its manicured grounds, splendid marinas, and upmarket shops rest at the base of densely forested hills. In the distance, a monumental ridge of high, treeless mountains still bore patches of snow, which, set against the cerulean sky and the gray, towering peaks, made for one of the more stunning vistas along the coast. The mountains in winter boast numerous ski resorts that are popular among Europeans.

Gemiler Island, just half a mile long and a quarter mile wide, once held a dense Byzantine settlement, the remains of which, seen one lazy sunny morning from the deck of *Indigo*, looked as if they might be fun to explore. Up close, what began as a promising idea soon became less appealing. Hiking up and down steep hills, climbing over low walls, and scampering into and out of grottoes demanded far more effort than the place seemed to warrant.

Growing weary of energetic pursuits, I took the tender for a cruise along the mainland coast. While motoring at idle speed, lost in a state of insouciance that failed to rise even to the minimal requirements of a daydream, the notion came upon me out of the fog that on the shore nearby stood a person. I blinked a few times and focused a vacant gaze in that general direction and, sure enough, there on the beach stood a nymph clad in minimalist swimwear that would have easily fit into a shot glass. And she was beckoning to me seductively. Few sights are more inspiring to the mariner.

Every man who has ever set out to sea dreams of coming upon such a beguiling scene. Yet he also knows what men have known since the time of Odysseus, that waving nymphs have as their sole object in life the wish to lure mariners onto rocks and their certain demise. Many are the ships that have come to grief upon the tempting charms of Nymphs Who Wave from Shore.

I regret to report that in resisting the temptation of these troublesome vamps, the record of mariners is not an exemplary one. It is a most regrettable fact, borne out by the events of history, that when faced with a seductive siren waving to them, mariners can be relied upon, as a rule, to do precisely the thing that they ought not to do.

These thoughts, and others, passed through my mind in the way that an arrow pierces the atmosphere, hitting nothing and having as a result no effect whatever. So I cranked over the tender's helm and set off to rescue a fair maiden in distress.

As I approached the shore, there appeared in my path a rock shelf just beneath the surface, an obstacle to the heroic rescue I so fervently wished, even then imagining the gratitude the damsel would surely bestow upon the knight errant who saved her from some hideous fate.

Seeing the obstacle to my progress, our lady on the shore leapt into the briny deep and began flailing away at the Mediterranean in a manner that, I believe, was intended to suggest that version of the freestyle in which the hair is kept free of unwanted moisture lest it damage a stylist's latest creation. Through a sea made frothy by her exertions, she made her way to the tender and, with my gallant help, climbed aboard, deeply chilled from the immersion. My heroic rescue was complete.

Well . . . not quite.

No sooner had she got into the tender than another equally comely lass began waving from the same shore in much the same tantalizing way. This one, too, jumped into the sea and, selecting a stroke more in the manner of a retriever on fetch, began making her way toward the tender. Once she was safely aboard, a third appeared.

Now I was beginning to think I had stumbled upon an international convention of Nymphs Who Wave from Shore. Saving one from whatever evil lurked about seemed like the noble thing to do. The Code of Chivalry called for nothing less. But nymph-saving can be a strenuous affair. When the second, never mind the third, appears, the mariner may start to feel that there are just too many of these creatures wandering about tempting men and vessels, and most likely the best course is just to leave them to Fate. That is what the wise man would do.

Never one to pass up temptation (though one who frequently has regretted not having done so), I rejected this sensible idea and grabbed up what I dearly hoped was the last of this growing platoon of femme fatales who kept popping up on the beach. I didn't know what the daily bag limit for nymphs might be, but I felt fairly certain that I had by now exceeded it.

No sooner had the third climbed aboard than there appeared onshore another person, this one a lone male known to the nymphs. To my usually genial countenance, there came the look of one who has just received a home foreclosure notice. He, like the shore wavers, was youthful and, unlike them, sported a scruffy beard that brought to mind the thorn kraal favored by the African cow herder. The hair on his head hung well below his earlobes and complemented his beard as if it were a roof over the kraal. The lad apparently intended that his appearance should insinuate into the viewer's mind that here stood a graduate student in philosophy, and this it did nicely.

After introductions all around, it turned out that these, along with others still onshore, were not alluring nymphs at all but graduate students from Bosporus University in Istanbul on a spring break camping trip. In the custom of college students the world over, it was beer they were after, not the wrecking of ships—a revelation that summoned empathy for their plight and, as I had been in their position a time or two in the past, my offer of assistance.

Winding our way among the islands at top speed, we soon found an emporium on a nearby beach from which we secured the needed refreshment, then repaired to the comfortable setting of *Indigo*—but not before recovering from their campsite a set of bongo drums and a guitar. Two of the nymphs were the lead singer and drummer in a reggae band popular in Istanbul. After a light meal, they performed some of their sprightly tunes for the enjoyment of us all. Before we knew it, and despite our best efforts at self-restraint, a moderately vigorous celebration broke out.

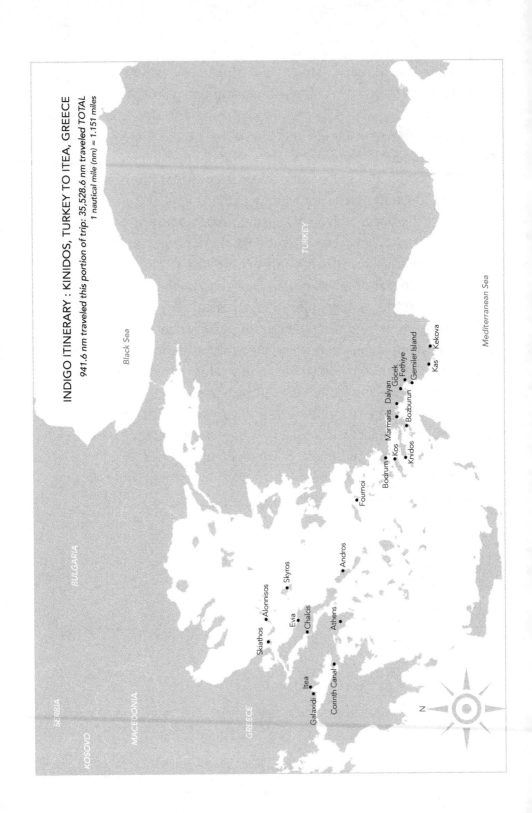

INDIGO ITINERARY : KINIDOS, TURKEY TO ITEA, GREECE

941.6 nm traveled this portion of trip: 35,528.6 nm traveled TOTAL
1 nautical mile (nm) = 1.151 miles

TWENTY-SIX

Athens and More Greek Islands

Over several weeks, I visited the Greek islands of Kos, Fournoi, Andros, Skiros, Alonissos, Skiathos, Evia, and Khalkis, and I can say, without intending to malign the places, that all but one are unremarkable. They are nice places to visit with sunny, rock-strewn beaches, friendly locals, and all that, but just not memorable.

Island of Alonissos

Alonissos is the exception. We went there because I had months earlier read and saved a magazine article touting it as a quiet refuge from the multitudes, and this it surely was, not least because we arrived before the season began.

After a stroll around the island's charming harbor of Patitiri lying in languid repose under warming rays of a kindly Aegean sun, I rented a car and took off for the nearby former capital of Palea Alonissos.

Up a steep, winding road at the peak of a mountain, I came to the village, parked in a designated remote car park, and ambled along its pedestrian walks and staircases, halting at a few miniature plazas to take in the panoramic vista of the surrounding mountains and the gleaming Aegean in the distance. Foreigners with an eye for a bargain have been buying up the once-neglected houses and restoring them. There are wine bars, a few restaurants, and some curio shops, but there is nothing about the place to suggest that it attracts the package tour crowds that plague so many of the Greek islands. It has a pleasant air, tranquil and unpretentious.

After a time, I came upon two distinguished-looking gentlemen about my age walking up a lane in my direction, carrying sacks of groceries. Among the activities one expects to see distinguished-looking gentlemen pursuing, grocery-sack-carrying up lanes of Greek villages is not on the list.

I introduced myself, and they returned my salutation in a most amiable manner. Thus did I come to know Daniel Zeldine and his longtime friend and colleague Dominique Raoux-Cassin, both recently retired from the French diplomatic corp. After exchanging introductions and pleasantries, Daniel invited me to join them for a drink in his recently purchased vacation home, an invitation I happily accepted.

Daniel's vacation getaway actually consists of three homes, each two floors high and standing adjacent to one another separated by common walls—three row houses, really. He bought three hoping that, when combined, they would provide room enough for his daughter and other family members to come for long visits. Across the narrow lane from his are similar dwellings owned by a cousin.

All the homes and shops in the village are built of local brick, are painted white, and have flat roofs and flat, unadorned facades. At the ground floor, each has a single door opening onto a laneway and, at the second floor, a single window covered with slatted shutters painted a dark hue.

The front door of the dwelling Daniel occupied opened directly into the only room on the ground floor. Each of the two floors consisted of just a single room measuring about a hundred square feet and had a ceiling height of about six and a half feet. Into this cramped space was squeezed in one corner a tiny staircase, without railings or balustrades, that spiraled tightly to the upper floor to emerge through a hole of about nine square feet.

In the unit serving as Daniel's temporary living quarters, the upper floor window opened onto a tiny terrace on which we sat watching the day fade away over the sea and chilling clouds roll in. For warmth and sustenance, Daniel produced a bottle of intoxicant made from grappa and a local honey.

When it got too cold to sit outside, we adjourned to a tiny family-owned restaurant for an excellent meal and local wine. Afterward, they joined me on *Indigo* for brandy, where they regaled me with tales from their various posts around the world.

It turned out to be one of those happy, utterly fortuitous encounters that make travel so very enjoyable. We swapped email addresses and promised to keep in touch.

Then *Indigo* set sail for Athens.

Athens, Greece

After departing Alonissos, we anchored overnight in quiet coves, first at Skiathos, then at Evia, and made brief visits ashore on each. Rounding the north end of Evia and proceeding south down a channel between the island and the mainland, we arrived just offshore of Athens in the early morning light.

This city of somewhere between four million and six and a half million inhabitants—nobody knows the number with greater precision—sprawls across the low hills and littoral of the Attica Basin, encompassing an area of 150 square miles. From the sea, its buildings appear all to be whitewashed and low-rise, except for those in the small financial district, and densely packed. The mountains in the background are gray limestone, treeless and arid and girded by a dingy layer of the ever-present mixture of exhaust fumes and dust for which Athens is known.

We docked in the yacht marina at Piraeus, the port suburb of Athens from which cruise ships plying the Aegean Sea arrive and depart. As so often with port towns, Piraeus is uncommonly ugly, stuffed with shabby apartment buildings and menaced by dense traffic. At night, it seems like a fine place for muggers to lurk about.

All around its several harbors are outdoor coffee bars, where locals gather to drink frappes, among much else. In the Greek rendition, a frappe is a concoction of sweet coffee whipped to a milkshake-like viscosity, heavily fortified with extra caffeine and served cold in a plastic cup. I drank one and promptly developed a throbbing headache between the eyes, sweating palms, tremors, and a mild disorientation lasting twenty-four hours. That was from just one. Greeks typically consume four or five of these in the course of an afternoon and evening. Little wonder they are so boisterously chatty and party until the sun comes up. Judging from the youthful customers in these places at all hours of the workday, an urge to gainful employment does not appear to be among its effects.

It was in the Greek islands that I first encountered the proliferation of open-air coffee bars. There—and in Athens, too—these greatly outnumber restaurants and serve as public places for socializing and people watching at all hours of the day and night. In nearly all towns and villages around the Mediterranean, it is more fashionable to sit at small tables outdoors sipping coffee than to sit at large bars indoors gulping whiskey.

Whatever may have been the appeal of Athens in the time of Pericles, little of it remains. The city's parks and buildings are ill kept, its streets trash strewn and traffic choked. Many buildings are in obvious need of repair or, better yet, demolition. A pall of smog, trapped against the mountains by wind blowing in off the sea, hangs over the city, giving its air an unhealthful hue.

Back in the 1930s, that infestation of the planet known as the International Style of architecture began to infect almost all Greek architects. As the population of Athens exploded in the 1950s and 1960s, large areas in and near the city's center were cleared of offending Neoclassical style buildings, and in their place were erected excrescences in this vernacular, jumbles of bland boxes now grown moldy and in need of paint. One of the style's founders and leading exponents, Walter Gropius, designed the US embassy in Athens, which is unfortunately still in use. There is little about the city center that is handsome.

Some of the suburbs are more appealing. It was to one of these that Katrina and Labros, the young couple I had met on Patmos Island many months before, invited me for a fine, home-cooked dinner of traditional Greek fare. Their apartment is modest, cozy, and caringly appointed. One of its bedrooms serves as a small shop where Katrina practices cosmetology on a modest scale.

At the time of my visit, Labros worked as an aircraft machinist for a Greek subcontractor to Boeing, and after six years of exemplary performance, he remained stuck at the entry level. Coming from the distant island of Crete, he had no mentor to pull him up the ladder, and without family or political alliances, advancement in Greece is nearly impossible, regardless of merit. I knew that in the US he could earn double his current salary, have better benefits, and find immediate employment. Yet Labros and Katrina declined even to consider moving. They just did not want to live so far from their close-knit families, even though these could do nothing to help in his career. In Greece, kinship is all-important.

Even for the traveler who is not an admirer of ancient ruins, one of the few sights worth seeing in Athens is the Parthenon. Happily, it can be seen from almost anywhere, sitting as it does in grand repose upon the Acropolis, a hatbox mesa rising 200 feet above the scruffy city. Seeing this noble monument to man's better nature rising from a city wrought by man's lower nature is deeply disheartening. Athens's grim chaotic history is a living lesson, with almost daily reminders on the fragility of democracy.

The Corinth Canal and the Gulf of Corinth
From Athens, we cruised through the Saronic Gulf, its shore lined with much of Greece's heavy industry. Petrochemical refineries, tank farms, factories, naval bases, and mills abound. Trash-strewn, oily water near shore discourages swimming.

The Corinth Canal cuts through the narrow isthmus connecting the Peloponnese Peninsula with the rest of Greece, reducing the distance between the Aegean and Ionian Seas by 150 miles. Begun in the time of Nero, worked on sporadically over many years and only completed in 1893, it slices through limestone rising to 250 feet above sea level at the highest point. Its cut is 3.2 miles long and a mere eighty feet wide with a draft of twenty feet. Vessel traffic is one-way, reversing as the need arises.

Upon arriving at the canal's eastern entrance, we delighted at the sight of small cruise ships, various commercial vessels, and yachts emerging magically from the rugged hills and moving across the land as if on wheels. When the last of these eastbound vessels passed out of the canal, we joined a convoy westbound, falling into line as directed by the canal authority.

Once through the canal, we found ourselves in one of the Med's least known and most visually extraordinary bodies of water. Just eighty miles long and varying between five and twenty miles wide, the Gulf of Corinth is encircled by parched, treeless mountains rising to 8,000 feet, still splotched with snow in late spring. On the narrow alluvial plain that fringes the shoreline are fishing villages and sandy beaches, citrus groves, and vineyards.

Cruising through the Gulf was one of our most remarkable experiences in the Med. A clear sky overhead, calm waters under the keel, and surrounded by high mountains looming over us in every direction, it was scenery much like that from an Alpine lake in Bavaria.

At night, the Gulf became a fantasyland as lights from villages along the shore and from those high up on the mountain faces sparkled in the dry air like cheery holiday decorations on a grand scale. Not to be outdone, Mother Nature added the intense glory of a lustrous full moon rising above the mountain crests. Nothing I have seen on this Earth excelled that night on the Gulf of Corinth for sheer visual ecstasy.

Our first stop in the Gulf was the picture-perfect village of Ormos Galaxidhiou, adjacent to a pine-covered waterfront park. Here, we anchored and went ashore for dinner at one of the many open-air cafés that line its tiny harbor. A gaggle of noisy kids playing in the plaza in front of our dining table threatened the tranquility we sought, so I instructed Stew Gillian to buy them all ice cream, thinking this would keep the blighters occupied and quiet during our meal. In doing so, I failed to take account of the fundamental principle of economics holding that when anything desirable is free, demand for it will soon become infinite. Faster than you might think, the noisy kids who had once numbered ten became twenty, all clamoring for more ice cream.

Just across the Gulf is the quiet village of Itea, which offers a marina for vessels visiting the nearby Temple of the Oracle of Delphi. In another of those foolish moments, which on occasion come to us all, I suspended my sensible aversion to ancient ruins and took a taxi high up the steep, deeply gouged slopes of Mount Parnassus to join a great horde of similarly misguided tourists. While the views looking out over the Gulf were dazzling, the temple museum, densely packed with visitors even in late May, was not. I made a high-speed, broken-field run through its collection of variously shattered statuary and temple parts and departed.

During a memorable lunch at a small café hanging precariously from the mountainside, a breezy freshness in the air, I gazed impassively over olive and citrus groves to the distant Gulf of Corinth just as those ancients who had come to visit the Temple of Apollo at Delphi once had done. Whatever divinations may have emanated from here, horoscope-like, the vistas from it are enchanting.

Greek Islands of the Ionian Sea

Exiting the Gulf of Corinth at its western end through narrow straits into the Gulf of Patras, we came upon the Greek islands of the Ionian Sea. With beautiful beaches, pine-clad mountains, and stunning coastlines rising from the iridescent water, these are among the fairest islands in the Med. Differently from those of the Aegean, these fertile islands, though rugged and mountainous, are partly covered over in a lush, semitropical tapestry of vineyards, olive groves, wheat fields, and orchards. Cliffs up to 600 feet high line their western shores, providing dramatic scenery above and secluded beaches below.

It was on one of these beaches, at Shipwreck Cove on the island of Zakynthos, that we took the tender to shore and there enjoyed a picnic in relative isolation[1]. Though we had a fine time with plenty of local wines and cheeses, cold beer, and snacks, the beach brought home yet again a characteristic of nearly all Med beaches that I found both surprising and mildly disappointing. Because the parched hills and steep mountains that form the islands are mostly limestone, the beaches at their base are comprised of rocks. On some, these are small pebbles, on others rocks up to the size of tennis balls. Those at our picnic site were of the latter variety and impossible to walk on comfortably without shoes of some sort, or lie upon without a soft pad.

We next stopped at the picturesque waterfront village of Fiskardo on the island of Kefalonia. Its harbor was filled with small craft lying at anchor and its quay lined with restaurants, bars, and shops of surprisingly high quality. There is about it that pleasing air of authenticity found in towns not entirely given over to the tourist trade.

Here I met a Frenchman from Paris, his young daughter, and her friend, who had been sailing for several weeks among these islands in a boat of not more than twenty-five feet or so. Father and daughter were born and raised on the island of Corsica, which they praised so lavishly that I added it to our itinerary. They also extolled the Greek islands of the Ionian as among the finest sailing grounds in the Med. I have found no cause to dispute them.

Just north of Kefalonia lies the island of Lefkas, separated from the Greek mainland by a narrow causeway. Here we visited overnight the busy resort town of Nidri, perhaps most notable as the town located about a mile from Skorpios, the tiny island once owned by Aristotle Onassis. On the same island is the village of Lefkas Town, where narrow pedestrian walks wind among well-tended homes and shops of exceptional quality. Differently from other villages on the island, the second floors are made of timber as protection against the recurrence of earthquakes, one of which flattened the town in 1953.

---

1. The photo of *Indigo* on the front cover of this book shows the cliffs defining the Cove in the background."

Overhanging the walkways are flower-festooned balconies, and through inviting archways are tiny, secluded gardens. It is one of the most delightful villages I have visited anywhere, and one to which I would happily return, though not during the summer season.

Corfu, our next stop, is the most famous and largest, and the least appealing, of the Ionian Islands. Once popular as a haunt of royalty and celebrities, it is today a favorite of Brits on package tours and heavily populated by Brit expats.

While at first sight dispiriting, Corfu Town, where we docked, is said eventually to grow on you—although I took little comfort in this assurance, as the same can be said of fungus. Its old town is a confusion of tattered shops located near the cruise ship docks, usually aswarm with wandering tourists. Though supposedly cleaned up for the 1994 EU meeting, from its appearance today, you would never know it. Tottering old Venetian-style apartment buildings in need of repair and laundry lines festooned with underwear give the place an air of shabby, bygone gentility. Outside the old town, it gets better, but the traffic-choked streets discourage traveling far. Anybody planning an excursion to the Ionian Islands would be wise to avoid this island in favor of those farther to the south and more remote.

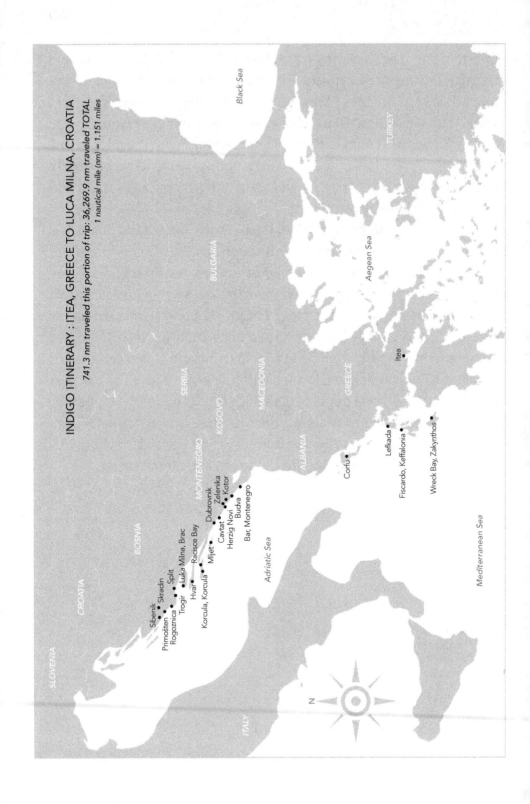

INDIGO ITINERARY : ITEA, GREECE TO LUCA MILNA, CROATIA

741.3 nm traveled this portion of trip: 36,269.9 nm traveled TOTAL

1 nautical mile (nm) = 1.151 miles

TWENTY-SEVEN

Nearly Naked in Croatia

Departing from Corfu on June 16, we left behind the last of the Greek islands of the Ionian Sea, entered into the Adriatic Sea, and made our next landfall in a region that was to be one of the most fascinating places we visited.

We traveled up the Balkans coast to the picture-perfect village of Cavtat, similar in appearance to Carmel, California, of sixty years ago.

Cavtat, Croatia

My favorite part of Cavtat, apart from the village itself, is the adjacent seafront park with a shoreline pedestrian walk skirting the rocky shore and shaded by a dense forest of pines. About a mile or so long with park benches thoughtfully placed in shady spots along the way, it makes a perfect place for idle strolls.

Halfway along its length, there is a rude facsimile of a tiki bar, a makeshift affair with six seats under the shade of its thatched roof. Its owner had for years sought permission from the town to build the place but never could get an answer, yes, no, or maybe, so he just built it anyway and had been there six years doing just fine, thank you. You have to admire the man's spirit.

It was along the seaside walk that I first became aware of a most unusual feature of Croatian beaches. Few of them are made of pebbles like those we found in the Greek islands, and fewer still are made of sand. Most of the beaches in Croatia are heaps of naturally formed slabs of rock, great and small, on which people lie about in a relaxed pose without benefit of soft padding between them and the rock. It was quite ordinary to see people of all ages stretched out supine in the sun, their head resting—if that is the right word here—on bare, hard rock. On first sight of this, I thought of seals sunning themselves.

The other fact of Croatian—indeed Balkan—life that became apparent in Cavtat and repeatedly during my long stay is the thought-less disregard of bathers there for the delicate sensibilities of visitors from more puritanical-minded countries—like the US, for example. I can say with confident assurance that there is not a man over the age of his teens that does not wear on public beaches what we in the West call a Speedo, invariably black. He wears this bathing attire without regard to his age or to the condition of his physique. To take an example, I saw many men in their seventies and eighties wearing these garments, men whose gluteus maximus had long ago gone minimus.

Nor did I see a single woman, regardless of age, that did not wear a bikini. I am the first to say that this bit of swimwear, when worn by an attractive, lissome young woman, is one of nature's finest bless-ings, a gift from the gods. Those worn by tall, leggy, Serbian women are most especially so. A bikini worn, however, by an older and more voluptuously proportioned woman usually fails in its attempt to enclose all the flesh that its wearer has attempted to cram into it.

Setting aside my attempts at humor on the subject, I actually came to admire the casual disregard of these people for the opinion of others on the very personal subject of their physiques. They seem to be saying, "Here is my body, flawed as it may be, and I do not care what you think of it. I will display it as suits my comfort, not as suits your inhibitions."

This disregard for the conventional standards of Western prud-ery has its origins in the Soviet era. Citizens behind the Iron Curtain learned that Western ideals of public deportment had their origin in Puritan religiosity and as such were denials of the true nature of man, the nature that only atheist Communism properly celebrated. Accordingly, it was not only acceptable for people to display themselves as Mother Nature intended, but they were encouraged to do so.

For that reason, Croatia today abounds in what are known there as naturist camps, the last vestiges of Communism and a harmless rebuke of Western censoriousness. Nowhere else on Earth are there more of these, or are they more enthusiastically attended. Scandinavians, Germans, Austrians, and Slavs from all over Europe flock to Croatia in summer to lark about in the buff. Naturists claim that strolling around in the altogether—or "sky-clad"—is disinhibiting in a breezy, free-swinging sense, claims I have no cause to dispute.

Here, I have a confession to make. I considered joining in the frivolity, going so far as to get directions to the camp nearest my hotel. I also received instructions from the concierge on nudist camp etiquette, an area of social encounter offering endless opportunity for hapless faux pas. I thought to myself, *If not here, where, and if not now, when?*

At the last minute, though, I abandoned the idea when a single word popped to mind: *sunburn.* Of the many afflictions a man wishes not to befall his most treasured appendage, scorching easily makes the list. And as a light-skinned, blue-eyed, once-blonde male, I am easily scorched.

Dubrovnik, Croatia

Lord Byron called Dubrovnik the Pearl of the Adriatic, George Bernard Shaw said it was Paradise on Earth, and a general under Napoleon dubbed it, just before capturing it, an Oasis of Civilization.

The Serbs and Montenegrins, during the Yugoslav Wars, called it a target and very nearly destroyed the place by raining down upon it thousands of artillery shells in 1991 and 1992. At the time the bombardment began, the citizens of the town were unarmed, defenseless, and had done nothing to provoke the Serb army except vote not to join a greater Serbian nation.

Today, the damage repaired and the famous town restored to its prior grandeur, it remains one of the world's gems, deservedly a UNESCO World Heritage site. Marble-paved squares, steep, cobbled streets, elegant palaces, convents, churches, fountains, and museums, all built from the same sand-colored, finely milled limestone, are enclosed by enormous protective walls. Built to keep out invaders, a task at which they failed, the walls now shelter this enchanted town from the modern world outside and, most importantly, from traffic. Only pedestrians fill its streets.

I was there in the swelter and crowds of the summer season, a timing that in the daytime detracted from my enjoyment. At night, though, after the cruise ships have departed, the locals begin their habitual promenade and the city takes on a magical air that lightens the step and brings a smile to the most sullen face. It ranks for me as one of the finest examples of a restored old town.

Island of Korcula

Off the rocky shores of this jagged coastline is the large island of Korcula, a cluster of smaller ones—including pastoral Mljet, half of which is a pristine national park—and the mountainous Peljesac Peninsula. The area produces some of Croatia's finest wines, both red and white, which we were pleased to sample and add to our stores, and serves up notable seafood.

Korcula's old town, where we tied up to the quay for a night, is tiny by comparison to others in the region but popular as a summer resort.

Split, Croatia

Much of my time in Croatia, I spent in and around the city of Split. Croatia's second largest city is a remarkable town for the reason that the Roman emperor Diocletian chose to build his retirement home there, now a UNESCO World Heritage site. Completed in 305 AD, much of it is still standing. It is built of lustrous white stone quarried from nearby Brac and includes marble from Italy and Greece, and columns and sphinxes from Egypt. Far from being a museum, within its walled area of just 7.5 acres are enclosed 220 buildings of widely varying vintage, including homes for 3,000 people and shops, cafés, bars, and restaurants. Along its waterfront is a promenade crowded every night with strolling tourists and locals enjoying the breezes wafting in from the sea. It is one of the most fascinating Roman ruins in existence.

During the summer season, the Split promenade, called the Riva, fills each night with all manner of street performers and kiosks offering specialty foods and local wines and beers. Outdoor concerts nearly every night offer something for most any taste, though some require a fluency in Croatian to grasp fully what is happening on stage. For its Riva, summer music festivals, and the grand old palace ruins, Split ranks among my favorite places, even with the summer crowds.

Hvar, Croatia

While on *Indigo*, the crew and I spent three nights docked on the quay in the old town of Hvar on the island of the same name. It ranks as my favorite—and judging from the crowds, everyone else's favorite—island on the Dalmatian coast. Offering many excellent restaurants and hotels and an exuberant nightlife, it is about all you could want in a fun place to visit.

Just next to the town harbor is a large, densely treed national park with a nicely shaded pedestrian path skirting its seaward edge. About a half mile along this path, I came to a tiki bar perched among the rocks along the shore, memorably called Bubba Gump's Hula Hula Bar. The moment I arrived, the heavy wake of a passing ferry had just come ashore, which, as it struck the rocks, splashed chilly seawater onto the customers and into their refreshments, to the raucous delight of all. This, I quickly concluded, was a fine place to waste lots of time. It didn't hurt that bikini tops seemed to be in short supply.

~~~

Farther north along the coast from Split, I visited the towns of Trogir, Rogoznica, Sibenik, Primosten, Zadar, and numerous others, all similar in that they are waterfront and built around old towns that have become shopping and entertainment destinations. In a protected bay at Sibenik is the opening into a deep limestone chasm that leads through a winding course to the village of Skradin. We boarded a van there and traveled farther upstream to the Krka National Park, whose distinguishing feature is a series of waterfalls uniquely formed from the calcium carbonate-laden river.

Still farther north, I passed through the port city of Rijeka to the small resort town of Opatija, one of many such towns on the Kvarner Riviera, once the favored diversion of notables from Vienna during the days of the Hapsburg Empire. Its shore, still lined with handsome villas and vintage hotels, is now also home to upmarket shops and swish restaurants.

One night I attended a piano concert given by a professor of music from a nearby university and held in a room in one of the old villas. He was a talented performer and played a wide selection of genres from American jazz and pop tunes to Mozart and Croatian classical. Always a soft touch for such things, I bought his CD.

The Istrian Peninsula

I played that CD during my drive through the Istrian Peninsula, reputed to be the culinary center of Croatia. Its wines, while surely adequate, are not up to the standards of the southern regions around Hvar and Dubrovnik, but its cuisine is superb. While I was there, the truffle season was at its peak. Sniffed out by trained dogs, these tasty fungi, both black and white, grow all over central Istria. Any restaurant will add them to a dish for a modest cost.

In the central part of the peninsula, it seems that atop nearly every hill is yet another old town. One features artists, another features musicians, and another fine food and local wines. When not catering to wandering tourists, these sleepy villages are devoted to harvesting grapes, hunting truffles, and cultivating orchards. Even during the season, tourists are far fewer than on the coasts. I visited Buzet, Motovun, Buje, and Groznjan, and I liked them all quite a lot.

Slovenia

On the peninsula's west coast, I headed north into Slovenia, just because I had never been there. I stayed several nights in one of the finest hotels I have ever encountered. The Palace is a magnificent refurbishment of a classic old hotel in the resort town of Portoroz. Just up the highway is the Italian port city of Trieste.

Slovenia is clearly richer than Croatia. It also still harbors animosity for its immediate neighbor left over from the Yugoslav Wars. Nobody would convert Croatian currency, called kunas, into euros, and each time I tendered it, a clerk turned me down with a polite disdain as if it were crawling with deadly bacteria.

Across the street from the hotel is a beach facing a bay off the northern Adriatic. Its street side is lined with touristy shops, bars, and restaurants, and its bay side is crowded with beach chairs arranged in a grid seven rows deep from the water and spaced three feet apart. The chairs rent by the hour to anyone wishing to sunbathe among a thicket of others.

Rovinj, Croatia

I next drove south along the Istrian coast through all of the resort towns along the way before arriving at Rovinj (Row-veen). My hotel there, called Monte Mulini, is modern and nicely sited on a hill sloping gently to a placid bay. It's a short walk to the exceptionally large old town.

The hotel's best feature, however, is its immediate proximity to one of the finest public parks I have yet encountered anywhere. The park is enormous, covered in old-growth forest and interlaced with pedestrian paths along which are spaced inviting, tree-shaded bars and restaurants. Its seaside walk, about two miles long, twists and winds around the craggy shore and carries a constant parade of locals and tourists. Some come for a favorite swimming spot, some to ride bikes, but most, like me, are there just for a quiet, contemplative stroll among natural beauty.

Croatia is full of these parks that were begun in Tito's time but continued, enlarged, and improved thereafter. There is scarcely a waterfront anywhere in the country that is without its pedestrian-only sea walk. The notion that the owner of waterfront private property has the right to exclude the public from walking along the shore is foreign here. If there is a salutary remnant of the former Yugoslav Republic, this may be it.

On a day trip, I drove to Pula and did a drive-by sighting of its notable attraction: the sixth largest Roman amphitheater in the world, with a seating capacity back then of 20,000. It really is impressive, and is today the site of frequent concerts during the summer. In the same place gladiators once entertained crowds, Norah Jones, Andrea Bocelli, and Placido Domingo perform in concert.

TWENTY-EIGHT

The Balkan Experience

Upon returning to Split, I promptly planned my next excursion by car, this one to Sarajevo, capital of Bosnia, site of a horrific, four-year siege during the Yugoslav Wars.

I drove south from Split along Croatia's southern Dalmatian coast to Metković before entering Bosnia. The border crossing was perfunctory and of little consequence. I made my way east up a two-lane highway through Mostar and Jablanica to Sarajevo.

As the road ascended from the coastal plains to the low piedmont and finally to the mountains where ski resorts abound, the signs of war became more frequent—lone farm buildings shattered by mortars and commercial buildings pockmarked by small arms fire.

Sarajevo, Bosnia

Upon arriving at the outskirts of Sarajevo, I at first saw freshly painted buildings and thought that perhaps the war hadn't reached here. Then I learned that it had reached here, all right, and in appalling fashion. The freshly painted buildings were among the few on which the disfigurements of war had been slathered over with stucco and paint. Nearly all the rest still bore the scars of deadly battle—deep, lasting, ugly scars, much like those left on the minds of the Bosnians who'd survived.

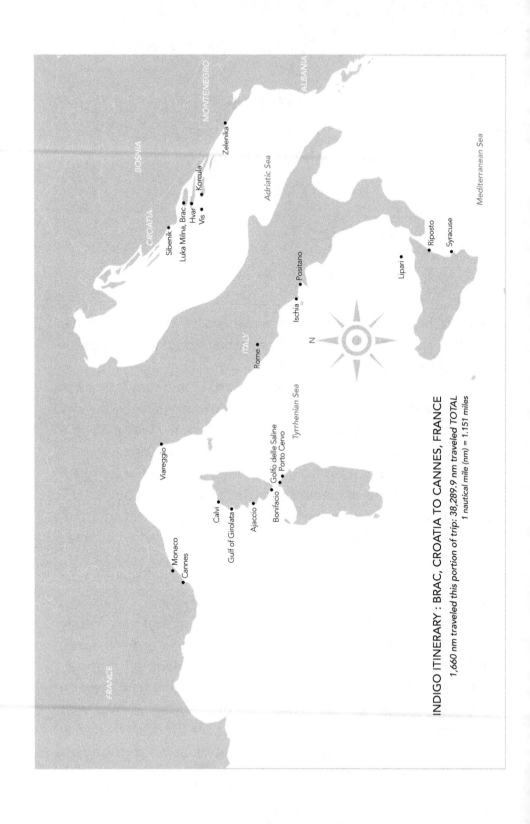

INDIGO ITINERARY : BRAC, CROATIA TO CANNES, FRANCE

1,660 nm traveled this portion of trip: 38,289.9 nm traveled TOTAL

1 nautical mile (nm) = 1.151 miles

Topography is one key to understanding the suffering that the people of Sarajevo endured from April 1992 to February 1996, during the longest siege of a capital city in modern history. The city of nearly 526,000 (before the war) predominantly Muslim citizens sits at the bottom of a bowl almost completely encircled by low, forested hills. The only relief in the encirclement—and the only substantial stretch of flat land—is a gap in the far western suburb on which sits the only airport, a topographic anomaly that was to have deadly consequences.

When the Serbian army of 13,000 arrived, it took up positions along the crests of those encircling hills, which included more than 200 batteries of artillery, tanks, mortars, machine guns, rocket launchers, and snipers with long-range scopes. The Sarajevans in the bowl below were at first poorly armed and mostly civilians, whose only wish was to be left in peace. Instead, they became targets. Over the course of the siege, an average of 329 shells per day hit the city. On one memorable day, July 22, 1993, 3,777 shells rained down.

Serbians living in Sarajevo had long lived and worked quietly among the Bosnians, even marrying into Bosnian families and living in Bosnian neighborhoods. When the Serb army arrived, however, many abandoned their families and friends and joined the invaders. It was, and remains, an apostasy of breathtaking dimension. Still more appallingly, after the war, these Serbs returned to the city and their families and (former) friends, and today they live and work alongside those whom they had sought to annihilate.

When I arrived in the city and checked into my hotel in the center of its old town, I hired a guide, and together we toured the war-ravaged city. Hardly any building was without damage; some were only bare skeletons remaining after artillery or mortar rounds had pierced their roofs. Enormous apartment blocks bore gaping holes. Even the garishly painted Holiday Inn showed telltale marks of battle.

From a hilltop, the guide pointed to a patch of stark-white grave markers where once existed a soccer field. As I surveyed the cityscape from that hill, I observed patches of white markers, both great and small, splotched across the landscape. Former parks, sports fields, even gardens were now cemeteries. The death toll in Sarajevo from nearly four years of siege was an estimated 11,000, of which over 5,000 were civilians. Another 50,000 were wounded.

The only possible way to get food and water to starving families required a near-suicidal 1,000-yard dash across the open-airport runways to Bosnian-held land and back. Ostensibly controlled by UN peacekeeping forces, the airport was, in fact, a killing field.

One day the guide took me to a very special rudimentary museum of sorts. From inside a small, battered house in a neighborhood alongside the airport, a tunnel—today known as the Tunnel of Hope—extended under the runways to emerge 3,150 feet away in the Bosnian-held safe territory. Dug by hand by volunteers working round the clock, the tunnel was two feet and seven inches wide and barely five feet high. On its floor was a rude set of rails welded from lengths of angle iron. On these rails, a wooden trolley once carried food, water, medicine, even diapers, and, most important, soldiers and weaponry to the desperate people of Sarajevo. During its operation, twenty million tons of food passed into the city, and a million people passed both into and out of it.

In the museum, I sat in a tiny room and watched a brief film of live scenes from the siege. In one extraordinary segment, tank rounds repeatedly slammed into some of the enormous apartment buildings I had passed on my way to the city. After viewing that film, I became convinced that Serbian regular and paramilitary forces intended to exterminate Bosnians, military and civilian alike, including women and children. There was no other reason for directing fire into the defenseless homes of civilians.

In Sarajevo's old town were numerous square blocks of pedestrian walkways lined with shops of every description, museums, restaurants, and the ubiquitous coffee bar. Here and there were modest mosques with attendant schools and handsomely renovated hotels and shopping arcades. In the evenings, locals and a few tourists promenaded, dipping into shops here and stopping for coffee there.

Sarajevo had a pleasing, restful air about it, and the people seemed affable enough. In the four days I stayed, I came to like the place and its people, and I am glad I went. That said, after wandering around in the old town and learning firsthand about the siege, and perhaps viewing the bridge where Archduke Ferdinand's assassination kicked off the Great War, there is not much to keep a tourist's attention.

On my drive back to Split, Bosnian police stopped me for passing through a miniature village a touch quickly. Two smartly attired officers stepped from a modern compact car. One spoke English. After scolding me for my flagrant violation of the law, he said that because I was a foreigner, I'd have to go to jail until a judge heard my case. The fine, he said, would be 200 euros. I offered, in the interest of efficiency, to pay the fine to him immediately so he could deliver it to the judge. He thought this was a great idea.

A Few Words About Muslims

This seems to be a good point at which to record my impressions of the Muslim citizens I encountered. With the exception of the United Arab Emirates, I sensed neither animosity toward nor resentment of an obviously American visitor. In contrast, I was at all times regarded in a cheerful manner, fully in keeping with the nature of the encounter. Many of the Muslims I met in Oman and Turkey, in particular, evolved into real and lasting friendships.

What most impressed me about the people of these countries was their wholesomeness. I never felt unsafe at any hour or at any location. I never saw public drunkenness or rowdiness (by the locals), even in those liberal-minded countries where consuming alcohol was commonplace. I observed a nearly complete absence of licentiousness, drug use on a disruptive scale, publicly troublesome teenagers, slovenly personal appearance, and most of the other social pathologies that plague and coarsen the Western world. Published statistical profiles of these countries bear this out.

I could never quite shake from my mind that I was in the midst of an obviously and pleasingly decent community of like-minded citizens. Families were close-knit, children were well behaved and scrubbed, and attire was sensible, largely unfashionable, and worn neatly without being salacious. People were extraordinarily polite to one another, always exchanging the traditional greetings of friend-ship. Men openly embraced each other with real affection and held hands with their wives in public unselfconsciously. The insistent bass and driving rhythms of rap, hip-hop, and techno were almost entirely absent. Ostentation was discouraged, with the notable exception of the United Arab Emirates. Everyone I encountered was invariably polite and helpful.

For all of these salutary features, I give full credit to Islam, although it is achieved at a price of regimented conformity few of us would be willing to pay today. We did pay the price once, before the cata-clysms of the '60s revolution, and as we look back on it now, through the murky lens of hindsight, we are wistful, hoping those days might come again, almost begging to pay the price of renewed conformity.

I noted that the Western notion of multiculturalism would've been unthinkable in this homogeneous society. The corruption of their culture, the debasement of the moral choices they'd made for them-selves and their families by the powerful lure of Western modernism was a fear they expressed to me often. That is why, even though they may choose to emigrate to London, Paris, or New York, they'd be unlikely to assimilate fully for at least a generation or two, if ever.

Vienna, Austria

Kitty and some friends from Jacksonville arrived for a girls' trip, a week of fun cruising among the islands of the Dalmatian coast. Our son, Grant, came with them, and wishing to leave the women to themselves, he and I hopped on a flight to Vienna.

Vienna ranks in the top three or four cities in the world on nearly everybody's list, and with good reason. With the help of a friend from the area, I booked a hotel immediately fronting on St. Stephen's Platz in the very heart of the old town, and we walked everyplace we went. I wanted to be sure Grant got exposure to the city's fine arts and history.

Among the memorable places we visited were the Upper and Lower Belvedere Palaces and their gardens, the Rathouse, an all-Mozart concert adjacent to the Spanish Riding School, the Museum of Modern Art, and St. Stephen's Cathedral. We dined at some superb restaurants and drank at a few classy bars.

It was our good fortune that the annual summer music festival was underway while we were there. In the lush park around the Rathouse, vendors set up kiosks selling local foods including lots of sausage (of course), beer, champagne, and wine. There were even full bars and restaurants set up, a few of these mounted on scaffolding the better for their patrons to view and hear the music. I say "view" the music because the entertainment consisted of a giant video screen on which notable past performances of the Vienna Philharmonic and various guest artists were shown. It was all a civilized affair with a great deal of socializing among the audience, so much so that I doubt many saw the screen or heard the music. There was about it the air of a gala social event with background music.

From Vienna, Grant and I drove into the small town of Klagenfurt, turned south, and made our way through a high pass in the mountains to Ljubljana, Slovenia, noted as Europe's smallest capital. We had lunch in the town center alongside the languid Ljubljanica River, then drove on to Zagreb.

Zagreb, Croatia
Situated along the banks of the Sava River and on the slopes of Medvednica Mountain, Zagreb is the capital of Croatia and, at a population exceeding 800,000, its largest city. Nearly all of the country's scientific and research institutions and major companies are headquartered there. The place bustles with energy that fills the air in its two old towns, especially on warm summer nights. Though people outside of Europe are only dimly aware of Zagreb, if they know of it at all, it is one of central and southeastern Europe's leading cosmopolitan centers.

As we drove through its outer suburbs, Zagreb looked dispirited, just another slightly seedy Eastern European city. When we came to the heart of it, though, a new, more promising scene opened before us. Classical-style buildings from the era of its days in the Austro-Hungarian Empire, freshly scrubbed and painted, lined its leafy streets. Numerous parks, immaculately maintained, hummed with locals and tourists alike enjoying the sunny day. Its Gornji Grad, or Upper Town, an ancient hillside neighborhood built of stone, was thronged with fun seekers strolling the narrow pedestrian lanes and outdoor stair-cases among cheerful terrace bars and outdoor restaurants. The side-walks of Donji Grad, or Lower Town, a tamer place of shops, cafés, museums, and parks, too, were lined with strolling crowds taking in the early evening air.

We stayed two nights at the palatial Esplanade Zagreb Hotel, built in 1925 for passengers of the Orient Express. Its restaurant is one of the best I have encountered anywhere in Europe, complemented by a bar and terrace.

From Zagreb, we drove on a new four-lane, limited-access high-way that would take us to Sibenik, where we would rejoin *Indigo*. To give you some idea of Croatia's infrastructure, it is the finest highway I have ever driven. I could maintain a hundred miles per hour with ease and complete safety.

After saying goodbye to Kitty, her friends from Jacksonville, and Grant, we hoisted anchor and set off for Montenegro.

Bar, Montenegro
With a population of less than 700,000 and a land area slightly smaller than Connecticut, Montenegro is the least consequential of the Balkans countries, yet it is also undoubtedly the most scenic, a min-iature impecunious version of Austria. "Wild Beauty" is the national tourism slogan, and that it surely has. Its coastline, just 180 miles long, is renowned for steep cliffs, beautiful beaches, and translucent waters, its interior for craggy mountains, Alpine lakes, and primeval forests.

As the primary port of entry, the city of Bar is a jarring contradiction to the country's beauty. One of my guidebooks, whose intended readers are youthful backpackers and so less fussy than I, says, with a gift for understatement, "Bar is unlikely to be anyone's holiday highlight." It will appeal to those whose tastes run in the direction of Soviet-era brutalist architecture.

At the heart of the busy town center are three adjacent, identical concrete structures that closely resemble gigantic, upside-down toilet bowl plunger cups and exude all the playful charm of an abattoir. The part of their concrete that has not fallen away to reveal rusty rebar is badly worn, moldy, and in need of paint. The retail shops that the plunger cups are there to house need tenants, and their glass storefronts and paved walkways need cleaning. Much of the rest of the city reflects a similar state of dereliction, and as a result, our stay there was brief.

Budva, Montenegro

For our next stop, we chose the beach resort town of Budva, and there secured dockage along the quay in the old town. Just a few steps away is a sliver of beach frequented by locals, along with a smart bar/restaurant to accommodate them. Across the way is the old town itself, a former medieval trading center now converted, like all such old towns in the Med, to a shopping and entertainment center.

Not more than fifty yards away begins a great arc of beachfront on which are some twenty or more bars, restaurants, coffee shops, and the like. As in the Greek islands, the beach consists entirely of pebbles of various sizes, giving its shore the appearance of a paid-out gravel pit.

As I was sitting on *Indigo's* aft deck, a parade of people passing by on their way to and from the beach distracted me from a book I was reading. Of those in the parade, I noticed two uncommon and glaringly obvious features. The first was that the women were young, minimally clad, and stunningly attractive, leading me at first to believe that the quay to which we had tied must be the site of the Miss Montenegro pageant now evidently well underway. Thus did I come to learn a fact the entire male population of the planet, with the lone exception of your humble correspondent, already knew: Serbian (including Montenegrin) women are among the most beautiful in the world.

The other feature of this parade was that all those in it, including females, were much taller than any group I had ever seen before. It was as if the national basketball teams had chosen this place and time to go for a swim. Curious, I consulted my smartphone and found the answer. The people who populate the areas around the Dinaric Alps of the Western Balkans are the tallest in the world. The average height of a man there is six feet one and a half inches, and the women are not far behind. My supposed basketball teams were just average folks.

Just south of Budva, one of the finest five-star resort hotels in Europe was under reconstruction on a tiny island. The terracotta-roofed, two-story vintage dwellings, which were once the favored hotel of Sophia Loren, Doris Day, and Queen Elizabeth II, had fallen into disrepair under the Socialist Federal Republic of Yugoslavia. Called Aman Sveti Stefan (Saint Stephen), the island hotel was a slice of Mediterranean heaven surrounded by the sun-spangled Adriatic. Oleanders, pines, and olive trees scented the air.

On our last night in Budva, some of the crew and I attended the season opening of a popular tiki bar featuring an authentic Brazilian samba band. There I met Serbs, Greeks, Brits, Russians, Croats, Swedes, and Germans, and a black girl from North Carolina and her Swedish husband. Apart from her, I was the only American. I was also the only man with gray hair, and as usual, the earliest to leave.

From my brief encounter with its nightlife, I sensed the town is one that mature adults should avoid in the season. Raffish and very much a beach resort town, it still was a fun place and worth a visit.

Montenegrins and Serbians are distant and unreceptive to strangers. I sought many times to make eye contact with them but never succeeded. Even among the well-lubricated customers of a bar, I sensed tolerance but not welcome.

An incident in Budva makes the point. A bar I attended in the old town was crowded, so much so that I could not get the bartender's attention nor even squeeze myself up to it. Standing next to me was a young Serbian man occupying more of the bar than he needed. Between him and his neighbor was room for me, but he had placed his drink in front of that space as if to capture it for himself. I tried to gain his eye contact and tried by word and gesture to suggest that he move his drink to a position more directly in front of him.

He declined to respond or even to acknowledge my presence, so, doing my best to effect an inoffensive manner, I took hold of his drink and moved it a foot. It is no simple matter to move a man's drink in an inoffensive manner, and in this attempt I may have failed. Not bothering to look at me or say a word, he moved it back. He was half my age, a full head taller, and had the physique and bearing of a soldier. He also seemed to have a disposition easily inclined to homicide. As I thought about it, I realized that he might have indeed been a soldier in the recent wars, and if so, it was likely that an F-16 with *US Air Force* painted on its side had bombed or strafed him, an experience that would understandably dampen his affection for Americans.

Croatians and Slovenians are more affable. They are predominantly Roman Catholic, subscribe to Western liberal traditions, and are friendly toward the West. I frequently heard Croats say they were not like those "Easterners," meaning Serbs. During the Yugoslav Wars, Croatia came to the aid of Bosnians fighting the Serbs—although they are said to have done so mainly for profit, a fact that still irritates the Bosnians as well as the Serbs.

Just to make things complicated, there are the Muslims. These predominate in Albania, Kosovo, and a major part of Bosnia, but also live in scattered towns all over the Balkans. They align with neither West nor East but with the world of Islam, though they are far more tolerant than are the Muslims of the Arabian Peninsula (excluding the kind-hearted people of Oman). Walking around in Sarajevo, the capital of Bosnia, you would hardly know you were in a Muslim country, save for a few older women in headscarves. Even the mosques are

310

modest buildings that blend into the neighborhoods, quite unlike the grand structures of the Arab world.

Herceg Novi, Montenegro

Few places in the world are as sublime as the Bay of Kotor, often described as Europe's most spectacular fjord. Its rugged, mountainous shore, opalescent waters, colorful subtropical gardens, and ancient terracotta-roofed villages give it the air of a fantasyland and rank it, along with the Gulf of Corinth, among the most captivating bodies of water I have ever seen.

To get there, we traveled north from Budva along Montenegro's scenic mountainous coast lined with high cliffs and rocky headlands and, at the bay's opening into the Adriatic, turned in to its narrow entry constricted by converging peninsulas. The bay, shaped roughly as an hourglass, consists of an outer and an inner bay separated by a narrow stricture. Once inside the outer bay, the entry peninsulas hide the Adriatic from view, giving the beguiling effect of being in a large inland lake surrounded by steep hills, rocky shores, and, in the distance, high mountains.

Our first stop was the delightful town of Herceg Novi. Plastered onto the face of an exceedingly steep hill, bougainvillea, oleander, and flowering cacti garland its buildings and lanes, and enormous date palms line its waterfront. This verdant, subtropical landscape suggests South Florida, yet the mountains just behind the city are dappled in snow well into late spring. I know of no other place where subtropical plants flourish so near snow-covered mountains.

The town square sits at the top of a long, steep series of stairs— or, if you prefer, at the end of a short taxi ride—and at night it is buzzing with activity around the numerous outdoor cafés, coffee bars, and smart shops. Walk up another flight of stairs, pass through an ancient stone archway, and you come upon a tiny plaza on which is a pleasing old Orthodox chapel still used today and thoughtfully surrounded by alfresco bars and restaurants. From the plaza looking out over the bay, the views are spectacular and grow more so with each sip of rakija, a fortified brandy drunk neat or applied to the skin as an antifungal agent.

Along the shore is a pedestrian walk connecting many of the surrounding lakefront villages on which the locals promenade each evening beginning around six p.m., taking in the night air and practicing their impressive skills at avoiding eye contact with outsiders.

Kotor, Montenegro

From Herceg Novi on the outer bay, we passed through narrow straits into the more compact inner bay bordered by mountains, gray and treeless in the distance, steep hills swathed in subtropical greenery, and timeless villages standing mute as they have for centuries.

Just as I was certain that I had seen all the best the bay could offer, we rounded a turn into an arm at the end of which stands the remarkable old town of Kotor. Up close, it is like so many old towns, built of timeworn stone blocks, walled in against predatory raiders, and now humming with shoppers and tourists. From our vantage, though, it took on a different character. Although the town is directly on the bay's shore, a nearly vertical wall of bare scabrous mountain rises immediately behind it, giving the scene a theatrical quality unlike any place I have seen before.

Old Towns in the Med

Since arriving in the Med, I had encountered countless towns and cities whose primary appeal to tourists is what I have been referring to as an old town. Built most commonly from about 1000 to 1500 AD, roughly in the middle and late years of the Medieval Period, some expanded well into the eighteenth century. They invariably feature a high surrounding wall with crenellations, moats, heavy gates, and other devices to discourage invaders and are built of limestone quarried nearby.

The earliest structures used unfinished stones mortared into place, while later versions used milled stones. Laneways are paved in cobbles of the same stone, most worn smooth over time, and vary in width from about twelve feet to as little as six. Buildings are usually three to five floors high, built close together (thus the narrow lane-ways) except where more widely separated to make room for plazas, have pitched roofs of terra cotta tiles, and few, small window openings always with simple slatted shutters. Later structures exhibit some refinements, like articulation and relief at window and door openings and at eaves, done in the vernacular of the dominant occupants at the time. All of them have churches or cathedrals and small chapels.

Hotels in old towns all over the Med have much in common. Because they must accommodate themselves to the medieval structure, the rooms are small by modern standards, have low ceilings and little ambient light due to tiny window openings—if they have any at all. Interior walls are nearly always the unfinished, rough surfaces of the exterior walls. While modern appointments and plumbing vary, there is the inescapable sense of occupying a cave. Claustrophobics will find them unappealing.

The best old towns I encountered were in Vienna, Florence, Rhodes, Palma (on the island of Majorca), Zagreb, and Dubrovnik. Others of note are Hvar, Rovinj, and Split in Croatia; Herceg Novi and Kotor in Montenegro; Hania on the island of Crete; Saint-Tropez on the Cote D'Azur; Seville; and Barcelona. The best exclude all traffic other than pedestrian, are immaculate, and have tasteful signage for shops, streets, and plazas. They have also resisted slathering over the original stone facades with stucco in a misguided effort to modernize their appearance.

Much of the appeal of these old towns comes in the absence of vehicle traffic and in the narrow, winding labyrinth of lanes that offer surprises around nearly every corner. Wandering around aimlessly in old towns, taking in the sights and smells, stopping for a coffee or meal in some open-air plaza is a true delight. They are even more appealing at night when illumination gives them still more character and the plazas are crowded with people having a good time.

TWENTY-NINE

Rome, Florence, and the Italian Coast

Before leaving Montenegro, we took on a full load of fuel[1] and set a direct course for Syracuse on the east coast of Sicily.

The best feature of our visit to Sicily was that Chris Jensen, my old friend from Pensacola who had cruised with me and two other friends along the Brazilian coast, and had joined me again in Tahiti, once again met up with *Indigo*.

Syracuse, Sicily

We docked stern-to right in the heart of Syracuse's old town, and from there Chris and I wandered the town's narrow lanes and inviting plazas. Of special interest was the Duomo, or cathedral. Located on a plaza lined with shops, restaurants, and alfresco coffee bars, it sits upon the same foundation and uses the same fluted Doric columns as an ancient Greek temple to the goddess Athena. Adding to the architectural confusion, its entire facade is exuberant baroque, while inside a Greek font rests on a Norman bronze lion beneath a medieval, wood-paneled ceiling.

Unlike the old towns of Croatia, the old town of Syracuse was in disrepair. The buildings badly needed painting, drain pipes hung disconnected, and the streets needed cleaning. There was nothing about it to suggest that tourists were welcome.

1. *Indigo* had a fuel capacity of 10,000 gallons.

The town is popular among the Mafiosi of Sicily for the reason that it is a demilitarized zone, off-limits to the competing clans by mutual agreement. After all, they need a place to vacation without that nagging worry of assassination.

Riposto, Sicily

Our next stop was Riposto, just up the coast but still on Sicily's eastern shore. Riposto is the port nearest to Mount Etna, the world's most active volcano. Our tour guide drove us an hour and a half through the unsightly countryside and up to the mountain's scenic peak. Along the way, he explained that the emergence of several hundred fumaroles, which appear on the volcano's surface as topographic pimples, has tamed Etna's destructive power by providing harmless outlets that literally let off steam. This, I later learned, is nonsense fed to gullible tourists. The volcano's unpredictable violent eruptions, occurring as recently as 2000, 2001, and 2002, destroy homes and shops and throw fireballs 2,000 feet into the air. Yet, curiously, whole towns still live in its shadows and within easy range of its destructive power.

Island of Lipari

From Riposto, we passed through the historic Strait of Messina, 1.9 miles wide at its narrowest point, and traveled a short distance to Lipari in the Aeolian Islands group just off Sicily's northeast coast. After docking at a quay in the center of town, Chris and I wandered the friendly laneways of the old town, visited an ancient Spanish citadel, now a museum, and drove a rental car around the entire verdant island. Vistas over the Tyrrhenian Sea to other islands in the group a few miles away are stunning.

Lipari was once the source for much of the world's pumice, a by-product of volcanic eruptions. You can buy the stuff from roadside vendors or just pick it up from most of the beaches.

In the tender, we crossed a narrow channel to the aptly named island of Vulcano. Along one side of its harbor, another impressively massive volcano rises steeply, and here and there across its face spew geysers of steam. Just at the shore is a natural hot mud bath for those who find sitting up to their neck in radioactive slime appealing. To cleanse yourself, you can jump into a sea warmed by underwater fumaroles. One slight flaw in Mother Nature's spa is the unmistakable sulfuric aroma that permeates the air.

We departed Lipari at night and cruised close by the famed island of Stromboli, known since ancient times for its constant impressive eruptions. Just as we passed, as if on cue, blasts of molten red starbursts rose high into the night sky just as they have done for centuries.

Positano, Italy

Our next stop was an anchorage off the coast of the Amalfi peninsula at Positano, where we took the tender ashore and wandered around the lower part of the small town. With the town stuck on the face of an exceedingly steep massif, walking its streets is an exhausting workout best avoided by energy conservers like me, so I hired a car and driver to take us to the best of the peninsula's offerings. These included lunch at a restaurant hanging over the edge of a high cliff, affording pleasing views over the sea far below, and the delightful artsy village of Ravello favored by the many celebs that haunt the area in spring.

Rome, Italy

In Rome, we tied up *Indigo* in a modern marina near the mouth of the Tiber River. From there, Chris and I ventured the forty-five-minute drive into Rome on several days to see the required tourist sites, including the Spanish Steps, Trevi Fountain, Coliseum, the Roman Baths, Circus Maximus, Campo di Fiori, Piazza Navona, and the like.

The line of tourists waiting to get into the Vatican Museum and St. Peter's Basilica wrapped almost entirely around the Vatican itself, requiring at least a hot, sweaty two-hour wait. To avoid it, I paid a guide $50, which entitled us to jump to the head of the line and join a throng shuffling through.

From the art collection, the guide and I made our way first to the

Sistine Chapel to join with a dense crowd of other upturned heads viewing *The Last Judgement*, Michelangelo's famed fresco painting. The ceiling was, at sixty-eight feet, far higher than I had imagined it to be, and the room was dimly lit—not ideal for viewing great works of art. The painting itself, widely regarded by experts as the finest attainment of any artist ever, is an impressive work, no doubt. Its scale alone is enough to awe the uninformed viewer like me. When you learn that the work required four years of sustained labor while the artist lay on his back, you begin to appreciate it more, even before assessing the techniques and compositions he employed, judgments I am not qualified to render.

On the way to St. Peter's Basilica, we walked along a sunlit corridor whose walls and ceilings were covered with exquisitely detailed geometric ornamentation. Here the guide challenged me to identify which of this work was trompe l'oeil and which was joinery, a challenge at which I failed miserably. You simply cannot tell. Once inside St. Peter's, we wandered around in its dazzling, almost decadently sumptuous, interior, gazed in solemn respect upon Michelangelo's *Pieta*, and departed.

Chris left the next day for home, and my longtime friends from Jacksonville, Buck Fowler and Mike Shad, joined me for a ten-day respite from their daily lives.

Island of Sardinia

With Mike and Buck aboard, we left Rome and set out for Sardinia.

Our first stop was Porto Cervo at Costa Smeralda on Sardinia's northeast coast. On a large swath of that coast bought by the Aga Khan in the 1960s, there now stands an enormous, swanky development with five hotels, several marinas, and more than 2,000 homes, many owned by Russians and Arabs. Just to give you an idea of the place, Buck and Mike took me to a poolside lunch at Hotel Cala di Volpe, where the bill, which included three bottles of a modest but adequate local wine, could have made a down payment on a car. At a smart shopping center just a hundred yards from the marina was about every high-end shop you could imagine, plus a few more. You can have a lot more fun for a lot less money anywhere on Florida's Redneck Riviera.

Golfo delle Saline

After two days in the rarified atmosphere of the Aga Khan's (former) playground, we headed north along the coast to an anchorage in the Golfo delle Saline. There, Buck, Mike, and I took the tender for a joy ride among the nearby islands, stopping at a popular resort town, Santa Teresa di Gallura, for lunch and an idle stroll along the waterfront. As it was late September, the tourists were long gone and the weather was mild and breezy, perfect for doing mostly nothing.

Bonifacio, Island of Corsica

Next day, we enjoyed a delightful cruise from Sardinia's north coast across a four-mile-wide strait to Bonifacio, Corsica. Approaching the town, the first thing you see is a wide expanse of precipitous, chalk-white cliffs rising 230 feet from the sea. Perched precariously on top are an old town and citadel and, unseen from the sea, a secure natural harbor that cuts deep into the cliffs. After docking on the town quay, we went for a walk along the waterfront and stopped for lunch at one of the numerous outdoor cafés.

One day we decided to drive into the high mountains of southern Corsica to view a noted waterfall. I think we all imagined that we would find the place, park the car, walk twenty yards, see the thing, and return to the park bar for some refreshments.

But it was not to be. After something like a half hour's hike over rugged terrain, Mike, the wisest of us, said that was about all the exertion a waterfall deserved and turned around and retreated to the park refreshment stand. Buck and I continued along the way and got lost for a brief period before Buck also headed for the barn.

Yours truly, as always certain the objective is just around the next corner, continued stumbling over moonscape and bush until an hour later coming upon a desultory waterfall that was nowhere near worth all the effort. When I at last arrived at the park bar, Buck and Mike, employing commendable restraint while sipping cool refreshment, resisted saying, "We told you so!"

After a few days and nights wandering among the winding lanes of Bonifacio's old town and enjoying some of the local cuisine, we drove to the golf club set atop high cliffs. There, on the veranda enjoying spectacular views over the Corsican coastline, we enjoyed one of the finest lunches any of us had ever had. In the distance, we could watch windsurfers ripping along on the thirty-knot winds that kept *Indigo* in port two days longer than planned.

Corsica is infamous for the vendetta. Back in the nineteenth century, these became so commonplace that during one brief period, something like a third of the male population died from knife wounds incurred in these honor killings. The noted French author Guy de Maupassant wrote a fictional account of one of these in his short story entitled, appropriately, "A Vendetta." As you might expect from a small, isolated island of remote mountain villages, these arose mostly from unauthorized canoodling. The modern remnant of this practice (the vendetta, not the canoodling) is a plethora of shops in every town selling authentic, Corsican-made vendetta knives. Some are even suitable as flatware for the dinner table.

When the wind and seas abated, we set off aboard *Indigo* to cruise along the ruggedly scenic west coast of Corsica, stopping first at the capital city of Ajaccio, birthplace of Napoleon Bonaparte but otherwise of little note. Along the way, we had the rare pleasure of seeing a sperm whale up close. From there, we coasted along a spectacular rocky shore of high mountains and deeply indented bays to the Golfe de Girolata set within the Scandola Nature Reserve, where we anchored for the night.

Calvi, Island of Corsica

From the anchorage, we traveled next day a short distance north along the coast to the resort town of Calvi. Mike and Buck opted to stroll through the old town and up a steep hill to a well-preserved citadel while I, having seen many Mediterranean old towns by this point, rented a car and drove deep into the high coastal mountains of the Parc Naturel Regional de Corse.

There, I passed through remote ancient villages, along narrow lanes barely a car's width, and marveled at impressively rugged mountains rising to 9,000 feet. The roads, such as they are, are poorly marked, so I easily got lost. I kept driving ahead until reaching what appeared to be an important road—really a paved narrow lane—and headed toward the sea. I stopped for lunch at a rustic inn, where the menu was entirely in Corsican, an ancient dialect of Italian, so I had no idea what it said. The only other patron that day was a large guy eating what looked like a delectable dish, so I just pointed to it and indicated I'd have the same. Whatever it was, it was delicious.

Viareggio, Italy

From Calvi, we rounded Cape Corsica and made our way across the Ligurian Sea to Viareggio, the birthplace of *Indigo*. The city is home to nearly every Italian yacht builder, including Benetti, Azimut, Perini Navi, and *Indigo's* builder, CBI Navi, among others, and accordingly looks industrial around its busy waterfront.

In due course, we found the seaside resort area and strolled along admiring the architecture, thankful we had arrived long after the summer season. The city is famous for its collection of Liberty-style (art nouveau) buildings, which come in a variety of beach resort colors and ornamentation. Just a few blocks from the sea is a large neighborhood of narrow streets and two-story buildings of this style. Their facades reminded me very much of New Orleans's French Quarter.

While walking along the beachfront, you cannot miss just to the east the high peaks of the Garfagnana, a wild area of massifs noted for its extensive deposits of fine marble. What appear to be snow-covered peaks are the lustrous faces of active quarries. The town of Cararra is nearby.

After saying goodbye to Mike and Buck and welcoming Kitty, we set sail for Florence.

Florence, Italy

When Kitty and I were much younger, we had visited Florence and disliked the place so much we swore never to return. It was hot, crowded, and noisy, and its important buildings were covered with scaffolding. Traffic congestion made driving impossible, and the streets were unsightly with litter. I remember wondering how the Florentines could treat their patrimony with such obvious disregard.

I'm happy to say that Florence today is transformed. Vehicle traffic has been severely restricted in the old town, and the streets, lanes, and piazzas are litter-free and scrubbed nightly. At the time of our visit in late September, the weather was cool enough to invite long walks, but not so cool as to inhibit outdoor dining. In the major piazzas, there were street performers and cheerful crowds, and a delightful air about the place.

Our hotel, while certainly satisfactory, was near the Piazzale Michelangelo atop a hill looking over the old town, which meant we faced either a cab ride or a considerable hike into town. Next time, I would stay right in the center of the old town at the newly renovated and luxurious Hotel Savoy.

We visited most of the obligatory museums and gardens, like the Pitti Palace, the Boboli Gardens, the Uffizi, all the major piazzas, the Ponte Vecchio, and the Duomo. Just walking around the newly improved old town, though, was the real delight. Taking in the brisk night air, watching the street performers, having a glass of wine at an outdoor café—these were the most memorable moments for us both.

From Florence, we drove up into the Garfagnana region of the Apuan Alps. We wound our way on narrow lanes among tiny villages, medieval trading towns, and modern ski resorts, got lost on the poorly marked roads, and eventually made our way into Liguria at the city of La Spezia at the head of a gulf of the same name. Praised for its beauty so eloquently by so many poets, it is today known as the Gulf of Poets.

Portovenere and Cinque Terra, Italy

A peninsula that runs south from the city, surely one of the most agreeable places on the entire Med coast, ends at the picture-postcard town of Portovenere, where we stayed a few nights. It is just a touch more raffish than Portofino up the coast. It doesn't have that look of a cultivated garden, but it's also not nearly so jammed with tourists. We both liked the place very much and enjoyed walking along its attractive harbor front.

Along the westward shore of the peninsula are the five remote villages that together form the famous Cinque Terre. From every description, you would think Cinque Terre is a series of remote, sparsely populated, rustic villages hanging precariously from sheer cliffs and that they rarely see outsiders. The reality is quite different. As we drove down the switchback road toward one of the five towns, we wondered why parked cars lined every inch of the way, and at the bottom discovered the reason. They were the cars of tourists come to hike the cliff trails, just like us.

In town, the place was a mob scene of young and old, outfitted in the latest L. L. Bean Cinque Terre hiking outfits, complete with a pair of Kevlar walking sticks—this to stroll along on prepared surfaces as challenging as a path through Central Park. Just so you don't strain yourself, there is a train that runs among the towns, allowing you to select the section of trail you'd like without having to overdo it.

We drove to Riomaggiore, parked in a garage, and took the train to Consiglia, where we learned that our intended trail back to the car had closed for repairs. Kitty took the return train. Never one to take the easy way out, I got around a locked gate that blocked off the closed trail by clamoring up a brief stretch of cliff and crawling under a construction fence, then walked along the deserted stretch of cliff back to the car—an hour and a half at a leisurely pace.

It was a sunny day, perfect for a stroll, and the views from the cliff were memorable. But other than my walk along the closed section, there were just too many people—and this was the off-season. It felt too much like Disney World: large crowds standing around, dense lines of people shuffling along to the same places, lunching in the same cafés.

Portofino, Italy

Nowhere along the Mediterranean is there a more agreeable stretch of shore than the Portofino Peninsula. The steep, seaside hills are a verdant garden. Narrow paths wind amid hidden mansions looking out over a tiny harbor filled to capacity with yachts great and small. Throughout the hills and shorelines of the area are networks of walking trails that lead to nearby villages, some not reachable by car.

Our hotel, the Belmond Splendido, is a fine place to rid yourself of excess cash that may have built up in your bank account. We made the mistake of booking a room late and had to take a suite—more like a small apartment—and paid accordingly. The view was nice, though.

Apart from wandering among the paths, eating at local cafés, gazing vacantly over the lustrous sea, and shopping, there is not all that much to keep an active person entertained in Portofino. A few days is enough.

We drove back along the Italian Riviera to rejoin *Indigo* in Viareggio. Next stop: the French Riviera.

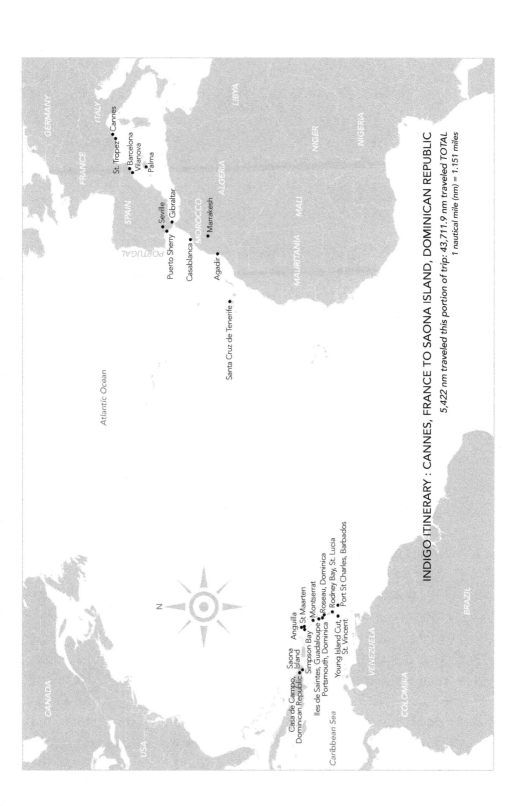

CANADA

USA

Atlantic Ocean

N

Caribbean Sea

Casa de Campo,
Dominican Republic

Saona
Island   Anguilla

Simpson Bay • St Maarten
Iles de Saintes, Guadaloupe • Montserrat
Portsmouth, Dominica • Roseau, Dominica
Young Island Cut, • Rodney Bay, St. Lucia
St. Vincent • Port St Charles, Barbados

VENEZUELA

COLOMBIA

BRAZIL

GERMANY

FRANCE
ITALY • Cannes
St. Tropez •
• Barcelona
Vilanova
Palma

SPAIN
PORTUGAL

Puerto Sherry • Seville
• Gibraltar
Casablanca MOROCCO
• Marrakesh
Agadir •

Santa Cruz de Tenerife •

MAURITANIA MALI

ALGERIA

LIBYA

NIGER

NIGERIA

INDIGO ITINERARY : CANNES, FRANCE TO SAONA ISLAND, DOMINICAN REPUBLIC

5,422 nm traveled this portion of trip; 43,711.9 nm traveled TOTAL

1 nautical mile (nm) = 1.151 miles

THIRTY

Sites Beautiful and Bizarre

Our first stop on the French Riviera was Monaco, both a principality and sovereign country of France. At less than a square mile, it is the world's smallest country, and the most densely populated.

Thanks to its reputation as a playground of jet-setters, I was fully prepared not to like the place. But I was to be pleasantly surprised.

Monaco

From the sea, this city/nation is not a handsome place. Its concrete-box high-rise condos and clumsy-looking hotels and public buildings, many dated from the 1970s and 1980s, give it the appearance of a quotidian seaside resort town of faded aspect.

Up close, it improves quite a lot.

We docked in the heart of the city's main yacht marina, the Port de Monaco on John F. Kennedy Avenue, from which we could walk just about anywhere. Steep hills deter excessive wandering, but Kitty and I overcame this by using the public elevators and outdoor escalators helpfully placed at convenient locations throughout the town. It is the only city either of us have seen with these public devices, especially the outdoor escalator. I visited the Jardin Exotique (Exotic Garden), which I found after an exhausting uphill hike, and loved its enormous collection of cacti and succulents from all over the world. Plastered, like the entire city, against a nearly vertical cliff, the garden offers stunning views over the Mediterranean from every shaded park bench.

We lunched at the obligatory Café de Paris and one night listened to live music in the bar of the Hotel de Paris. We passed up the opportunity to visit the famed Belle Époque Casino de Monte-Carlo, electing instead to stroll in its lovely formal gardens overlooking the sea. The Prince's Palace and its surrounding old town, both sited high atop a dramatic headland, made for an enjoyable walk and offered pleasant views across the sun-dappled Med.

Most of the offices in Monaco are wealth-management branches of the world's major banks and their associated accountants and lawyers. These functionaries, dressed smartly in the dark suits of the professional class, dot the cafés and bars during the lunch and cocktail hours. Those rare locals not employed as bankers, lawyers, or accountants seem to be mostly in their retirement years and are seen, along with tourists like us, sitting on benches among the manicured greenery of the city's parks.

Nearly every person in Monaco is smartly turned out, and its cityscape is crisply manicured, freshly painted, lush, and above all, tidy. Though I looked carefully, I could spot not a single piece of litter on the streets, and even in the hallways and stairwells of parking garages, there was not a hint of graffiti.

To sum up the place, Monaco is an astoundingly wealthy city glued onto the steep face of a coastal escarpment, with many fine restaurants, smart shops, a few less-than-notable museums, a world-famous casino (if you like that sort of thing), impeccably clean streets, and no crime. Its tree-shaded parks and immaculately restored old town invite idle strolls.

Just up the hillside from Monaco, off the Moyenne Corniche, is the medieval walled town of Eze, perched 1,400 feet above the sea. It's a tiny old town thoughtfully restored and now filled with shops and restaurants, including the five-star hotel and restaurant the Chateau de la Chevre d'Or (Chateau of the Golden Goat). There, Kitty and I lunched on an outdoor terrace with breathtaking views over the sea and equally breathtaking prices—like $50 for a small bowl of risotto. The French Riviera has many attractions, to be sure, but budget-friendly it is not.

By car, Kitty and I toured along the seafront of the Cote d'Azur, passing through village after village, and found most of them too densely developed for our taste. We very much liked the Cap Ferrat peninsula and, gracing its southern extremity, the Grand Hotel du Cap Ferrat, with fabulous gardens spilling across a low hill down to the sea.

Cannes and Saint-Tropez, France

The only reason to visit Cannes is to pick up an award at the annual International Film Festival. If there's not one waiting for you, I'd avoid the place. It's a small, slightly tatty city on the Med waterfront with a corniche and pedestrian promenade along the shore, a couple of historic hotels, casinos, nightlife, swanky shops, and excellent restaurants, and not much else. Its beaches are unremarkable and densely packed with people paying $50 per day for the privilege of sitting on them.

Following Cannes, we spent a few nights in Saint-Tropez, where I half expected to see Brigitte Bardot walking along the harbor front. Bardot, after all, had made it famous. The village's diminutive size makes it appealing and easily walkable. As usual for towns along the French Riviera, Saint-Tropez has a collection of waterfront outdoor restaurants and bars. All were crowded because our visit coincided with the few days set aside for end-of-the-year sales. It was a nice enough stop, but that's about it. During the season, or anytime near the season, the entire north coast of the Mediterranean should be avoided—it's far too jammed with tourists.

Barcelona, Spain

One of the world's great cities, Barcelona was a memorable stopover. Unfortunately, Kitty had returned to obligations in Florida by the time we reached there.

As the capital of Catalonia, the city's 3.2 million people speak Catalan, a unique language derived from the Latin Vulgate, similar to Spanish, closer to Italian, but different enough from both to cause confusion. Most inhabitants speak both Spanish and Catalan, though few speak English except in the better hotels and restaurants.

Catalans consider themselves somehow special and apart from their fellow Spaniards. They claim to be individualists and wear the label as if it were their signature quality. This has had its effects, most notably among the region's artists and architects. A long-simmering separatist movement finds most of its support on the far left.

Sprawled across the Catalan seashore, Barcelona at close range exhibits an utterly modern aspect. Abstract sculptures grace its plentiful and commodious public parks, strikingly modern buildings line its tree-shaded, wide boulevards, and the waterfront, recently renovated at the time of my visit, is a busy collection of outdoor cafés, bars, nightclubs, hotels, and apartments all tastefully designed in modern style.

Yet with all this modernity, the true heart of the city is the Gothic Quarter, another of the many old towns we have visited thus far. Masterfully preserved and appearing as though it just recently stepped out of its past, it is a labyrinth of winding, narrow alleyways and hidden plazas, shops, restaurants, and museums, all impressively clean despite heavy tourist foot traffic. At its center is the imposing Barcelona Cathedral where, in 1492, Columbus, having sailed the ocean blue, was welcomed home by Ferdinand and Isabella, the Catholic monarchs of the time. Though begun in 1298, it was completed only in the late nineteenth century, quite a bit tardy but in plenty of time for my visit. Apart from its eighty-five-foot-high vaulted ceiling, its main attraction is its intricately ornate neo-Gothic facade, about as far removed from modern as it's possible to get.

Hidden deep in the old town is the Picasso Museum, one of the city's most popular attractions. Housed within five adjoining former palaces—the term implying buildings far grander than they are—the museum holds some 3,000 pieces, mostly his early drawings and paintings. These early works bear none of the modernist characteristics for which the artist later became famous. Most are various sketches of the kind students turn out as exercises in the quest to develop their talent and find their signature style, but were fascinating to see nonetheless. By consensus of the world's experts, Picasso ranks with the finest artists who ever lived, just below the incomparable Michelangelo but in the same company as Rembrandt and Caravaggio. Why his disjointed depictions of animals and humans, especially females, should deserve such acclaim, I am at a loss to understand.

On my smartphone, I had a travel app for the city (LUXE City Guides) that I consulted frequently and used, together with Google Maps, to find my way around. To the app's discredit, however, it ignores a place that I found endlessly fascinating and to which I returned several times. That place, Las Ramblas, is one of Spain's most famous promenades and fills day and night with locals and tourists alike. No visit to Barcelona would be complete without an evening stroll there. Lined with street performers of every imaginable talent—and a few with no discernible talent at all—it is the longest pedestrian mall in Europe. Tarot card readers, mimes, musicians, magicians, and caricaturists are there to entertain you and to serve as grateful recipients of your excess funds. If you want to make further contributions to the local economy, there are versions of three-card Monte and ubiquitous pickpockets there to accommodate you.

Along one side of Las Ramblas is a nondescript building where I attended a performance of tango dancers and Spanish operatic singers. While the skills on display there may not have reached the highest levels of their respective arts, it was for the casual observer an easy hour and a half introduction to these, and well worth the time. Just up the way is an enormous covered farmers' market, formally named the Mercat de Sant Josep but locally known as La Boqueria, with about every edible object that Spain has to offer. It's a fun, colorful, though crowded, place for a morning stroll.

Just on the edge of the city is an enormous public park, the

700-foot-high promontory called Montjuic, on which are found an array of museums, nightclubs, art galleries, and such that now occupy buildings erected for the 1992 Olympics and some newly built since then. Here there is also a 1929 pavilion designed by the German American minimalist Ludwig Mies van der Rohe that is still today a remarkable and stately structure.

A museum in the park is devoted to archeology, and another to ethnology. At the hill's summit is the Castell de Montjuic, a gigantic, eighteenth-century castle built for the Bourbons containing an extensive collection of ancient weaponry. My favorite of the park's structures is the National Art Museum of Catalonia, otherwise known as the National Palace, an austere, grand, and grandiose building which houses, among much else, the world's finest collection of Romanesque art. It also has an exceptional restaurant from which you can enjoy spectacular views of the city's skyline.

In this most artful of the world's cities, we come now to its central figure, a man for whom Barcelona is itself an enormous museum of sorts and a testament to his—in my judgment—mildly deranged, or at least misarranged, talent. That man, Antoni Gaudí (1852-1926), and his disciples were the most important practitioners of a style that came to be known as Catalan Modernisme, also called Spanish or Catalan Art Nouveau, of which Gaudí's was an especially idiosyncratic version.

A pedestrian on the Passeig de Gracia would pass by glittering modern office buildings and tres chic shops, and for a time might think he is on Madison Avenue in Manhattan. Then he would come to a certain corner, look up and become dumbstruck by La Pedrera, a six-story apartment building designed by Gaudí and still very much in use today. The building looks as if it were built of paraffin that partly melted, forming wavy, bulging eyelids of molten wax over the windows and along the parapets. The building's rooftop is a thicket of vent stacks that are each a work of art, some resembling colorful mushrooms, and others clad in mosaics of ceramic tile. Inside, furnishings, and such mundane pieces as door handles and drawer pulls, all of forged iron and designed by Gaudí, are on display.

He also designed what is now a public park, called Park Guell, a fifty-acre site on the UNESCO World Heritage list that I was pleased to tour. These days, long lines wait to get in, but once inside, the place is a wonderland of weirdness. One building is a giant canopy supported by eighty-four crooked pillars, and others look like nothing so much as distorted gingerbread houses clad in intricate, undulating patterns of mosaic.

Gaudí's crowning work is a building so audacious in style and enormous in dimension that, even long before its completion, it is already Barcelona's iconic structure. As the Eiffel Tower is to Paris and the Flora-Bama Bar is to the Redneck Riviera, so the Sagrada Familia is to Barcelona. This wildly unconventional structure was begun in 1883 and became the all-consuming passion and life's work for Gaudí, who lived on its construction site as a recluse for fourteen years before his death. Fittingly, he is buried there. Work on the structure has stopped and started often, interrupted by the Spanish Civil War and shortages of funds, but continues today. Completion is expected—*hoped for* is the more accurate expression—sometime in the next thirty years, give or take a decade.

One night I attended a performance in the Palau de la Musica Catalana, a breathtakingly ornate concert hall designed by Lluis Domenech i Montaner, another practitioner of Catalan Art Nouveau, and opened in 1908. From my seat in the loge, I could look down upon a large Count Basie-style jazz orchestra playing what I guess were local tunes interrupted here and there by dramatic readings of something having to do with local history. Whatever it was, I couldn't understand a word. That was just as well. It was the building I had come to see, and it was memorable.

The exterior facade of the Palau de la Musica Catalana is one of the most remarkable and creative I have ever seen and, although riotously effusive, it remains tasteful to our modern eyes. When I got there, I stood outside and just gawked in amazement. Every available surface of its interior is a flourish of intricately detailed embellishment, even the interior of its thoughtfully included bar where I sat awaiting the start of the night's performance. In the hall itself, an enormous inverted stained-glass dome set between walls of intricately orna- mented stained glass hangs from the high ceiling.

The vestibule, staircases, and foyer, too, are extravagantly expres- sive spaces.

Palma, Balearic Island of Majorca
From Barcelona, we headed up the coast to the forgettable city of Villanova, where we took refuge from a passing storm before sailing on to Palma on the Balearic island of Majorca.

The largest harbor in the Mediterranean, Palma appears to be a city of two distinct halves—one appealing, the other not. As seen from the sea, the entire left half is a dense cluster of midrise concrete blight, while the right is an unusually large and wonderfully preserved medieval old town. Ashore, I didn't bother going into the left half of the city but spent all of my time wandering around in the old town. I found few old towns in Europe as sleek or as polished as Palma's, and few exceed it for top-notch shops and restaurants.

By a wide measure, the old town's most visually striking feature is its spectacular Gothic cathedral, known locally as the La Seu, on the harbor front. If it is not the largest such cathedral in the world, it is to me the most impressive, more so even than St. Peter's in Rome. None other than Gaudí remodeled its interior, including in his work a bizarre canopy that hangs above the altar. A large cove to the right of the altar was designed by a student of Gaudí's and looks as if it is a space in which Tomás de Torquemada once extracted confessions of heresy in the Spanish Inquisition. The cathedral is astonishingly beau- tiful, especially when illuminated at night, a perfect example of Gothic architecture; it alone is worth a visit to Palma.

Gibraltar
Known to the ancient Greeks as the Pillars of Hercules, two enormous slabs of rock less than nine miles apart—one on the African side in Morocco and the other on the European side in Gibraltar—define the

Strait of Gibraltar. In all my years of seeing this famous strait on charts and maps, I never dreamed it was so narrow or its defining rocks so large.

Gibraltar is hardly a country of consequence. It's actually a British Overseas Territory occupying less than three square miles. It's a wealthy tax haven and little else. For the Brits, the tax shelter requires they own property there, which they do in large numbers, thus explaining the forest of high-rise condos. Most are empty most of the time.

Ashore, the town resembles a prototypical English village, complete with men sporting enormous bushy mustaches, menus featuring Sunday roast with Yorkshire pudding, and pubs named the Rose and Crown or the Squat and Gobble.[1]

According to my tour guide, the cruise ships that visit here come for just one reason: the apes. At the top of the rock are several families of Barbary apes, about the size of well-nourished chimps, which for some incomprehensible reason seem to fascinate visitors.

Gibraltar's favorable tax status extends to bunker fuel sold at $3 per gallon compared to $5.70 everywhere else in the Med, with the result that its harbor, not surprisingly, is a vast parking lot of ships waiting to fill up on the cheap fuel, a bargain we were pleased to accept ourselves.

Seville, Spain

On our way to the historic city of Seville, we passed through the Strait of Gibraltar on a nearly perfect morning when the sea, blessedly calm, shone luminous in the early light.

To reach Seville by boat, it is necessary to travel fifty miles up the languid, silt-laden Guadalquivir River—the same river from which the Spanish crown launched many ships in its explorations and exploitations of the New World and, thanks to hurricanes, pirates, and reefs, recovered fewer than it launched. Surrounding the river's channel is a vast and verdant delta of cattle ranches and crop farms, and along

---

1. I made up that last one.

the channel's edges are hundreds of eel traps from which the slimy creatures are hoisted, later to appear on the plates of diners less discriminating about what they eat than I.

In the city center, we tied to a quay along the right bank, and from there I began my explorations. The first stunningly obvious, and pleasantly redolent, feature of the city's landscape is that nearly every one of its major streets is lined with rows of orange trees which, when I was there, were fully laden, although with a fruit so sour as to be inedible. They provide an agreeable softening and a dash of cheerful color to the otherwise dour medieval cityscape.

In the old town's center is the obligatory Gothic cathedral without which no Spanish city is complete, although this one is unique in that attached to it is the Patio de los Naranjos, or "patio of oranges." From the cathedral, the visitor can take fascinating strolls through the maze of narrow streets and picturesque laneways that make up the Barrio de Santa Cruz, once the Jewish ghetto. Here are flower-festooned patios, hidden plazas, boutique hotels, fine restaurants, bars, and expensive homes. There are also the ubiquitous tapas bars, where you can sip sherry and have gazpacho.

I managed to visit most of the notable tourist destinations, like the former royal palace, called the Real Alcazar; the Hospital de los Venerables with its splendidly restored and sumptuous baroque chapel; and most visually stunning of all, the dazzling Plaza de Espana set in the midst of the cool, leafy Parque de Maria Luisa. The Museo de Bellas Artes, Spain's second finest art museum, exceeded in its eminence only by Madrid's Prado, was worth the visit, more for the exceptional building than the collection of Spanish art and sculpture.

The city's active nightlife would have been fun had it begun before midnight. But in the Latin tradition it didn't, so instead I sampled various sleekly modern bar/restaurants and a few traditional places, as well, and always managed to return to *Indigo* early enough to enjoy a full night's rest and be prepared for the following day's jaunts.

THIRTY-ONE

The Road to Marrakech

Morocco's culture, rich and varied, is predominantly Berber with strong influences from the French and Spanish. Though there is much corruption, it is a constitutional monarchy, generally liberal, decidedly pro-Western, and especially friendly to the US. Sunni is the principal Islamic sect, but surprisingly, Jews have lived in the country more or less peacefully and undisturbed for centuries. Once numbering about 265,000 in the 1940s, they are down to about 5,500 now as a result of migrations to France and Israel.

On the darker side, Morocco is a major producer and transshipment point for drugs flowing into Europe.

Casablanca, Morocco

In few places is the power of Hollywood to impress images into our minds more apparent than here, and nowhere are those images so false. I had seen the movie *Casablanca* enough times to have a clear picture of the place—its low, white stucco structures, dusty streets, and a sleek nightclub called Rick's Café—and those are the expectations I took with me as we left Seville in December and headed south.

When we arrived offshore, I was astonished to see a city of more than three million inhabitants living on trashy streets amid grim high-rise buildings of moldy concrete. So much for Hollywood images. Driving around the city and its seaside suburbs—with a driver named Abdul, no less—brought little relief.

The city has the world's third-largest mosque, which holds 20,000 supplicants inside and another 80,000 on its expansive veranda, standing magnificently on the ocean shore. Given the propensity of Middle East and North African tyrants to outdo each other in the grandiosity of their grand mosques, these figures are surely inflated. Its single minaret is the world's tallest at 650 feet, or so it is claimed. There is also a faux-Rick's Café with a piano bar called As Time Goes By.

I went one night to a traditional tagine dinner and floor show. For those who don't know—like me before this visit—tagine is a method of cooking in a clay pot, the results of which are hardly distinguishable from lamb stew except for the couscous. The show included various singers and dancers, all of whom insisted on employing Arabic music, which to the Western ear sounds like unmelodic, off-key yodels.

Casablanca, I soon concluded, is a city easily stricken from the traveler's list of places to visit. We were stranded there for several days waiting for a storm to pass. Once the sea returned to its customary condition, we set out. While en route, we learned that the storm we had waited out sank five sailboats, and on one of these, a ninety-foot catamaran, resulted in two fatalities. Winds blow in the ocean off North Africa with uncommon strength for days on end, causing dangerous seas. This, after all, is the spawning ground for the hurricanes that inhabitants of the Caribbean and Florida know all too well.

Agadir, Morocco

A seaside resort city, Agadir sports colorfully landscaped boulevards, a beachfront promenade, and a modern marina/condo/retail complex where we were pleased to dock. There is little of the tumbledown squalor so evident in Casablanca. Here, too, the severe strictures of Islamic life are nowhere to be seen. Casinos, Western-style nightclubs, bars, beach resorts, and even brothels abound, all repugnant to the imams but delightful to their flocks.

On the Road in Morocco

Wishing to see the interior of Morocco and particularly its vast desert, I rented a car, bought a map, and set out for the exotic city of Marrakech on the flat plains northwest of the High Atlas Mountains. To get there, I took a route deliberately off the main highway and through these mountains so that I might gain an impression of local village life.

What I saw on the way to my first stop was an endless procession of careworn, dusty villages, almost entirely without benefit of greenery and littered with trash. Every village was much like every other in its dispiriting appearance. Two- and three-story, flat-roofed, unadorned buildings built of cinder block on simple concrete frames and smeared over in khaki-colored stucco line both sides of the road, each adjoining the other in row-house fashion. In every case, the ground floor is a shop of some kind, and the upper floor houses the extended family that built and owns the building.

Men all over Morocco dress in a floor-length, snug-fitting, long-sleeved robe called a djellaba. They come in a variety of colors, all of them dull. Its most peculiar feature, seen on no other Arab or North African robe, is its tall, conical attached hood resembling that of a KKK white-sheet outfit, giving the wearer the look of an imperial wizard or, more benignly, a Smurf. Their choice of footwear is often brightly colored leather slippers whose pointed, upturned toes contribute to a generally cartoonish appearance.

The women are among the most vividly attired people I have ever seen anywhere. Their long robes and headscarves come in a wide variety of bright fabrics varying from garish solids to wildly floral patterns, some neon in their iridescence. Against the relentlessly dreary village backdrop, these striking hues offer a meager touch of cheer. On many occasions, I saw farm trucks transporting these women to or from some agricultural job. With all of them standing in the breeze of the truck bed, the scene brought to mind a very large open box of richly colored crayons traveling down the road. I rarely saw women wearing the burqa.

Taroudant, Morocco

For lunch, I stopped in the first large town I came to, called Taroudant, a regional market center. It is a medina, the term for a traditional Arab town enclosed by high ramparts, a name derived from Medina in what is now Saudi Arabia, where Muhammad found refuge from persecution. The town's four miles of enclosing ramparts are smoothly finished in stucco and freshly painted in red ochre, roads around them are tastefully landscaped and recently repaved, and the enormous gated entries through them into the town are marked by an array of flagpoles with flags flapping in the wind. These features suggest that inside the high walls there must be something like an historic theme park—but once the visitor passes through a gate, he gains an altogether different impression.

What the walls shield from view is an authentic and active Moroccan market town, warts, scars, and all. Narrow laneways, barely wider than a car and often blocked by donkey carts, twist and wind through the town in such a haphazard pattern that it's impossible to know where you are. The air is filled with dust kicked up by the ever-present desert wind, bringing with it pungent smells of donkeys, fishmongers, and exotic spices, and the ground is littered with trash.

In no time at all, I became hopelessly lost in the confusing labyrinth, unable to find the central square that I sought. A black motorbike pulled up next to me, belching blue smoke from its tailpipe. It was a Japanese model built at least twenty years ago and ubiquitous in the crowded towns and cities all over the Middle East and North Africa.

The driver was a lad of about eighteen dressed in the omnipresent soiled caftan and sandals. With a big, toothless grin, he asked, "Mister, where you wish to go? To town square?"

I nodded while trying to hold back a coughing fit inspired by swirling dust and exhaust fumes.

"Mister, you follow me or you be lost and never find this good place. Many foods there. You follow me. I take you there."

I nodded again, and he led me on a bewildering trail through the town until finally we came to a congested parking area at the edge of a souk, where a man standing there as if an attendant directed me to a parking slot. According to my newly acquired guide, Golub by name, the man was one of his many cousins. *Of course he is*, I thought.

Golub turned out to be an affable and helpful fellow. He took me on a delightful tour through the bafflement of laneways, stopping for lunch at a popular café located alongside the public square. Instead of escorting me to the ground floor where the locals, all men, were eating and jabbering away, Golub directed me to a shady table on a rooftop veranda with a nice view of the square.

When I asked why he wished to separate me from the locals, he grinned and said, with surprising prescience for such a young man, that he thought I might like to have wine with my meal and, after all, this was a devoutly religious town where alcohol was strictly forbidden. With that, he disappeared and returned shortly with a bottle of a strictly forbidden, though outstanding, French rosé properly chilled and wrapped discreetly in old newsprint, thus revealing himself to be a clever and resourceful guide whose attitude toward Islamic constraints could only be described as flexible. I didn't know what the penalty was for an American caught drinking alcohol in a pious Muslim town, and hoped I wouldn't find out.

After lunch, Golub took me down a few grimy back alleys to a tiny house that, like all the others, lacked refinements and needed paint and a good cleaning inside and out. There I was introduced to a man who led me inside to its cramped front room, where three matronly women were squatted on the floor operating primitive, hand-powered grinding machines. They were, I was informed, gnashing argan nuts in the process of turning them into a rare and costly oil for which he claimed an assortment of fanciful properties. I passed up the chance to buy direct from the manufacturer.

It was in this town that I first saw black African men dressed in the same getups as the locals. They were from the desperately poor neighboring country of Mauritania and had come to the slightly less poor Morocco to find jobs. If Mauritania is on your list of places to visit, I recommend you remove it. Only trouble and bad food await you there, so Golub and others told me.

Marrakech, Morocco

Upon leaving Taroudant after my excellent lunch and unlawful rosé wine, I took a road that ran high up into the snow-dusted Atlas Mountains on its tortuous path to Marrakech. It turned out to be at once the most scenic and most treacherous road I've ever traveled. That a part of it was marked as dangerous on my Michelin map should have been a hint had I bothered to notice before setting out. Scenery along the way was much what I expect a road through the Hindu Kush would reveal: nearly treeless mountains, roads in disrepair with their cliffside edges unprotected by guardrails, and goat herders clogging the way with their flocks. So severe are the mountains that progress up them is made in tightly wound switchbacks. Here and there are tiny villages plastered onto the precipitous ground, their houses made entirely of dried mud bricks with flat mud roofs.

Unable to make more than about twenty miles an hour, night descended long before I reached Marrakech, adding an extra dimension of excitement to the driving. With help from a GPS, I reached my hotel just before midnight. Part of a huge golf resort on the outskirts of town, the place is called Palmeraie Golf Palace, named after the expansive palm grove in which it is located. It looked as if it could belong somewhere in Florida, but with some distinctly Moroccan design features. During my brief stay, it was host to a convention of French doctors.

Marrakech, known as the Miami of Africa, is one of the best places

I've ever visited, and I would gladly return there often. This Berber city of a million inhabitants sits on a plateau at the intersection of the Sahara, the High Atlas Mountains, and the Anti-Atlas Mountains. It was once the capital of a great empire, and is today the principal city of south Morocco and the country's third largest city after Casablanca and Rabat. Its fabulous palaces, luxuriant palm groves, and wildly exuberant central market hold a powerful fascination for visitors, including me. I loved the place.

Like all first-time visitors to the city, I headed straight for the enormous medina. Its ramparts, at twelve miles long, up to six feet thick and thirty feet high, are impressive and kept in immaculate repair. Within these are souks (specialized markets) carrying just about every product Morocco offers, like brass and copper items, carpets (of course), jewelry, leather goods, clothing, fabrics, skins, fruits and vegetables, live chickens, basketry, and much, much more. There are also many fashionable shops and swish restaurants, mostly with a French flair. As in Taroudant, the ramparts hide a confusion of narrow streets, alleyways, and paths going this way and that, often blocked by the ubiquitous donkey carts and blanketed in smells, not all of them pleasant.

At the heart and soul of the medina—indeed of all Marrakech— stands the riotously seductive and always fascinating Jamaa al-Fna square—or Jamaa, as it is locally known, said to be the world's busiest square, a claim I do not dispute. As darkness settles in, Jamaa begins to take on a character like no other place I know of, becoming a gigantic, multifaceted open-air spectacle. Water sellers, snake charmers, mystics, palm readers, dancers, acrobats, magicians, musicians, storytellers, showmen, con artists, soothsayers, and tooth-pullers gather to practice their trade on locals and tourists alike. The air soon fills with leaping flames and dense smoke from grilling meat, the aromas of spices and cooking food, the sounds of exotic music, and the hectoring of insistent merchants. As the night wears on, the music becomes louder and more hypnotic, and soon you begin to think you have stumbled into a joyous Moroccan version of Dante's Inferno.

Outdoor food vendors selling everything from fresh-squeezed orange juice to sausages, soups, salads, and lamb kebabs, all outstanding, make it unnecessary to dine in a restaurant. You can just buy what you like and take it with you as you walk around, astounded by the feverish delirium that surrounds you. Jamaa alone is worth the trip to Marrakech.

Within the medina's ramparts is also the more sedate and decidedly tidier kasbah, a term meaning a fortified citadel. From the Jamaa, it is entered through a massive portal called the Bab Agnaou. Inside are the Royal Palace and a variety of souks, food stalls, restaurants, and hotels.

Wishing to be nearer the action and to avoid having to search for a parking spot, I moved to the legendary La Mamounia Hotel, surely one of the finest in the world, and at 800 euros a night for a basic room, one of the dearest, too. Its magnificent twenty-acre garden is lush with olive and orange trees and stately palms, and it is just a ten-minute walk from Jamaa. You will not stay in a finer, more sumptuous hotel anywhere.

Most of the low-rise structures throughout the Moroccan interior, including ramparts, kasbahs, palaces, enclosing walls, and even modern desert villas (although not Hotel La Mamounia) are built using a construction method called pisé, a French word for "rammed earth." These look as if they were made of stucco or adobe, have smooth surfaces, and are almost uniformly the color of red clay or khaki. If you can picture a desert fort used by the French Foreign Legion in movies of the 1940s, you'll have a good idea of pisé-built structures. Other buildings are built of dried mud bricks, sometimes with chopped straw added, and often have flat roofs made of dried mud. The warm coloration and use of rounded edges and their simple, unadorned surfaces give these buildings a softer and more restrained appearance than if they were built of concrete. While the exteriors of so many Moroccan structures are unadorned, the interiors are often extraordinarily ornate, employing intricate geometric patterns, mosaics, and rich hues.

Ouarzazate—Africa's Hollywood

Leaving Marrakech, I traveled up and through the high passes of the High Atlas Mountains, their pinnacles dappled in snow, on my way to the town of Ouarzazate (whar-za-zat). The entire drive was another scenic wonderland of remote villages; ancient, strategically sited kasbahs; and flocks of sheep and goats grazing in the most precarious places. For most of the way, a narrow river flowed at the bottom of the steep-sided chasm along which I was driving and into which I wished not to plummet. It joins others draining the escarpment that together form the Draa River, into whose valley I would soon be driving on my way to the far desert.

About the very last building you would expect to find in the eastern Moroccan interior at the edge of a vast desert is a Hollywood-style movie studio, but that is just what I found there. Not just one, but two. Atlas Film Studios, enclosed by high ramparts and covering 322,000 square feet of desert, is guarded at its spectacular gates by two gigantic pseudo-Egyptian sphinxes from which you quickly conclude that behind these gates there could be nothing other than a film studio. Across town is the Andromeda Italian Film Studios of similar size. I was astonished to find that these are the town's principal employers and have produced hundreds of films over the years, including some notable in the US market, like *Lawrence of Arabia*, *Gladiator*, *Cleopatra*, and *The Man Who Would Be King*. I had unknowingly stumbled upon Africa's Hollywood.

As if to press home the point, the public spaces in my hotel, where all the film crews are housed during shootings, were decorated with props and set pieces from various films produced in the past by these studios. There was, for example, the throne of Ramses II from *The Ten Commandments* and another throne, this one from *Cleopatra*.

Promotional posters advertising various films from the 1960s and 1970s cluttered the walls.

Ouarzazate is also home to one of the world's finest kasbahs, a fortified citadel and palace for the area's tribal chieftain. This one, a UNESCO World Heritage site, is quite large by customary standards and has outer walls and colossal entry gates intricately decorated in geometric patterns found only in Morocco.

Villages of Morocco

I drove into the eastern Moroccan desert, passing through the towns of Agdz, Zagora, Tamegroute, and Tagounite, wishing to see the monumental sand dunes of Ch'gaga and a Tuareg encampment.[1] Along the way, I passed through ostentatious topography such as I have rarely seen before. In sequence, I came upon low hills, rolling plains, haphazard fields of enormous volcanic boulders, vast divots deeply scoured in the Earth's surface by ancient rivers, and scabrous mountains. The entire panorama looked as if the Earth's surface had been turned inside out. It is this arresting scenery that explains the two film studios and, indeed, as I drove along, I passed a working film crew set up at an especially appealing site.

At each of the towns were ksars, the iconic village fortifications of the area, all of them ancient but still in use today. Built of pisé, their enclosing walls and entry gates are inscribed by village artisans in intricate geometric patterns and are popular with tourists, including me. From the prolific fortifications in Morocco, you would conclude correctly that in the old days—actually not all that long ago—the area was full of marauding bandits eager to confiscate the hard-gotten gains of farmers and craftsmen, and even the farmers and craftsmen themselves, who could be sold as slaves. Tribal warfare was rife then, held in check now by the state.

As the road wound its way into ever-higher mountains, all devoid of even a hint of organic growth except a few planted date palms,

1. Right away, you can see that the Berber language and English diction are not on friendly terms.

I came upon a most sobering accident scene. A large flatbed truck loaded with hundred-pound sacks of couscous had plunged from the road over a cliff—there was of course no guardrail—and down a steep mountainside. The driver had not survived. From that point onward, I drove more carefully.

Soon the road descended from the desiccated mountains into the Draa Valley and followed alongside the river's course, passing through ancient villages and their equally ancient adjoining ksars. Stopping at a few of these and passing slowly through others, I was able to gain a sense of village life. Women, vibrantly adorned and balancing earthen jars or scraggly swathes of river reeds on their head, were more numerous than the donkeys with whom they seem to compete as bearers of burden. Men chopped palm fronds and reeds, occupied roadside vendor stands, or lay about doing nothing at all. Poorly nourished donkeys pulling primitive carts loaded with palm fronds ambled along on the road's shoulders, and frolicsome kids sat astride haggard donkeys, whacking them with sticks in a fruitless attempt to encourage more speed.

Here and there, roadside vendors hawked freshly picked dates. It was the season for these, so I stopped and bought a bunch, tasted one, and threw the rest away. Although a major part of the Moroccan diet, these dates are so cloyingly sweet that they are almost certainly a contributor to the rotted dentition that affects the entire countryside.

But for the roadway and its passing vehicles, and a few modern handheld implements like the machete, life here is much as it was a thousand years ago. Its desultory pace follows the seasons and produces no discernible improvement in the villagers' lives year by year. Summers are blisteringly hot, up to 130 degrees Fahrenheit, and there is precious little electrical power—so, save in a few stores for tourists, there is no air conditioning. Few people can afford cars or trucks so, despite having to cover considerable distances, they walk. Roadways are lined with walkers, donkey carts, and donkey riders.

The Draa River, without which these villages could not survive, flows swiftly through multiple channels as it passes out of the High Atlas Mountains, joins with other rivers, and gathers volume. But at its easternmost extremity, it slowly weakens, then simply ceases to exist, an ignominious end for an important waterway. At its terminus, the last of the precious water has all finally evaporated or leeched into the desert soil, sapping its life-giving power and leaving all beyond an arid, trackless wasteland.

It was this wasteland that I now wished to see and drove on in that direction.

While roaming aimlessly around the town of Zagora generally in the direction of the desert, I was approached by a man on foot asking if I needed a guide. His name was Omar. He wore a traditional djellaba robe and open-toed sandals and, like many Moroccan men, sported a neatly trimmed beard. He was articulate and clearly intelligent, and spoke excellent English, almost without accent. This, more than anything else, prompted me to hire him.

Omar climbed into my car, and together we headed south out into the desert. Along the way, he explained the local culture, the function of ksars, the role of Islam in the villages, and much more.

We first visited the encampment of a small band of Tuaregs just at the edge of the desert, where Omar introduced me to the group's leader, Mohamed, a diminutive, smiling fellow draped in the radiant blue cloth favored by the Tuareg everywhere. They had pitched their four black, thick, camel-hair tents in the open desert floor several miles from any permanent structures, five miles from the nearest village, and at least thirty yards from each other. From this arrangement, it was easy to see that the impulse to congregate is not part of their culture. Although there was a small copse of palms nearby offering modest shade, they avoided it.

Tuaregs are an ancient Berber nomadic people who populate, although in the sparest sense of that term, the Saharan interior of North Africa. When they need supplies, they trek into the nearest village with money earned from whatever source is available to them, buy what they need, and return to their isolation. It is civilization they shun, preferring instead the solitary life of the idle wanderer in a harsh land where few others live.

Both Omar and Mohamed insisted that I climb aboard one of the clan's camels couched nearby and go for a brief ride around some dunes—for a slight fee, of course. Not wishing to give offense, I went along, feeling the whole time like a kid at the pony rides. But as I thought about it, no matter how foolish I appeared, how many times does a guy like me get to ride a Tuareg camel in the Moroccan desert? If you're wondering, camel riding is ponderously slow and wobbly. You'd prefer a horse, or better yet a dirt bike.

Apart from gently fleecing tourists like me, the Tuareg earn money by collecting from the desert and selling bones and teeth that once belonged to an impressive assortment of critters, like prehistoric dinosaurs, raptors, and sharks that once populated the Sahara in teeming numbers. There is an energetic market in these, both for the authentic version and, for the unsuspecting buyer, the fabricated knock-offs.

We still were not at the end of the paved road marking the deepest point into the desert it was possible to go without a four-wheel-drive vehicle. That point was at the village of M'Hamid at the edge of the great sand dunes of Ch'gaga. When I asked Omar and Mohamed about going there, both promptly said that it was forbidden, and that the road was closed off at a military checkpoint where I would be turned back. The village, it seems, is the site of a French Foreign Legion outpost whose purpose is to stem incursions by radical Islamist elements in nearby Algeria who wish a lot of no-good upon the insufficiently devout and Western-friendly Moroccans and the Western tourists they harbor.

Disappointed, I got back in the car with Omar and headed for the village of Tamegroute. There I met and dined with the proprietress of Jnane-Dar Diafa restaurant and inn, a Swiss woman named Doris Paulus. In a sustained eruption of youthful folly, she had come to the area some thirty years ago with her then-boyfriend to start the business. They split, he ran off, but she stayed on in that relentlessly dutiful way that seems to characterize the Swiss. Now, all those years later, here I sat in the desert under a camel-hair tent dining with her and Omar and hearing her tale, doing my best to feign interest.

After an extended lunch, Omar and I drove back to his village of Zagora, where he invited me to join him, his father, and uncle for tea in the shop they own together. In keeping with tradition, they and their families live in the several floors above the shop and own the building, built by their hands, that houses it all. He introduced me to the father and uncle, who, like Omar, insisted on smiling broadly, thus exposing blackened badlands where once teeth had stood. The shop's inventory consisted mostly of Moroccan tourist schlock of the sort I had seen all over Marrakech.

As the three of us sat down around the tiny gas burner holding the teapot, I began to feel like an innocent mouse in a strange back-yard surrounded by cats. Here, though, the cats were largely tooth-less. Foolishly, I had poked around in the shop and apparently had begun to display some interest in an especially handsome silver-han-dled dagger with matching scabbard, and a walking stick fashioned from camel bone, both handmade by Tuareg tribesmen—or so I was assured. It was then that the bargaining began.

I won't burden you with the tedious process by which we finally agreed on a price I was willing to pay for a modest addition to my collection of junk from around the world. But I can say that a few days later, I learned that the items I had bought—which I regarded at the time of purchase as particularly fine, rare, and handsome—were mass-produced, of poor quality cleverly disguised, and could be had for a small fraction of what I'd paid.

As I was departing and we were saying our goodbyes, Omar's young son tried to collect a fee for "watching" my car. These guys were good.

~~~

After spending the night at my hotel in Africa's version of Hollywood, I left the next day to drive through more magnificent scenery the several hundred miles back to *Indigo*. One day I'd like to return to Morocco. Next time I'll spend a week or so in Marrakech, then rent a four-wheel-drive vehicle and head off into the mountains and desert, allowing several weeks to see it all. I didn't get to see the famous dunes of Erg Chebbi nor any of the panoramic topography around them. Next time, I will.

There is a good reason for those two film studios being where they are, and it's the scenery. Few places in the world offer such a variety of stunning vistas, warped and twisted landscapes, and villages a thousand years old whose people go about life as they always have. Morocco goes onto my list of the best places I have ever visited and one to which I will return soon.

THIRTY-TWO

Perils in the Jungles and Cities of South Africa

In early February 2011, following an uneventful voyage of 380 nautical miles from Agadir, Morocco, to Tenerife in the Canary Islands, I flew to Johannesburg, South Africa, to meet up with Kitty and Grant to spend what turned out to be an unexpectedly enjoyable three weeks there.

We started by traveling the short distance to Pretoria, where an overnight stay at an inn awaited us. I knew that Johannesburg—or Jo'burg, as it is commonly called—is more notable for its rate of violent and property crimes than for the attractions it offers. Pretoria—nearly a suburb—visibly reflects its neighbor's unsavory reputation. Although our inn had been converted from a grand mansion located on a leafy boulevard amid other fine mansions, many now serving as various embassies, a masonry wall twelve feet high topped off with both coiled concertina wire and straight lines of electrified wire surrounded it. Security cameras activated by motion sensors were more numerous than were birds perched in the trees.

Upon our arrival outside its gate, the inn's manager visually inspected us and our car through a viewing port, confirmed our identification with the driver and our reservation, and approved us for admittance. A solid corrugated steel gate slid back on tracks, allowing our car to enter, and quickly closed behind us. It was all an unpromising start to our travels in South Africa and carried with it the conspicuous suggestion that these two cities are not yet fit for safe travel. Seldom has a carefree getaway begun on such a foreboding note.

Next day, we drove out to the airport to a small terminal building and boarded a twin-prop plane for the hour-long flight to our destination: the Singita Ebony Lodge located in the famed Sabi Sand Game Reserve. This is a private game preserve of some 140,000 acres surrounded by Swaziland, Mozambique, Botswana, and Zimbabwe. It also adjoins the vast Kruger National Park, which at nearly five million acres (7,700 square miles) is one of the world's largest parks. None of the preserve or the national park is fenced off from the other, so for the area's resident creatures, it's all just one big happy hunting ground if you happen to be a predator—or a succulent buffet line on which you are a featured item if you're not.

Sabi Sand Game Reserve, South Africa

Upon landing on the lodge's private airstrip, we were greeted by the manager, who had brought a safari Jeep to ferry Kitty, Grant, and me to our rustic two-bedroom cabin. Complete with stone fireplace, this would be home for the coming week.

Paved walkways winding through tall grass and scrub trees separate the lodge's public spaces from its cabins. Lurking on and near these after dusk are hyenas, leopards, and assorted other unfriendly types attracted by the aromas wafting from the lodge kitchen. Management cautioned us that if we wished to leave the safety of our cabin after dusk, we should call reception for a guide who, armed solely with a flashlight and experience, would escort us. That pretty much dampened any interest we may have had for late-night strolls in the bush.

Management also cautioned us never to leave our cabin without locking its heavy, solid-wood entry door. One of us—okay, that would be me—failed to do this when he left the cabin in broad daylight, reasoning that it wasn't necessary as he'd be gone not more than twenty minutes. Later that afternoon, the housemaid pointed out to us that during that brief period, a wily baboon, who had obviously watched me leave, had entered through the unlocked door, gone straight to the minibar, and opened it. He removed a basket of assorted snacks, neatly opened each packet, consumed its contents, replaced the wrappers in the basket, and returned the basket to its usual place. He then closed the minibar door, left the cabin, and closed the cabin door securely behind him. Few human thieves are so fastidious.

As our guide during our stay there, the lodge's manager assigned us the most senior and experienced of its guides. Leon was a tall, genial white man of Boer descent with a slightly diffident, professorial manner. A former high school biology teacher from a village in Zimbabwe with eighteen years' experience guiding tourists in the African wilds, he had encyclopedic knowledge about Africa and the impressive array of its animals we would encounter. He never failed to guide us to the most interesting of these and describe them in considerable detail.

The daily routine began at six a.m., when we reported to the lodge public area for coffee and light snacks before setting out in one of the new open-top Land Rovers specially designed for African animal viewing. Joining us for each outing was a black African tracker from a nearby village. He sat on a small fold-up seat mounted on the left front fender, from which he spotted game with uncanny perception. I was pleased to note on our first excursion that Leon carried along a high-powered, bolt-action rifle fully loaded and ready to go, if needed. As matters ensued, he didn't need to use the rifle, though he removed it several times from its scabbard when doing so seemed the prudent thing to do.

Following a morning of stalking whatever beasts happened to be out that day, we returned to the lodge for a lunch from which the staff often had to chase uninvited marauding monkeys. Lunch and a restful midday nap behind us, we set out in the late afternoon for a longer trek into the wilds that extended into the night. During these morning and evening explorations of the African bushveld, we saw just about all the species that inhabit the area that time of year. There were elephants, lions, leopards, black rhinos, and Cape buffalo (collectively known as the Big Five), giraffes, zebras, hyenas, wildebeests, hippos, wild dogs, baboons, and monkeys, all in impressive profusion. In addition, a wide assortment of various antelopes wandered about in what I thought was a foolishly insouciant manner, given that many carnivores on whose menu they appear surround them. Among these were the duiker, klipspringer, steenbok, springbok, and the abundant impala. These animals, along with some of the strangest birds we've ever seen, were so plentiful that you could hardly travel a hundred yards without something or other coming into view, usually up very close.

We sat within fifty feet of a leopard that we watched climb into a low tree. He perched on one of its limbs for a short nap, then descended and ambled along a dirt road to another tree that apparently agreed with him more.

Leon drove us to a pride of young lions lying upon a dried streambed, seemingly asleep in the warm African sun. As we sat there watching cautiously from just twenty feet away, one flicked open a cold black eye, and then opened both, raised its head, and stared straight at me. I smiled in a manner intended to offer my high regard for lions and everlasting goodwill toward the species, but he failed to reciprocate. Leon had already unsheathed his rifle and had it ready, though I am pleased to say it wasn't needed.

One morning as we were driving along one of the reserve's two-rutted tracks, we alarmed a group of monkeys inhabiting a tree. They began screeching and scrambling up to the highest limbs. The cause, we learned, was that they had spotted a leopard on the hunt.

Leon got us into position to watch as the leopard hunkered down and slinked along in the tall grass, trying to get close enough to a small herd of impala to surprise and nab one for lunch. These frail creatures, not much larger than a goat, are so quick afoot that no leopard can hope to run one down. They're the local version of fast food. Ambush is the only way to catch an impala, and the monkeys' alarm had blown that chance for the leopard.

At the airstrip where we had landed earlier in the week, we watched a pack of vicious wild dogs—a truly wild animal different from the feral version of domesticated dogs—attempt a sneak attack on a young wildebeest, only to be thwarted by a vigilante posse of older bulls.

One day Kitty, Grant, and I drove ten miles or so over dirt tracks to a hamlet of a thousand or so inhabitants. This was where most of the black lodge staff lived, all of whom belong to a large tribe common in South Africa and once part of the Zulu nation. With land so plentiful, the clean, modest, masonry homes were set on parcels of a half acre, neatly fenced against small creatures that might nibble away their gardens. Each home's yard was tidy as, indeed, was the whole village. A communal standpipe every few blocks provided freshwater, and septic tanks were used for sanitary disposal. All the local roads were unpaved but smoothly graded. In the backyard of many homes was a small, round, one-room thatched-roof hut that served as a private temple for worship directed at the owner's gods, built round so that evil spirits would not have a corner in which to lurk.

Our guide took us around to a few homes where makeshift tourist attractions awaited. At one, three young boys performed a Zulu dance of some sort that involved a lot of stomping on the bare ground and beseeching of some god or other—something like an African Macarena. Other stops revealed local crafts, a male a cappella choral group, that sort of thing. In the area of commercial skills, the natives here have a long way to go.

On the evening before our departure, the lodge treated the three of us to a delightful outdoor barbecue under the clear African night sky. Leon joined us at our table for a fun evening of conversation about his life growing up in Zimbabwe, going to school, and later teaching biology there, and now guiding tourists at Singita. The lodge manager and his wife, too, joined in and helped us learn more about a

354

way of life so different from our own. We noted that brightly glowing kerosene lanterns surrounded our dining area and that a loaded hunting rifle was close to hand. Prudent measures, we thought.

Cape Town, South Africa

Upon our return to Jo'burg, we boarded the famed Blue Train—South Africa's version of the Orient Express on which it is modeled—for a one-night, two-day trip across vast, sparsely populated plains to our destination in Cape Town.

Widely regarded as one of the world's most beautiful cities, Cape Town is, at 3.5 million inhabitants, the second most populous city in South Africa, after Johannesburg. It also is the capital of South Africa, though only for legislative matters, and the provincial capital of the Western Cape.

On arrival, we checked into the Cape Grace Hotel, sited conveniently on the central harbor. This area has been attractively developed into both residential and commercial spaces, the latter of which are dense with shops and restaurants, and filled most days with locals and tourists alike wandering about in the pleasant sea air. From our balcony, we looked over the looming presence of the 3,300-foot Table Mountain, dramatically defined by its sheer vertical cliffs. Table Mountain, along with Lion's Head and Devil's Peak, form the city's topographically theatrical backdrop.

On most evenings, a strong onshore wind blowing against the far side of the mountain builds pressure sufficient to push a continuous mass of warm, moist air up its steep slope, over the flat surface of its plateau, and down the nearside. As the air rises and warms, it forms a thick blanket of banker-gray cloud that calls to mind a bad toupee gone awry. As a rule, it arrives at about the cocktail hour and so provides a wholesome spectacle to those seated outdoors at their favored bar.

During our stay in Cape Town, we visited most of the notable tourist attractions and did a few oddball things, as well. Grant dived in the frigid waters of the Indian Ocean, safely encaged behind steel bars, as great white sharks circled close by. One even knocked into the bars as if to test their resistance.

We spent a day touring the wine-growing region of Stellenbosch, a stunningly beautiful place vastly more appealing than Napa Valley, thanks to the enormous, sheer-walled peaks of bare gray rock that define its boundaries and the comparative absence of crowds and traffic. An exceptional lunch at one or the other of the swank winery restaurants, seated outdoors in a balmy sunshine amid pastoral beauty, is about as pleasant as a meal gets.

Throughout our stay in Cape Town, we were accompanied by the ever-affable John Mason, former British army officer who, with his partner Lloyd Bernard, had served as our security detail aboard *Indigo* during the passage through the pirate-infested Gulf of Aden. He and his team of highly experienced former military security experts provided discreetly armed security for us in Cape Town, where it was appropriate. Given the rising rate of violent crime in South Africa, including Cape Town, abetted by the enormous leap in the population of ghetto-like shantytowns, it seemed like the prudent choice to hire them. Their services allowed us to visit some places to which we otherwise would not have ventured but from which we benefited greatly.

One of Cape Town's most repugnant features is its proliferation of immense, teeming shantytowns, known there by the sanitized evasion "townships." At the time of our visit, there were thirteen of these in varying sizes, the largest inhabited by an astonishing 1.4 million people—although in fact, the number is no more than a speculation.

We drove through several of these shantytowns and strolled on foot through one so that we might gain some understanding of them. Their inhabitants are black Africans from South Africa and neighboring countries who have come to Cape Town in search of a better life through means both commendable and nefarious.

All of the townships are on flat, treeless plains outside the city and are easily visible from one or more major traffic arteries. A few preexisting roads along their periphery are paved, but internal roads, most of them not wide enough for vehicles, are dirt tracks.

The typical shanty, a single room of about fifteen feet square, six feet high, with an earthen floor, is made of corrugated tin sheets nailed over primitive wooden box frames. The low, flat roof consists of tin sheets often held in place by cinder blocks. Each shack is jammed up against the next with barely a foot or two between them. Where the city provides electrical service, power poles linked to the shanties by sagging lines dot the landscape. In many townships, there is no evidence that electrical power is available at all.

Most of these townships have a freshwater standpipe every few hundred yards, where potable water is collected in pottery jars or plastic buckets, and a few open-air groupings of concrete sinks in which the women wash clothes. None of the shanties has even rudimentary plumbing, so in most cases the city provides large clusters of portable toilets.

Despite what the innocent Westerner might suppose, these townships bustle with commercial enterprise. At busy street corners, there are lines of open-air barbecue shacks one after the other, with grills blazing, aromatic smoke rising, and customers standing in line. Rusting, battered shipping containers, their sides and doors crudely hand-lettered, serve as beauty parlors, convenience stores, repair shops, flea market stores, and more. In short, many of the emporia commonly found in any large community are here and seem to be thriving, although at the most rudimentary level.

By some estimates, somewhere between half and 70 percent of all black Africans carry the HIV virus, with a startlingly high percentage of these cases rapidly developing into AIDS. Without adequate resources to pay for costly treatments, deaths from the disease are at epidemic levels, leaving behind a tragic number of orphaned infants and young children. For this reason, all of the townships have numerous makeshift orphanages scattered throughout their area. Staffing these are older women who work for little or no pay.

Because Kitty and I wanted Grant to see, by the starkest of contrasts, how very fortunate he is, we decided to visit one of these orphanages. The one John Mason chose for us was a modest cinder block, two-story home with additional rooms added in the rear. Bunk beds filled its cramped spaces, accommodating the dozen or so kids housed there, from infant to about eight years old.

In another township we walked into one of the masonry buildings to find squalid, unlit, trash-strewn rooms. Behind one door was a tiny, stifling space containing a shabby bunk bed on which lay an obese, middle-aged woman. As I entered, she raised her head, looked in my direction for a few seconds, then plopped her head back down and closed her eyes without saying a word.

Back out in the streets, cheerful, runny-nosed kids greeted us and insisted that we hold hands with them. After a few blocks, we came upon the outdoor communal laundry, where women went about their washing chores with impressive vigor and a great deal of gossip.

Despite the ramshackle, insalubrious conditions of the townships, their inhabitants were always dressed in clean clothes and seemed themselves well scrubbed. It is surprisingly common for township residents to gain an education and employment, learn to speak and write English fluently, and in general move up the socioeconomic ladder while remaining in the community from which they sprang. They do this both because the cost of living there is considerably less than elsewhere, and because they have long-standing attachments there.

~~~

Following our three weeks in South Africa, which we enjoyed immensely, Kitty and Grant returned to Florida, and I returned to *Indigo* at Tenerife to begin our final preparations for crossing the Atlantic.

INDIGO ITINERARY : SAONA ISLAND, DOMINICAN REPUBLIC TO FT LAUDERDALE, FLORIDA

1,776 nm traveled this portion of trip: 45,487.9 nm traveled TOTAL

1 nautical mile (nm) = 1.151 miles

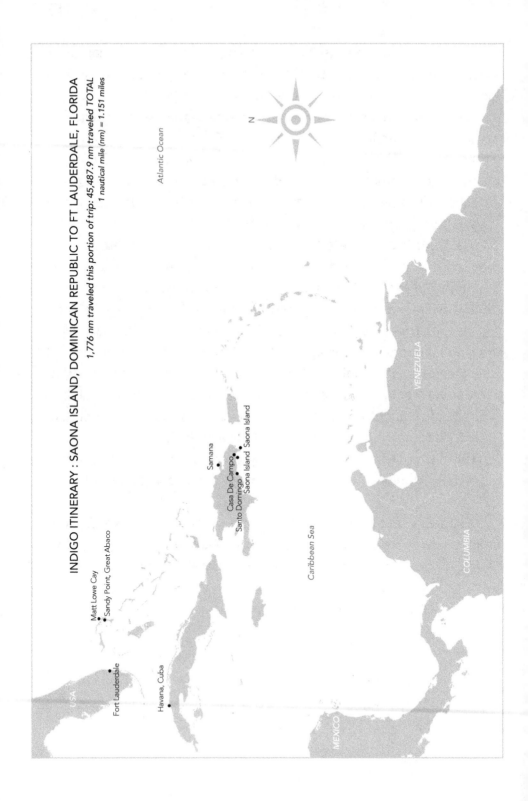

Atlantic Ocean

N

Matt Lowe Cay
Sandy Point, Great Abaco

Fort Lauderdale

Havana, Cuba

USA

Samana

Casa De Campo
Santo Domingo
Saona Island   Saona Island

Caribbean Sea

VENEZUELA

COLUMBIA

MEXICO

THIRTY-THREE

Heading Home by Way of Havana

The distance from Tenerife to Barbados is 2,617 nautical miles, which we covered at an average of 8.4 nautical miles (9.7 statute miles) per hour in thirteen days. As with other long passages of our journey, a routine quickly developed that for me amounted to rank indolence and for the crew amounted to shift work as they stood periodic watches and attended to their various duties. I caught up on a lot of reading, blog writing, emailing, and the like, to say nothing of frequent naps.

Return to the Caribbean Islands

Like nearly all Caribbean islands, Barbados has some fabulous beaches and balmy breezes, though because it is closer to the equator than most, it is sweltering at any time but winter. It is known as the England of the Caribbean with good reason. Most of its nonnative inhabitants, whether permanent or temporary, are Brits, and signs of that abound. Most restaurants on Sunday serve a proper English roast dinner with Yorkshire pudding, and the bars offer about the same beers, ales, and light fare found in any London pub.

From Barbados, we traveled west to the lee of the Windward Islands at Saint Lucia, where we turned north toward home, using the mass of these islands to block the wind-driven waves coming off the Atlantic. At Anguilla in the far north extremity of the Lesser Antilles, we turned west, bypassing Puerto Rico to arrive at Casa de Campo, Dominican Republic.

With a population of nearly ten million and, at 85 percent, the highest literacy rate in the Caribbean, the Dominican Republic has much to recommend it—but proximity to a felicitous neighboring country is not among its best features. It occupies the eastern two-thirds of the island of Hispaniola, and is verdant, fecund, and comparatively safe for human habitation. Haiti, its immediate neighbor, occupying the other third of the island, is the opposite of all of these: barren, infertile, and dangerous. I am not aware of anywhere else in the world where two adjoining countries are so starkly in contrast.

My longtime close friend Jack Burnell joined me for a week in the Dominican Republic at the capital city of Santo Domingo. Together we idled away time with leisurely walks, lunches on *Indigo*, dinners in local restaurants, and car tours to the notable attractions, few as they are.

We admired the superb Spanish Colonial architecture of the city's old town. Dating from 1496, it is the oldest permanent European settlement in the New World.

Jack, ever inquisitive, climbed an exhausting stone stairway to the top of the sturdy fortress guarding the harbor's entrance, where he enjoyed a great view of the harbor—imagining himself to be a conquistador, I'm guessing. As an avid practitioner of energy conservation, I declined to join him but instead sat on a tree-shaded bench and watched tourists go by.

Later, as we strolled through a leafy town square in the heart of the old town, we came across a store with a dazzling assortment of rums and cigars tastefully displayed on shelves and glass cases covering two large floors. We had happened upon Man Heaven without the inconvenience of having to die to get there.

Back on *Indigo*, we traveled the short distance to Bayahibe, a nearby beach resort town where locals board large catamarans for a five-mile trip to Isla Saona, one of the world's most picturesque beaches. Intrigued, we hopped into the tender and visited the beach and joined a few hundred locals lying about under the shade of a magnificent palm grove, sipping on rum drinks conveniently sold from rustic, thatched-roof huts. So identical is the beach to the universal mind's eye picture of the idyllic tropical paradise that many advertisements around the world—and more than a few Hollywood films—feature it as just that. It is at least as perfect a beach as any I have ever seen, including those of Polynesia and Thailand.

Havana, Cuba

After Jack's departure, *Indigo* made her way around the east end of Cuba and westerly along its extensive north shore to Havana. We reported as required to Marina Hemingway and tied up to a concrete seawall in a former resort complex of apartments, hotels, and modest villas whose designs appeared to date from the 1950s. The grounds and buildings were poorly kept. Castro's compound, in which he was living at the time, was just across the street.

To get into the resort or to leave it required passing through two police checkpoints—not to prevent cash-bearing tourists from leaving the area to spend money in the city, but to prevent impoverished Cubans from boarding vessels and leaving the country. Uniformed and plainclothes cops are numerous in Havana, and snitches, hoping to ingratiate themselves and their families with these, even more common. During our entire stay, at least two plainclothes cops hovered on foot around *Indigo* twenty-four hours a day.

As we tied up, a friendly man in his midthirties with an exuberant mass of unruly red hair greeted us in flawless, unaccented English. The Fixer, a nickname I will use to protect his identity, turned out to be an invaluable guide through the intricacies of socialist/black market Cuba.

For guys, the first thing you notice upon arriving in Havana is the cars. When Castro arrived, those who could do so departed and left behind their US-made cars, all of them dating from 1959 and earlier.

Most of these, still painted in their original hues and with original interiors, radios, and the like, are now government-owned taxicabs. Their motors and running gear, long since worn-out, have been replaced by Japanese-made, fuel-efficient five-cylinder diesel engines and five-speed manual shift transmissions with their modern shift mechanism linked to authentic hand levers mounted on the steering column.

During our four-day stay, I saw an astounding variety of car makes and models, all reminiscent of my youth, and often rode in a 1948 Chevy four-door sedan. It had rolled and pleated red velour seat covers and a backseat large enough for a small party—the sort of car that lends itself well to furtive canoodling in lovers' lanes.

There were also DeSotos, Buicks, Willys Jeepsters, Studebakers, Edsels, Nash Ramblers, Oldsmobiles, Plymouths, Dodges, gloriously finned Cadillacs, lots of Chevys and Fords, including Corvettes and T-birds, two- and four-door sedans, convertibles, and faux-wood-paneled station wagons, all of which were produced before 1959. There is hardly a better way to travel around Havana, or anywhere else, than in a gleaming red 1958 Impala convertible with the top down and its chrome shined to perfection. In Havana, you can travel in such splendid style for the mere price of a cab ride.

The Fixer escorted me on several day and night excursions into the central city's tourist area, a recently tarted-up old town of magnificent Spanish Colonial architecture. There, I mingled in crowds of tourists just arrived off whatever cruise ship was in port and with those bused into town from a long stretch of beachfront hotels nearby. There are boutique hotels, bars, and a few decent restaurants. Shops selling tourist goods of a middling sort line the shaded parks and charming plazas, and everywhere you look, lines of those delightful old cars pass by, adding color and character to the place. Of the old town's new hotels, all in buildings converted from some prior use, the Saratoga is said to be the finest.

Just a block off the main pedestrian walks, though, the streets and buildings are careworn and dilapidated, buildings not painted since the Revolution, concrete spalls, exposed torn and rusted rebar, shutters hanging loose on their hinges. What the tourist sees is merely a facade, a thin veneer of respectability.

Despite cops and snitches, Cuba is one vast black market in which employees and enterprising thieves steal goods and services of every description and sell them to distributors or backyard assemblers, who then sell on to retailers and the public, local and tourist alike.

The Fixer told me that a friend of his works at an airport pumping gasoline for state-owned aircraft and vehicles. Each day when he goes to work, his wife prepares his lunch and puts it into a backpack, which he wears openly. Also in the backpack is a flask made of flexible plastic sewn into its lining. At day's end, with his backpack stuffed with the empty wrappers and leftovers from lunch, the better to disguise his illicit mission, he fills the flask with stolen gasoline and goes home. The half gallon it holds brings a high price on the black market and, when accumulated over a year, amounts to what for him is a hefty supplement to the pittance the government pays him: about $15 per month for the average worker.

Another example is the Cuban cigar. Street peddlers accost nearly every tourist walking through the old colonial zone and surreptitiously offer in hushed tones a "deal" on authentic branded Cuban cigars. These are invariably cigars made from floor sweepings designed to look like the authentic item. They sell for $2 to $10 each, while the branded, higher quality version in the state-owned cigar store sells for $30 to $50.

Wishing to buy eight boxes of authentic branded cigars of the highest quality, but not wanting to buy them from the state, I worked with the Fixer to obtain these through the black market. As he explained, the state-owned cigar factories supplement their workers' pay by giving them two to three cigars a week for personal consumption. The workers accumulate these and steal quite a few more, then sell all of them to an assembler. He combines these with cigars from other workers, and those from casual thieves, adds authentic paper cigar rings, fancy boxes and wrappings (also stolen), and sells the finished product to men like the Fixer, who sell them to tourists like me. By purchasing his goods from factory workers, the assembler assures that the products he sells are of the same quality as that of the state-owned stores. Moonlighting cigar rollers, using inferior tobacco waste and reject wrappers, produce the shoddy cigars sold to the innocent tourist.

For eight boxes containing 200 high-quality cigars, I paid $5 per cigar. The Fixer, along with his accomplice—a small, wiry man with a scarred face, aptly called Scarface—delivered them to me in a black nylon duffel bag while we sat behind blackened windows in the backseat of the Fixer's car parked out of sight from enquiring eyes. I tested a select few and paid over the cash.

As we drove back to the boat in a car loaded with illicit loot, the senior man on duty at a police checkpoint in the Marina Hemingway resort waved us through. Of course, he was a cousin of the Fixer and got a small piece of the deal for his troubles. At the boat, two plain-clothes cops, detailed to *Indigo* to make sure that we didn't help any Cubans escape, stood in the way of getting the bag full of illegal cigars onboard. With a modest amount of cash in US dollars in his hand, the Fixer got out of the car, went over to the two cops, slipped the cash into their hands, and said they looked as if they could use some exercise and that maybe a brisk walk would do them some good. Presto, the cops left, and the cigars and I got safely onto the boat.

That I am not writing this from inside a Cuban prison is testament to the Fixer's skills. I know in retrospect that this was a foolhardy thing to do, but the excitement of it was just too much to resist, along with the pleasing thought of stiffing Castro. I gave all of the cigars to friends in the US and Bahamas.

One night, the Fixer escorted me to a cabaret in which the famed Buena Vista Social Club performed. They are a mixed ensemble of musicians, singers, and dancers who have entertained tourists in Havana and all over the world for years. Many of them, now well into their seventies and a few in their eighties, may have lacked the passion of younger performers but had lost none of their skill. The two-hour program was dazzling to see, and the audience of fellow tourists and I loved it.

I went for lunch to the historic National Hotel and visited briefly the Capri and Riviera Hotels, all once owned by the mob in the person of Meyer Lansky. The National is still a special place occupying a promontory looking over the sea and a lush garden. Inside, you have the sense of living in the 1940s or 1950s. At the bar, cocktails from that time, like the Gibson, Rob Roy, and for Havana the iconic Cuba Libre, are popular. Black-and-white autographed photos of celebrities and authentic furnishings and other interior appointments from the era decorate the public spaces. But when you step outside and see a line of shiny American cars all from the mid-to-late 1950s waiting to take you on a tour of the city, some of their drivers in period costume, you wonder for just a moment if you have not somehow made a temporal wrong turn and wound up in a bygone time.

I went for dinner one night to the only privately owned restaurant in Havana, called La Guarida, the small cave. It is located on the top floor of a three-story walk-up apartment building in what was once an upmarket neighborhood but is now, like all of its surrounding buildings, a shabby tenement.

There was no signage on the street or the building to indicate the restaurant's presence. The street was unlit, and inside the building's entry, a single bare lightbulb glowed in its foyer. The Fixer and I walked up the dusty staircase, past urchins playing amid clothes hanging out to dry. Wood trim and doors at each of the apartments had gone without paint since the Revolution, and the common areas had not been cleaned for months. We walked past cast-off steel drums that once held Castrol but were now plumbed into the apartments and used as water storage tanks. At the top floor, a single small sign identified one apartment as the home of La Guarida.

The Fixer pressed a buzzer on the wall next to the tall, unpainted wood door, and an attendant opened it without ceremony and admitted us into a cramped foyer jammed with people waiting for tables.

Cozy rooms off a central hallway were full of tightly packed tables, all full, and there was a friendly, energetic air about the place. The host seated us in one of these rooms with tasteful art hanging from its walls, and there we enjoyed a decent, though not exceptional, dinner with wine at a cost that seemed reasonable.

To get into town from the marina requires a drive of about ten miles, passing through an area whose principal street is Fifth Avenue. Once a district of graceful mansions set in lush gardens, it is now home to administrative offices for various government agencies. Consequently, those stately old homes and their once-luxuriant tropical gardens have sunk deeply into disrepair. The most prominent of the homes are now foreign embassies, all maintained to a higher standard.

I liked Havana very much, most especially its hardworking, clever, and decent people and would eagerly return there. On my next visit, though, I'll want to tour the whole country just to see what life is like outside the big city.

~~~

US law required that, before returning to US waters, our captain file with the Department of Homeland Security a form listing our last five ports of call. He had done that via email, and of course, the list included Havana.

As we departed Havana and coasted along the north shore of Cuba, we were overflown by a US Navy patrol plane, which made two passes. One pass came low over our stern, and I'm sure that was so the pilot or observer could read our name from the transom. I can only assume that the flyover was in response to our having visited Cuba.

Home
On April 4, 2011, we proceeded into the harbor in Fort Lauderdale and docked just across the canal from the very dock from which we had departed on our round-the-world adventure exactly five years and two days before.

Afterword

Nekkid suggests an escapade,
spontaneity, passion, a zest for life.
For a nekkid person, it's not hard to
conjure the image of a wry, expectant
smile or a smirk of eager anticipation
or a twinkling eye and gleeful grin.
Nekkid is just plain fun.

—Phil Phillips

As Captain Steve expertly guided *Indigo* into her berth, I stood at the railing of the foredeck and looked out over the Fort Lauderdale harbor. It was good to be back in the US, and I was looking forward to spending time with family and friends.

I knew this wouldn't be my last ocean voyage. I had greatly enjoyed "getting nekkid." For one thing, I had a lot of fun and met a lot of new friends. The voyage also expanded my horizons, especially regarding what I thought I knew about other cultures. Experiences I'd had during the journey challenged—in some cases dismantled and reformed—attitudes I'd inherited from my Pensacola upbringing. Extreme acts have a way of doing that, stripping away the unnecessary and giving you a look at what's important and what isn't.

Such a trip isn't for everyone. Any well-conditioned, well-respected man might scoff at the notion of getting nekkid. Such a man might worry about what others will say. Such a man, to me, has sold his soul, and in exchange for what? A desk in a corner office? A precious collection of neckties? To be nekkid is to be spontaneous, passionate—in essence, to be free. It is to be, as the late, great Lewis Grizzard so succinctly said, "up to somethin'."

You don't need a yacht to get nekkid. All you need is the will to do it. Every man, or woman, ought to get nekkid whenever possible. This was my adventure. I hope it will inspire you to go get your own.

Itineraries

Here are the ship's logs for the voyage described in this book, covering 45,487 nautical miles with 261 stops along the way, both at anchor and at commercial docks and marinas. In addition, there are included here the logs of two subsequent voyages.

The first of these was a journey from Florida, north to Labrador and the west coast of Greenland, across the frozen wastelands of far northern Canada, through a sector of the Arctic Ocean, and into the Bering Sea, through the Bering Straits to the Aleutian Islands, Kodiak Island and along the coasts of South Central Alaska and British Columbia ending in Victoria, BC. This added to Indigo's Slow Boat wanderings an additional distance of 12,234 nautical miles with 58 stops en route. The north most portion of this voyage includes the infamous Northwest Passage, which we were pleased to make without serious incident.

Finally, there are the logs of a cruise through the balmy western Caribbean to Cartagena, Columbia, through the exotic San Blas Islands, a roundtrip through the Panama Canal, visits to several Central American islands and returning to Florida, a distance of 3,551 nautical miles with 17 stops.

Taken together, these three voyages, all aboard Indigo, comprised a grand total of 61,243 nautical miles, or a distance equivalent to 2.83 times the equatorial circumference of the Earth, with 336 stops along the way.

M.Y INDIGO ITINERARY FT LAUDERDALE TO FRENCH GUIANA

From	To	Distance	Depart	Days	Arrive	Nights in Port
Ft Lauderdale	Elbow cay	230	27 mar	1	28 mar	6
Elbow Cay	Casa De campo	780	3 apr	3	5 apr	14
Casa De campo	Samana	304	19 apr	3	21 apr	3
Samana	San Juan	180	9 may	1	10 may	1
San Juan	Tortola	72	11 may	1	11 may	1
Tortola	Virgin gorda	26	12 may	1	12 may	1
Virgin gorda	Anguilla	71	13 may	1	13 may	1
Anguilla	St martin	20	14 may	1	14 may	10
St Maarten	St Barths	16	24 may	1	24 may	1
St Barths	Antigua	77	25 may	1	25 may	2
Antigua	Isle De Saints	81	28 may	1	28 may	1
Isla De Saints	Dominica	22	29 may	1	29 may	2
Dominica	Martinique	35	29 may	1	29 may	1
Martinique	St Lucia	48	30 may	1	30 may	1
St Lucia	St Vincent	57	31 may	1	31 may	1
St Vincent	Bequia	10	1 jun	1	1 jun	1
Bequia	Mustique	12	2 jun	1	2 jun	1
Mustique	Tobago cays	19	3 jun	1	3 jun	1
Tobago Cays	Grenada	56	4 jun	1	4 jun	1
Grenada	Trinidad	80	5 jun	1	5 jun	8
Trinidad	Paramaraibo Surinar	560	13 jun	3	16 jun	2
Paramaraibo Surinar	Kourou French Guiana	187	18 jun	2	19 jun	1
Kourou French Guiana	Fortaleza	1041	20 jun	4	25 jun	31

TOTAL MILES FOR THIS SHEET = 3984

TOTAL MILES SO FAR = 3984

M.Y INDIGO ITINERARY Fortaleza to Florianopilis

From	To	Distance	Depart	Days	Arrive	Nights in Port
Fortaleza	Natal	255	23 jul	2	25 jul	2
Natal	Joao Pessoa	78	27 jul	1	27 jul	3
Joao Pessoa	Ihla Itamarica	55	30 jul	1	30 jul	2
Ihla Itamarica	Recife	15	7 aug	1	7 aug	2
Recife	Salvador	385	10 aug	2	12 aug	8
Salvador	Morro Sao Paulo	33	20 aug	1	20 aug	1
Morro Sao Paulo	Camamu	40	21 aug	1	21 aug	1
Camamu	Ilheus	59	22 aug	1	22 aug	2
Ilheus	Port Seguro	130	22 aug	2	23 aug	1
Port Seguro	Abrolhus	96	24 aug	1	24 aug	1
Abrolhus	Guarapari	193	25 aug	2	26 aug	1
Guarapari	Buzios	163	27 aug	2	28 aug	2
Buzios	Cabo Frio	21	30 aug	1	30 aug	1
Cabo Frio	Rio De Janeiro	73	31 aug	1	31 aug	8
Rio De Janeiro	Saco de Seu	64	9 sept	1	9 sept	1
Saco de Seu	Angra do Reis	11	10 sept	1	10 sept	1
Angra do Reis	Parati	26	10 sept	1	10 sept	1
Parati	Ihlabela	73	11 sept	1	11 sept	1
Ihlabela	Paranagua	239	12 sept	2	13 sept	1
Paranagua	Portobelo	126	13 sept	2	14 sept	1
Portobelo	Florianopolis	26	15 sept	1	15 sept	3
Florianopolis	Florianopolis	8	18 sept	1	18 sept	

MILES BROUGHT FORWARD = 3984

TOTAL MILES THIS SHEET = 2169   TOTAL MILES SO FAR = 6153

M.Y INDIGO ITINERARY FLORIANOPOLIS TO VINA DEL MAR

From	To	Distance	Depart	Days	Arrive	Nights in Port	
Florianopolis	Imbituba	60	6Dec	1	6 Dec	1	
Imbituba	P Del Este	600	7 Dec	3	10 Dec	7	
P Del este	Buenos Aires	280	17 Dec	2	18 Dec	15	
Buenos Aires	Mar Del Plata	270	6 Jan 07	2	7 Jan 07	2	
Mar Del Plata	Puerto Madryn	480	10 Jan	2	13 Jan	2	
Puerto Madryn	Santa Cruz	514	16 Jan	3	19 Jan	2	
Santa Cruz	Ushuaia	467	22 Jan	2	24 Jan	3	
Ushuaia	Caleta Lientur	158	5 feb	1	5 feb	1	
Caleta Lientur	Puerto Williams	68	6 feb	1	6 feb	3	
Puerto Williams	Ushuaia	27	9 feb	1	9 feb	3	
Ushuaia	Puerto Williams	27	12 feb	1	12 feb	6	
Puerto Williams	Punta Arenas	307	18 Feb.	3	21 Feb.	3	
Punta Arenas	Porto natales	500	25 Feb.	9	3 mar	2	
Porto Natales	Cal jamie	64	9 mar	1	10 mar	1	
Cal Jamie	Cal Amalia	113	10 mar	1	10 mar	1	
Cal Amalia	Pto Eden	104	11 mar	1	11 mar	1	
Pto Eden	Estero Atracadero	101	12 mar	1	12 mar	2	
Estero Atracadero	Pto Quellon	301	14 mar	2	16 mar	1	
Pto Quellon	Castro	72	17 mar	1	17 mar	1	
Castro	Pto Mont	102	17 mar	1	18 mar	0	
Pto Mont	Valdivia	264	29 mar	2	31 mar	11	
Valdivia	Vina Del Mar	440				14	
Vina Del Mar	Valparaiso	13	13 nov	1	13 nov		

MILES BROUGHT FORWARD = 6153

TOTAL MILES THIS SHEET = 5332

TOTAL MILES SO FAR = 11485

M.Y INDIGO ITINERARY VALPARAISO TO TANNA

From	To	Distance	Depart	Days At sea	Arrive	Nights in Port	
Valparaiso	Juan Fernandez Is	370	27 nov	2	29 nov	1	
Juan Fernandez Is	Easter Is	1675	30 nov	8	8 dec	2	
Easter Is	Pitcairn is	1120	10 nov	5	15 dec	1	
Pitcairn Is	Mangareva Gambier Is	296	16 dec	1	17 dec	2	
Mangareva	Papeete	918	19 dec	4	23 dec	16	
Papeete	Moorea	12	8 jan	1	8 jan	12	
Moorea	Papeete	12	20 jan	1	20 jan	14	
Papeete	Moorea	12	3 feb	1	3 feb	2	
Moorea	Maroe Bay Huahine	79	5 feb	1	5 feb	1	
Maroe Bay Huahine	Fare Huahine	19	6 feb	1	6 feb	1	
Fare Huahine	Raiatea	21	7 feb	1	7 feb	1	
Raiatea	Tahaa	10	8 feb	1	8 feb	2	
Tahaa	Maupiti	48	10 feb	1	10 feb	2	
Maupiti	Bora Bora	23	12 feb	1	12 feb	8	
Bora Bora	Apataki	337	20 feb	2	22 feb	1	
Apataki	Papeete	275	23 feb	1	24 feb	15	
Papeete	Huahine	104	10 mar	1	11 mar	4	
Huahine	Raratonga S. Cook Is	562	14 mar	3	17 mar	3	
Raratonga	Niue	623	20 mar	3	23 mar	2	
Niue	Tonga	239	23 mar	3	26 mar	5	
Tonga	Nandi Fiji	442	31 mar	3	2 apr	6	
Fiji	Port Vila Vanuatu	512	8 apr	2	10 apr	3	
Port Villa	Tanna	130	13 apr	1	14 apr	1	

MILES BROUGHT FORWARD = 11485   TOTAL MILES THIS SHEET = 7839   TOTAL MILES SO FAR = 19324

M.Y INDIGO ITINERARY Tanna to Phi Phi

From	To	Distance	Depart	Days At sea	Arrive	Nights in Port	
Tanna	New Caledonia	555	14 Apr	2	16 Apr	13	
New Caledonia	Brisbane	740	29 Apr	4	2 May	171	
Brisbane	Surfers Paradise	137	20 Oct	1	21 Oct	11	
Surfers Paradise	Keppel Is	300	1 Nov	2	3 Nov	1	
Keppel Is	Hamilton Is	315	4 Nov	1	5 Nov	2	
Hamilton Is	Whitehaven	12	7 Nov	1	7 Nov	3	anchor
Whitehaven	Cairns	237	10 Nov	2	11 Nov	9	
Cairns	Benoa Bali	2100	20 Nov	9	29 Nov	12	
Bali	Kalimantan Bali	471	12 Dec	2	14 Dec	2	anchor
Kalimantan	Pulau Belitung	265	16 Dec	1	17 Dec	1	anchor
Pulau Belitung	Singapore	220	17 Dec	1	18 Dec	55	
Singapore	Penang	350	11 Feb	2	13 Feb	2	
Penang	Langkawi	70	15 Feb	1	15 Feb	12	anchor
Langkawi	Butang Is Thailand	35	27 Feb	1	27 Feb	2	anchor
Butang	Ko Tarutao	50	1 Mar	1	1 Mar	2	anchor
Ko Tarutao	Phi Phi	30	3 Mar	1	3 Mar	2	anchor
Phi Phi	Ko Lata Hai	8	5 Mar	1	5 Mar	2	anchor
Ko Lata Hai	Railay Beach	45	6 Mar	1	6 Mar	4	anchor
Railay Beach	Hong Is	18	11 Mar	1	11 Mar	1	Anchor
Hong Is	Ko Yao Yai	43	14 Mar	1	14 Mar	3	Anchor
Ko Yao Yai	Yacht Haven	35	17 Mar	1	17 Mar	3	Marina
Yacht haven	Patong Beach	70	20 Mar	1	20 mar	2	Anchor
Patong	Phi Phi	40	21 mar	1	21 mar	2	anchor

MILES BROUGHT FORWARD = 19324   TOTAL MILES THIS SHEET = 5722

TOTAL MILES SO FAR = 25046

M.Y INDIGO ITINERARY PHI PHI, THAILAND TO MYKONOS, GREECE

From	To	Distance	Depart	Days	Arrive	Nights in Port	
Phi Phi	Railay Beach	23	24 Mar	1	24 mar	1	Anchored
Railay	Chicken Is	4	24 Mar	1	24 Mar	1	Anchored
Chicken Is	Hat Surin	36	25 mar	1	25 Mar	3	Anchored
Hat Surin	Yacht haven	54	29 Mar	1	29 Mar	9	Marina
Yacht haven	Port Blair Andamans	440	8 April	2	10 April	7	Anchored
Port Blair	Male Maldives	1612	17 April	9	26 April	3	Anchored
Male	Uligan Is Maldives	50	29 April	1	29 April	3	Anchored
Uligan Is	Mumbai India	771	2 May	5	6 May	3	Alongside
Mumbai	Dubai	1150	9 May	6	15 May	37	Alongside
Dubai	Muscat	330	21 June	2	22 June	38	Marina
Muscat	Djibouti, Djibouti	1395	30 July	8	06 August	1	Anchored
						1	Alongside
Djibouti, Djibouti	Hurghada, Egypt	1120	08 August	6	13 August	5	Marina
Hurghada	El Gouna	17	18 August	1	18 August	4	Marina
El Gouna	Port Suez	173	22 August	2	23 August	1	Anchored
Port Suez	Port Said	90	24 August	1	24 August	3	Alongside
Port Said	Rhodes, Greece	378	27 August	3	29 August	2	Marina
Rhodes, Greece	Limin Amforos, Karpathos	88	01 September	1	01 September	1	Anchored
Limin Amforos, Karpathos	Ay Nikolaoas, Crete	80	02 September	1	02 September	4	Marina
Ay Nikolaoas, Crete	Thira, Santorini	80	05 September	1	05 September	2	Mooring
Thira, Santorini	Manganari Bay, Ios	19	07 September	1	07 September	1	Anchored
Manganari Bay, Ios	Andiparos	30	08 September	1	08 September	2	Anchored
Andiparos	Mykonos	39	10 September	1	10 September	2	Marina

MILES BROUGHT FORWARD = 25046

TOTAL MILES THIS SHEET = 7952

TOTAL MILES SO FAR = 32998

M.Y INDIGO ITINERARY MYKONOS, GREECE TO KINIDOS, TURKEY

From	To	Distance	Depart	Days	Arrive	Nights in Port	
Mykonos, Greece	Skala, Patmos	73	12 September	1	12 September	2	Marina
Skala, Patmos	Bodrum, Turkey	54	14 September	1	14 September	2	Marina
Bodrum, Turkey	Turkbuku	30	16 September	1	16 September	1	Anchorage
Turkbuku	Kusadasi	56	17 September	1	17 September	4	Marina
Kusadasi	Cesme	63	21 September	1	21 September	1	Marina
Cesme	Foca	45	22 September	1	22 September	1	Alongside
Foca	Ayvalik	48	23 September	1	23 September	1	Anchor
Ayvalik	Gallipoli(gelibolu)	100	24 September	1	24 September	1	Anchor
Gallipoli	Istanbul(Atakoy Marina)	117	25 September	2	26 September	1	Marina
Istanbul	Constanta, Romania	203	30 September	2	01 October	2	Marina
Constanta	Constanta	50	02 October	1	02 October	1	Alongside
Constanta	Sulina	102	03 October	1	03 October	1	Alongside
Sulina	Tulcea	38	04 October	1	04 October	2	Alongside
Tulcea	Ismail, Ukraine	20	06 October	1	06 October	1	Alongside
Ismail	Constanta, Romania	159	07 October	2	08 October	4	Alongside
Constanta	Mangalia	30	12 October	1	12 October	16	Shipyard
Mangalia	Mangalia	23	28 October	1	28 October	10	Shipyard
Mangalia	Istanbul, Turkey	189	07 November	2	08 November	4	Marina
Istanbul	Kusadasi	350	12 November	3	14 November	16	Marina
Kusadasi	Bodrum	80	30 November	1	30 November	4	Anchorage
Haulout Aegean Shipyard			04 December				
Aegean Shipyard	Bodrum	3	12 April	1	12 April	6	Marina
Bodrum	Kinidos	26	18 April	1	18 April	1	Anchorage

MILES BROUGHT FORWARD = 32998

TOTAL MILES THIS SHEET = 1859

TOTAL MILES SO FAR = 34857

M.Y INDIGO ITINERARY KINIDOS, TURKEY TO ITEA, GREECE

From	To	Distance	Depart	Days	Arrive	Nights in Port	
Kinidos	Bozburun	36.5	19 April	1	19 April	1	Anchorage
Bozburun	Marmaris	61.3	20 April	1	20 April	2	Marina
Marmaris	Dalyan	23	22 April	1	22 April	1	Anchorage
Dalyan	Gocek	31.5	23 April	1	23 April	2	Marina
Gocek	Fethiye	13.5	25 April	1	25 April	2	Marina
Fethiye	Gemiler Island	14.9	27 April	1	27 April	1	Anchorage
Gemiler Island	Kas	43.7	28 April	1	28 April	2	Marina
Kas	Kekova	16	30 April	1	30 April	1	Anchorage
Kekova	Kas	18	01 May	1	01 May	0	Anchorage
Kas	Bodrum	136.5	01 May	2	02 May	6	Marina
Bodrum Marina	Bodrum Cruise Port	2.5	07 May	1	07 May	2	Marina
Bodrum	Kos, Greece	10	09 May	1	09 May	3	Marina
Kos	Fournoi	58.3	12 May	1	12 May	1	Anchorage
Fournoi	Andros	78	13 May	1	13 May	2	Anchorage
Andros	Skiros	67.5	15 May	1	15 May	1	Anchorage
Skiros	Alonnisos	39.2	16 May	1	16 May	1	Marina
Alonnisos	Skiathos	23.5	17 May	1	17 May	3	Marina
Skiathos	Evia	52.1	20 May	1	20 May	1	Anchorage
Evia	Khalkis	39	21 May	1	21 May	1	Anchorage
Khalkis	Athens	98.2	21 May	2	22 May	4	Marina
Athens	Corinth Canal	31.2	26 May	1	26 May	1	Anchorage
Corinth Canal	Galaxidhiou	41.2	27 May	1	27 May	1	Anchorage
Galaxidhiou	Itea	6	28 May	1	28 May	1	Anchorage

MILES BROUGHT FORWARD = 34857   TOTAL MILES THIS SHEET = 941.6   TOTAL MILES SO FAR = 35528.6

M.Y INDIGO ITINERARY ITEA, GREECE TO LUCA MILNA, CROATIA

From	To	Distance	Depart	Days	Arrive	Nights in Port	
Itea, Greece	Wreck Bay, Zakynthos	105	28 May	2	29 May	1	Anchorage
Wreck Bay, Zakynthos	Fiscardo, Keffalonia	45	30 May	1	30 May	1	Anchorage
Fiscardo, Keffalonia	Nhidri, Levkas	17.9	31May	1	31 may	1	Marina
Nhidri, Levkas	Levkas, Levkas	8.5	1 June	1	1 June	1	Marina
Levkas, Levkas	Corfu Town, Corfu	65	03 June	1	03 June	5	Marina
Corfu, Greece	Bar,Montenegro	180	08 June	2	09 June	1	Marina
Bar,Montenegro	Budva	15	10 June	1	10 June	1	Marina
Budva	Kotor	30.5	11 June	1	11 June	2	Marina
Kotor	Hercig Novi	14	13 June	1	13 June	2	Marina
Herzig Novi	Zelenika	1.5	15 June	1	15 June	0	Marina
Zelenika, Montenegro	Cavtat, Croatia	23.5	15 June	1	15 June	2	Marina
Cavtat	Dubrovnik	12	17 June	1	17 June	1	Marina
Dubrovnik	Polace, Mljet	33	18 June	1	18 June	1	Anchorage
Mljet	Racisce Bay, Korcula	19	19 June	1	19 June	1	Anchorage
Racisce Bay	Korcula, Korcula	3	20 June	1	20 June	1	Marina
Korcula, Korcula	Hvar, Hvar	33.7	21 June	1	21 June	3	Marina
Hvar	Trogir	29	24 June	1	24 June	1	Marina
Trogir	Rogoznica	18	25 June	1	25 June	1	Marina
Rogoznica	Skradin	25	26 June	1	26 June	1	Marina
Skradin	Sibenik	8.8	27 June	1	27 June	1	Marina
Sibenik	Primosten	11.3	28 June	1	28 June	0	Anchorage
Primosten	Split	27.6	28 June	1	28 June	5	Marina
Split	Luka Milna, Brac	15	04 July	1	04 July	1	Anchorage

MILES BROUGHT FORWARD = 35528.6

TOTAL MILES THIS SHEET = 741.3   TOTAL MILES SO FAR = 36269.9

M.Y INDIGO ITINERARY BRAC, CROATIA TO CANNES, FRANCE

From	To	Distance	Depart	Days	Arrive	Nights in Port	
Luka Milna, Brac	Vis, Vis	21	05 July	1	05 July	1	Marina
Vis	Korcula, Korcula	45	06 July	1	06 July	1	Marina
Korcula	Hvar, Hvar	38	07 July	1	07 July	2	Marina
Hvar	Tudor	30	09 July	1	09 July	2	Anchorage
Tudor	Marina Mandelina, Sibenik	31	11 July	1	11 July	1	Marina
Sibenik	NCP Shipyard, Sibenik	1	12 July	1	12 July		Dry Dock
Sibenik	Zelenika, Montenegro	158	03 Sept	2	04 Sept	0	Alongside
Zelenika, Montenegro	Siracusa, Sicily	384	04 Sept	3	06 Sept	4	Stern To
Siracusa, Italy	Riposto	44	10 Sept	1	10 Sept	0	Marina
Riposto	Lipari	82	10 Sept	1	11 Sept	1	Stern To
Lipari	Positano	151	12 Sept	2	13 Sept	1	Anchorage
Positano	Amalfi	6	14 Sept	1	14 sept	1	Stern To
Amalfi	Ischia	42	15 Sept	1	15 Sept	1	Stern To
Ischia	Rome	95	16 sept	2	17 Sept	3	Marina
Rome	Puerto Cervo, Sardinia	130	20 Sept	2	21 Sept	1	Stern To
Porto Cervo	Golfo delle Salina	10	22 Sept	1	22 Sept	1	Anchorage
Golfo delle Salina	Bonifacio, Corsica	21	23 sept	1	23 Sept	5	Stern To
Bonifacio	Ajaccio	47	28 Sept	1	28 Sept	1	Stern To
Ajaccio	Golfo Girolato	39	29 Sept	1	29 Sept	0	Anchorage
Golfo Girolato	Calvi	26	29 Sept	1	29 Sept	1	Stern To
Calvi	Viareggio, Italy	110	30 Sept	2	01 Oct	18	Shipyard
Viareggio	Monaco	121	19 Oct	2	20 Oct	3	Marina
Monaco	Cannes	28	23Oct	1	23 Oct	1	Anchorage

MILES BROUGHT FORWARD = 36,629.9   TOTAL MILES THIS SHEET =   1660   TOTAL MILES SO FAR = 38289.9

M.Y INDIGO ITINERARY CANNES, FRANCE TO SAONA ISLAND, DOMINICAN REPUBLIC

From	To	Distance	Depart	Days	Arrive	Nights in Port	
Cannes	St. Tropez	25	24 Oct	1	24 Oct	3	Marina
St Tropez	Barcelona	238	27 Oct	2	28 Oct	10	Marina
Barcelona	Vilanova	33	07 Nov	1	07 Nov	7	Marina
Vilanova	Palma, Mallorca	130	14 Nov	2	15 Nov	3	Marina
Palma	Gibraltar	465	18 Nov	3	20 Nov	3	Marina
Gibraltar	Puerto Sherry, Spain	77	23 Nov	1	23 Nov	1	Marina
Puerto Sherry	Seville, Spain	86	24 Nov	1	24 Nov	3	Alongside
Seville, Spain	Casablanca, Morocco	265	27 Nov	2	28 Nov	4	Alongside
Casablanca	Agadir, Morocco	265	02 Dec	2	28 Nov	7	Marina
Agadir, Morocco	Santa Cruz de Tenerife	380	10 Dec	3	12 Dec	23	Marina
Santa Cruz de Tenerife	Port St Charles, Barbados	2617	04 Jan	13	16 Jan	24	Marina
Port St Charles, Barbados	Young Island Cut, St Vincent	91	09 Feb	1	09 Feb	1	Anchorage
Young Island Cut,St Vincent	Marigot Bay, St Lucia	57	10 Feb	1	10 Feb	1	Marina
Marigot Bay	Rodney Bay, St Lucia	9	11 Feb	1	11 Feb	2	Marina
Rodney Bay, St Lucia	Roseau, Dominica	92	13 Feb	1	13 Feb	1	Anchor/Stern To
Roseau, Dominica	Portsmouth, Dominica	20	14 Feb	1	14 Feb	2	Anchorage
Portsmouth, Dominica	Iles de Saintes, Guadaloupe	22	16 Feb	1	16 Feb	1	Anchorage
Iles de Saintes, Guadaloupe	Little Bay, Montserrat	72	17 Feb	1	17 Feb	1	Anchorage
Montserrat	Sint Maarten	90	18 Feb	1	18 Feb	1	Anchorage
Simpson Bay	Isle de Sol, St Maarten	3	19 Feb	1	19 Feb	1	Marina
St Maarten	Sandy Ground, Anguilla	20	20 Feb	1	20 Feb	1	Anchorage
Anguilla	Casa de Campo, Dominican Republic	351	21 Feb	3	22 Feb	4	Marina
Casa d Campo	Saona Island	14	27 Feb	1	27 Feb	1	Anchorage

MILES BROUGHT FORWARD = 38,289.9

TOTAL MILES THIS SHEET = 5422   TOTAL MILES SO FAR = 43711.9

M.Y INDIGO ITINERARY SAONA ISLAND, DOMINICAN REPUBLIC TO FT LAUDERDALE, FLORIDA

From	To	Distance	Depart	Days	Arrive	Nights in Port	
Saona Island, Dom. Rep.	Catalina Island	19	Feb 28	1	Feb 28	0	Anchorage
Catalina Island	Santo Domingo	51	Feb 28	1	Feb 28	5	Alongside
Santo Domingo	Casa de Campo	58	March 05	1	March 05	8	Marina
Casa de Campo	Samana	155	March 13	2	March 14	1	Anchorage
Samana, Dominican Republic	Havana, Cuba	826	March 15	5	March 19	3	Marina
Havana, Cuba	Sandy Point, Great Abaco	365	March 22	2	March 23	1	Anchorage
Sandy Point, Great Abaco	Matt Lowe Cay, Abacos	72	March 24	1	March 24	4	Anchorage
Matt Lowe Cay	Ft Lauderdale, Florida	210	March 28	2	March 29	6	Marina
Port Everglades	LMC, New River	20	April 04	1	April 04	65	Shipyard

MILES BROUGHT FORWARD = 43711.9   TOTAL MILES THIS SHEET = 1776   TOTAL MILES SO FAR = 45487.9

M.Y INDIGO ITINERARY NORTHWEST PASSAGE FT LAUDERDALE TO BAFFIN ISLAND

From	To	Distance	Depart	Days	Arrive	Nights in Port	
LMC, Ft Lauderdale	Pier 66, Ft Lauderdale	20	June 08	1	June 08	4	Alongside
Ft Lauderdale, Florida	St John's River	285	June 12	2	June 13	1	Anchorage
St John's River	Jacksonville, Florida	30	June 14	1	June 14	1	Alongside
Jacksonville	Jacksonville	14	June 15	1	June 15	0	Alongside
Jacksonville	Jacksonville	12	June 15	1	June 15	3	Alongside
Jacksonville	Philadelphia, Pennsylvania	799	June 18	5	June 21	5	Marina
Philadelphia, Pennsylvania	Portland, Maine	499	June 26	3	June 28	2	Marina
Portland, Maine	Halifax, Nova Scotia	360	June 30	3	July 02	10	Marina
Halifax	Baddeck, Cape Bretton	196	July 12	2	July 13	4	Alongside
Baddeck, Cape Bretton	Cornerbrook, Newfoundland	235	July 17	2	July 18	1	Alongside
Cornerbrook, Newfoundland	St Anthony, Nfld	271	July 19	2	July 20	2	Alongside
St. Anthony, Nfld	Port Marnham, Labrador	76	July 22	1	July 22	1	Anchor
Port Marnham, Labrador	Hawke Harbour	53	July 23	1	July 23	1	Anchor
Hawke Harbour	Cartwright, Labrador	89	July 24	1	July 24	2	Alongside
Cartwright	Nanortalik, Greenland	583	July 26	4	July 29	1	Alongside
Nanortalik	Akunaq Bay, Eggers Island	105	July 30	1	July 30	2	Anchor
Akunaq Bay	Qeqertarssutsiaq	150	August 01	1	August 01	1	Anchor
Qeqertarssutsiaq	Kvanefjord	175	August 02	1	August 02	1	Anchor
Sanmissoq, Kvanefjord	Nuuk	165	August 03	1	August 03	3	Alongside
Nuuk	Manermiut	308	August 06	2	August 07	1	Anchor
Manermiut	Illilisat	61	August 08	1	August 08	1	Alongside
Illilisat	Qarqat Bay	5	August 09	1	August 09	1	Anchor
Qarqat Bay, Greenland	Pond Inlet, Baffin Island	582	August 10	4	August 13	0	Anchor
Pond Inlet	Tay Sound, Baffin Island	36	August 13	1	August 13	1	Anchor

MILES BROUGHT FORWARD = 45488

TOTAL MILES THIS SHEET = 5109   TOTAL MILES SO FAR = 50597

M.Y INDIGO ITINERARY BAFFIN ISLAND TO PRINCE RUPERT

From	To	Distance	Depart	Days	Arrive	Nights in Port	
Tay Sound, Baffin Island	Cambridge Bay, Victoria Island	762	August 14	4	August 17	1	Alongside
Cambridge Bay	Alaska Bay, Chantry Island	240	August 18	2	August 19	1	Anchor
Alaska Bay	Tuktoyaktuk, NWT	452	August 20	3	August 22	1	Alongside
Tuktoyaktuk	Kodiak, Alaska	2,204	August 23	10	Sept 01	2	Marina
Kodiak	Homer	146	Sept 03	2	Sept 04	12	Marina
Homer	Sunday Harbour, Port Dick	70	Sept 16	1	Sept 16	1	Anchor
Sunday Harbour	Goat Harbour, Puget Bay	120	Sept 17	1	Sept 17	1	Anchor
Goat Harbour	Columbia Glacier-Cordova	170	Sept 18	2	Sept 19	2	Marina
Cordova, Prince William Sound	Icy Bay to Yakutat	310	Sept 21	2	Sept 22	1	Marina
Yakutat	Hubbard Glacier-Yakutat	75	Sept 23	1	Sept 23	3	Marina
Yakutat	Lituya Bay	106	Sept 25	1	Sept 25	1	Anchor
Lituya Bay	Elfin Cove	60	Sept 26	1	Sept 26	1	Alongside
Elfin Cove-Glacier Bay	Juneau	145	Sept 27	1	Sept 27	4	Alongside
Juneau	Tracy Arm	77	Oct 01	1	Oct 01	1	Anchor
Tracy Arm-Endicott	San Juan Islands	92	Oct 02	1	Oct 02	1	Anchor
San Juan Islands	Petersburg	48	Oct 03	1	Oct 03	1	Alongside
Petersburg	Wrangell	40	Oct 04	1	Oct 04	1	Alongside
Wrangell to Anan Bay	Fools Inlet	36	Oct 05	1	Oct 05	1	Anchor
Fools Inlet	Yes Bay, Behm Canal	87	Oct 06	1	Oct 06	1	Anchor
Yes Bay to Bailey Bay	Walker Cove	57	Oct 07	1	Oct 07	1	Anchor
Walker Cove	Ketchikan	67	Oct 08	1	Oct 08	3	Alongside
Ketchikan	Brundige Inlet, Dundas Island, Canada	57	Oct 11	1	Oct 11	1	Anchor
Brundige Inlet	Prince Rupert	46	Oct 12	1	Oct 12	2	Alongside

MILES BROUGHT FORWARD = 50597

TOTAL MILES THIS SHEET = 5467

TOTAL MILES SO FAR = 56064

M.Y INDIGO ITINERARY PRINCE RUPERT TO VICTORIA, BRITISH COLUMBIA

From	To	Distance	Depart	Days	Arrive	Nights in Port	
Prince Rupert	Exposed Bay, Klewnugget Inlet	51	Oct 14	1	Oct 14	1	Anchor
Klewnugget Inlet	Bishop's Bay	68	Oct 15	1	Oct 15	1	Anchor
Bishop's Bay	Khutze Inlet, Graham Reach	42	Oct 16	1	Oct 16	1	Anchor
Khutze Inlet	Shearwater Resort, Denny Island	71	Oct 17	1	Oct 17	2	Alongside
Denny Island	Illahie Inlet	43	Oct 19	1	Oct 19	1	Anchor
Illahie Inlet	Port McNeill, Vancouver Island	84	Oct 20	1	Oct 20	2	Alongside
Port McNeill	Kanish Bay	83	Oct 22	1	Oct 22	1	Anchor
Kanish Bay	Powell River	49	Oct 23	1	Oct 23	1	Alongside
Powell River	Nanaimo	50	Oct 24	1	Oct 24	1	Alongside
Nanaimo	Vancouver	36	Oct 25	1	Oct 25	17	Alongside
Vancouver	Victoria	81	Nov 11	1	Nov 11		Alongside

MILES BROUGHT FORWARD = 56064

TOTAL MILES THIS SHEET = 658

TOTAL MILES SO FAR = 57722

M.Y INDIGO ITINERARY Fort Lauderdale to Panama Canal to Fort Lauderdale

From	To	Distance	Depart	Days	Arrive	Nights in Port	Nights at Anchor
Ft Lauderdale	Casa de Campo DR	938	Jan 28 2017	5	Feb 01 2017	4	
Casa de Campo	Cartagena, Columbia	640	Feb 05 2017	4	Feb 08 2017	6	
Cartagena, Columbia	Porvenir, San Blas, Panama	212	Feb 14 2017	2	Feb 15, 2017	0	0
Porvenir, San Blas, Panama	Isla Carti, San Blas	7	Feb 15, 2017	1	Feb 15, 2017		1
Isla Carti	Dog Island, San Blas	10	Feb 16, 2017	1	Feb 16, 2017		1
Dog Island	Punta Escribano, Panama	15	Feb 17, 2017	1	Feb 17, 2017		
Punta Escribano	Isla Linton	27	Feb 17, 2017	1	Feb 17, 2017		1
Isla Linton	Shelter Bay Marina, Colon, Panama	39	Feb 18, 2017	1	Feb 18, 2017	1	
Shelter Bay Marina	Gamboa	29	Feb 19, 2017	1	Feb 19, 2017		1
Gamboa	Flamenco Marina, Panama City	20	Feb 20, 2017	1	Feb 20, 2017	4	
Panama City	Red Frog Marina, Bocas Del Toro	193	Feb 24, 2017	2	Feb 25, 2017	4	
Bocas Del Toro	Isla San Andres, Columbia	209	Mar 01, 2017	2	Mar 02, 2017		1
Rada El Cove	Rada El Cove (day trip)	25	Mar 03, 2017	1	Mar 03, 2017		2
Rada El Cove	San Andres Harbor	12	Mar 05, 2017	1	Mar 05, 2017		6
Isla San Andres	Stock Island Marina, Key West, Florida	891	Mar 11, 2017	5	Mar 15, 2017	3	
Key West	Palm Harbor Marina, West Palm Beach	196	Mar 18, 2017	2	Mar 19, 2017	9	
Palm Harbor Marina	Roscioli Shipyard FT Lauderdale	58	Mar 28, 2017	1	Mar 28, 2017		

CPSIA information can be obtained
at www.ICGtesting.com
Printed in the USA
LVHW081952130520
655432LV00010B/284